The Promise of Alliance

NATO and the Political Imagination

IAN Q. R. THOMAS

ROWMAN & LITTLEFIELD PUBLISHERS, INC
Lanham • Boulder • New York • Oxford

ROWMAN & LITTLEFIELD PUBLISHERS, INC.

Published in the United States of America
by Rowman & Littlefield Publishers, Inc.
4720 Boston Way, Lanham, Maryland 20706

12 Hid's Copse Road
Cummor Hill, Oxford OX2 9JJ, England

British Library Cataloguing in Publication Information Available

Library of Congress Cataloging-in-Publication Data

Thomas, Ian W. R.
    The promise of alliance : NATO and the political imagination / Ian Q.R. Thomas.
        p.   cm.
    Includes bibliographical references and index.
    ISBN 0-8476-8580-2 (cloth : alk paper). — ISBN 0-8476-8581-0 (pbk. : alk. paper)
    1. World politics—1989- . 2. North Atlantic Treaty Organization.   I. Title.
D845.T48   1997
355'.031'091'821—dc   97-14246

ISBN 0-8476-8580-2 (cloth : alk. paper)
ISBN 0-8476-8581-0 (pbk. : alk. paper)

Printed in the United States of America

The Promise of Alliance

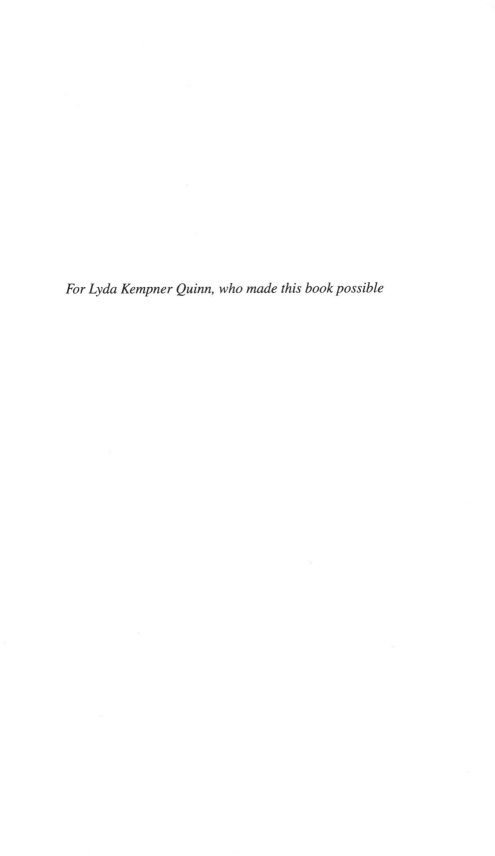

For Lyda Kempner Quinn, who made this book possible

Contents

Preface

When I began this study in November 1990, expert and popular opinion on both sides of the former Iron Curtain was suggesting that Europe, which had so recently thrown off the symbols and substance of Cold War hostility, needed a new security "architecture" to replace the alliance blocs of the previous era. NATO, it was said, was an anachronism that had to go.

Amid such pronouncements about its imminent demise, the alliance as an institution took steps to persuade the world of its continuing utility. On an almost daily basis there flowed, from Brussels and other allied capitals, a stream of rhetoric that seemed to have the intent of communicating NATO's importance for a changed world—a world that had witnessed the end of communism and, ultimately, the end of the Soviet Union itself, and that now faced uncertainties and instabilities that, according to the rhetoric, NATO was eminently and perhaps uniquely suited to address. NATO's political and military leaders began to proclaim the alliance's significance in ever wider terms that, more often than not, referred to the nonmilitary utility of NATO and its capacity to act as a force for stability in an uncertain post-Cold War world. An organization created to defend the West against the Soviet Union was now being justified in terms that did not—and could not—make reference to the past specters of communism and Soviet aggression.

These events and declarations prompted me to set about studying the changes that had previously occurred in the aims and purposes that NATO was declared and believed to be serving. At first I assumed that the changes in the conceptions of the nature and promise of NATO that had taken place during the forty or so years' span between its foundation and the end of the Cold War were responses to objective events, presented with a gloss of propaganda. But I came to see that the rhetoric had something of a life of its own, that it was an independent factor that had contributed, perhaps importantly, to NATO's cohesion. To see how far this was the case and why it happened, this study examines the relationship between changing conceptions and alliance cohesion, between rhetoric and actual policy, and between official declarations and public diplomacy. It examines the period from 1948 to 1996, but in the last chapter I have succumbed, briefly and tentatively, to the historian's temptation to speculate about the future.

There is a sizable industry, comprising scholars, journalists, and current and former officials, that produces so many articles, books and monographs about NATO that it may seem that there is no need for another. But the role of rhetoric in the evolution of NATO is a subject that, remarkably, has been neglected. The reason, I suspect, is because it is a subject that was hard to write about objectively, and for anyone to be seen to be writing about objectively, while the Cold War was on. Now that the Cold War is over, I hope I have managed to do just that. I have made use of the work of many scholars. My debt to them is revealed in my notes. I, of course, bear full responsibility for any faults or errors contained herein.

Acknowledgments

I have been working on this book for six years, and there are many to whom I owe my thanks. Professor Robert Neild, my dissertation supervisor at the University of Cambridge, has been an enthusiastic and generous teacher. I owe my warmest gratitude to Professor Neild for engaging me in the study of the Cold War and for guiding me through the many pitfalls faced by the graduate student. His high standards of scholarship, keen analytical mind, and rigorous intellect helped sharpen my own thinking about international relations and improved this book in immeasurable ways. Professor Richard Ullman of Princeton University, whom I first met in 1991 when he was the George Eastman Visiting Professor at Oxford University, was the first to encourage me to explore conceptions of NATO and was an early supporter of the idea that the topic deserved a book-length treatment. As my unofficial supervisor, Professor Ullman was a constructive critic and devoted teacher who provided insightful guidance and unstinting support, as well as friendship. Dr. Simon Duke of the Central European University in Budapest read and commented on many early drafts, providing critical analysis on innumerable occasions.

There are others to whom I owe my gratitude. Gail Ullman, whose editorial expertise and good cheer never wavered in support of this project, patiently helped me to transform a dissertation into a book. Niko Pfund generously provided editorial and technical assistance and answered my many questions with infinite patience and wise advice. Iain Johnston offered his considerable talents as a book designer to help create the layout and cover for the book. I would especially like to thank Steve Wrinn, Robin Adler, and Dorothy Bradley at Rowman & Littlefield Publishers for their editorial and technical support. Tina Bone typeset the manuscript with patience and great skill. Liz Cunningham compiled the index.

This book could never have been written without the resources of the Cambridge University Library; and I would like to express my gratitude to the staff, and in particular to those of the Official Publications Department, for their patient help. I am also indebted to the Master, Fellows, and students of St. Edmund's College, Cambridge, who provided intellectual sustenance and collegial support, both during my years as a graduate student at the college and, later, when I retured as a Visiting Scholar to revise the manuscript.

As work on the book progressed, Captain Sebastian Bather of the 2nd Battalion, The Royal Gurkha Rifles, gave me an opportunity to share my thoughts about the nature and purpose of NATO with his fellow officers and men at the Brunei garrison, Borneo. Their ready friendship, exemplary military professionalism, and firm grasp of the complexities of politico-military affairs allowed me to test my academic hypotheses and helped broaden my understanding of alliance politics.

Special mention should be made of Dr. Burtram B. Butler, to whom I owe my deepest gratitude for his unfailing friendship and invaluable counsel. I am indebted to Professor Henry Steele Commager, who since my freshman year at Amherst College has been a source of inspiration and enlightenment.

I should also like to thank the people who, through their friendship, supported and sustained me while I completed this book. They include Espen Gullikstad, Hugh Henry, Mark McMonagle, Stewart Nettleton, Bart Quigley, and Kim Sundell. My loving wife, Zuhra Haleem, has been unfailingly patient and always supportive. An immeasurable debt of gratitude goes to my mother, Lyda Ann Thomas, who nurtured and advised me and whose unbounded love and support helped me to persevere. This book is dedicated to my grandmother, Lyda Kempner Quinn, whose love, generosity, and sage advice made it possible.

Chapter 1

Introduction

Of the many international organizations created in response to the Cold War, none has undergone such profound changes in its goals and objectives as the North Atlantic Treaty Organization (NATO). Since its creation in 1949 and throughout the Cold War, the Atlantic alliance served as the principal organizational manifestation of a unified Western response to the perceived Soviet threat. As this threat declined and ultimately ceased to exist in the late 1980s and early 1990s, NATO was faced with the prospect that it too might wither away, but the alliance was able, with a surprising durability, to weather the changing tides of the Cold War and emerge into its aftermath. Consider for instance how NATO, after more than three years of diplomatic wrangling, turned the tide of the war in Bosnia in a matter of days. Indeed, the alliance in the post-Cold War period has been a crucial actor in international politics, and has claimed for itself a dual role as the source and guardian of a new pan-European security system. Formed to defend the West against the Soviet threat, NATO in the post-Cold War era has endeavored to promote new, more expansive conceptions of its form and function to justify its continued relevance.

This is nothing new. Throughout the forty-eight years of NATO's history there have been many changes in conceptions of its form and function, of its strategy, and of the military and nonmilitary tasks it was declared and believed to be performing. That the ability to make these changes has been an important mechanism in preserving NATO's unity is a point that few would dispute. Yet how the changes in conceptions came about and what their role has been in the life of NATO are matters that have not been studied. That is a gap that this book aims to fill. It does so by asking three questions: What were the changing conceptions to which the members of NATO subscribed? What were their origins? What purposes did they serve? As a preliminary, it is useful to begin with a discussion about the nature of alliances in general, and about the dynamics of alliance formation and maintenance.

Alliance Theory in Political Science

One central tenet of alliance theory holds that no alliance lasts without an adversary. At the end of the Cold War and with the collapse of Soviet power, some commentators invoked this notion to predict the imminent dissolution of NATO. Having lived on and defied both alliance theory and casual prediction, NATO may represent the alliance with a future—an alliance, that is, that meets the political needs of its members despite the absence of a clear threat to their security and regardless of the nature and scope of any residual threat posed by the former adversary.[1]

The standard theoretical literature on alliances tends to focus on the formal characteristics of alliances, why states join alliances, and why they leave. Quincy Wright and Hans Morgenthau, for example, viewed alliances as instruments of collective defense against external enemies or internal disturbances, as natural mechanisms of the contemporary international system that express a shared intent to pool resources in an attempt to balance the power of rival states.[2] Stephen Walt, noting that powerful states do not always represent a threat, has revised this definition by suggesting that states align with one another not out of mechanistic balance-of-power concerns but in response to more precise calculations based on the perceived need to balance threats.[3] In contrast, George Liska has observed that states place a premium on internal stability and security, and he has argued that states therefore join alliances only out of an indirect concern for international stability.[4]

Glenn Snyder has made a special contribution to alliance theory by drawing a distinction between "general" and "particular" state interests and by noting that the former have led states to seek alliance while the latter, when they are in competition with the particular interests of other alliance members, can cause considerable tension within, or even the dissolution of, an alliance.[5] In this context, Robert Jervis has theorized about the consequences for alliance cohesion when states within an alliance hold conflicting perceptions of interests and threats.[6] Some formulations, such as those posited by Francis Beer and Robert Osgood, stress the transitory or organic nature of alliances and the need for states within an alliance continually to cultivate the communal fidelity and cooperation of their partners.[7] Other attempts to explain the nature and purposes of alliances have focused on behavioral approaches or economic models.[8]

Theorists differ about the degree to which alliances require political maintenance. Similarly, there is no clear consensus as to how far alliances are expressions of preexisting informal alignments based on a broad convergence of political, military, economic, and ideological interests. Nor is there agreement on how far the international system—whether bipolar or multipolar in character—affects the process of alliance formation.[9] It is, however, generally agreed that alliances are instruments of political maneuvering that can be used to restrain allies as well as adversaries, to keep the peace, and to wage war. In this sense, alliances may change in the light of changing interests, perceptions, or requirements; and there are generally recognized forces that bring states together, as well as forces that pull them apart. But alliance theory is less useful when it comes to explaining the mechanisms or instruments that hold alliances together over time, particularly when, as in the case of NATO, the original conditions under which the alliance was formed have changed radically.

The Corpus of Existing Knowledge: NATO

To place NATO within the context of this theoretical discussion, it is important to note that the standard histories of NATO pay only passing attention to the mechanisms and instruments of unity within the alliance. Many scholars have chosen to focus on the elements of discord and disunity that have allegedly plagued NATO throughout its history. NATO has been variously described as "entangling," "unhinged," and "troubled."[10] It has been called "the troubled partnership," "the limited partnership," and an alliance "in crisis."[11] Some scholars, seeking to draw corrective lessons for the future from NATO's troubles, have emphasized its positive nature. In this regard, NATO has been accorded labels such as "enduring" and "the transatlantic bargain."[12] For those more inclined to study NATO's origins, notions of political pragmatism, urgency, or expediency have been embraced as signifying NATO's early essence.[13]

Confusion and debate within the scholarly realm about what NATO was doing and what it stood for mirrors some of the more curious features of the alliance itself. The ability of the alliance to keep renewing itself through the identification of new aims and their repetition has spilled over into the public and academic domains. Many of the ideas generated by NATO's leaders surrounding the purpose and function of the alliance have come to form important elements in academic approaches to the study of NATO. The complex reasons for this phenomenon will become more clear in the chapters that follow, but suffice it to say here that the tendency of the academic community and of NATO's political and military leadership to work closely together, to move easily and frequently between the public and private realms—indeed to hold jobs at one time or another in both realms and therefore to share many of the same assumptions and expectations about how international political life operates—are important elements in the explanation.

Alongside the confusion over how to describe the alliance and the competition among authors to produce provocative new book titles, there has been much fine scholarly work. The scholarly literature on NATO falls into five broad categories: the political and legislative origins of NATO; the state and nature of transatlantic relations; national perspectives on the alliance; the impact of out-of-area events on NATO; and strategy. Timothy Ireland, for example, has written an excellent work on the political and legislative origins of the North Atlantic Treaty, mostly from the American perspective.[14] John Baylis has done the same from the British perspective.[15] These studies complement earlier ones written by Nicholas Henderson and Lord Ismay, who were directly involved at the highest levels of the alliance in its formative years.[16]

Transatlantic tensions within the alliance and how to ease them have also received much attention, particularly from American scholars like Henry Kissinger, Harlan Cleveland, and David Abshire, who wrote extensively both before and after government service.[17] These studies, not surprisingly, tend to be prescriptive and policy oriented. There are also many insightful studies of Anglo-American relations, as well as of the dynamics of American, British, French, and German participation in NATO.[18] The impact of events beyond the formal geographical purview of the alliance has been admirably covered by Elizabeth Sherwood and by Douglas Stuart and William Tow.[19] In the strategic realm, Jane Stromseth, Katherine Kelleher, and Paul Buteux have made important contributions to an understanding of NATO's strategy and of politico-military relations within the alliance.[20]

These diverse works share one important feature: they treat changing aims and declarations as a natural product of policy debate among the allies. They proceed from the assumption that changing notions of what NATO stood for and was doing were reactions to objective events, and they have tended to regard new declarations and aims as a product of those changing forces.

Conceptions of NATO

This work takes a different approach. It treats changing declarations about the nature and purpose of NATO as essential clues in the search for an explanation of NATO's impressive longevity. It is based on the belief that to understand how and why these declarations kept changing will be to shed some light on what held the alliance together—how its political response system worked, and perhaps how it may be expected to work in the future.

Throughout this work these declarations of aims are referred to as "conceptions." By conceptions we mean ideas, images, notions, or plans that have been used to describe, rationalize, or justify NATO. As we shall see, they were both political and strategic in nature; they were sometimes expressed in the widest terms, ascribing to NATO tasks or objectives not traditionally associated with alliances; they were often changed; and they were extraordinarily diverse.

The Evidence

The evidence on which this book is based consists primarily of the major public statements and other acts of public diplomacy by the central leaders of the four principal NATO allies—the United States, the United Kingdom, France, and the Federal Republic of Germany—and of NATO itself, acting through its collective decisionmaking and consultative bodies, as well as through its secretary general, to follow the rhetorical drama of the Cold War and its aftermath. The events and forces that gave rise to these statements and actions are also examined, but this work is not a history of NATO. It is a history of the changing conceptions of NATO that were propagated among its principal members at the elite level. It does not attempt to assess the impact of conceptions on the public, except when a gap between the two had important implications for alliance politics or contributed to changes in conceptions. The approach is chronological, with each chapter focusing on a period that came to be defined and shaped not only by historical forces, events, and personalities but also by conceptions of NATO's form and function, its changing roles and objectives.

This approach means that there is no treatment of the smaller states of the alliance. That is because the main conceptual corpus has been shaped, constructed, supported, or challenged largely by the four primary allies— among which France in particular, though not always, has played the role of dissenter. The importance of the views of the four is reflected in the tendency of the alliance as a whole to adopt and express them through collective communiqués, declarations, and policy statements. There are no clear or compelling examples of when the smaller or weaker members of NATO formulated a conception that was significantly inconsistent with the views held by one or more of the big four. Adherence or opposition to the conceptions of the main allies provided the others with leverage for influence—indeed, far more so than the formulation of alternative conceptions.

The Role of Rhetoric

Rhetoric is the art of using language to persuade others: it is used to inform and enlighten; to convey, conceal, or distort information; and to engender consensus or nurture opposition. The study of rhetoric contributes to the study of international relations because a major part of the process of shaping or understanding the international environment occurs in the act of describing that environment.

Words, like actions, have consequences. Political language plays on and creates truth, and it has a self-perpetuating quality. Language in general is a vehicle for human action; and political language helps political leaders rationalize their decisions and actions. More generally, language serves the general need to comprehend the political world. Language thus not only serves as a tool to interpret events but also, when used repeatedly, becomes part of a generally accepted political reality.[21]

Words were principal weapons in the Cold War. Like many wars before and since, the Cold War had strong ideological features; it was not just about national security. To wage Cold War, for many Western political elites, was to embrace a moral imperative, to engage in a contest between good and evil. In this struggle, language became a determining factor in the perceptions, thoughts, justifications, and actions of policymakers. Political rhetoric helped inform an environment of threat perceptions and responses; and ideas expressed publicly by officials gave public significance to events and policies and served as a basis in words for belief and action.[22]

Rhetorical expressions by senior allied leaders were occasionally either dutiful or decorative. But the intent was to inform, to persuade, to express ideas about people, events, policies, objectives, and history. Rhetoric became the medium for propagating conceptions about the nature and promise of NATO.[23]

The following chapters demonstrate how notions of the nature and function of NATO changed over time, how those conceptions have arisen both from the politics of the alliance and from the politics of its member states, and how they might influence future choices about the direction of NATO. Conceptions were produced by events internal and external to the alliance; and they were extraordinarily diverse and often changed, though rarely discarded. Once enunciated, conceptions take on the status of doctrine; they are passed from generation to generation of leaders; and they are invoked with almost religious zeal. The sheer diversity of conceptions suggests that NATO is a rather malleable instrument, and one that has meant many things over the years. Changing conceptions are thus a reflection of NATO's flexibility, expressions of consensus within the alliance, and a key mechanism of alliance unity. The malleable nature of NATO has given the alliance an ability to change to meet the changing requirements of international political life and, ultimately, to survive.

Chapter 2

Creating Western Defense

Notions of how to secure peace in Europe changed rapidly and radically in the first half decade of the postwar era. As the Cold War heated up in Berlin and then in Korea, Western political and military leaders sought ways to revitalize and rearm Western Europe, prevent communist advances, and frustrate the Kremlin. The liberation of the European continent had been a guiding principle behind the Allied effort against the Axis powers. With the breakdown of four-power collaboration in 1947 and 1948, the guiding principle for the Western democracies changed from liberating to defending Western Europe. As part of this process, occupied Germany was transformed from an enemy to a partner.[1] "We could not," recalled U.S. Secretary of State Dean Acheson, "begin too soon to transform the occupying forces into a new concept and new organization, a force for the protection of Europe."[2]

The protection of Europe came to be symbolized by the North Atlantic Treaty. This chapter demonstrates how the instrument of the treaty became, over time, an end in itself, obscuring its original purpose as the goal of European unity became increasingly subordinated to the means of European unification. With this process in mind, it seeks to answer questions about conceptions of NATO and their origins. What were the early conceptions of European security in the immediate postwar era and how did they influence the political evolution of the North Atlantic Treaty? How and why did these conceptions change as Cold War tensions changed? Because of the central role played by the United States in formulating early conceptions of NATO and of postwar European security, the rhetoric and actions of its leaders receive considerable attention in the pages that follow.

The North Atlantic Treaty and the Birth of NATO

The Background to the North Atlantic Treaty

In a speech at Harvard University in June 1947, Acheson's predecessor, George C. Marshall—Acheson replaced him in early 1949—set forth the basic principles of U.S. postwar policy for the rehabilitation of Europe:

> It is logical that the United States should do whatever it is able to do to assist in the return of normal economic health in the world, without which there can be no political stability and no assured peace. [The purpose of U.S. policy] should be the revival of a working economy in the world so as to permit the emergence of political and social conditions in which these institutions can exist.[3]

This was perhaps the earliest attempt by U.S. officials to establish firmly and publicly the linkage between economic recovery and political stability. As events unfolded, the national security interests of the United States were inextricably linked to the economic recovery of Western Europe—a process which initially relied almost entirely on promises of American support. These promises, as we shall see, began increasingly to take the form of security guarantees.

The principles set forth at Harvard became known as the Marshall Plan, and they were put into effect by the Economic Cooperation Act of 1948, which appropriated money for assistance to Western Europe.[4] Despite Marshall's generous offer of U.S. aid and the sweeping commitments implied by President Harry S Truman's plan, the Truman Doctrine, to provide military assistance to Greece, it was widely hoped that the real initiative to revitalize Europe would come from the Europeans themselves.[5]

The initiative, when it came, was led by British Foreign Secretary Ernest Bevin. In a January 1948 speech to the House of Commons he called for the formation of a Western union among the United Kingdom, France, Belgium, the Netherlands, and Luxembourg in the political, economic, and military spheres:

> If we are to preserve peace and our own safety at the same time, we can only do so by the mobilization of such a moral and material force as will create confidence and energy in the West and inspire respect elsewhere, and this means that Britain cannot stand outside Europe and regard her problems as quite separate from those of her European neighbors.[6]

Bevin's call for union was accepted by the continental powers, and on 17 March 1948 the Brussels Treaty was signed.[7] The treaty was aimed principally at preventing renewed German militarism in Europe, though it looked toward defending against the possibility of aggression from the Soviet Union.[8]

One of Bevin's central concerns was how to engage a long-term commitment from the United States for the security of Western Europe.[9] He believed that "this alone could restore the balance of power in Europe which had been shattered by the eclipse of Germany, the emergence of a strong Russia and the post-war weakness of Western Europe."[10]

French leaders embraced the Brussels Treaty for similar reasons. Burdened by wars in its colonial empire, France urgently needed dollars to support its economy. Like Bevin, French leaders faced difficult choices, and they turned to the United States for help in restoring France's former grandeur, to oppose the growing influence of the French Communist Party, and in controlling the Germans. The Marshall Plan called for the inclusion of Germany, and France was wary of any plan that called for the potential restoration of German economic and military power.[11]

The United States offered immediate support for the treaty. In a special address to Congress, President Truman announced the unprecedented act of peacetime conscription, saying that it was "of vital importance that we keep our occupation forces in Germany until the peace is secured in Europe." Referring to the treaty, he added:

> This development deserves our full support. I am confident that the U.S. will, by appropriate means, extend to the free nations the support which the situation requires. I am sure that the determination of the free countries of Europe to protect themselves will be matched by an equal determination on our part to help them do so.[12]

The Western Europeans, with Bevin in the lead, were heartened by this forthright expression of support, but they continued to press for a formal commitment. The Western Union, though a good start, was insufficient on its own. In Bevin's view, the restoration of European morale and the consolidation of the new union required the addition of American resources and power.[13]

The United States, with its historical antipathy to alliances, was reluctant to undertake any such obligations. However, events in Prague, where the Soviets had recently engineered a coup, and in Berlin, where they were attempting to force the Western powers out by means of a blockade, had a profound effect on Congress. By mid-1948, a move was under way in the United States to make its intentions more clear.[14]

The Vandenberg Resolution, named after its author, Republican Senator Arthur H. Vandenberg, was passed by a vote of 64 to 6 on 11 June 1948.[15] It is widely regarded as being the forerunner to the North Atlantic Treaty.[16] The resolution emphasized two principles. The first was that in any security treaty signed by the United States there would be no automatic commitment to go to war—Congress, in keeping with its constitutionally mandated powers, would reserve the right to declare war. The second was that no unilateral benefits would accrue to the other parties to the treaty; security should flow both ways. This second principle would negate later suggestions, made by the State Department's Policy Planning Staff (PPS) under George Kennan, to offer the Europeans unilateral guarantees of U.S. military support.

Kennan, director of the PPS, believed that the United States should encourage the Europeans to set up security organizations but not be a participating member.[17] Kennan favored the "dumbbell concept" of Atlantic security, which envisaged separate security entities, with the Europeans on one end and the Americans and Canadians on the other. By way of declarations, the North Americans, under this conception, would make it known that they considered the security of the European unit as important to their own. A formal treaty between the United States and its European allies would not be an appropriate response to the Russian threat, which Kennan regarded as being of a primarily political nature. He argued that the American effort to assist Europe should aim not to combat communism as such, but rather focus on the postwar economic imbalances that made Western European societies vulnerable to totalitarian exploitation of all kinds, fascist and Nazi as well as communist.[18]

Both the Czech coup, which had highlighted the threat posed by indigenous communism, and the Berlin blockade crystallized feeling in the United States about the need for a military alliance between the United

States and its European allies.[19] Though he opposed a treaty, Kennan did believe there was a need for a strong military posture in the West. If there was a valid long-term justification for a formal defense relationship by international agreement, which could promote security in the North Atlantic area, it would have to be based on the assumption that a treaty would help develop defensive power in the area, act as a deterrent, and thus serve the goal of containment.[20] "On the other hand," wrote Kennan in a PPS paper, "it is important to understand that the conclusion of such a pact is not the main answer to the present Soviet effort to dominate the European continent, and will not appreciably modify the nature or danger of Soviet policies."[21] Marked disparities in armed strength might be manipulated by the Soviets through intimidation tactics, but Kennan did not believe the Soviets wanted war. The real risk, he reasoned, would come from diverting resources away from European economic recovery; and the cost of failure in this area was potentially greater than the risk of not rearming.[22]

As the American elite debated the form and substance of a possible future commitment to European security, the British tried urgently to communicate their own growing sense of insecurity.[23] In March 1948 the British Embassy in Washington sent a top secret *aide memoire* to the State Department.[24] It outlined Norwegian fears, recently communicated to the British Embassy in Oslo, about being compelled to negotiate a pact with the Soviet Union similar to that made by the Finns one year previously. The Norwegians were seeking to gauge the level of assistance they might be able to expect when they resisted Soviet threats, which they were determined to do. Generalizing from the Norwegian experience, the note drew attention to the probable emergence of two serious threats in the near future: a strategic (military) threat represented by Russian moves against the Atlantic states, and the political threat posed to efforts to build a Western union. Impending Russian moves against Norway were said to be bringing matters to a head, and "only a bold move can avert the danger." The note went on to express Bevin's view that the most effective course would be to conclude "a regional Atlantic Pact of Mutual Assistance, in which all the countries directly threatened by a Russian move to the Atlantic could participate."[25]

Bevin declared that the security of North America, Europe, and the free world were inseparably bound. To secure these bonds, he proposed working for three security structures simultaneously: the first was to conclude the impending Brussels Treaty—only five days from signing—with U.S. backing; the second would be an Atlantic security scheme with close U.S.

participation; and the third would focus on the Mediterranean and on Italy in particular. An Atlantic security system "could at once inspire the necessary confidence to consolidate the West against Soviet infiltration and at the same time inspire the Soviet Government with enough respect for the West to remove temptation from them and ensure a long period of peace." The alternative would be a repeat of the grim lessons of history: aggression, followed by appeasement and then war.[26]

The document is significant for at least three reasons. First, it demonstrates the British desire, shared by other European states, to link the United States firmly to any security system for Europe. Second, it illustrates Bevin's ability to appeal to the American desire for Europeans to act on their own initiative, by proposing not one but three schemes for European (and international) security. Third, it is an early treatise on the need not only for reassurance in Western Europe but also to deter the Soviets.

The early postwar period witnessed the emergence of a consensus in the West about the two central concepts that would guide future discussion about how to secure peace in Europe. The notions of self-help and mutual aid, enshrined in the Marshall Plan and the Vandenburg Resolution, paved the way for a U.S. political and military commitment to defend Western Europe. The concepts also helped to establish an obligation on the part of the United States' European allies to provide, with U.S. economic assistance, for the defense of Western Europe. The gradual coming together and intermingling of strategic, economic, geopolitical, and ideological considerations ultimately prompted policymakers on both sides of the Atlantic to consider the idea of mutual security guarantees. These guarantees took form in the North Atlantic Treaty, which, along with the Marshall Plan, was designed to thwart the Soviets, soften the appeal of communism, and hasten the recovery of Western Europe.

The notions of self-help and mutual aid formed the conceptual foundation for the North Atlantic Treaty and for future transatlantic relations, but they also later became the focal point of acrimonious debate about whether the West Europeans were fulfilling their part of the "transatlantic bargain." As the Cold War set in, these separate but related issues—the belief that only the United States could act as the principal guarantor of European security, the transatlantic tension resulting from American doubts about the willingness of their partners to provide for themselves, the symbolic power of an alliance to promote confidence, and the need to deter the Soviets—would receive increasing attention.

The Washington Talks: Negotiating the North Atlantic Treaty

Talks began in Washington early in 1948 among the five Brussels Treaty powers, the United States, and Canada, according to Nicholas Henderson, second secretary at the British embassy and a participant at many of the negotiations, "to determine how best to deter the Russians and fortify confidence and reinforce the security of the democratic countries of Western Europe."[27] The participants agreed that a defense system for the North Atlantic area would restore confidence and be a major contribution to the security of Europe.

At this early stage—the negotiations would last for fifteen months—the role of the North American allies had not been fully determined. Nor was there any clear consensus about the need for a formal treaty. However, at the time, according to Henderson:

> it was the decision of the Soviets both to bring [Eastern Europe] under their complete control, including the elimination of all democratic elements, in flat defiance of what was agreed at Yalta and later at Potsdam, and to threaten to extend the Soviet sway to Western Europe, that finally produced a western response eventually to be embedded in the North Atlantic Treaty.[28]

There was considerable division of opinion in the State Department about several elements of the proposed treaty, including, as we have seen, even whether such a treaty was desirable. However, as both Marshall and Acheson moved slowly but assuredly toward acceptance of the idea that a security treaty with U.S. participation was essential to the defense of Europe, these divisions were muted.[29] Although there eventually was broad agreement among all the negotiating parties about the necessity for a treaty and about the general principles that would guide the negotiations, the Washington Talks considered four outstanding points of principle:

1. *Whom to include in a treaty.* Questions over membership had their origins in the debate about how to treat Germany, whether to regard it as a former enemy or as a future partner. In their discussions surrounding both the Brussels Treaty and the North Atlantic Treaty, policymakers placed great emphasis on how to restrain Germany. This emphasis was based on the then prevailing assumption that resurgent German militarism was Europe's greatest menace and that, to prevent it, Germany must remain indefinitely under Allied control. Such a draconian, retaliatory approach was ultimately abandoned in favor of one that sought to co-opt West German power and

resources in support of containing, or encircling, the Soviet Union. Though jettisoned, early conceptions that regarded Germany as a defeated enemy—not ally—served as an explicit example of the psychology then prevailing in Washington and other allied capitals that had suffered German aggression.[30]

The debate about membership as it pertained to the treaty negotiations was essentially a continuation of this debate, with some important additions. The central issue revolved around the fear that those countries left out of the pact would become the next targets (if they were not already) of Soviet subversion or outright attack. The parallels with the debate about Germany (e.g., how to treat a defeated enemy) were most pronounced when it came to discussing Italian membership.

Italy presented particular problems. It was not a North Atlantic state or a member of the Brussels Treaty. Military opinion in the United States and Europe was skeptical about the possibility and extent of an Italian military contribution; some foresaw a drain on scarce resources.[31] On the other hand, the exclusion of Italy could lead to an unfortunate internal domestic political outcome, and political leaders were concerned about the power of the Italian Communist Party. Unlike Greece and Turkey—two future, non-North Atlantic members of the alliance—Italy was a former enemy state that had no connections with American economic and military assistance programs. Despite problems relating to geography and military significance, political concerns carried the day. Acheson expressed fears that Italy "might suffer from an isolation complex and, with its large communist party, fall victim to seduction from the east." He noted the "importance of strengthening Italian resistance to Russian domination."[32]

The French, who were initially opposed both to Italian and Norwegian membership, changed their position when they decided to press for the inclusion of their North African territories. By pressing for Italian membership and appearing to compromise over the Norwegian issue, the French hoped sufficiently to broaden the scope of the pact to include French North Africa. This stance was later altered to include only the Algerian departments.[33] A compromise was reached in February 1948: Norway was invited to join the negotiations; Italy was invited to consider the completed treaty in March; and the Algerian departments of France were included in Article 6 of the North Atlantic Treaty, which defined the area covered by the treaty (see below).

A prime constraint on the negotiations when it came to discussing membership was the problem of ends and means. In one respect, the greater the membership of the alliance, the easier it would be to apportion limited American resources—because this was expected to prevent piecemeal requests for aid, which would increase the overall total—and share responsibilities by limiting redundancies. On the other hand, the very fact that those resources were scarce compelled the negotiators to search for ways of limiting invitations to membership. The attempt to strike a balance between means and ends, between embracing every anticommunist state on the continent (and even beyond) and limiting membership to those that could actively support the terms of the treaty (without sacrificing those who could not) was an issue that was never really solved. The debate about membership had begun over how to regard the former enemy states of Germany and Italy; it now became a debate over whom to regard as an ally.

2. *Categories of membership.* Although in the end only one form was agreed on as being acceptable, the participants at the Washington Talks originally considered at least two types of membership. The first was membership of maximum commitment for reciprocal assistance and full partnership in military planning. The second was membership involving limited commitment, where, for example, bases or facilities would be provided in return for a commitment by full members to defend the territory of limited members. Kennan took the idea of limited commitment even further and suggested neutrality for some members and "graded membership" for others.[34]

The idea of different categories of membership was rejected by the Permanent Commission of the Brussels Treaty, to which agreements reached in Washington were submitted for consideration. The Permanent Commission, reports Henderson, "thought that countries would either have to join the pact or not join, and that difficulties would arise if some were permitted to join on easier conditions than others."[35] The issue of graded membership was, for the time being, settled.

3. *Duration.* The Brussels Treaty representatives favored a long term for the North Atlantic Treaty—up to fifty years. The United States and Canada thought that twelve to twenty years would be sufficient. The Canadians broke the deadlock by proposing a review of the treaty after it had been in effect for half its duration, which was agreed at twenty years.

4. *Coverage.* This point was closely related to the question of membership, except that it involved more than questions of allies and former

enemies. As far as the treaty negotiations were concerned, this was the finer and more difficult of the two points of principle. Membership was a broader concept that could, for instance, include Belgium and France but not their overseas territories.[36] The debate about the area to be included had to be precise: the treaty was to be read as a legal obligation, and the definition of the area in which aggression would bring into operation the pact's provision for military assistance (Article 5) was one that could not afford to be vague. It was finally agreed that an armed attack on one or more of the signatories would be considered an attack on all, and the obligation of mutual military assistance for defense purposes was declared to be applicable to the territories or possessions of the signatories in the North Atlantic area north of the Tropic of Cancer.[37]

Each of these four points would create numerous textual difficulties when it came time to translate broadly agreed principles into the working language of a treaty. The obligation clause was particularly important. The Americans sought wording along the lines of the Rio Treaty, which made clear reference to the constitutionally mandated powers of Congress to declare war, while the Europeans wanted the clause to be more binding and immediate in its implications. Other problems arose from the debate about the military organization that would flow from the treaty. The French wanted the machinery of the treaty to take over the military planning for the entire area covered by the treaty, which reflected a French desire to strengthen the Anglo-American engagement to continental defense. The Americans and British opposed this, and formal military planning of the type the French sought did not begin until late 1950, when the Korean War provided planners with a new sense of urgency.[38] A third area of concern focused on collaboration in nonmilitary areas and on consultation. The Canadians pressed strongly and successfully for a vague commitment on the part of the signatories to pursue closer cultural, economic, and social ties. Article 2 of the treaty reflects this commitment. Article 4 called for the allies to consult whenever any one of them felt that its security or territorial integrity was threatened.

Insight into the textual difficulties surrounding the negotiations is provided by Henderson in his description of those relating to the wording of the treaty's preamble:

> All the representatives recognized the importance of the Preamble. It was hoped that the Preamble would summarize the purposes of the Pact in simple language which could have popular appeal throughout the world.

Unfortunately, this proved a difficult task. Listening to the debates on the Preamble, it was difficult at moments to believe in that singleness of spirit of the North Atlantic community which the Preamble itself was meant to epitomize and proclaim. It was finally decided to state briefly and in simple prose the main objectives of the parties in concluding the North Atlantic Treaty.[39]

Justifying the Treaty: Public Opinion and Political Elites

Simplifying the Threat

Early conceptions about providing for the security of Europe rested on assumptions about the centrality of economic recovery, which would restore confidence and generate prosperity. Perceived Soviet hostility altered this conception to include an increased military element that would be institutionalized by treaty and that would be comprised of more than the postwar occupation forces of the United States, United Kingdom, and France. The notion, propounded by Kennan, that military commitments were necessary only insofar as they bolstered public confidence without detracting from economic recovery, was soon eclipsed by uncertainty over how much additional military force would be enough. Conceptions about restoring confidence thus soon came to include the idea of a defensive alliance formalized by a treaty that would illustrate the resolve of the West. What began as a treaty and essentially a confidence-building measure evolved, within a few years, into a full-blown military organization.

The transition, however, was gradual. Ironically, one event that hastened the process was the effort to justify to Western public opinion the need for a treaty. Kennan reports that "to justify a treaty of alliance as a response to the Soviet threat, it was inexorably necessary to oversimplify and to some extent distort the nature of this threat. To the Soviet mind this was a suspicious circumstance."[40] In immediate practical terms, the simplification of the threat made it easier to sell the treaty to a war-weary public and to skeptical legislatures. More broadly, it helped to resolve—at least in the short term—the complexities and ambiguities of international politics. The early and intense focus on the Soviet threat and the identification of that threat with all forms of communism compelled Western policymakers to approach a wide range of international problems in terms of how those problems fitted within their conceptions of anticommunism and containment. Those problems not necessarily—or at least not initially—associated with the Soviet threat, particularly the power vacuums in Germany and Japan, the need for reform and recovery in Europe, civil disruption in Africa and Asia, and revolutionary nationalism in the Third World, would henceforth be viewed largely in terms of their Cold War political value and how or whether they could be addressed or manipulated to advantage. In the domestic arena, rhetoric that described a monolithic and implacable foe helped garner the political support and public approval required for expenditures and actions, including those aimed at marginalizing isolationists or alleged appeasers.[41] A simplified threat made things easier; black and white were preferable and conceptually easier to grasp than shades of gray. The North Atlantic Treaty marked one of the defining moments of the Cold War; it signaled that deterrence and containment, rather than reassurance and engagement, would be the preferred means of dealing with the potential Soviet adversary.[42]

American and British Conceptions of the North Atlantic Treaty

The early public release of the treaty, some three weeks prior to the date marked for its signature, formed part of an overall campaign in Europe and North America to garner the legislative support and broad public approval that was needed for ratification.[43] American acceptance was crucial, and the Truman administration's efforts to promote the treaty provide an important early record of what the treaty was perceived to represent.

In a radio address to the nation on 18 March 1949, Acheson drew attention to the painful but unmistakable lessons of the twentieth century, lessons that had proved that the security of North America and Europe were inseparably linked. The North Atlantic Treaty, he declared, was designed to bring "a corrective influence to a precarious world."[44] Because it was in harmony with the UN Charter, it would give "added strength to the United Nations. It is designed to help bring about world conditions which will permit the United Nations to function as contemplated at the San Francisco Conference." Like the UN, the treaty would promote peace by making clear the consequences of the use of force.[45]

Although Acheson framed his first public appeal in terms of the treaty's consistency with the principles of the UN, he and his colleagues on both sides of the Atlantic regarded it, from the beginning, as something more than an extension of the UN Charter. Not only was it wholly consistent with the grand design for world peace as envisaged by the charter, it also was regarded as the formal acknowledgment of a community of interests that bound North America and Western Europe.[46] Acheson also noted its potential political, psychological, and military value.

By promoting collective defense, for example, the North Atlantic Treaty would complement the European Recovery Program (ERP). Acheson proclaimed that they "are both essential to the attainment of a peaceful, prosperous and stable world."[47] Article 3 of the treaty provided for mutual aid—a concept, as we have seen, at the very heart of the Marshall Plan—and the promise of mutual military assistance contained in the treaty would therefore be an extension and enhancement of the broader concept of a previously agreed commitment to mutual aid.[48]

Thus, the first public pronouncements by U.S. officials about the North Atlantic Treaty stressed its consistency with the UN Charter and drew attention to its ability to further widely accepted and promulgated goals of U.S. foreign policy. From the beginning, it was cast as part of the larger process of securing world peace: "If we can secure North Atlantic peace," said Acheson, "we shall have gone a long way to assure peace and security in other areas as well."[49] In addition, Acheson chose to characterize the treaty as part of an ancient historical process of political evolution driven by the principles of democracy, individual liberty, and the rule of law. The treaty was "the product of at least 350 years of history, perhaps more. It is clear that the North Atlantic Pact is not an improvisation. It is the statement of the facts and lessons of history."[50]

The essence of the treaty, then, as first publicly enunciated by the Truman administration, was that it was an instrument of peace consistent with the UN Charter that would be made more effective through its ability to make clear the determination of the North Atlantic powers to provide for their own defense. Although the treaty was characterized as the formal acknowledgment of underlying realities and long-standing common interests, it was also viewed as being part of a process. If the identity of interest among the North Atlantic nations was stable and rooted in historical continuity, then the act of sustaining and securing that identity was not. Thus, Acheson closed his second public statement on the text of the proposed treaty with a dual reminder about both the process and its means: "To have genuine peace we must constantly work for it. But we must do even more. We must make it clear that armed attack will be met by collective defense, prompt and effective. That is the meaning of the North Atlantic Pact."[51]

Indeed, Acheson's most effective argument for the treaty was, not a plea for international peace, but a calculated appeal to the self-interest of the United States.

It had long been an article of faith in American political history that the cost of freedom was unceasing vigilance, but the application of this axiom to the postwar era in general and to the process of rebuilding and defending Western Europe in particular would have important consequences. Efforts at being eternally vigilant to secure the freedom of the West would require Americans to put aside their traditional preference for isolation from world affairs. Standing eternally vigilant also meant that the North Atlantic Treaty, now the primary instrument of a new American activism in Europe, would itself require unending attention and constant public reaffirmation. In short, the process and the goal of securing world peace would become confused and merged with the means.

British political leaders had taken the initiative to promote the concept of a North Atlantic Treaty, and their rhetoric closely resembled that of the Americans. In a speech to the House of Commons on 18 March 1949, Bevin stated that the Atlantic Pact was "a purely defensive arrangement" consistent with the principles of the UN and the inherent right of individual or collective self-defense recorded in Article 51 of the UN Charter. Although the Brussels Treaty had made some progress toward restoring a sense of security in Europe, "this new Pact," declared Bevin, "brings us under a wider roof of security, a roof which stretches over the Atlantic Ocean and gives us the assurance of great preponderance of power" against any threats. Bevin went on to state that the treaty would give confidence to the states of Western Europe and speed their economic development.[52] In private, he expressed his belief that a North Atlantic Treaty would have the additional effect of helping the French government convince the opposition of the wisdom of further unifying the western zones of Germany and beginning to integrate them into the alliance. These hopes appear to have been validated by events, because, within one week of the signing of the treaty, a consensual Allied policy on Germany had been agreed, after years of prolonged and inconclusive argument.[53]

Like Acheson, Bevin believed in the power of the treaty both to bind Europe together and to promote positive future change.[54] For Prime Minister Clement Attlee and his cabinet, the Atlantic alliance was conceived as the first step toward the establishment of a global security system, and Bevin's comments reveal the extent to which his conceptions of European security were linked with those of North America and, by implication, the world.[55] British leaders had placed their long-term hopes for peace, prosperity, and security firmly on NATO's rising star.[56]

Signing the Treaty: The Rhetoric of Hope and Determination

After months of negotiation among the principal North Atlantic powers and three weeks of public discussion, the treaty was signed in Washington on 4 April 1949. Truman declined to sign the treaty, preferring instead to leave the honor to Acheson.[57] The remarks made at the signing ceremony, offered by the representatives of the eleven original signatories (Greece and Turkey were invited to accede to the treaty in 1952), are significant, both for their rhetorical richness and for the clues that they provide about how the treaty was viewed by the men who signed it—many of whom were participants in the negotiating process. Their rhetoric was flowery, and some patience is required when sifting through it, but an examination of it yields important insights.

Paul-Henri Spaak, the Belgian prime minister and minister for foreign affairs, described the treaty as "an act of faith in the destiny of Western civilization." Lester Pearson, secretary of state for external affairs for Canada, declared that "our treaty is no mere Maginot Line against annihilation, no mere foxhole from fear, but the point from which we start for yet one more attack on all those evil forces that would block our way to justice and to peace." Gustav Rasmussen, minister for foreign affairs for Denmark, called it "a solemn reaffirmation" of the UN Charter "designed to strengthen the system of the United Nations." Robert Schuman, French minister of foreign affairs, called it a "sign of France's absolute determination to maintain peace." Carlo Sforza, the Italian foreign minister, referred to the treaty as "a complex and articulate instrument" and said that he hoped it would "prove to be like the English Magna Carta: on one side intangible, on the other side a continuous creation ... [it] will constitute one among the noblest and most generous events in human history." Joseph Bech, representing Luxembourg, expressed optimism that "it may give the world a salutary period of lasting truce." Dirk Stikker, the Dutch foreign minister, said it marked "an end of an illusion" (the UN) and "the birth of a new hope of enduring peace." Halvard Lange, the Norwegian foreign minister, called it "a pact of peace"; while José Caeiro Da Matta, signing for Portugal, expressed similar sentiments and characterized it as "a precious instrument of peace." Ernest

Bevin, representing Britain, declared that the North Atlantic Treaty was part of a larger "process of enthroning and making paramount the use of reason as against force." Truman, who made the closing remarks at the ceremony, called the treaty "a simple document" and "a solemn pledge ... a shield against aggression and the fear of aggression—a bulwark which will permit us to get on with real business of government and society."[58]

We would not expect to find much disagreement among men who had spent the previous fifteen months in arduous negotiations over the terms and implications of a treaty and who had come together in the first place out of a shared sense of danger and common interest, and we therefore should not be surprised that their comments were positive and even idealistic, especially at so public a gathering and before the treaty had been ratified. Allowing, then, for the understandable propaganda value of the event and for the necessity to give the treaty maximum positive exposure, what can be said about these comments? What do they reveal about conceptions of the treaty and about the underlying assumptions and political expectations of the statesmen who signed it?

Some of these conceptions, like the treaty's consistency with the UN Charter and its nonaggressive, peaceful nature, have already been examined. However, the remarks at the signing ceremony highlight some of the less obvious but no less important notions surrounding the functions of the treaty and the processes that it was expected to further.

Like the treaty itself, the ceremony marks both a beginning and an end. The beginning was a change not in the West's political objectives, which remained constant, but in the collective judgment, initiated by Britain and led by the United States, of the means of their attainment. In the initial postwar period Western leaders had been cautious, relying on the UN to achieve a settlement and bring peace to a divided and devastated European continent. By the spring of 1949, with the North Atlantic Treaty signed and yet with the fear of Soviet invasion still widespread in Europe, the West, and particularly the United States, began to display publicly that it was prepared to take on the larger risks of supporting an alliance that involved the threat and possible use of force, while still seeking to gain the maximum advantage from the message this would convey without having actually to resort to war.

This same period also marks an end—the end of reliance on the promise of the UN. With the signing of the treaty, there emerged hope that Europe's internecine quarrels and hatreds would be extinguished, forever laid to rest by the positive collective force of the North Atlantic Community. The UN had been vested with great hopes and received considerable public exposure not unlike that later given to the North Atlantic Treaty. With these hopes waning, and with the process of selling the notion of an alliance to Western public opinion following soon thereafter, it was even more important not to allow the end of the previous era to overshadow the effort to promote an alternative path.

That the event was marked by rhetoric and the shared imperative to sound enthusiastic is obvious, but that does not exhaust its importance. For it was staged to establish at a conscious if not subconscious level, both for the statesmen present and for the masses of the ordinary Western public, the link between the instrument of the treaty and the higher purposes of Western political endeavor. It was an identification that revived the ancient myth of the crusades and the idea that only by banding together in common cause could Western civilization be saved from the communist hordes. The pomp and rhetoric of the ceremony, with so much emphasis placed on the treaty's ability to further the ends of Western civilization, can be regarded as part of a larger effort to condition psychologically the North Atlantic nations for the ideological struggle that lay ahead.

Ratifying the Treaty

In June 1949 the treaty was submitted for ratification to the Senate Committee on Foreign Relations.[59] Aware of the Senate's historical reluctance to enter into treaties of alliance, Acheson declared that "if it can be called an alliance, it is an alliance only against war itself."[60] Acheson told the committee that the treaty was consistent both with the UN Charter and with the U.S. Constitution; it would avert war by showing the determination of the West; and it would increase U.S. national security and was therefore in the best interests of the country.

Each of these issues posed potential (though in the end not fatal) hurdles to ratification, but Acheson's principal argument was that although the treaty represented a new political arrangement and a new commitment for the United States, it was also an accurate reflection of the future course of U.S. foreign policy: "Since the course of action envisaged by the treaty is substantially that which the United States would follow without the treaty, there is great advantage to the United States and the entire world in making clear our intentions in advance."[61] The salience of this notion would be borne out by subsequent events, especially the Korean War, when the United States arguably did not make its intentions clear. At the time, however, one of the treaty's strongest early selling points was that, in addition to its many other attributes, it was a clear statement of political intent designed to be read—and understood—by its signatories and their potential adversaries alike.

Acheson stressed the psychological value of the treaty, declaring that it would "free the minds of men in many nations from a haunting sense of insecurity." A general sense of well-being, he reasoned, would enable the United States to realize substantial savings in connection with both the ERP and with the domestic military establishment. This then was the linkage between the psychological and economic value of the treaty: by addressing insecurity it would promote fiscal responsibility. Before this linkage could be established, however, a strong declaration of the intent to defend against aggression was needed. There could not be a more propitious opportunity for such a demonstration as the North Atlantic Treaty.[62]

But the treaty also offered more specific and perhaps more lasting contributions to world peace: by promoting the unity and security of the North Atlantic region and by symbolizing agreement to seek a unified approach to common problems, it would make possible the integration of the western zones of Germany into Western Europe and facilitate a lasting solution to the German problem. Moreover, the treaty would achieve these results while simultaneously strengthening British ties to the continent and reassuring France.[63] Through coordinated mutual aid and self-help (the twin pillars of U.S. foreign policy and of the treaty itself), the signatories would derive "maximum benefits with minimum costs and bring far greater strength than could be achieved by each acting alone."[64] In sum, the treaty was cost-effective, practical, in harmony with U.S. and international law, and could potentially solve some of the major outstanding international issues—what to do about Germany and how to prevent renewed militarism on the European continent.

The treaty was debated by the Senate from 5 to 21 July 1949. Its two strongest proponents were Senators Tom Connally and Arthur Vandenburg, who, in presenting the treaty to the Senate, echoed some of the administration's arguments but who also presented some new ones in favor of ratification. Connally stressed that the treaty was something new that, in binding the United States to Europe, would create a radical change in European political relations.

Already we see that the treaty is not typical of the ad hoc alliances, used so extensively in modern European history, to meet a particular crisis or wage a particular war; nor is it typical of the treaties designed to achieve a delicate balancing of power. Alliances and coalitions have usually been directed against or have sought protection from a definite opponent. The North Atlantic Treaty is directed against any armed attack within a specified area.[65]

With American participation, the treaty would put an end to balance-of-power politics in Europe.

While the treaty did not designate an opponent in advance, and could therefore be characterized as an instrument of peace, it did restrict U.S. obligations, and those of its allies, to one area, and would therefore not constitute the open-ended worldwide commitment about which many senators had expressed deep misgivings. The treaty was new and would usher in a new era in European relations precisely because the United States was involved: this salutary presence would put an end, once and for all, to Europe's periodic wars.

It would be misleading to dismiss the senator's views as little more than American arrogance or political naiveté, for the political history of the United States has been strongly colored by the belief in America's destiny as a "light to the world" and as a crusader for good.[66] Thus, Connally could reasonably, if not entirely correctly, argue that the North Atlantic Treaty would be "the logical extension of the principle of the Monroe Doctrine to the North Atlantic area."[67]

Although Connally shared the Truman administration's view that the strength of the treaty lay in its ability to broadcast political intent in advance, his reference to the principles of the Monroe Doctrine highlighted the differences between conflicting conceptions of how best to advance U.S. interests in Europe. As a statement of political interest, the Monroe Doctrine sought to extend American protection to the newly independent South American republics and to protect U.S. hegemony in the Western hemisphere. The North Atlantic Treaty was more than a statement of interest, because it bound the United States in advance to come to the aid of its allies. The obligatory nature of the treaty set it apart from any doctrinal approach, which is the course of action George Kennan had been advising.

Kennan repeatedly expressed his belief in the temporary—not permanent—nature of the alliance, and he had urged his political masters not to sign a treaty, preferring instead a less formal type of guarantee in the form of a statement of interests.[68] Once the notion of a treaty had been accepted, Kennan's abiding conception of NATO was one of a political guarantee extended, through U.S. participation, to Western Europe to enable it to recover its economic and political stability as a precondition for seeking a pan-European settlement with the Soviets.[69]

Senator Vandenburg's testimony, which followed Connally's by one day, characterized the treaty as a force for peace. Addressing concern among his colleagues that the treaty would perpetuate the division of the continent by blocking peace initiatives, he declared that "there is no hypothesis of honorable peace into which the North Atlantic Treaty does not fit. It stands in the way of nothing but armed aggression and nobody but armed aggressors. It cannot possibly handicap any successful peace efforts in other directions. It can only supplement and strengthen them."

The real threat to world peace and security lay not in the new defensive arrangements implied by the treaty, but rather "from embattled, greedy communism at home and abroad." The United States was the ultimate target of communist conspiracies ("Every vigilant American knows this is true," declared Vandenburg), and it needed the North Atlantic Treaty to minimize the threat.

> Those who share jeopardy must show vigilance against it. That is what this treaty does. It reduces the jeopardy by anticipating it. It reduces the jeopardy by sharing it. Indeed it may well extinguish the jeopardy—and I believe it will—by the clear demonstration that this united self-defense against aggression will be invincible.[70]

In sounding the tocsin against communist conspiracy, Vandenburg did more than appeal to anticommunist sentiment: he drew attention to the breadth and seriousness of the threat and to the consequent necessity of a broad and united response. If the communist threat was pervasively ranged against the Western democracies, then the only realistic response was a common one in the form of the North Atlantic Treaty. It not only conformed to the broad principles of American—and Western—political ideology, it also was clearly in the national interest.

> My view is that this treaty is the most sensible, powerful, practical, and economic step the United States can now take in the realistic interest of its own security; in the effective discouragement of aggressive conquest which would touch off world war three; in the stabilization of western Germany; and, as declared by its own preamble, in peacefully safeguarding the

freedoms and the civilization founded on the principles of democracy, individual liberty and the rule of law.[71]

On 21 July the Senate voted 82-12 in favor of ratification. The treaty entered into force on 14 August 1949.

From Treaty to Organization

Creating the NATO Machinery

The outbreak of the Korean War in June 1950 brought the Cold War to a new level of intensity.[72] When North Korean troops crossed the 38th parallel marking the postwar division of North and South Korea, Western political leaders saw the hand of Moscow at work, and many regarded the invasion as the first move by the communists in an attempt at global domination. Viewed in conjunction with the collapse of Nationalist China in the summer of 1949, this new catastrophe in Asia seemed momentarily to negate everything Western diplomats had achieved in Europe—the Truman Doctrine, the Marshall Plan, the North Atlantic Treaty. In terms of conceptions of European security, the war in Korea helped transform the instrument of the North Atlantic Treaty, which heretofore had been regarded largely in terms of its ability to restore confidence, into the organization that became NATO.[73] In short, the war helped put the "O" in NATO.[74]

This process began at the December 1950 meeting of the North Atlantic Council (NAC), where the foreign ministers of the member states formally approved the idea of a united command and appointed NATO's first supreme commander, General Dwight D. Eisenhower.[75] Eisenhower was provided with an international staff and charged with the duty of integrating the forces from Western Europe and North America that had been assigned to NATO.[76] The NAC also accepted in principle the idea of German participation, but it would be six years before this became fact. Acheson's account of the meeting records that

> the defense ministers of the treaty states agreed on an ingenious recommendation, called a strategic concept, and passed it on to be considered by the NATO Council. The concept was not a plan but a collection of principles for devising an integrated defense. No European nation was to attempt a complete military establishment, but rather each was to make its most effective contribution in the light of its geographical position, economic capacity, and population.[77]

This, the first of NATO's many strategic concepts, was known as "balanced collective forces."

The acceptance of the strategic concept was a landmark for the alliance. Subsequent meetings in the early 1950s would approve force goals and debate and approve extended membership of the alliance. But the decision to apply the principles that underlay the strategic concept marked the crucial turning point in the evolution from treaty to organization. The defense of Western Europe was no longer conceived as being upheld by the collection of states that had signed the North Atlantic Treaty, but rather by the organization that the signing had spawned. It is an important distinction.

The notion that European states would forgo attempts to maintain or create a complete military establishment was a radical departure from past practice. This period marks the emergence of NATO as a transnational institution, and is an early indication of the alliance's remarkable ability to forge consensus, overturn long-standing tradition, and identify and nurture common interests. The speed and success of these early efforts to create institutional machinery for regional collective defense helped establish in the minds of Western political elites and military leaders the notion that the alliance was capable of handling difficult and challenging tasks. It reaffirmed their faith in the power of collective undertakings, in the indivisibility of transatlantic security linkage, and in the indispensability of the alliance.

By September 1951, Acheson began to describe the development of NATO as "a process of growth toward unity."[78] The North Atlantic states, he declared, now needed to translate into reality the hope and determination they had expressed in the treaty. The treaty would soon move, he said, "from a paper plan of defense" to an integrated defense force under unified command.[79]

The evolution of the alliance from a set of formal undertakings to a military and political organization was based on a changing commitment, and on changing conceptions of what was to be the purpose of the alliance. For the Americans, the conception of a collective security treaty early in 1948 had been one of a political commitment to go to war to aid any ally that had been a signatory to the treaty. Against a backdrop of European initiatives and Soviet actions in Berlin and the war in Korea, the political commitment to defend an ally in need was enhanced to embrace a commitment to prepare for the defense of Western Europe. What had begun as a treaty evolved into an organization; and the symbolic and psychological value of the treaty soon gave way to material preparations. The United States was initially reluctant, beyond its role as occupier of Germany (and, thus, guarantor against German revanchism), to commit itself militarily to the defense of Europe. But the creeping growth of a militarized view of the Cold War undermined the original program of European unity through economic recovery, despite Kennan's warnings about the primacy of political issues.[80]

Over time, the United States embraced a militarized view of the Cold War, and its policies were ultimately shaped by the notion that a Soviet attack could only be deterred with military strength. The efforts for the military defense of Europe found institutional form in NATO. For Kennan, the North Atlantic Treaty was the result of misplaced emphasis and a lack of balance between political and military considerations.[81] Whether we agree with this hypothesis is not important. The important point is that, for the vast majority of political and military planners in the United States and Europe, rearmament through NATO became a precondition for economic recovery and peace. Once accepted, this theme would be religiously and re-peatedly invoked by NATO's leaders. Its continuous reaffirmation reflected a deeper faith in the notion that to secure peace, the West had to prepare for war.

What, we might ask, could have been important enough to risk the continued division of Europe, when so many in the West had pledged themselves to work tirelessly for its unification? The answer lies not so much in Kennan's views about an imbalance between political and military considerations, but in an awareness that the coming together and intermingling of political and military elements had helped to obscure original purposes. In this context, the division of Europe was not the ultimate price to be paid but a refinement of the objective itself.

The North Atlantic Treaty was conceived and adopted in an environment of fear and uncertainty of the immediate postwar period, when ideas and prospects for European unification came to rest not on Europe as a whole but on *Western* Europe. The treaty—and later the organization—came to symbolize peace and security, and the division of Europe was a tragic but acceptable price to pay for rescuing its western portions.

There was some logic to all of this. The United States and its Western European allies had just waged a costly and protracted war against the Axis powers. With the perceived lessons of this conflict in mind and with a growing consensus supporting the view that the Soviets were in many ways as bad as Hitler and his associates, the course became clear. Political and military leaders were determined not to allow the Soviet behemoth to dominate the Eurasian landmass.[82] NATO, it was believed, would help them achieve this objective.

NATO and the Concept of a North Atlantic Community

Throughout 1950 and 1951, Acheson shaped his vision of the new alliance in several important speeches. In an address to Congress late in May 1950, he declared that "the North Atlantic Community is emerging as a political reality of the greatest importance," the continued strengthening of which "will benefit free peoples everywhere" and advance Western interests far beyond the borders of the North Atlantic region.[83]

Beneath Acheson's conception of an emerging North Atlantic Community lay one of the fundamental political axioms of the Cold War—namely, that a united community of North Atlantic nations would be a strong community, and that a strong community would promote and preserve peace. As he told the Congress: "In our unity, there is strength. And, in our strength, there is unity."[84]

The process of determining how and when the community would be strong enough was, presumably, to be left up to its leaders and, through them, to NATO. The difficult process of defining the terms of the treaty would pale in comparison to the effort of defining how much was enough and of proportioning scarce resources. The problems associated with matching ends with means would vex alliance leaders throughout the Cold War, and would threaten, at times, to undermine the much-vaunted solidarity of the nebulous entity called the North Atlantic Community.

To those, like Acheson, who invoked it, the North Atlantic Community was no mere label of political expediency. Its growth, in concert with the development of organizational machinery to enhance the effectiveness of the North Atlantic Treaty, was part of "a clear conception which we have all had" that the security of one member of the alliance was tied to the security of all.[85]

The notion of indivisible transatlantic security was widely accepted early on in the Cold War, and seems to have been spared the political scrutiny it deserved. With the option of national choice buried under the avalanche of evidence that indicated that only a common approach was feasible, the issues of the day came to be focused not on whether there was security linkage, but on how the implications of this linkage, now established as fact in the minds of policymakers, could be managed.

The North Atlantic Community was not simply an appendage of the North Atlantic Treaty. The treaty, the organization, and the community of member states were held to be the formal and organizational manifestations of something far larger than a military arrangement: "the treaty," declared Acheson, "did not create something new as much as it recorded a basic reality—a unity of belief, of spirit, and of joint interest which was already felt by the nations of the North Atlantic Community."[86] Although the treaty was said to have emerged out of a long-standing community of interests and values, it is significant that before the treaty was signed there were only scattered, oblique references to a North Atlantic Community. After the spring of 1949, however, the concept of a North Atlantic Community became a central feature of many official public utterances about NATO.

A community, by nature, is organic: it is a growing and evolving body of people leading a common life under some form of shared social and political organization. A community can acquire a sense of its identity only in relation to other communities, whether past or present. In the early years of the Cold War, both recent and ancient history contributed to the notion of a North Atlantic Community. Recent history showed that, unlike the rigid Soviet-dominated community that was emerging through force in the East, the North Atlantic Community was based on shared principles, cultural heritage, and common consent. Ancient history also established the North Atlantic Community as something new: never before had the possibility appeared so likely that Western Europeans, with North Atlantic partners, would put an end to centuries of internecine conflict.

The North Atlantic Treaty was conceived as the formal expression of this community—a community that had evolved out of long historical processes and that had been quickened by the Soviet threat. Sharing the very attributes of the community that had given birth to it, the treaty, according to Acheson, had "broad and constructive intent." He observed that:

> The North Atlantic Treaty is far more than a defensive arrangement. It is an affirmation of the moral and spiritual values which we hold in common. It represents the will of the peoples of the North Atlantic community not only to safeguard their freedom, but to seek increasing fulfillment of it. The central idea of the treaty is not a static one; it is conceived rather in the spirit of growth, of development, of progress. What we seek is to pursue the opportunity for a living heritage of freedom to continue to grow.[87]

Compelled by the dangers of communist expansion and subversion, the North Atlantic states had first to give priority to the establishment of an integrated defense. But these dangers, warned Acheson, must not cause the West to lose sight of its larger objectives of building strong economic, social, and political institutions—institutions without which all objectives, both short- and long-term, would be unattainable. The North Atlantic Community could fulfill its potential only after it had provided a strong defense—indeed, a strong defense under NATO would be the vehicle for the attainment of the higher stages of human development.

The notion of the treaty as a motive force, something mechanical in its ability to propel Europe toward a more secure future and, at the same time, adhesive in its potential to bind the states of Western Europe to each other and to North America, is novel and far-reaching in its implications. Schemes for the unification of Europe under various political, military, or religious guises are as old as the idea of Europe itself.[88] What is striking about this conception is that the force uniting and balancing Western Europe, protecting it from itself and from its enemies, is an external one. For the first time, we see the possibility that at least a portion of Europe could be united and pacified through the actions of a non-European power.

Others took this notion even further. Discussing the idea of the proposed North Atlantic Treaty in April 1948, Canadian statesman Louis St. Laurent declared that it "would not be merely negative. It would create the dynamic counter attraction to Communism—the dynamic attraction of a free, prosperous and progressive society, as opposed to the totalitarian and reactionary society of the Communist world."[89] NATO, then, would not only attract its allies into a closer, more stable, and more secure association; it would also become a magnet for the oppressed or disaffected states of the Communist bloc.

The defense efforts of NATO were sometimes cast as being an unfortunate but necessary first hurdle to the attainment of the more profound political and social objectives of the North Atlantic Community. One among many examples of this phenomenon can be found in the communiqué of the North Atlantic Council at the conclusion of the Lisbon meeting in February 1952.

> The partnership between the nations of the North Atlantic Treaty is not just for defense alone but of enduring progress. The members of the Council look forward to the time when the main energies of their association can be less concentrated on defense and more fully devoted to cooperation in

other fields, for the well-being of their peoples and for the advancement of human progress.[90]

NATO thus was cast as the necessary, though regrettable, first step toward a higher level of development for humanity.

Public Opinion and NATO

The appeals to higher purposes made by Acheson and his associates on the NAC were not simply pretense, aimed to deflect potential domestic criticism of the alliance by stressing its social relevance. The early 1950s marked the emergence of a conscious recognition that NATO was on trial before a global audience comprised of potential enemies, as well as potential allies. The scrutiny of allies and adversaries made it imperative for the alliance as a whole, as well as for its individual leaders, constantly to move forward, look ahead, rationalize, and promote the alliance as a broad-based and broadly conceived instrument of political and social achievement, and ever to seek to increase its capabilities and effectiveness. Part of this process, which included impassioned pleas to public opinion, focused on the wider and looser concept of a North Atlantic Community and on the need to promote NATO on grounds not associated with military defense. Generating new conceptions about the promise and purpose of the alliance was also a key element.

At an address made at the opening of the Lisbon summit, Acheson declared,

> Once we have become sufficiently strong, we shall still be on trial. Our wisdom and creativeness will be challenged. We shall need to be resolute of spirit, restrained in temper, and audacious in concept, but when I look back over the last years I take heart for the years ahead. The problems they will bring will be no more formidable or complex than those we have already faced or surmounted. We will succeed because we *must* succeed.[91]

The notion that NATO could be a vehicle to something more than military security was propounded even more emphatically by Averill Harriman, U.S. director for mutual security, at a public ceremony marking the third anniversary of the signing of the North Atlantic Treaty. NATO, he declared, "has become one of the most powerful facts of international life. It is the foundation of the structure of security the free nations are building around the world." As opposed to the old European system of war and diplomatic intrigue and the current Soviet system of dictatorship, the North Atlantic states "are participating in a new development in the history of nations. NATO is the new concept."[92]

It is true that the states of North America and Western Europe had many shared political interests—the most manifest being the perceived need to defend against the Soviet threat—as well as a similar, if not always harmonious, cultural and historical heritage. But the notion of shared experience was adopted by NATO's leaders to further their political objectives. If larger goals were realized in the process, so be it; but the overriding immediate objective was the establishment of an integrated defense, and one tactic of garnering the public support and sacrifice required for its attainment called for a broad-based appeal to higher values.

According to Harriman, a strong NATO would make aggression impractical and "then … NATO may serve as an instrument for the fulfillment of the great aspirations of mankind."[93] Harriman shared the axiomatic reasoning of many of his contemporaries among the political elite: a strong, healthy, and free society would promote peace and security; and peace and security would promote a strong, healthy, and free society. This reasoning implied that the preparation for war would bring peace and other social goods—but the process had to begin with NATO. As Harriman described it:

> Through NATO, we are working for the common defense against aggression. Through NATO, we are working for economic expansion and the prosperity of all our peoples. Through NATO, we are working to foster freedom. Through NATO, we are seeking to release the intellectual and social forces which are our common heritage.

This, he concluded, "is the philosophy behind all our joint efforts in the North Atlantic Treaty Organization."[94]

Thus, NATO was conceived as being a force for positive change, imbued with moral force flowing from the political mandate of its members when they signed the North Atlantic Treaty and committed themselves to regional collective defense. NATO was already a success: it had, according to Harriman, "forced new patterns of thought" in Europe regarding historical prejudices.[95]

A few months earlier, in Canada in November 1951, Acheson had laid the foundation for the shift in emphasis from seeking ratification of the North Atlantic Treaty to fostering a strong base of popular political support. The security of the West, he declared, now required a unity of people as well as a unity of governments. The durability of our alliance ... depends now upon the support it receives in our towns and villages, and not just in our capital cities. [The chief imperatives of the free world] today require not so much genius and inspiration at the top as comprehension and determination all the way down.[96]

Once the treaty had been signed and ratified, NATO's leaders turned their efforts of political persuasion to the public. Acheson's earlier admonition to the NAC about NATO being "on trial" was part of this phenomenon. Ironically, the recognition of the importance of public opinion for NATO meant that the jury who would judge NATO's success and determine its effectiveness would not be the Soviets and their communist allies, who had been branded the enemy, as much as it would be the masses of the ordinary Western public. Those who were to receive the benefit of the protection of the alliance would decide its fate.

One among many examples of the intensified public relations effort was a 1952 address by William H. Draper, the U.S. special representative to NATO, before the Atlantic Council Conference at Oxford University. After reciting the official U.S. view of the origins of the Cold War and of Soviet misbehavior, Draper invoked the theme of an emerging Atlantic Community and the principles that lay behind it. He also took issue with those who claimed that NATO was a purely military alliance. Although Soviet expansionism had forced military arrangements to come first, Draper declared that the West had not abandoned its other objectives. Alluding to the provision for enhanced social and cultural contacts contained in the North Atlantic Treaty, Draper observed that "no longer is NATO only a phrase or an idea. It is a going concern, and one that is growing in strength and effectiveness."[97] The global struggle against communism was nothing less than "a battle for the minds of men."[98] It was a battle in which NATO was at the forefront.

The Americans were not the only ones involved in the great psychological battles of the Cold War. Five years after the signing of the treaty, Lord Ismay, NATO's first secretary general, observed that NATO was "a great international experiment." He observed that one of the alliance's main functions was to counter anti-NATO and communist propaganda, by "acting as a forum for consultation about psychological warfare." NATO's role in the civilian field, according to Ismay, was "based on a firm and universally accepted concept of the purpose and techniques of preparing the civilian front."[99]

Western European Unity and NATO

The European Defense Community

Although the British had provided the original initiative behind the Brussels and North Atlantic treaties, it was the French who made the next significant strides toward achieving the goal of European unity by means of collective defense. In May 1952, France, West Germany, Italy, and the Benelux states signed the European Defense Community (EDC) Treaty.[100] The scheme was the most comprehensive yet produced for European defense and has been regarded as the nucleus for true European governance. It was inspired by the Pleven Plan, named after French Defense Minister René Pleven, who in 1950 had called for the creation of a European Army, into which national units would be integrated at "the smallest possible unit."[101] West Germany would be rearmed but denied both a General Staff and separate armed forces; its battalions would be distributed among the brigades of the other allies. Integration was designed to save resources, improve effectiveness, and limit the power of Germany to make war. German rearmament, now deemed essential to a successful defense of Western Europe, would take place within the EDC, which would be closely tied to NATO. The force would operate under a European defense minister, who would be responsible to a European Assembly and a European Council of Ministers. There was to be a common defense budget.

Like conceptions of NATO and of an Atlantic Community, those surrounding European unification have tended to rest largely on the assumption that a true community cannot evolve without a military organization to protect it. At its inception, it was hoped that the EDC would provide the momentum for lasting Franco-German reconciliation. It seemed the logical successor to the European Coal and Steel Community (ECSC), which had been launched to promote economic and political integration in Western Europe, particularly between France and Germany.

At a press conference following the Lisbon NAC meeting, Acheson stressed that the EDC would be "closely interlocked" with NATO. Similarly, the Lisbon final communiqué declared that the obligations and relations between the EDC and NATO should "be based on the concept of two closely related organizations [with the EDC working] within the framework of, and reinforcing" NATO.[102] This period helped establish the notion that any European efforts had to be "interlocked" with (and subordinate to) transatlantic ones. At the opening of a conference in Paris on the EDC in

February 1951, Schuman declared that "Atlantic defense and European defense ... do not exclude each other. They occupy different planes. Within the framework of Atlantic armed forces there will be a European army as a permanent instrument of the security of our continent and as an essential instrument of European integration."[103]

In conceptual terms, West European unity could exist only at the center of an Atlantic Community. Without this hierarchy, declared Acheson, "you will have disunity and weakness throughout the Atlantic Community." He also observed that European unity was "as inevitable as the movement of the stars in their courses."[104] At his farewell press conference a few weeks later, Acheson more fully propounded his conception of European unity and its relation to NATO.

> Unity in Europe could be compared to a centripetal force operating in the center of the Atlantic partnership, because strength attracts strength— weakness repels strength—and as this strength grows in Europe, there will be an inevitable drag closer of Great Britain and then of North America into closer and closer association in the Atlantic alliance.[105]

Here again we see axiomatic reasoning at work. A stronger Western Europe would mean a stronger Atlantic alliance, and a stronger alliance would mean a more peaceful world. This process also worked in reverse: if European unity did not continue, a centrifugal force would be set in motion, first Europe and then North America would drift apart, and chaos would reign. "It seems to me," concluded Acheson, "that these are fundamental axioms of political life. They are not ones that one can argue about."[106]

Acheson does not appear to have considered the negative effects that such reasoning might have on the Soviets and their allies. He relied on his axioms, which proved to him beyond doubt that a strong NATO would deter Soviet aggression. Nor does he appear to have considered the possibility that, instead of strength being cumulative, as he suggested, a "strong" NATO might alienate potential allies by giving the impression that the Atlantic alliance was entering an arms race with the Soviets that made both sides equally dangerous.[107] Such reasoning, however, would conflict with the prevailing view that a strong NATO was the prerequisite to a European settlement with the Soviets.[108]

The result of failing to discuss the assumptions and implications of axiomatic political reasoning was to constrain policy options. This was the case because the axioms from which policy flowed allowed for only those policies that would conform to the parameters of the original assumption.

For example, once it had become an article of faith that the security of Western Europe and North America were inseparably linked, it was only a short step to the conclusion that this linkage had to be formalized by an alliance. An alternative axiom, such as the one that held that the United States had no business other than business in Europe and that had been prominent in the early part of the century and during the interwar period, might have produced different policies, as it had in the past (i.e., some form of American isolationism).

The tendency of policymakers to start with a set of "fundamental axioms of political life" and, from there, to shape and implement policy may have contributed not only to an arms race dynamic founded on the unshakable belief that more was always better, but also to the emergence of a political mind-set that refused to reexamine its basic tenets and their origins. A political mind-set of this nature, unwilling to question various "certainties" about the complexities of international political relations, may have contributed to some of the more long-standing political impasses of the Cold War. The American effort to force French ratification of the EDC provides an interesting example of the consequences of axiomatic reasoning. We turn now to a discussion of that effort and its aftermath.

The Politics of Axiomatic Reasoning

By the middle of 1953, the first supreme allied commander, Europe (SACEUR), Eisenhower, had moved into the White House, the Korean War had ended, Stalin was dead, and the EDC Treaty had not yet been ratified by France. In this context, the policies of the Eisenhower administration were shaped toward three objectives. The first, regarding NATO, was to introduce the "long-haul concept," which was designed to remove the sense of economic and political urgency from the alliance that had been generated by the Korean War. This was to be accomplished by making the NATO budget sustainable over a long period.[109] The long-haul concept, declared U.S. Secretary of State John Foster Dulles, "means a steady development of NATO, which, however, will preserve, and not exhaust, the economic and fiscal strength of member nations."[110]

The long-haul concept was invoked to justify the end of large-scale U.S. economic aid to Western Europe.[111] This reduction reflected the second of Eisenhower's objectives, which was to increase the security of the United States and its allies while decreasing overall expenditures. The plan, which came to be known as the "New Look," had some of its origins in the development of U.S. tactical nuclear weaponry, which appeared to provide the means for more security at less cost.[112]

The third objective of the new administration was to try to force the ratification of the EDC Treaty. This was an inherited approach, resulting from conceptual conformity with the Truman administration's view of the necessity for EDC and its perceived status as the European core of NATO. But it also reflects the desire to reduce spending by getting better results from the collective allied effort. In short, EDC had now been embraced by the Americans on the basis of its fiscal as well as security benefits. Speaking about the signatories to the EDC Treaty, Dulles said that "unless their military and economic power is to be combined ... the whole NATO organization has a fatal weakness. The European Defense Community is needed to give NATO a stout and dependable heart."[113] Military strength would be increased through economic health, and economic health would be increased through military strength.[114]

Despite strong Anglo-American statements of support for the treaty, the French continued to resist ratification. In February 1953, French Foreign Minister Georges Bidault told Dulles that French support hinged on four issues: agreement on the protocols interpreting the treaty; a strong British association with continental Europe to offset the expected rise in West German military power; a settlement of the Saar dispute with West Germany; and active U.S. support for the war in Indochina.[115]

Although at least one author has argued that the French were stalling over the EDC largely to gain U.S. concessions and support for the war in Indochina—and thus to perpetuate colonial rule—it is clear that other factors were at work.[116] One factor was French national pride, which had been aroused over the French defeat in World War II, the heavy losses suffered in Indochina, and the idea, popular among opponents to the treaty, that the EDC would sacrifice the traditions of the French military at the cost of reviving a German army.[117] As Bidualt's cable illustrates, the French feared a purely continental conception of European security in which the United Kingdom would not be a formal participant. Without British participation, France faced potential dominance from a revived Germany.

By the end of August 1954, when the French National Assembly rejected the treaty, the EDC had become not only the symbol of Franco-German reconciliation but also the yardstick of European reconstruction. Its rejection, therefore, was regarded as a grave event that threatened to undermine the entire Western coalition.[118] The French chose ultimately not to ratify the

EDC Treaty because the price was deemed too high (e.g., German rearmament for a costly token of political unity), but also because the United States, once it had decided on German rearmament, had left France with the unpalatable option of having a rearmed Germany either in NATO or in the EDC.

Dulles had warned the French at the NATO foreign ministers conference in Paris in December 1953 that failure to ratify the treaty would have important consequences. Failure, he said, "would compel an agonizing reappraisal of basic U.S. policy."[119] German rearmament was now a requirement of alliance maintenance, rather than an expression of national choice. This threat may have pushed the French too far, prompting an already bruised national ego to assert itself against the treaty. Rigid U.S. policy was thus partially to blame for the defeat of the EDC, because it divided the French political community and intensified the ideological debate.[120]

What most observers have tended to overlook, however, is that, as suggested above, the State Department, because of its tendency to think in axiomatic terms, had little choice other than to be rigid. Once it had been accepted as axiomatic that there was to be a hierarchy of integration, with European union coming after and yet supporting an Atlantic Community, then the EDC became an essential component of the conception for Western defense. One consequence was that alternatives to the EDC—such as rearming Germany within NATO—were considered unrealistic or farfetched.[121] It is all the more remarkable, then, that just over one month after this grave event "the NATO solution" had been accepted, signed, and was on its way to unanimous ratification by member governments.[122]

The EDC had been conceived in part to extend NATO's designated authority. By merging European troops and arms into a single formation, NATO would have, in Dulles's words, "a stout and dependable heart." But the failure of the EDC is arguably less important than the debate over it, which brought into focus the contentious issues facing the Western alliance.

One of these was the issue of whether a costly and divisive token of European continental self-defense was a practical and worthy goal when the Europeans were doing so little to provide for their own defense. The notion of making West German rearmament tolerable by cloaking it in the idea of Europe as expressed by the Schuman Plan failed to gain French backing because the concept of a united Western Europe was, for now at least, too closely linked with the reality of West European dependency on NATO and, ultimately, the United States. By agreeing to the North Atlantic

Treaty and the formation of NATO, the United States had ensured France's security at a minimal cost to the French; and this made it possible for France partially to reject the EDC on the ground of national economic self-interest.[123]

The French defeat of the EDC provided an important lesson about what had been until then accepted as a fact of international political life, namely, the notion that the capacity for independent national action was severely constrained under the conditions of the Cold War. Indeed, one of the basic arguments for the creation of NATO—and one that became a central feature of NATO's political canon—was that no nation could go it alone.[124] Although the French were a few years away from making their first forays into the arena of true national independence, the outcome of the debate over the EDC provided an important warning to those who argued for alliance unity at all costs. The French, in resisting American pressure and forcing on the alliance what had previously been regarded as an unacceptable compromise, set the stage for future conflict. The U.S. response to Suez two years later would confirm for French leaders the notion that, contrary to allied conventional wisdom, national assertiveness, backed by an independent nuclear capability, was the only secure, reasonable, and honorable course.

The NATO Solution: WEU and German Rearmament

Following the French rejection of the EDC, Dulles hurried to West Germany in mid-September 1954 to meet with Chancellor Konrad Adenauer, and then on to London to confer with British Prime Minister Anthony Eden. The three leaders "agreed upon the need for speedy action and favored the early convening of a preparatory conference to consider how best to associate the German Federal Republic with Western nations on a basis of full sovereignty."[125] This agreement led to the London Conference, which implemented the "NATO solution" for continental European defense.

At the conclusion of the London Conference, the assembled allied leaders issued a declaration of their intent to end the occupation of Germany "as soon as possible." In conjunction with this goal, the Brussels Treaty would "be strengthened and extended to make it a more effective focus of European integration."[126] For this purpose, the Federal Republic of Germany (FRG) and Italy were invited to accede to a modified Brussels Treaty, which would be "modified" largely by abandoning its anti-German tone, expanding the Council of Ministers, creating an Assembly for Western European Union

(WEU), and a WEU Agency for the Control of Armaments. In addition, "the conference recorded the view of all the governments represented that the North Atlantic Treaty should be regarded as of indefinite duration."[127] The purpose of this move, according to Eden, was to help allay any remaining French fears about German rearmament.[128] These agreements were confirmed at the follow-up Conference in Paris from 20 to 22 October 1954.[129]

It is perhaps not surprising that, because of its close association with NATO, the WEU was vested with many of the same hopes and attributes. It was not, wrote Adenauer, "by any means a primarily military alliance. It is an instrument of European integration in all fields."[130] Dulles praised the concept, declaring that it "had been made possible by the North Atlantic Treaty." It was, like NATO, a force for peace and, by eliminating Franco-German hostility, "promises to create a new Europe."[131] Eisenhower's letter to the Senate, urging it to approve the protocols on ending the occupation and ratify the accession of West Germany to the North Atlantic Treaty, expressed a similar view and declared that the new arrangements would go far beyond a defensive alliance. They would promote a new sense of understanding among Europeans "which will inspire greater cooperation in many fields of human endeavor."[132] Thus, part of the "NATO solution" included not only the absorption of the WEU into NATO but also a return to the concept, temporarily shaken by the defeat of the EDC, that European unity would evolve under an Atlantic Community as expressed by NATO.

Continental and Atlantic Conceptions of Security

The dramatic failure of the EDC and the subsequent adoption of an alternative plan in which West Germany joined NATO through the WEU reflected an array of attitudes over the critical issue of military organization for continental defense. These different conceptions of European security, however, should not simply be placed under two distinct categories in which there is either a continental or an Atlantic conception of security, for there was more than one version of each.[133]

The early continentalists, with Frenchmen such as Schuman and Pleven at the forefront, viewed the EDC as a means of slowly disengaging Europe from Atlantic, Anglo-Saxon control. De Gaulle, in this sense, would be the rightful heir to these early efforts, though they were not nearly as confrontational as de Gaulle's approach would come to be. Another mode of continentalism came to be expressed by the WEU, which extended the original vision of European unity from five to seven states and which guaranteed a British continental contribution for the first time.

Although the members of NATO and of the WEU repeatedly stressed that their institutions would be "interlocked," with NATO leading and with the WEU in a supporting role, this early period in which the WEU replaced the EDC by default established the possibility that a continental conception of security was still attainable, if only Europeans would assert themselves. The possibility of this happening fluctuated throughout the Cold War, becoming less so when East-West tensions were high and more likely when they declined.

Like continental conceptions, Atlantic conceptions of European security also took different forms. One view held that although European security was important, the primary U.S. mission lay in other areas. Its role in Europe would be to assist in the long-term effort to build a European framework within which Germany could be bound and anchored. The United States would work to promote a European identity that was allied with and receptive to American leadership. The EDC was viewed as the best way to achieve these objectives.[134] Any conflict between broader U.S. objectives and the European identity would be settled—in favor of the United States—by reference to the core of political and security interests that they shared; the primacy of security over other concerns would give the United States the advantage in resolving disputes.

A second view held that the United States, through NATO, needed to be deeply engaged in Europe to protect it from the threat of Soviet invasion and subversion. The role of the United States was to be expressed by a troop presence that would help defend against the Soviet Union and by economic and military aid that would create enduring democratic political systems supported by a vigorous Western European economy and defense. The EDC, under this conception, would serve as an appendage to NATO, making its defense efforts more effective and strengthening the Atlantic framework.[135]

David Calleo has written that the pluralist vision of postwar order as envisaged by George Kennan was effectively ended when the United States assumed direct leadership for European defense under NATO. European independence had been built into the Marshall Plan, but because European self-reliance was not emphasized under NATO, Kennan's dumbbell concept gave way to an "American-directed NATO."[136] This view needs modification.

European self-reliance *was* pursued under NATO in the form of the EDC and later through the WEU, both of which were cast as the "European pillar" of the alliance. The failure of these efforts did not put an end to pluralism. Indeed, the political struggle associated with the failure may only have added greater luster to the promise of a European identity and to the notion of a Europe free from American as well as Soviet influence. These ideas would become the substance of Charles de Gaulle's vision of an alternative European order under French leadership. Thus, pluralism did not die for everyone, even though Kennan conceded defeat for his hopes so long as the Cold War endured.[137]

Despite Calleo's argument, it was not American acceptance of NATO leadership that softened the appeal of pluralism as much as it was a change in the collective judgment about how postwar order could best be secured. Pluralism held that the United States would act to balance Soviet power while Western Europe recovered; and it stressed the temporary nature of these relations and the emergence of an independent Europe—though one still closely associated with the United States—that would be strong enough to defend itself. If anything ended the notion of pluralism, then it was the acceptance of an axiom that derided true pluralism as an obsolete and dangerous notion.

U.S. forging of NATO under its leadership was a symptom of changing conceptions of international political life. It was a logical, though perhaps not inevitable, act of political and military engagement in Europe that flowed from a shared belief in the necessity for collective action. Where transatlantic security was inseparable and independent national action a fallacy, the best place for action was not at home but in Europe.

National Conceptions of NATO

One further point needs to be made, and this concerns the national motives for supporting NATO. This chapter has focused largely on U.S. motives and on the pronouncements and actions of the alliance as a whole, but that does not diminish the importance of European conceptions of NATO's form and function. In general, the Western allies held numerous common objectives and, though there were often conflicts of opinion or method, they agreed on more issues than not.[138]

As we have seen, both the French and the British had strong domestic political reasons for enlisting American support for West European defense.

American aid not only allowed them to rebuild their shattered economies and cities after the war and helped to secure them against the Soviet threat, but it also offered the possibility of retaining colonial possessions: U.S. troops in Western Europe and the American commitment to NATO freed French and British resources for imperial duties.

For British leaders, the commitment to NATO and, later, to continental European defense in the form of the WEU, had important benefits. One of these was to promote the dual aim of, according to Eden, "bringing the Germans and the French together, and keeping the Americans in Europe."[139] A British contribution was regarded as being essential not only to the defense of Western Europe but also to the defense of the United Kingdom and the Empire.[140] The British role in forging a compromise after the defeat of the EDC also paid dividends by further enhancing the Anglo-American special relationship. The results of the Paris Conference seemed to confirm Britain's claim to the role of partner to the Americans in NATO, and it set a precedent for future bridge-building between the United States and the continental allies.[141]

The French drew different lessons from this early period. They had achieved limited success by pressuring the United States and Britain for greater political and material support for the war in Indochina, as well as for increased commitments to continental defense. The tactic of withholding French support for allied initiatives, which began as early as the Washington Talks (on the issue of Italian membership) and which became most pronounced over the EDC, proved to be an effective means of gaining concessions, both in Europe and beyond. Subsequent Anglo-American resistance to these tactics resulted in further alienation and a more complete faith in the notion of national self-sufficiency.

The political objectives of Chancellor Konrad Adenauer initially were constrained by West Germany's status as a defeated former enemy. His room for maneuver was increased by the allied decision to proceed with re-armament—a move that made many Germans uncomfortable. Adenauer's success in overcoming domestic reluctance to rearmament earned him the political support of his future allies and helped him implement his foreign policy agenda.[142]

The lessons of history were arguably stronger for Germans than for other Europeans, and, like their counterparts in other states, West German political elites drew their own conclusions from the immediate postwar period.[143] After the horrors of Nazism, the destruction of the war, and the division of Germany, two things seemed clear: first, neutrality was not an option, because the Soviets could not be trusted to respect it; and second, it was imperative for the Federal Republic to join the Western community of nations. Thus, Adenauer's foreign policy goals sought first to achieve West German sovereignty and then tightly to bind the new state to a united Europe, which in turn would be tightly bound to an Atlantic Community.[144] The process of rearmament, followed by integration into a strong and united NATO, was perceived to hold the key to the ultimate reunification of Germany.

In May 1955, the occupation of the western zones of Germany was ended and the Federal Republic was formally recognized by the Western powers. That same month it acceded to the North Atlantic Treaty. Adenauer declared that "West Germany is now a member of the strongest alliance in history. It will bring us reunification."[145] The prospects for reunification were improved by German participation in Western defense, according to Adenauer, because it gave Germans "the only possible chance of exercising any influence on the decisions of the Western Allies vis-à-vis Soviet Russia."[146]

Conclusion

The early history of the alliance established some of its more lasting features. By 1955, NATO was conceived as being a multifaceted organization, capable of solving problems, providing security, and promoting change. As this chapter has illustrated, NATO would:

- Stabilize the world by promoting peace both in Europe and beyond. By serving as the foundation of the security efforts of the free world, NATO could influence events beyond its geographical purview and serve Western interests out of area.

- Revitalize the UN and permit it to function as originally conceived.

- Complement the ERP and other basic goals of U.S. foreign policy. The North Atlantic Treaty would mean a new Monroe Doctrine for Europe. Because it was founded on the concepts of mutual aid and self-help, NATO was in the interest of all concerned, and would demonstrate the benefits of a unified approach.

- Form the vanguard in the fight against communism and keep the Soviets out of Western Europe.

- Prevent renewed German militarism while promoting German reunification, as well as broader European unity and recovery;

- Stand as the formal manifestation of a North Atlantic Community founded on common interests and shared political ideals. As such, it expressed long-standing political realities and the facts and lessons of history. At the same time, it was a new form of political association involved in a process of "growth toward unity" that would change forever the nature of relations among the states of Europe by changing ancient patterns of thought.

- Promote Western civilization and help fulfill humankind's greater aspirations, by serving as a repository and defender of moral values. Symbolizing the moral superiority of the West, NATO would help "roll back" communism and serve as a powerful "counter attraction" to it.

- Promote public understanding about the danger, nature, and scope of the Soviet threat, and lead the fight against communist propaganda by coordinating psychological warfare.

- Serve as a political forum for East-West as well as for interallied diplomacy.

A strong NATO was the precondition for the achievement of these goals. The multiple connotations about the nature and promise of NATO flowed from a set of axioms that described certain fundamental realities of international political life; they were held as articles of faith precisely because they were deemed to be a true reflection of the lessons of history. They included the notions that:

- The security of Western Europe and North America was inseparably linked. As stated in Article 5 of the North Atlantic Treaty, the security of one member of the alliance was tied to the security of all; an attack on one member would be regarded as an attack on all. The nebulous concept of strength was embraced by NATO's leaders as the key to the prevention of any aggression against the alliance. There was strength in unity, and unity in strength. It was a reciprocal and simultaneous process: more strength meant greater unity, and greater unity necessarily meant more strength.

- Independent national action was dangerous and obsolete.

- A sound defense could rest only on a solid economic and social foundation, and a sound economic and social foundation required a sound defense.

- Military collaboration and rearmament were the preconditions to unity, from which point strength and, ultimately, peace would flow.

- The search for peace was an endless task and, by implication, so too was the search for strength and unity.

The application of these axioms had mixed results. On one hand, they simplified the infinite complexities of international political relations and, in so doing, assisted policymakers in "selling" both their political objectives and the programs for their realization to tired, skeptical, and sometimes hostile publics and legislatures. On the other hand, the process of simplification often constrained the possibilities for examining alternative approaches, by locking policymakers into a mind-set that was not open to ideas that challenged their fundamental assumptions.

The application (or, in the parlance of political scientists, the operationalization) of these axioms also had other important consequences. They instilled in NATO's leaders an identity crisis that took the form of deep concern—almost obsession—with the perceived need constantly to promote and advance the ends and means of the alliance. At times it appears that they held little faith in the strength of their own national political systems to resist outside aggression or subversion, so much so did they warn against it and so vehement were their claims about NATO's essential role. The habitual focus on creating more strength and greater unity may have had a profound negative impact both on the Soviets and on neutral and nonaligned states. Within the alliance, it almost certainly produced a rigidity in outlook that discouraged dissent and, by sowing resentment against what some perceived as dogmatism and ideological bullying, laid the foundation for future conflict.

Chapter 3

Managing Western Defense

This chapter explores how and why conceptions of NATO changed in response to the events of the period 1956-1966. These years were marked initially by the ill-fated 1956 Anglo-French attack on Suez and the simultaneous Soviet invasion of Hungary and, at the end, by the French withdrawal from NATO's Integrated Military Organization (IMO) in March 1966. The intervening period witnessed the Berlin crisis (1958-1963), the U-2 affair (1960), and the Cuban missile crisis (1962). Meanwhile, the United States was becoming ever more deeply entangled in Vietnam. It was a period within which there were repeated attempts at East-West reconciliation and summitry; a period that also produced the signing of the first significant arms control treaty, the 1963 Partial Test Ban Treaty. These events occurred against the backdrop of decolonization in the Third World and growing political and economic integration and cooperation in Western Europe.

The effect of these events was to produce alternating periods of confrontation and détente, which had a curious impact on NATO. In periods of confrontation, the alliance focused, true to its nature, on bolstering the strength and credibility of its military forces to meet the perceived Soviet military threat. In periods of détente, when there was a marked relaxation of strained relations, the military pressure holding the alliance together eased and the leaders of NATO, with the United States at least *primus inter pares*, were faced by the prospect that the alliance might relax, lose cohesion, and "let down its guard." The allied response was to turn to wider and looser conceptions of NATO's form and function that were consistent with the original declaration of aims in the Washington Treaty. Three main political conceptions were invoked—the Atlantic Community, interdependence, and an Atlantic Partnership—and these were accompanied by a series of strategic notions designed to hold the alliance together militarily on a long-term basis now that the West no longer enjoyed nuclear supremacy. The tenability of these political and strategic conceptions was in time challenged by the French under Charles de Gaulle, whose opposition to a U.S.-led NATO ultimately resulted in the French withdrawal from the IMO. But the other members of NATO followed the U.S. lead and joined in the formulation of these new conceptions.

This chapter is divided into five sections. The first three sections examine political concepts and ask how and why political notions were invoked in response to internal disorder and an uncertain external threat. What purpose did these political notions serve, what were their origins, and what was the difference between them? The fourth section examines strategic concepts and explores how perceived changes in the strategic environment contributed to conceptual change. In what way were new strategic concepts in this period linked to political notions? Why did they evolve as they did? What purposes were they meant to serve? The fifth section draws some conclusions.

The Reign of the Atlantic Community

The interrelationship between NATO and the concept of an Atlantic Community, as we saw in chapter 2, was symbiotic and the two eventually became synonymous. The founders of NATO simultaneously created both NATO and the Atlantic Community—that is to say that NATO's raison d'être was to defend the Atlantic Community and at the same time NATO was the Atlantic Community in the sense that it was the only overtly organizational expression or manifestation of that entity. The term *Atlantic Community* designedly conjured up a group of nations with shared values, interests, and traditions. Beyond this, the concept remained ambiguous.

The concept of an Atlantic Community formed an important part of NATO's early political rationale and was invoked by North American and

European political leaders in their attempts first to negotiate and later to ratify the Washington Treaty. The outbreak of the Korean War, however, turned attention to the immediate practical task of creating standing forces to meet the perceived Soviet threat to Western Europe. When the military threat appeared partially to recede in the mid-1950s, alliance leaders, led by John Foster Dulles, responded by reviving the notion of an Atlantic Community. In the aftermath of the Suez crisis and the Hungarian invasion, when the Soviet threat seemed more menacing again, the notion of an Atlantic Community was invoked as a conceptual framework through which NATO could respond to a changing international environment and the shifting demands of alliance. Thus, the concept in the mid-1950s was invoked first as a response to a decline in East-West tensions and, later, as a response to an increase in those tensions and to intra-alliance friction over Suez.

Developing NATO in a Period of Relative Peace

In the wake of the 1955 Geneva Summit[1] came a decline in East-West tensions, but just as the long-professed objective of détente began to come into view, alliance leaders began to warn about the possibility of a false détente and the dangers of complacency in the Western camp.[2] The possible onset of détente also was seen to justify the wisdom of Western policy as articulated by and through NATO. The chronological flow of events was interpreted as a causal relationship between the decision to rearm Germany in NATO, as embodied in the 1955 Paris Accords, and the softening in the Soviet position.[3] Although the decline in tensions was directly attributed to the growing strength of NATO, the future was said to hold even greater (though undefined) challenges in a world in which the Soviet threat remained.[4] The Soviets had changed their tactics—that was all—and only the preservation of Western unity could prevent an erosion of the Western position and win the "battle for men's minds."[5]

Although Soviet society and policy were perceived to be changing, Soviet aims were seen as remaining predominantly belligerent. Western leaders tended to view the change in the Soviet stance as a mere change in Soviet tactics.[6] Their distrust of the sincerity of the new Soviet tactics appears to have rested in part on the bitter experience of the previous Soviet "peace offensive" of 1948-1950.[7] John Foster Dulles, for example, warned that the Soviets had not abandoned their ultimate objective of conquest and subversion and would continue "with pressures to disrupt and destroy international security arrangements" in the free world.[8] Alongside the uncompromising interpretation of Soviet intentions, there was concern over the public image of NATO, and fear that Soviet propaganda was causing doubts and questions about the alliance's relevance.[9] "All the doubts and questions," declared one senior State Department official in April 1956, "have their roots in misconceptions about the premises of the Atlantic Alliance and about the true character of the international situation now confronting this country."[10] Other U.S. officials strove publicly to underline the significance of NATO by drawing attention not to what had happened but to what had *not* happened: "Since NATO came into being," declared U.S. Under Secretary of State C. Burke Elbrick, "there have been no military hostilities of any kind in the European area and the communists have not gained a single inch of additional territory. I think this speaks for itself."[11]

Peace in Europe was said to illustrate the importance of NATO. True, there are great problems in demonstrating why things have not happened: there is no saying whether NATO had an optimum strategy or whether it was only minimally effective at deterring Soviet forces that may never have intended to invade anyway. But allied leaders chose to err on the side of caution, and the search for a new and improved NATO was on.

NATO was conceived as a good investment, a sort of insurance against possible future problems.[12] But the premiums for this policy had to be paid on time—and in advance if possible—because the West could not write a check after the accident.[13] Advance payments were necessitated by the costs and requirements of weapon modernization and maintenance. To keep pace with the sweep of modern technology, NATO battle plans, training programs, infrastructure, and equipment required constant revision and updating. So, too, did the alliance itself. In the words of Elbrick: "We will continue to face a great many problems. NATO is not the kind of operation that we can ever expect to wrap up and forget about. It requires constant attention and constant effort by all members of the alliance."[14]

President Eisenhower addressed these issues in April 1956, when he observed that "a group of free nations can stay together fairly easily when you have got a definite threat to their very existence right in their faces." But with the Soviets moving into the economic and political sphere and with some of the military threat apparently lifted, "now it becomes very difficult ... through spontaneous cooperation to achieve a unity to oppose the other man."[15] Thus, the main dilemma confronting Western leaders in an era of relaxed tensions was how to maintain Western unity in the absence of a compelling need to maintain that unity. NATO became the logical focal point of these efforts because it had always been cast as the organizational embodiment of Western unity.

In a series of speeches in April and May 1956, Dulles put forth official U.S. conceptions of NATO. Like the president, Dulles appreciated the value of fear in forging bonds of alliance: "Fear," he observed, "makes easy the tasks of diplomats, for then the fearful draw together and seek the protection of collective strength. Allies no longer feel the same compulsion to submerge differences as when they faced together a clear and present danger."[16] Declaring that NATO contained "the possibilities of great development," Dulles stressed the importance of maintaining unity and increasing "cooperation *for* something rather than merely against something. Let us exalt freedom by showing better what freedom can do."[17]

The notion that NATO should place greater emphasis on working for something rather than merely against an adversary appears to have been closely linked with earlier notions about NATO's potential to act as a counterattraction to communism and as the embodiment of the higher ideals of Western civilization. With an apparent lessening of East-West tension, it was argued that the time had now come, in Dulles's words, "to advance NATO from its initial phase to the totality of its meaning."[18]

Soon after, Dulles declared that NATO had "a basis for continuing validity" because it had not been designed to serve limited purposes. It was his view "that an organization of this kind either grows or tends to dry up." Dulles characterized this process as "a law of nature" and "inevitable." If NATO was to be viewed as an organization created only for the duration of the Soviet threat, then "you do not look ahead through long vistas of time." A short-term outlook of that trend was one option, or you could consider that NATO "is an organization which reflects the spirit of Western civilization, which has been a great and vital factor in the world for a great many years but the efficacy of which ... has been greatly diminished by the disunity between its members."[19]

Dulles argued that the ultimate objective of Western postwar diplomacy had been to heal disunity in Western Europe. This had been the guiding principle behind bringing the FRG into NATO and in creating the WEU. But if NATO, the highest organizational embodiment of Western unity and the organization responsible for healing the divisions of Western Europe, were to be regarded merely as temporary and emergency, then the postwar order would lack "the element of a permanent healing of those divisions and the creation of unity." To ensure the long-range future peace and prosperity of Europe, transatlantic organizations must "have the quality of permanency and not be merely emergency ties."[20]

Thus, when the Soviet threat appeared to recede, taking with it the compelling need to bond together, U.S. policymakers turned to arguments about the continuing importance of unity. The search for "a quality of permanency" in transatlantic relations was now, at least for the short term, justified on the grounds of intra-Western political purposes no longer tied to the Soviet threat.

At its annual spring meeting in Paris early in May 1956, the NAC was persuaded to give substance to Dulles's proposal.[21] The principal decision of the council was to develop further the Atlantic Community, particularly in the economic and political fields. The NAC's final communiqué reflected the views of top U.S. policymakers when it observed that the alliance's collective security efforts had stopped Soviet aggression in Western Europe and induced the Soviet government to adopt "the so-called policy of coexistence."[22] The council appointed Lester Pearson, Gaetano Martino, and Halvard Lange to be a Committee of Three on Nonmilitary Cooperation to advise it on ways of improving NATO's cooperation in nonmilitary fields and "to develop greater unity within the Atlantic Community."[23]

The Suez Crisis and the Concept of an Atlantic Community

Much has been written about the impact of the Suez crisis on NATO, and there is no need to repeat it here.[24] Suffice it to say that the British and French action, undertaken in collusion with Israel, and accompanied by attempts to mislead rather than consult their NATO allies, caused a major temporary breach in the alliance, which soon needed urgently to be repaired. What concerns us here is the impact this had on conceptions of NATO.

The alliance was quickly patched up at a meeting of the NAC in December 1956, only three weeks after the fighting ended, when useful texts to express the newly restored unity and point the way forward were conveniently found in the Report of the Committee of Three on Nonmilitary Cooperation.[25] The report identified two main challenges to NATO. The first challenge concerned the external threat and was posed in the form of a question: "Can a loose association of sovereign states hold together at all without the common binding force of fear?" As Dulles had done in April, the Three Wise Men, as the authors of the report were known, echoed the rhetoric of the moment and advised the members of NATO to take a long-term view of the Cold War and maintain their vigilance at a time when "ultimate [Soviet] objectives remained unchanged." The change in Soviet tactics was cast as an attempt to "ensnare" the newly independent countries, and, to defeat this plot, NATO was urged to make its "purposes better understood in non-NATO countries." Thus, the report served in part as a continuation of the propaganda "battle for the minds of men." The second challenge to NATO identified in the report was the need to "prevent centrifugal forces of opposition and indifference from weakening the alliance"—a pointed reference to Suez.

The recommended response to these challenges was twofold. First, NATO was urged to become more than a military alliance by turning the Atlantic Community "into a vital and vigorous political reality." Second, and in conjunction with the first recommendation, the members of NATO were encouraged "to make consultation in NATO an integral part of the making of national policy." These recommendations were justified by invoking the North Atlantic Treaty, which, with its references to the nonmilitary aspects of security and its provisions for consultation,was said to hold "the promise of the grand design of an Atlantic Community." Thus, in the aftermath of the Suez crisis, nonmilitary cooperation was urgently recommended to increase the unity and cohesion of NATO by building an Atlantic Community and by increasing consultation—a move that, on the surface, was designed to achieve the general objective of preventing a recurrence of Suez while addressing perceived changes in Soviet tactics.

But such rhetoric masked a deeper concern. It would have been futile simply to declare that focusing on alliance cohesion and the nonmilitary aspects of security would prevent a recurrence of Suez. Suez involved British and French perceptions of core interests at stake. If similar events were to be prevented in the future, it would not be because of statements emphasizing alliance cohesion but because London and Paris had been made to realize that without Washington's approval they could no longer accomplish their foreign policy goals.

The fact that NATO had been threatened internally by unilateralism among its members, rather than by an external threat from the Soviet Union, made talk of community appear hollow, but this contradiction between rhetoric and reality did not prevent U.S. Under Secretary of State Christian

Herter, who would soon replace Dulles as Secretary of State, from being euphoric about the Atlantic Community. In July 1957, he declared that

> I believe that it has now become quite clear that the concept of the Atlantic Community will be able to withstand the removal of the direct threat or any other changes in policy. It has become part of the basic strength of the free world which is necessary not only to meet an imminent danger but also as a force in changing the future relationships between nations.[26]

In surviving the "grave tests" of recent months, NATO was declared to have "gained a new vitality."[27] Implicit in this statement was the notion that the longevity of NATO—its mere existence in a tumultuous era—conferred not only legitimacy but also relevance. The lesson, according to Herter, was "quite clear": NATO could outlive the Soviet threat and, as the nucleus of an Atlantic Community, become a force for good in the world. This conception described the Atlantic Community in its originally ambiguous but idealistic tones.

Although Herter's rhetoric was largely consistent with that of the pre-Suez period, we can detect a slight change in the substance of the concept of an Atlantic Community in the immediate post-Suez era. For this change we must turn to the ailing Dulles, who, as in previous years, took the lead in formulating American conceptions of NATO. According to Dulles, NATO's mandate was not merely to meet the Soviet threat but to "everywhere try to develop the unity and dynamism of the free world." Military security was viewed as essential but not sufficient, and Dulles termed the emphasis on military security "a negative concept." Increased consultation in NATO was praised by Dulles as providing the means to realize the more positive goals of the Atlantic Community. Consultation would do more than prevent a repeat of Suez; it "*will help to demonstrate* that the nations of this community are not solely concerned with matters of military defense to create a defense against Soviet aggression. We are also developing a political climate good for all people everywhere who want to see peace and justice and human welfare."[28] The difference between pre- and post-Suez conceptions of an Atlantic Community rests in the emphasis placed on consultation in the post-Suez period.

The decision further to develop the Atlantic Community through increased consultation was motivated in part by the perception that changing Soviet tactics required a corresponding change in NATO.[29] Because the interests of NATO's members were recognized as not being confined to one area, increased consultation also seemed to provide a solution to the problem of coordinating policy out of area and simultaneously bolstering the cohesion of the Atlantic Community as expressed through NATO. Although there was widespread agreement that increased consultation would be inherently good, there remained no clear definition of what was meant by the development of an Atlantic Community—or in fact what exactly was meant by the concept itself. Nevertheless, the ambiguous concept of an Atlantic Community had broad political appeal and the community's development was widely regarded as being the precondition to greater allied unity.[30]

Dulles's views about the potential benefits of consultation were embraced by both Canadians and Europeans.[31] Indeed, one of the Three Wise Men was Canadian, two were European, and none was American. But the greatest support for the concept of an Atlantic Community emanated from Britain and North America, where enthusiasts later claimed to have identified historical forces that were pulling toward a single Atlantic political authority, with NATO at its core.[32] The most challenging European response to the proposal for invigorating the Atlantic Community through increased consultation came from France. In September 1958, Charles de Gaulle, who had returned to power in June, pressed the notion of consultation to its extreme and proposed a tripartite directorate among the United States, United Kingdom, and France to coordinate allied policy on a global scale, including the use of nuclear weapons.[33] Despite its emphasis on consultation, the directorate was regarded as anti-NATO and emphatically anti-German. Eisenhower quickly rejected the idea—an action that appears to have pushed France further along its course of independence.[34]

In the wake of Suez allied leaders focused on combating, in Dulles's words, "the divisive forces which are always at work in an organization of this kind." Division in NATO had come as a result of the tendency to elevate national concerns over common objectives. Unity, declared Dulles at a press conference in December 1957, was now "of transcendent importance." The proposals for increased consultation had come as a reaction to Suez, and were cast in general terms cloaked in the old rhetoric of an Atlantic Community. The intent of this rhetoric was to restrain the members of NATO from embarking on future military adventures without consulting the other allies, and especially the United States.

Dulles concluded his press conference with what was to become a defining characteristic of public pronouncements by senior allied leaders: "The time has come," he announced, "to put forth a fresh new effort to revitalize NATO."[35] Where he departed from most of his colleagues was with his remarkably candid confession about the frequency of those fresh new efforts: "That kind of thing is going to have to be done every five or six years."[36] Dulles was only partially accurate: the effort to revitalize NATO would become a continuous one.

The Reign of Interdependence

The concept of interdependence, which entered the NATO canon in the late 1950s as part of the ongoing effort to revitalize the alliance, was accompanied by a slightly stronger version of the rhetoric surrounding the notion of an Atlantic Community. The concept of an Atlantic Community had a strong voluntary flavor about it and did not immediately imply the need for cooperative action: it was an essentially passive concept that suggested that the members were free to join or leave the community. In contrast, the concept of interdependence implied that the members of NATO could not escape the consequences of interaction. There was nothing voluntary about interdependence: it was interpreted as being a fact of international political life in the nuclear era, when the need to act jointly was imperative.

The concept of interdependence held the spotlight from December 1957, when the term first appeared in a final communiqué of the NAC, until the spring of 1961, when U.S. President John F. Kennedy used it to underpin his concept of an Atlantic Partnership. The concept of interdependence was shaped by an axiomatic faith in the notion that the security of North America and Western Europe were inseparably linked. Interdependence was also closely related to the notion that, in the nuclear era, independent national action was fallacious and dangerous. In theory, it implied a weakening of state sovereignty and suggested a more equivalent sharing of responsibility.[37]

NATO in the Era of Interdependence

Events in Suez and Hungary had not been the only incidents that provided a sense of urgency to the efforts to reform NATO. The successful Soviet launch of *Sputnik* early in November 1957 shocked the West and was seen to embody a dramatic and increasingly threatening growth in Soviet capabilities. Dulles noted that its effect on the West would be "an increasing tendency to draw together."[38] In practical terms, it led to the deployment of intermediate-range ballistic missiles (IRBMs) to Britain, Italy, and Turkey. Other NATO counties refused to host them—hardly "together."

It was in this context that the NATO heads of state and government met in December 1957 in Paris.[39] In their final communiqué, the representatives of the NATO allies announced that, because of the international situation, NATO must "organize its political and economic strength on the principle of interdependence, and must take account of developments outside its own area."[40] NATO's leaders also called for increased economic and political cooperation—by now a standard feature of most NATO communiqués—and, in an apparent response to *Sputnik*, established the NATO Science Committee, which was to be headed by a science adviser who would report to the secretary general. With this move, a new chapter was added to NATO's growing conceptual canon, and henceforth its leaders would claim that NATO performed, among its many others functions, the role of an alliance for science.

Eisenhower's second inaugural address is a good example of the rhetoric of interdependence:

> No people can live to itself alone. The unity of all who dwell in freedom is the only sure defense. The economic need of all nations, in mutual dependence, makes isolation an impossibility; not even American prosperity could long survive if other nations did not also prosper. No nation can longer be a fortress, lone and strong and safe. And any people seeking such shelter for themselves can now build only their prison.[41]

Such language, though perhaps equally applicable to the concept of an Atlantic Community, highlighted the sense of urgency and the necessity for common action that underlay the concept of interdependence.

Interdependence was elevated in an attempt to explain the complex problems and challenges of the Cold War and to justify increased defense expenditures. Alastair Buchan, a keen promoter of interdependence and the British director of the International Institute for Strategic Studies (IISS), noted that "what is required is an intellectual appreciation of the problems and dangers of the next decade, and intellectual appreciations are notoriously hard to sell to treasuries and Parliaments." He called interdependence one of the "kind of central ideas around which it is possible for the NATO powers to cohere."[42]

"NATO," declared Dulles in September 1958, "is basically an exercise in interdependence." For those members who cherished their independence, Dulles had a characteristically ingenious formulation: independence, he said, "can only be preserved by the practice of interdependence." Increasing interdependence was both a goal and a reality, and, like the need for increased unity in NATO, it was being proffered as the best possible course NATO could adopt in response to a strong and united enemy. The Soviets and their allies had achieved strength and unity through dependence and domination; NATO sought to achieve those same qualities through interdependence. Again, Dulles's view is illustrative:

> It is self-evident that no single nation can be truly independent and the master of its own destiny if it stands alone against the massive menace of 900 million people and their military and economic resources, solidified by international communism into a monolithic, aggressive force dedicated to world domination.[43]

These public assertions characterizing the Sino-Soviet bloc as a unified monolith were not in accord with Dulles's private thoughts on the matter, but the public remained ignorant of this.[44] Official rhetoric from Washington continued, long into the Kennedy and Johnson administrations, to depict international communism as a cohesive threat to the free world.[45] It appears that the Soviet threat was exaggerated—and on at least one occasion, the 1960 election case of the so-called missile gap, wildly inflated—to bolster a domestic consensus in the United States in support of containment and defense expenditures that might otherwise have weakened, and to make the case for increasing interdependence among the NATO allies.

The notion of interdependence was applied in many ways. The military implications, being, in Dulles's words, "self-evident," called for task sharing in defense, greater specialization of the functions of different members of NATO, and a division of labor to overcome the rising costs and complexities of weapons. The burden was declared too large for any one nation to go it alone.[46] None of this was new. NATO had been dealing with these problems from the start. What was new was that interdependence, with its overtones of permanence, was now invoked as the reason for action, in place of the cries of crisis that had roused NATO in its early days but had now worn thin.

Rhetoric aside, interdependence had less to do with the politics of the Cold War than with the international economy. But the axiomatic linkage that had been drawn between economics and the Western defense effort prompted Western leaders to cast the economic manifestations of interdependence in terms of the NATO framework. Although not organized through NATO, the Western European postwar economic recovery was directly attributed to NATO's protective shield. Thus, economic and military interdependence were portrayed as being mutually dependent—a relationship that confirmed the wisdom of imbuing with axiomatic faith the notion that a strong economy and society required a strong defense, and vice versa.[47]

The slogan of interdependence was applied also in the larger realm of foreign policy, and its principle was invoked on a range of issues, from allied consultation on summits to the reunification of Germany, the suspension of nuclear testing, and general disarmament questions. Out-of-area issues like those concerning Jordan, Lebanon, Quemoy-Matsu, and Formosa appeared to underscore the importance of interdependence, which required ongoing consultation among the NATO allies. Consultation on out-of-area issues was not intended to enlarge the treaty area, but was based on the recognition, according to Dulles, of "the fact that misunderstandings anywhere impair cooperation in the treaty area."[48] This global security linkage, which implied that trying to distinguish between NATO and non-NATO issues was fallacious, rested on "the concept of the indivisibility of the peace."[49]

Vietnam and the Concept of Interdependence

Interdependence was invoked by the United States in its attempt to cultivate European support for its evolving policy toward Southeast Asia. But America's European partners were beginning to worry that the U.S. commitment in Vietnam was misguided and also that it would undermine U.S. support for NATO in particular and for European security in general—a concern that reflected the continuing European preoccupation over the proper role of the United States in European affairs and a fear that either too much or too little U.S. involvement would lead to war with the Soviets. Dulles met these fears by invoking interdependence. He declared, in what seems like a lawyer's hint to the Europeans, that "the principles at stake [in Southeast Asia] are the principles upon which NATO rests. If the principles are not valid and not sustained in Asia, it cannot be confidently assumed that they are valid and will be sustained in Europe."[50]

A question that was not addressed by the United States at this time was whether, if a European state went on a military adventure comparable to Vietnam, the United States would support such an endeavor. The unsuccessful French pleas for assistance in 1954 before Dien Bien Phu and the failure of the United States to support Britain and France at Suez suggest that the United States was not prepared to let its allies determine when and where interdependence was to be applied. The logic of the "indivisibility of the peace," which conceptually linked all issues in all areas of the free world, would eventually lead the United States into an ever-wider role in Vietnam and into increasingly bitter debates with its allies. The ultimate lesson of Vietnam, for some, would be that security was in fact divisible. But in the late 1950s, with official rhetoric describing a monolithic and ever-expanding adversary, no issue or region could be considered beyond the purview of the alliance—provided that the United States set the agenda. Paradoxically, the United States sought to promote free societies but was often annoyed when its allies sought to express independent foreign policies.[51]

The Kennedy and Johnson administrations continued to invoke interdependence as a means of trying to elicit allied support for the U.S. policy toward Southeast Asia. In June 1961, Kennedy traveled to Europe to consult with allied leaders before meeting with Nikita Khrushchev in Vienna. "Our problem," he told the North Atlantic Assembly, "is to give new life [to NATO] and to consider jointly how we can play a more significant role in other parts of the world now threatened by communist subversion or infiltration."[52] It was "a matter of vital strategic significance" for the NATO allies to concern themselves with events in the Southern hemisphere, "where we are now in danger, and where freedom is now in danger."[53] Speaking in Frankfurt, Kennedy said that to question interdependence "would only give aid and comfort to the men who make themselves our adversaries and welcome any western disarray."[54] Lyndon Johnson too emphasized the concept of interdependence, especially as it applied to Vietnam.[55]

European Reactions to Interdependence

Confronted with this flow of American rhetoric, NAC communiqués duly incorporated the concept of interdependence as part of the NATO canon. But the French went along reluctantly and later rejected the concept in favor of independent national action, particularly in the nuclear realm. The British, always keen to be especially close to the United States and eager to elicit continued U.S. support for their own nuclear program while retaining the appearance of independence, immediately were strong proponents of the concept. The December 1962 Nassau meeting (see below) would reward the British for their support. West German leaders, whose room for maneuver was limited and who were seeking to advance the prospects for reunification and increased influence in Washington, cautiously joined the Americans in promoting interdependence.[56] But support for the American view of the concept of interdependence extended only up to a point: for European allied leaders, interdependence did not mean that they were required to support the United States in Vietnam.[57] The ambiguity of the concept permitted this difference to remain implicit.

There are at least four reasons why the concept of interdependence replaced the rhetoric of an Atlantic Community in the late 1950s and early 1960s. First, the old rhetoric had worn thin, and it was no longer sufficient to invoke notions of community as a means of enforcing unity and conformity. Second, the rhetoric of interdependence offered a convenient conceptual tool for the United States as it attempted to enlist West European support for its global crusade against a perceived global challenge from the Soviets. Third, interdependence seemed to provide an answer to the question of how NATO could respond to out-of-area challenges now that the European allies had, under U.S. pressure, relinquished their colonial possessions and maintained only feeble forces east of Suez. As the United States assumed responsibility for the protection of many of these former colonies, interdependence was invoked both to mask and justify the extension of an American empire. Fourth, by the late 1950s, liberalization of trade, cheaper and faster air travel, and television had made the Atlantic much narrower and produced greater economic-cum-technological and cultural interdependence and a greater sense of closeness to events and peoples abroad. Politicians on both sides of the Atlantic sought through rhetoric to arouse this vague but growing sense of interdependence.

The Reign of an Atlantic Partnership

Although the concept of interdependence failed as a device to elicit European support for the U.S. adventure in Vietnam, it was employed by John F. Kennedy to promote his concept of an Atlantic Partnership.[58] The concept of an Atlantic Partnership, which entered American rhetoric early in 1961 and which died with the president late in 1963, formed the basis of Kennedy's approach to NATO, and was an important component of his "Grand Design," which called for the political and economic integration of Western Europe and the creation of a new transatlantic relationship based on new responsibilities for Europeans.[59]

The difference between the concept of interdependence and that of an Atlantic Partnership was that, in theory at least, the concept of an Atlantic Partnership was more explicit about the rights and responsibilities of Europeans. In the economic realm, America's European partners would be expected to contribute more to the developing countries while continuing the process of European integration. In the military sphere, they were to contribute more to NATO's conventional defense and forgo the quest for nuclear independence (and rely on the U.S. nuclear guarantee). As Western Europe continued along the path toward unity, it would receive an increasing share of nuclear control.[60]

As conceived by Kennedy, transatlantic partnership ultimately would comprise economic partnership between two equals, with a single community in military affairs and a single authority for nuclear weapons expressed through NATO. By encouraging European political evolution through the Common Market and the NATO forum, policymakers hoped that a shared community and interests would nurture a partnership that embraced policies that were in harmony with fundamental U.S. objectives.

From Interdependence to Partnership

In his inaugural address Kennedy emphasized American willingness to "pay any price, bear any burden."[61] But in his first message to the NAC, Kennedy stressed that the burden had to be shared. He pledged continuing U.S. support "to the basic concept of unity" that underlay NATO, but warned that the allies "must establish principles ... on which burden-sharing can be based."[62] Early in his term, Kennedy embraced the concept of interdependence and invoked it in an effort to extend American global leadership in partnership with European allies and the newly independent states.[63]

Interdependence had implied that economic, military, and political policy could no longer be separated: success in each policy realm was perceived to be contingent on success in the others. Kennedy's conception of the future rested firmly on this linkage: "It is time now," he wrote to Congress early in 1962,

> to write a new chapter in the evolution of the Atlantic Community. The success of our foreign policy depends in large measure upon the success of our foreign trade, and our maintenance of Western political unity depends in equally large measure upon the degree of Western economic unity.[64]

In its crudest form, this linkage suggested that the United States would attempt to use trade and arms agreements as bargaining chips to win allied support for burden sharing in Europe and Asia. But it was also an attempt to bring policy more in line with reality. For example, it would be unrealistic to foresee substantial progress on foreign trade matters when there was tension within the alliance over the U.S. role in Southeast Asia. By explicitly promoting this linkage, Washington could fashion a framework of incentives and penalties that might persuade its allies to follow its lead. This framework was offered to America's European allies under the guise of an Atlantic Partnership.

Kennedy's concept of partnership was a revival of earlier postwar axiomatic reasoning. It had its origins in an axiomatic faith in the notion that the security of North America and Europe were inseparably linked, that increased political consultation and integration were inherently good, and that a sound defense required a solid economic and social foundation (and vice versa). An Atlantic Partnership was meant to usher in a new era—an evolutionary advance, even—in transatlantic relations.[65] The benefits of increased trade would, according to Kennedy, advance "our efforts to prove the superiority of free choice." An integrated Western Europe in economic, political, and military partnership with the United States "will further shift the world balance of power to the side of freedom."[66]

Economic integration had helped nurture the impression that Western Europe was a distinct economic and political community that could form a European "pillar" of an Atlantic Partnership. This reasoning was supported by a mixture of fact and fiction. The supporting fact was the progressive postwar integration of Western Europe,[67] which was held together by the European Economic Community (EEC) and the Organization for Economic Cooperation and Development (OECD) and protected by NATO and the WEU. The supporting fiction invoked the fact of Western European integration to argue the case for the emergence of a larger, looser Atlantic grouping. The fiction held that, through NATO and the OECD, the so-called organs of Atlantic action, the Atlantic Community, reorganized and revitalized through an Atlantic Partnership, was emerging as the defender of the frontiers of freedom both in Europe and beyond.[68] The concept of interdependence, when applied in conjunction with a geopolitical code describing all security as indivisible, not only helped describe this trend, but was also used to promote its evolution.

According to Secretary of State Dean Rusk, the partnership envisioned a partial decline in the relative responsibility—and therefore influence—of the United States, but the overall effect on the free world, with the partnership at its core, would be salutary. He claimed it would have the additional effect of softening some of de Gaulle's objections to the U.S. role in Europe.[69] One senior U.S. official declared that "the policy is novel. It is a conscious encouragement by a major world power of the development of a co-equal power."[70] Again, this was fiction: there was neither a policy to support the concept nor an American intention to relinquish responsibility.

As early as August 1962, despite initial support for the concept from West Germany and Britain, cracks had begun to show in the edifice of the Grand Design.[71] The French, as we shall see, rejected the notion outright—but they were not the only ones to do so. Both European and American observers, agreeing with the main thrust of French objections, criticized the concept as a mask for U.S. hegemony.[72] Despite these objections, U.S. policymakers continued to claim that the benefits of an Atlantic Partnership were clear and compelling, and that it was only a matter of time before the "combination of strength and constructive purpose [of the partnership] ... will bring the Soviet world to the negotiating table."[73]

There was nothing new about Kennedy's concept. Since the founding of NATO, the United States had struggled to find ways of eliciting greater European support for its leadership—both in terms of securing Europe from the Soviet threat and in terms of fashioning a global response to that threat. Similarly, there was nothing new about the desire to unite Western Europe. In promoting an Atlantic Partnership, Kennedy had revived George Kennan's dumbbell concept of the late 1940s, which described transatlantic relations as being conducted between two spheres of equal weight.[74]

This revival came about for at least two reasons. The first has to do with Kennedy, who as a young, new president sought to establish the foundations of great change by conjuring up in rotund phrases visions and plans for the future. Alas, the concept of an Atlantic Partnership was more vision than plan—and an old one at that, wrapped in new rhetoric. There was also, for Kennedy, a preoccupation with the perceived need to create a new presidential identity—an identity, that is, that would express Kennedy's dissatisfaction with the policies of Eisenhower while legitimizing his own. Kennedy's conceptions of the future were used to demonstrate resolve and determination, to educate and arouse the public and allies, and—perhaps most important—to display a visible and substantial difference from his predecessor in his approach to the Cold War.[75]

The second reason for this conceptual change has to do with the nature of rhetoric: there is a need to keep renewing it, and when the regular cycle is exhausted (as partly illustrated by the rhetorical transition from an Atlantic Community to interdependence) or when a new leader wants to make his mark, oratory will change.[76] U.S. policymakers continued, where appropriate, to speak and write of community, but in the early 1960s notions of partnership were transcendent.

The Cuban Missile Crisis and the Concept of an Atlantic Partnership

So much has been written about the events of October 1962 that it is otiose to review them here.[77] What is important for the purposes of this study, however, is what happened afterward. In what had by now become a tradition of the aftermath of Cold War crises, U.S. policymakers, in the weeks immediately after the crisis, began an examination of the events surrounding it. Their conclusions, as in the cases of Korea, Berlin, and Suez, confirmed the central importance of NATO and of continued NATO unity. It is remarkable that a crisis that had the potential to undermine NATO's conceptual basis—and for the French at least did just that—served as a re-affirmation of its central tenets. The crisis also gave a boost to U.S. efforts to promote the concept of partnership.

In an address to the NATO Parliamentarians Conference in Paris two weeks after the resolution of the crisis, U.S. Under Secretary of State George Ball confidently claimed that the crisis "has served to set in clear relief the central significance of the Atlantic Alliance and the inter-relationship of the problems it faces."[78] According to Ball, there were at least three lessons to be learned from the Cuban crisis:

- As in every other major East-West confrontation, the Atlantic nations were involved—equally and inseparably—from the start. The removal of Soviet missiles from Cuba was in the European interest as much as in the American, because those missiles had been aimed at the strategic deterrent that protected Western Europe.

- The crisis showed the wisdom of a measured response—a response that could only continue to be employed if the allies increased the flexibility of their forces. The time spent seeking a political solution, rather than executing an air strike as some had suggested, decreased the chances for "nuclear incineration."

- The crisis proved the need for rapid response to sudden danger. The importance of European cooperation and support made "manifest the need for deeper, franker and more continuous exchange of views." Ball called for more contingency planning on a wide range of issues to develop what he termed "an Atlantic response."[79]

The Cuban crisis appeared further to confirm the relevance of several long-standing political conceptions of NATO, particularly those surrounding its evolution into something more than a military alliance. Ball, in what almost appears to be a Buddhist allusion, observed that NATO was now

> growing in a very different way. It has developed an inner life and an organic force of its own. And like all living organisms it has shown a capability of adjustment to change.... [NATO] has undergone a profound transformation into a major element in the Atlantic Partnership. It has never been more significant than it is today.[80]

It was now said to be more imperative than ever to continue these developments, especially in terms of increasing conventional strength in NATO. U.S. conventional superiority around Cuba had prevented the need for nuclear war and confirmed the wisdom of seeking greater flexibility. Thus, the availability of conventional land, air, and sea forces in the face-off over Cuba was used by U.S. officials to promote the acceptance of the concept of flexible response and encourage the European allies to contribute more to the conventional defense of Western Europe.[81] In addition, the language of partnership was used to coax Europeans in NATO to rely more comfortably on the U.S. nuclear guarantee.

For the United States, the outcome of the Cuban crisis proved the value of conventional forces.[82] In Western Europe, an opposing view held sway. America's European partners had been faced with nuclear war and, although there had been much American rhetoric about the importance of consultation, they were left largely unconsulted during the crisis. As we shall see, the French and British response was to commit themselves further to the development of independent nuclear forces, while West German leaders sought means within NATO to increase their say over the use of nuclear weapons.

The Rhetoric of Partnership and Its Implications

The rhetoric used to describe the Atlantic Partnership was taken directly from wartime speech. Throughout the Cold War, political and military leaders employed the language of total war to describe their conception of an unstable peace. A typical American justification for Atlantic Partnership illustrates the point:

> What we are talking about, after all, is not how to feather our own nests but how to mobilize our total resources in the interests of survival and prosperity; our survival and prosperity is [sic] bound up in turn with the fate of those countries which are struggling to create viable and prosperous societies and are prepared to look for help and guidance to whatever political and economic system may offer it to them.[83]

Here was the self-sacrifice reminiscent of the Second World War, when the United States stood as one with its allies against the forces of fascism and tyranny in Europe and Asia. Note the choice of words: Atlantic Partnership required the mobilization of *total* resources; survival *and* prosperity were at stake—a linkage that suggested that sacrifice now would lead to greater prosperity later. Note, too, the implication that ties of fate bound nations great and small together in common cause—this was indivisibility and interdependence at work. Lastly, this is a conception that described the interests and power of developing nations as almost wholly free of the deterministic forces of history or geographical reality, open to influence from either East or West (or both). The side that made the greatest effort and the best pitch would reap the spoils.

Did the language of community and partnership reflect a genuine commitment to the ideal of a pluralist Atlantic Community, or was it meant, as the French and others suggested, to obscure an interest in hegemony? It is likely that there was a mixture of idealism, ulterior motives, and confused thought. Whatever the motives, the rhetoric failed to describe reality. The concept of an Atlantic Community was a simple cliché that glossed over a more complicated reality.

Strategic Conceptions of NATO

We turn now to how concepts of how militarily to defend NATO changed in the period 1956-1966. Three main strategic concepts were invoked in this period: the shield, flexible response, and the multilateral force (MLF). They were adjuncts to the political conceptions of the period, as well as responses to the changing military situation.

From Trip Wire to Shield

Early NATO nuclear strategy relied on the American atomic monopoly to deter Soviet aggression.[84] This strategy emphasized the application of the "trip-wire" concept, which viewed the presence of U.S. troops in Europe as a trigger for Strategic Air Command (SAC) bombers in the event of a Soviet attack.[85] The conventional force goals adopted at Lisbon in 1952 were meant to reduce reliance on nuclear weapons, but as those goals were let slip, NATO continued to rely heavily on nuclear weapons throughout the mid-1950s, and conventional forces continued to be viewed as a trip wire.[86]

By 1957, senior allied military leaders had begun to call for the replacement of the trip-wire concept. This replacement was said to be necessitated by Cold War uncertainties—uncertainties about the duration of the conflict and about Soviet intentions. What NATO now needed was a "shield" force to defend NATO territory and defeat the enemy when he crossed the Iron Curtain.[87] Unlike the earlier trip-wire conception, shield forces would not undertake just a holding operation: they were assigned the actual task of reversing aggression. If, after the shield was struck and conventional forces (later armed with tactical atomic weapons) failed to reverse aggression, then the strategic nuclear sword would strike back. The shield concept would later form an important component of the strategy of flexible response.

Part of the reasoning behind this conceptual change can be traced to the rejection of the concept of massive retaliation—a concept with which few people, even Dulles, its original sponsor, had been comfortable.[88] Although he referred to massive retaliation as a concept "acceptable only as a last resort," Dulles argued in 1957 that NATO's new shield force "should increasingly include nuclear weapons."[89] Thus, uncertainties about Soviet intentions, uneasiness with the all-or-nothing dilemma of massive retaliation, and developments in tactical atomic weaponry helped foster conceptual change.[90]

The shield concept was used to justify the sharing of atomic secrets with Britain and the amendment, on two occasions, of the Atomic Energy Act.[91] It was also used to justify the placement of nuclear weapons in Europe under U.S. custody.[92] Without nuclear sharing with the United Kingdom and dual-key agreements with the other NATO allies, the concept was said to be an empty phrase. Dulles warned that the allies might move toward neutrality or refuse to participate in the common defense effort; proliferation would result; and the NATO policy of negotiation from strength would be undermined. Without nuclear sharing, the West could never hope to bring the Soviets to the bargaining table: it would be the victim, according to Dulles, of "one-sided disarmament" whereby NATO would "become a disintegrating collective defense effort."[93] The shield concept thus became part of the Eisenhower administration's efforts successfully to pressure Congress for a change in U.S. law in order to implement the "New Look" strategy, which paradoxically called for an increased reliance on the threat to use nuclear weapons while moving away from a strategy of massive retaliation and which was used in an attempt to compensate for manpower deficiencies.

The Concept of Flexible Response

By the late 1950s, the allies had been moving away from the Dulles-sponsored concept of massive retaliation, which called for an early nuclear response to any form of Soviet aggression against the West or its allies. NATO had however yet to announce a clear and coherent replacement strategy.[94] A strategy of "flexible response" would ultimately be adopted in 1967, but in 1960 flexibility remained a contentious issue.[95]

The concept of flexible response was intended to provide NATO with a range of options for a calibrated (or "escalated") response in the event of a Soviet attack: first conventional weapons, followed by short-range nuclear weapons, would be used before engaging in a full-scale nuclear exchange. NATO "shield" forces in Europe were conceived as forming the main component in this strategy, and were expected to be able to respond to a wide range of Soviet thrusts into NATO territory. The operational aspects of the concept, which called for tight central control of nuclear forces so as to ensure that their response was measured, were closely wedded to the notion that consultation would provide guidelines through which the allies could agree—in advance—on the level of response.

One problem with flexibility was that some European leaders remained unconvinced about its effectiveness as a guiding concept for the deployment and use of nuclear forces. U.S. Secretary of State Herter declared in September 1960 that a

> respectable posture of military defense within the Atlantic Community requires, in addition to modern weapons, forces of a balance and flexibility to meet any challenge, regardless of location or size, and a command structure appropriate to modern weapons technology.[96]

For some, this was a recipe that called for the politically impossible. The notion that the West had to be prepared to meet all challenges "regardless of location or size" reflected long-standing concern that the Soviets and their allies were capable of mounting challenges of all sizes in all locations. Of particular worry for the European allies was the creation of an "appropriate" command structure—one that would not commit them to nuclear war without some decision-making influence in Washington.[97]

With growing Soviet capabilities, would Washington risk its own cities to defend those of its allies? It was feared that the Americans might drag Europe into war through actions outside Europe or solve their nuclear dilemma by moving from a "suicide or surrender" scenario to one in which national salvation took precedence over alliance solidarity. The solution, widely embraced at the official level on both sides of the Atlantic, was to address the complex but related problems of nuclear command and control by increasing allied consultation. This move reflected continued faith in the notion that a closer knit Atlantic alliance was a prerequisite to peace. As Eisenhower informed the December 1960 NAC meeting in Paris, "we have formed habits of close political consultation. As we now face many complex problems which include but also transcend military defense, we must seek to strengthen and develop these habits in increasing measure."[98]

The issue of command and control of NATO nuclear forces in Europe had already been partially addressed with the deployment of IRBMs, which were dual-key arrangements. Thus, the Americans, who owned the weapons, required the consent of host nations before using them. In this context, the consultation issue, and later the debates over a multilateral force (MLF) and an Atlantic nuclear force (ANF), were part of an overall bid by Washington to undermine the appeal of independent deterrents and bind the European allies closer to the United States. The emphasis on consultation also reflects American recognition of the increasing economic strength and political cohesion of Western Europe in an era when the Soviet military threat was seen to be less menacing. With the European NATO allies on a more equal footing and less afraid of the Soviets, the United States was no longer in a position to lead in quite the same way as before, and it now sought to enlist European cooperation through consultative measures.

In a radical departure from NATO's existing strategy of early use of nuclear weapons, U.S. Defense Secretary Robert McNamara, in a secret speech to the NAC at Athens in 1962, outlined a strategy of "controlled and flexible response."[99] McNamara maintained that NATO could achieve a strong nonnuclear defense to defeat aggression short of an all-out Warsaw Pact attack. His subsequent public comments, with their emphasis on nonproliferation, the futility of national nuclear forces, and the need for a single target system under strong central control, were perceived as a direct attack on the French nuclear program and as pointed criticism of the British program.

The American emphasis on conventional forces also generated concern in Europe that the United States was qualifying its nuclear guarantee at the same time as it sought to deny its allies a nuclear option by insisting on central control. German leaders, who most feared a conventional attack and who believed that a U.S.-inspired conventional force strategy for NATO would weaken deterrence, were especially worried by flexible response. General Johannes Steinhoff, the inspector general of the West German Air Force, later wrote that the FRG was "concerned lest an excessively flexible response might lead to loss of territory."[100]

Nassau and NATO's Nuclear Defense

In comparison to the heated debate between the United States and its NATO allies over how to fashion an acceptable nuclear strategy, the Anglo-American talks held at Nassau in December 1962 were a sideshow. They nevertheless received much attention, and have continued to do so. For our purposes, the Nassau Agreement had one important feature: the United States and Britain attempted to make it more palatable to the other allies by invoking the concepts of interdependence and Atlantic Partnership.

The main purpose of the talks was to placate British anger over the cancellation of the Skybolt missile, which had been promised by the Americans and which was to form the basis of Britain's future deterrent.[101] In place of Skybolt, the United States agreed to supply the United Kingdom with Polaris missiles, which were to be fitted with British warheads for use in British submarines. In addition, some existing U.S. Polaris missiles would be assigned to NATO with a view to creating a NATO nuclear force—a force that it was later proposed should be known as the multilateral force. British submarines carrying Polaris missiles were to be assigned and targeted "in accordance with NATO plans," unless the British prime minister determined that "supreme national interests were at stake." At the same time, however, British nuclear forces would be used for the purposes of "international defense of the Western Alliance in all circumstances."[102]

Despite firm West German support for the Anglo-American rhetoric, which claimed that the new agreement would ease allied European fears over the control of nuclear forces, attempts to invoke notions of unity and interdependence to soften the hard edges of the communiqué were not very effective.[103] The French, who were offered but rejected a similar U.S. deal, began to ask some difficult questions. If, as stated in the communiqué, defense was "indivisible," why did the prime minister have an opt-out clause that allowed him to withdraw the missiles from NATO-designated targets? What circumstances would determine whether "supreme national interests" were at stake?[104] Although these questions remained unanswered, the Nassau Agreement was praised by the United States as "a new vehicle for pressing forward with the work of European integration and Atlantic Partnership."[105]

The French Challenge and the American Response

The French, who sought national security through nuclear independence, rejected the American offer of Polaris missiles on the ground that such an agreement—because it involved dependence on the United States—would be useless for the purposes of French national defense.[106] In January 1963, de Gaulle further angered his allies by vetoing the British bid to gain entry to the Common Market. He then signed the Franco-German Treaty, which he hoped would serve as the impetus for the emergence of a "European Europe" and which contained important passages referring to Franco-German military cooperation.[107] Although the West German leadership was split on the issue, Adenauer gave diplomatic support to the veto, which raised questions about whether the Federal Republic was committed to a Gaullist conception of Europe.[108]

Despite the French stance, which appeared to scuttle Kennedy's plan for a united European partner, Dean Rusk early in 1963 claimed that plans for a multilateral nuclear force for the alliance would go ahead. French obstruction, he said, "will not change one elementary fact, and that is that Europe and the North Atlantic *are and must be* moving toward growing unity and growing strength because these elementary facts of the present world situation make it necessary, and this has been the entire course of development since 1945."[109] In military terms, an Atlantic Partnership was now being sold by the Americans on the basis of Nassau and vague plans for a MLF. Acceptance of the new concepts was perceived to be not only imperative but also inevitable.

The growing French challenge to American views about proliferation and the efficacy of national nuclear forces elicited a strong response from senior U.S. officials. Walt Rostow, chairman of the State Department's Policy Planning Council, was a particularly outspoken opponent of nuclear independence. In an address to a foreign policy conference, he declared that "the acceptance [of the doctrine of national nuclear forces] could only mean the end of the North Atlantic Alliance, opening the way for the fragmentation and piecemeal diplomatic or military defeat of Western Europe."[110] This insistent tone and the dogmatic view that any deviation from current doctrine would open the way to an irreversible and calamitous chain of events had a striking similarity to the debates over the EDC a decade earlier. Then, as in 1963, the application by senior policymakers of a set of axioms about how international political life operated may have restricted policy options and served to undermine the credibility of the very doctrine they sought to uphold. Ultimate compromise on the issues of nuclear defense, which would come only in 1967 after the withdrawal of France from NATO's Integrated Military Organzation, would make such rigidity appear foolish, costly, and short-sighted.

At the time, however, the American line remained firm. U.S. leaders believed that the West should have only one nuclear force, and that this force should be under unitary, centralized control. Otherwise a nuclear exchange could not be controlled: for example, the United States might be trying to keep an exchange limited, and a British or French shot (say, on Moscow) might lead to a Soviet spasm response. Thus, national nuclear capabilities would undermine collective security and result in an unpersuasive and ineffective European capability with which it could neither defend itself nor deter Soviet aggression. National nuclear forces would also imply that there could be no protection without nuclear weapons—a dangerous proposition because it would fuel proliferation and, with it, the possibilities for accidental nuclear war.[111] But perhaps the main reason for American opposition to French and also to British nuclear forces was because they were thought to fuel nuclear ambitions in Germany.

For Rostow, the solution to the alliance's nuclear problems was to maintain the momentum toward increased unity in NATO by creating a unified nuclear deterrent "at its core." One idea was to achieve greater European participation in nuclear affairs by jointly devising and agreeing on guidelines for the targeting, control, and use of nuclear weapons and on the relationship between conventional and nuclear forces. Despite the vehemence of its rhetoric, U.S. opposition to national forces was inconsistent: the special (nuclear) relationship with the United Kingdom had been reconfirmed with the revision of the McMahon Act and the Nassau Agreement, while the French were left feeling snubbed and full of resentment.[112] Despite—or perhaps because of—the magnitude of de Gaulle's challenge, American policy makers continued to emphasize the importance of unity in NATO and in Europe and the inter-relationship between the two—a conception which stressed that unity in Europe would bring additional unity to NATO.[113]

The Multilateral Force

It was at this time, in the spring and summer of 1963, that U.S. officials began to promote the multilateral force (MLF) as the ultimate fix to European military anxieties. The MLF, a sea-based force consisting of twenty-five jointly owned, financed, and controlled allied surface ships, each armed with eight U.S. Polaris missiles and manned by mixed crews, was an ill-formed concept that had serious operational and technological shortcomings.[114] Proponents claimed that the MLF would:

- place Europeans, and especially the Germans, in the nuclear club without the associated problems, costs, and fears of national ownership;[115]

- offset Soviet IRBMs and enhance deterrence;

- reinforce U.S. involvement in Europe[116] (oddly, Americans often fell back on this justification, even as they were asserting that their engagement could not possibly be more forcefully expressed than by the existing nuclear guarantee and the presence of U.S. troops in Europe);

- promote greater unity and closer transatlantic and European partnerships.[117]

By addressing these issues, the MLF would provide NATO with an integrated nuclear force to be set alongside its integrated conventional force.

Kennedy had inherited the plan from the outgoing Eisenhower administration and, according to Arthur Schlesinger, Jr., "retained a certain skepticism about the multilateral force" even though he "accepted the need to reassure the Germans and show NATO that there were alternatives to Gaullism."[118] The Kennedy administration may however have confused the German desire for more influence over the use of nuclear weapons with a German appetite, which does not in fact appear to have existed, to possess or fire nuclear weapons. On the U.S. side, the MLF was reluctantly embraced as a way out of the conflicting goals of central control and nuclear sharing. In addition, by incorporating the British and by restraining others, the American protagonists of the MLF conceived it as a nonproliferation device.[119]

Late in 1964, British Prime Minister Harold Wilson announced his plan for an Atlantic nuclear force (ANF), which would be a multinational force comprised of an equal number of British and American Polaris submarines and a mix-manned surface fleet similar to the MLF.[120] This competing concept had the effect, which appears to have been intended, of killing the MLF and burying debate about a joint NATO nuclear force altogether.[121] European support for the concept, which was led initially by Britain and Germany, does not appear to have reflected a genuine desire for increased burden sharing or concern over the problems of proliferation, but rather a desire for increased influence in NATO's overall strategic and diplomatic policy.[122] The French were unequivocally opposed to the concept—an opposition that may have elevated the importance of Germany in the eyes of Washington.[123]

German support for the MLF, first announced by Adenauer in January 1963, was meant to achieve several important political objectives. Its aim was to demonstrate German loyalty to NATO and ease American fears, generated partly in response to references about military cooperation contained in the Franco-German Treaty, over nuclear collaboration.[124] In addition, support for the MLF in Germany was viewed as a means of mending fences that had been damaged as a result of Dean Rusk's post-Cuban missile crisis conversations with the Soviet foreign minister about the future of Germany and the possibility for a Partial Test Ban Treaty.[125] Adenauer's successor, Ludwig Erhard, in a statement to the Bundestag after his election as chancellor, also offered his support for the MLF and claimed that it would be a means to open up new forms of political and military cooperation.[126] Consistent German backing for the concept was thus aimed at further engaging the Americans in Europe, enhancing Germany's role in NATO and influence in Washington, and protecting West German interests surrounding the possible use of nuclear weapons and negotiations on the future of Germany.[127]

The United States abandoned support for the concept in 1965, as McNamara's preference for a consultative solution, encapsulated in the so-called Athen's Guidelines and the creation of the Nuclear Planning Group within NATO, became the focus of U.S. policy.[128] The MLF was not a well-conceived scheme, nor was the ANF, which was proposed in response to it. The proposal for multinational crews posed serious operational problems and failed to solve the control problem at the political level.[129] Consequently, the MLF was not even a satisfactory technological-cum-military solution to the alleged political problems it was supposed to solve.

NATO and French Strategy

It is tempting, when writing about French strategic concepts, merely to say that they were the exact opposites of those held by the Americans and leave it at that. Although it is generally the case that French theorists opposed their American counterparts, it is misleading to suggest that there was no more to it than that. Thus, French nuclear strategy needs to be examined on two levels: the conceptual and the political.

At the conceptual level, French theorists found intellectual challenges in opposing the American orthodoxy, in producing an alternative that fitted the needs of France and was French. Two French strategists laid the foundations for French nuclear strategy. One was Pierre Gallois, who argued that deterrence was credible only with respect to a nuclear state's own vital national interests.[130] Implicit in this analysis was the notion that in the nuclear era alliances were useless: no state could depend on another for defense; and thus independence and not interdependence should be the national goal.[131] Conventional forces, under this conception, were increasingly obsolete because the power of nuclear weapons ultimately would override any conventional force preparations.

André Beaufre propounded the theory of multilateral deterrence, which held that national nuclear forces increased deterrence. Multiple decision centers would increase the risks and uncertainty in the mind of an adversary and induce caution. French nuclear forces would be the "trigger" that detonated a rigid but powerful U.S. arsenal.[132] Flexible response, under this conception, was held to be a fallacy; there could be little, if anything, flexible about nuclear war.[133]

French nuclear strategy was linked with a challenge to the very concept of an alliance, and became anathema to the Kennedy and Johnson administrations.[134] Whereas the United Kingdom had viewed its nuclear weapons as a form of insurance in the unlikely event of U.S. paralysis and not as a substitute for the American guarantee, French leaders came eventually to view any outside agreement, whether with Americans or

Europeans, as unreliable.[135] Conceptually, this reasoning was cast in general terms that had nothing to do with the United States.

It was de Gaulle, however, who employed French strategic concepts in the service of diplomacy and, in so doing, castigated the Americans as hegemonic and callous about the needs of Europeans. Nuclear dependence on the United States, for de Gaulle, came to be synonymous with political dependence. An independent French nuclear deterrent, or *force de frappe*, would give France power and influence.[136] De Gaulle viewed American conceptions for a MLF and an Atlantic Partnership as attempts to discredit the French nuclear program, relegate France to the status of nonnuclear ally, and perpetuate American domination of NATO.[137] The independence of France was an objective of profound importance to de Gaulle, and should be viewed partly as a natural response to 150 years of military defeat followed by succor in this century from the Anglo-Saxons. Similarly, the vision of Europe de Gaulle was busy promoting was not so much based on French hegemony as on a vision of a united Europe that could countenance less interference from outside powers.[138]

The Franco-American debate over strategy had its roots in different concepts about the future of Europe and its relationship with the United States.[139] Kennedy's concept for a Grand Design, which rested on the framework of a transatlantic partnership expressed through NATO, envisioned a united Western Europe with close links to the United States. De Gaulle's competing vision offered a "European Europe," with France as its leader and with the EEC providing the mechanism for economic and social integration.[140] Despite his arguments to the contrary, de Gaulle was never able satisfactorily to address a compelling counterargument to his vision for a French-led Europe, namely, that his was simply a means of replacing American with French hegemony.[141]

On 7 March 1966, de Gaulle informed Lyndon Johnson that France, while retaining its obligations under the Washington Treaty, would withdraw from NATO's integrated command. NATO forces were given until 1 April 1967 to leave French soil, and NATO headquarters were moved from Fountainbleu to Brussels. NATO was in turmoil, with many allied leaders wondering whether the French move would set in motion an irreversible chain of events culminating in a U.S. withdrawal from Europe.[142] NATO, however, survived.

Conclusion

The forces propelling conceptual change from 1956 to 1966 in the political and strategic realms were both external and internal to the alliance. Externally, the perception of changing Soviet tactics and an uncertain Soviet military threat helped foster the acceptance of the notion that the Atlantic Community needed invigorating through increased consultation and, later, that the concepts of interdependence and flexible response should guide NATO's deliberations on nuclear strategy and out-of-area responsibilities. Internally, conceptual change was driven by the tension created from the French and British unilateralism at Suez, and by the election of a young new U.S. president who sought to provide NATO with a new rhetorical vision based on the concept of an Atlantic Partnership. Other crucial internal factors were West German rearmament, which by 1964 gave the FRG the strongest ground forces of any European member of NATO, and the economic and political integration and recovery of Western Europe. These factors forced the United States to seek improved means of consultation with its European allies, and to promote new concepts that embraced consultative methods. Beyond this, conceptual change can be accounted for by the need for new rhetoric. To avoid devaluation through repetition and to replace old rhetoric that had worn thin, new rhetoric was generated by U.S. policymakers in an attempt to enlist European cooperation.

At least three general points can be made about the political conceptions that were invoked: they were largely U.S.-generated; they were all ambiguous; and they were intended to keep NATO together politically under U.S. supervision. The political cooperation that was expected to arise from the application of these concepts was meant to feed over into other nonmilitary areas, ranging from the economic to the cultural, and into areas beyond NATO's purview, as in Vietnam.

In the strategic realm, Europeans in NATO, and especially the French, played a greater role than they had in the formulation of political concepts because, in comparison, strategic concepts had some precision. Competing conceptions of deterrence, for example, helped create the NATO crisis that resulted in the French withdrawal from the IMO in March 1966. Europeans tended to argue that building conventional forces would undermine the credibility of the threat of nuclear retaliation against Soviet aggression. Stronger conventional forces, it was often said, might "de-couple" the United States from Europe. In contrast, U.S. policymakers emphasized a strong conventional defense (to be provided mostly by Europeans) and enhanced (U.S.) central control. These broadly opposing viewpoints created obstacles to increasing conventional defense.[143]

More generally, substantive policy differences—and the failure or inability to recognize or address those differences—lay at the heart of the problem. Increased consultation, despite all its supposed benefits, did little, in the end, to resolve broad policy disputes: shared views and information did not ensure consensus, and disagreements lingered despite what came to be an almost habitual tendency to consult. Increased consultation was held axiomatically to be inherently good, but, in practice, it did not always live up to its promise.

The stability and harmony of alliance relations in the years 1956-1966 depended less on bold visions for the future than on cooperation on day-to-day problems close at hand. Although the tendency of allied leaders to use simple slogans to summarize broad policies—and to apply them with impressive axiomatic zeal—may have simplified the process of government, it laid the foundation for future conflict when it came time to implement those policies. For example, the Americans stressed the concept of flexibility so far that it contributed to new forms of rigidity—rigidity that would be overcome only after the schism with France had occurred.

NATO was often rhetorically cast as the nucleus of a new type of international community—a community that was given a sense of permanence rising out of the Soviet threat and from the range and depth of peacetime military relations. Moreover, NATO was conceived as a showcase for the forces of freedom: its role was to shape the future through an appeal to the "uncommitted" nations of the world and a demonstration, through words and deeds, of the strength and rightness of its cause.[144] These tactics were justified by reference to a conceptual framework within which the Cold War was seen as a struggle between opposing civilizations that held opposing concepts about the nature and worth of the individual.[145] NATO, as the prime defender of the West, was therefore viewed as the organizational embodiment of Western "humanist" concepts.

Allied leaders—both American and European—spent much time and energy stressing the monolithic character of their opponent, despite growing indications that this view was largely unfounded. In this warped yet politically appealing context, the view of a changing, adaptive enemy made notions of change imperative. NATO came to be viewed as an organic institution that required constant attention and nurturing if it was to survive the challenges of a changing environment. This rather linear conception, which described the alliance in the stark terms of growth or decay, sits uneasily with the history of the period, which appears to have been more cyclical than linear. Viewed cyclically, the period was one in which slight progress was initially made with the Soviets at negotiations and within which Soviet behavior appeared to change; following this, confidence in the policies of the West as expressed through NATO rose; tensions then declined and a new bout of concern over the relevance or long-term viability of NATO ensued, setting in motion NATO's prodigious talents at making collective exhortations to unity and solidarity. This cycle punctuates the history of the Cold War, as both East and West weather successive waves of confrontation and détente.

In contrast to the mythical monolith, NATO was viewed—sometimes correctly—as unwieldy, fractious, and in danger of atrophy, if not of disintegration. The nature of the enemy was invoked as a pretext for unity and conformity, but this did not change the fact that Europeans and Americans had different interests in important issues, ranging from inter- vention in Vietnam to the formulation of nuclear strategy. Interdependence, though in some ways a convenient concept for understanding the com- plexities of the Cold War, failed as a device to elicit European support for U.S. policy in Vietnam. More important, although it was sold as the con- ceptual underpinning of an Atlantic Partnership through which Western European integration could more quickly emerge, the rigid application of the concept of interdependence by the Americans produced the opposite effect. By seeming to dictate the terms of partnership, responsibility, and power, the United States alienated France. Ironically, uncompromising U.S. support for its own political and strategic conceptions may in fact have acted as a brake, rather than a motor, on European integration.

West German leaders in this period were strong supporters of the status quo, except when it came to the control over the use of nuclear weapons. This desire was mistaken by the United States as the rumbling of an eventual appetite for nuclear weapons or for a joint nuclear force with France. German leaders—first Adenauer, then Erhard—sought to shape the character of NATO by pushing strongly for integration and cohesion.[146] West Germany lay on the front line of an alliance whose strategy called for a tactical nuclear response to conventional aggression; and fear of nuclear use on German territory was reinforced by fear of the East, especially after the Berlin crisis. Alignment in NATO, and support for the American-generated proposals for multilateralism and partnership, offered a means of preserving national independence and influence in an international context.[147]

The United Kingdom viewed its influence in NATO as a function of its strategic role and accordingly sought an independent deterrent. It sought to grant or withhold its commitments to American-generated political and strategic conceptions to secure assistance in building its nuclear forces and to gain a share of political influence. In these machinations the United Kingdom was largely successful. Macmillan's strategy of judiciously crafting a policy based on the appearance of independence and the reality of dependence on the United States, which found its highest manifestation in the Nassau Agreement and which was cloaked in the rhetoric of interdependence, won Britain, for what it was worth, the role of junior partner to the United States in NATO.

The period 1956-1966 was one in which American leaders became increasingly dissatisfied with the "negative" concepts of massive retaliation and peaceful coexistence. Instead, they urged their European allies to return to basic principles as expressed in the North Atlantic Treaty and sought to transform NATO ever more into a political arrangement that defined itself by positive goals. These included building the Atlantic Community with a transatlantic partnership at its core and winning the allegiance of the newly independent states. The task of developing NATO in peacetime focused on educating public opinion and allies about the continued importance of unity. However, the postwar U.S. objective of a strong and united Western Europe proved incompatible with Kennedy's plan for the development of an integrated Atlantic Community under U.S. leadership, while the stringent emphasis on the need for unity and harmony limited the American ability to sanction often intractable allies. Conversely, it gave the United States' European allies an opportunity to assert their will. As NATO groped toward realizing the "totality of its meaning" by focusing on the politics of hope, the Soviets often lent a hand by forcing attention back to the politics of fear.

Chapter 4

Managing Détente

In contrast to the preceding years, as well as to those that followed, the years 1967-1975 were a period in which the role of rhetoric in international relations was vastly diminished. As the participants of the East-West confrontation became increasingly committed to the task of building a lasting détente in Europe and as actions began to speak louder than words, rhetoric for a short time ceased to be the principal political tool of the Cold War. In an era of cooperative ventures ranging from arms control to the pursuit of the more lofty humanitarian and social goals of the Helsinki process, when negotiation required an element of flexibility and when the need to invoke the Soviet military threat was both less compelling and less useful, the hyperbole surrounding NATO's form and function declined and was replaced by low-key rhetoric that sought to employ the language of restraint and goodwill in an effort to resolve Cold War antagonisms. NATO in this period came to be viewed as the natural Western mechanism for the management of détente. This chapter explains how and why this occurred.

The chapter is divided into three sections. The first traces the evolution of the view that NATO had a role to play in the détente process and examines the measures taken to adapt NATO to a policy of détente. It asks why and how far NATO and its members embraced détente, and examines how changing conceptions of the international environment contributed to a change in conceptions of NATO's form and function. The second section focuses on the tensions created within NATO as a result of détente and examines the responses taken to alleviate those tensions. How and why did a relaxation of East-West tension permit the members of the alliance to indulge in ventures that were perceived to threaten the solidarity of NATO? What measures were taken to repair intra-alliance damage, and what was the conceptual basis for them? The third section draws some conclusions.

NATO Embraces Détente

The Foundations of Détente

Détente is a French word denoting, as with a bow string, a relaxation of tension. Although the word was employed throughout the Cold War to describe periods when East-West hostility was in abeyance, its true reign emerged in the late 1960s and lasted until U.S.-Soviet relations began to sour in 1975. *Détente* has been commonly used to describe the policies of both superpowers, as well as the condition that obtained as a result. In addition, those policies, such as West German *Ostpolitik*, that were pursued by European leaders during this period have also been referred to as contributing to or comprising détente.

Détente was not a clearly defined concept. Nor did the various proponents of détente hold common conceptions of, or expectations for, the process.[1] Nevertheless, one aspect of the concept is clear. The rhetoric of détente was overwhelmingly restrained: on both sides political and military leaders eschewed belligerent hyperbole in favor of such phrases as "era of negotiation," "structure of peace," and "peaceful coexistence." For the West, détente was generally perceived to be a policy built on cooperative ventures such as trade accords and arms control—the success of which was to be linked to cooperative behavior by the Soviets and their allies on a host of international issues, including a negotiated settlement to the war in Vietnam, the question of Western access to and the continued freedom of West Berlin, and Soviet actions in Eastern Europe, the Middle East, and the Third World.[2]

In this prolonged period of restrained rhetoric the oratorical emphasis of policymakers shifted from invoking the Soviet threat as a means of persuading unruly allies and skeptical publics about the need to sustain and manage a strong and united Western defense to a policy of emphasizing positive changes in the international environment. These changes, in conjunction of course with a continued strong Western defense effort expressed through NATO, were hailed as being the basis on which détente could emerge. Three new factors of the international environment were perceived to pave the way to détente: the emergence of U.S.-Soviet strategic nuclear parity; the fragmentation of the Communist bloc; and the rise of an increasingly united and vocal Western Europe.[3]

In its early years the alliance had been guided by the axiom that rearmament was the prerequisite to détente. According to this reasoning, once NATO had achieved an (undefined) position of military strength relative to its Soviet adversary, it could then begin to negotiate from a position of strength rather than fear. Whether it was foreseen that the Soviets would respond by increasing their military strength does not concern us here. What is relevant for our purposes is that, by the late 1960s, the Soviets had achieved strategic nuclear parity with the United States.[4]

The achievement of parity coincided both with signs of a less hostile Soviet Union and with moves in Western Europe and, later, in the United States, to open negotiations with the Soviets and their allies on a wide range of military and political issues.[5] These early moves toward détente were, as we have seen in the last chapter, seen to justify the wisdom of pursuing "peace through strength."[6] Now that massive rearmament through NATO appeared to have been vindicated, allied leaders, with the Europeans in the lead, began actively to seek to involve NATO in the détente process.[7] This move was justified by reference to an axiom that held that détente was the prerequisite to a European settlement.[8]

In conjunction with the advent of strategic nuclear parity, some members of the Communist bloc, and particularly Czechoslovakia, appeared to be expressing themselves more freely than before—a significant international development that was hailed as offering new opportunities for changed relations. In an address to the NAC in April 1967, for example, U.S. Vice President Hubert Humphrey declared that "modifications in the once monolithic Soviet bloc ... require a new response."[9] In practical terms, the new response began with the United States and its NATO allies seeking improved relations with the Soviet Union and its Warsaw Treaty Organization

(WTO) allies on a bilateral basis.[10] These substantive moves toward improved relations were accompanied by a concerted effort to minimize the role of rhetoric. President Johnson, observing the trend toward better East-West relations in his 1967 State of the Union address, declared that "we have avoided both the acts and the rhetoric of the Cold War."[11] This sentiment was subsequently reiterated by Richard Nixon's first secretary of state, William Rogers, who declared in 1970, that "we're not engaging in rhetoric.... We're doing all we can to have reasonable discussions with the Soviets."[12]

The Harmel Report

As bilateral East-West contacts began to produce results, European and U.S. officials began to promote the idea that NATO, in the words of U.S. Secretary of State Dean Rusk, would now serve "to organize a durable peace."[13] As in earlier periods of perceived international transformation, NATO was viewed as an organic institution growing in response to changing conditions.[14] The initiative for NATO's role in détente was a European one and came from Belgian Foreign Minister Pierre Harmel, who late in 1966 urged the alliance to undertake a study of "the future tasks which face the alliance."[15] The results of the study became known as the *Harmel Report on the Future Tasks of the Alliance.*

The *Harmel Report*, which was adopted at the December 1967 NAC meeting at Luxembourg, explicitly affirmed the need for détente.[16] Characterized by one U.S. official as an attempt "to try to describe the goals we seek—to fill in a mental picture of the Atlantic system we wish to build," the *Harmel Report* became NATO's blueprint for détente.[17] It outlined two main functions for NATO. The first was to maintain the military strength and political solidarity of the alliance. NATO's second task, which would take the alliance into new territory, was "to pursue the search for progress towards a more stable relationship [with its adversaries] in which the underlying political issues can be resolved." Collective defense was said to be an essential precondition for the pursuit of détente; and while the *Harmel Report* blessed bilateralism as being consistent with the spirit of détente, it "must not be allowed to split the alliance." Thus, NATO was expected to serve as "an effective forum and clearing house for the exchange of information and views" on how best to conduct détente.[18] The *Harmel Report* was widely praised as providing NATO with a new sense of direction in the aftermath of the French withdrawal, when the allies were each pursuing complementary but largely bilateral détente policies.[19]

Thus, in addition to identifying détente as an important future function for NATO, the *Harmel Report* served as a means of pulling together the alliance when the French withdrawal from the IMO appeared to have threatened its continued vitality. In the aftermath of the expulsion of the NATO headquarters from French soil, NATO was proclaimed to be moving both geographically and conceptually to meet the challenges of a new era. The U.S. permanent representative to NATO, Harlan Cleveland, observed in June 1967 that: "NATO is not only moving, bag and baggage, from the Porte Dauphine in Paris to the old Evere airfield in Brussels; NATO is also moving from peacekeeping to peacemaking, from the management of a cold war to the management of détente."[20] America's chief spokesman to the alliance declared that "the Atlantic alliance is the natural Western agency for managing our side of détente…. We have stopped wishing for détente and have set about to seek it actively."[21]

The adoption of the *Harmel Report* led to the first NATO studies, conducted from 1968 to 1970, of the possibility for mutual and balanced force reductions (MBFR) in Central Europe. As these studies got under way, a series of public statements by the NAC illustrated its desire to pursue multilateral détente. At the June 1968 summit meeting at Reykjavik, the NAC restated its desire, first expressed in the *Harmel Report*, to explore East-West arms control in the form of MBFR.[22] The December 1969 NAC "Declaration on European Security" reaffirmed the Reykjavik proposal but stressed the necessity for "careful advance preparations" and the "prospects of concrete results."[23] At Rome in May 1970, the NAC was more specific, tying multilateral talks to progress on negotiations on Berlin.[24]

As NATO pushed for MBFR, the Warsaw Pact in March 1969 renewed an earlier call for a conference on European security.[25] Reciprocal acceptance of proposals for both MBFR and a conference on European security, later known as the Conference on Security and Cooperation in Europe (CSCE), was facilitated by the 1971 Berlin Agreement[26] and by *Ostpolitik*, which resulted in treaties normalizing relations between the FRG and the USSR, Poland, Czechoslovakia, and the German Democratic Republic (GDR).[27]

While the *Harmel Report* had explicitly recognized the bilateral aspect of détente, it had also observed that "certain subjects … by their very nature require a multilateral solution."[28] Multilateralism had particular relevance for Germany, where special postwar rights were exercised by the United

States, United Kingdom, France, and the USSR and where no peaceful solution to the division of the country could be agreed without multilateral negotiations. The appeal to multilateralism contained in the *Harmel Report* was thus designed partially to provide an opening for influence for the other allies as talks on Germany, which were expected to accompany détente, got under way; it served as a reminder that all the members of the alliance, and not just those who held statutory rights, had an interest in negotiations over the future of Germany. But it was the multilateral realm of MBFR that provided the alliance as a whole, and particularly the smaller allies, with an opportunity to enter the complex web of negotiations and linkages that comprised détente. By initiating a multilateral effort, NATO was expected not only to serve as the framework for military preparations against communist aggression, but also to provide the political framework for negotiations with its communist adversaries.

NATO and the Soviet Invasion of Czechoslovakia

These early moves for multilateral détente through NATO were interrupted in August 1968 by the Soviet invasion of Czechoslovakia, which came on the eve of the announcement of a second Johnson-Kosygin summit meeting and the start of Strategic Arms Limitation Talks (SALT).[29] While the invasion for a time threatened to derail détente, the process was put back on track when it became apparent that the Soviets would not seek to push their effort beyond pacifying the politically rebellious Czechs, by the recognition that the West could do nothing to reverse it anyway, and as a result of the November election of Richard Nixon, who issued an inaugural call for an "era of negotiation."[30]

As far as NATO was concerned, the Czech invasion was believed to have had the important consequence of reminding the European allies of their dependence on the American military presence in Europe.[31] It also underscored the gap between Western and Soviet conceptions of détente.[32] Change in the Soviet bloc had become an important component of détente. In the aftermath of the invasion, when the perceived fragmentation of the Soviet bloc seemed to be suspended, NATO was urged to close ranks, bolster its conventional forces, and be more wary of détente.[33] The invasion thus appeared to confirm the axiom that a meaningful détente required a strong collective defense posture: NATO should remain prepared for a return to Cold War hostility and a renewed Soviet military threat if détente failed.[34]

These so-called twin concepts of defense and détente would remain at the heart of NATO's political strategy for the duration of the Cold War, and were reaffirmed on numerous occasions.[35]

NATO's Role in Détente

NATO's role in détente was at first conceived to be largely a managerial one, with the NAC serving to "stimulate, monitor and guide" the process.[36] At least three advantages were expected to result from this approach. First, it was hoped that with the NAC performing the role of watchdog, the Soviets would be prevented from obtaining advantage in the many ongoing bilateral negotiations.[37] Second, the collective forum of NATO was expected to restrain the United States from seeking to build a special bilateral negotiating relationship with the Soviet Union—the so-called superpower condominium—above the heads of its European allies. Superpower condominium, it was feared, might lead to superpower agreement on issues of alliance-wide importance without reference to the concerns and interests of Washington's European partners. Similarly, it was claimed that, through consultation, the NATO forum would help restrain the European allies, and especially the Germans, from making hasty or ill-conceived deals.[38] Third, by protecting the European members from the threat of superpower condominium, NATO would make them "free to chart their own course in international affairs."[39] Thus, NATO was expected to provide some sort of political cover for each of its members as they pursued their own versions of détente, protecting them both from themselves and from the Soviets. The conception that NATO would restrain its members from acting unilaterally while serving as a forum for the exchange of ideas and information was not a new one, but it nevertheless fitted easily with the perceived requirements of a new era.

The wisdom of pursuing a multilateral approach coordinated through NATO appeared to be confirmed in 1969, when the Warsaw Pact altered its earlier proposal for a European security conference to include the United States and Canada. Because the original proposal had omitted the North American allies, it was regarded as a bid to drive a wedge between Western Europe and North America.[40] NATO's assumption of the role of détente management, which preceded the change in the WTO proposal, was said to provide "the best possible proof of its continuing vitality and ability to adapt to changing circumstances."[41]

As parallel MBFR and CSCE negotiations got under way in 1973, NATO's role in détente appeared to become more substantial. Unilateral force reductions had been rejected in favor of formulating a common approach through NATO. This method was praised as providing the best basis for gaining leverage in negotiations with the Warsaw Pact.[42] Although Henry Kissinger, who would serve first as Nixon's national security adviser and later as secretary of state under both Nixon and Gerald Ford, had declared shortly before Nixon's November 1968 election that "NATO is not equipped for détente policy," both he and Nixon appear later to have supported a limited détente role for NATO.[43] In his memoirs, Kissinger reveals that U.S. interest in MBFR was linked to a desire to combat the Mansfield Resolution, which attempted to mandate a significant withdrawal of U.S. overseas forces, including at least half of the 300,000 U.S. troops based in Europe.[44] Similarly, it appears that the European members of NATO advocated MBFR as a means of heading off unilateral U.S. force reductions.[45]

The task of formulating a common approach to MBFR may have appeared to provide NATO with an opportunity to be more than a clearinghouse for ideas, but there was an additional, bureaucratic feature to the alliance's advocacy of the multilateral approach to détente. In bureaucratic terms, NATO had, from its inception, demonstrated a proclivity to expand its activities in the political realm, particularly in periods of relaxed East-West tension. The late 1960s were no exception. As it became evident that détente would be the principal mode of political engagement for its members, the alliance naturally sought to play a coordinating role. NATO had a vested interest in being a spokesman for the West's approach to détente, if only out of some bureaucratic reflex aimed at preserving its institutional primacy. As the pace and success of bilateral détente increased, NATO's relevance came into question, as it had in earlier (and even shorter) periods of relaxed tension.[46] A natural desire to deflect criticism that NATO had outlived its usefulness was surely an unstated element in the adoption of détente.

If NATO as an organization embraced détente partly out of bureaucratic inertia and partly as a natural response to the perceived requirements of the day, its individual members appear similarly to have had self-interested reasons for promoting the concept that NATO had a role to play in détente. As we have seen, the Americans, despite Kissinger's early statement to the contrary, ultimately came to believe that multilateral détente through NATO could serve a useful purpose. The 1966 Mansfield Resolution, which is perhaps best regarded as the legislative manifestation of widespread domestic anti-Vietnam and antimilitary sentiment, was gaining support in the Senate.[47] With NATO formulating the MBFR agenda and cloaking itself in the mantle of détente management, the Nixon administration hoped to combat the public perception that NATO was inflexible and not working for a reduction of the military confrontation in Europe, thereby undermining congressional moves to limit the powers of the president concerning overseas troop deployments.[48] American lip service to the notion that NATO had a role to play in détente— a notion that explicitly recognized the necessity for improved allied consult- ation—had the added virtue of deflecting European criticism that the United States was weakening in its commitment to NATO while it pursued détente with the Soviets and while it undertook a reexamination of its foreign commitments occasioned by the war in Vietnam.[49]

As noted above, the European members of NATO had a collective interest, which they shared with the Nixon administration, in conducting MBFR through NATO to restrain the growing domestic American consensus behind the Mansfield Resolution.[50] Thus, European support for NATO's role in détente is partly a reflection of the long-standing conception that NATO could serve as a means of engaging the Americans in Europe and as a device for maintaining a substantial American military presence on the continent. It would be misleading, however, to suggest that this is the only explanation behind European support for the notion that NATO could serve a useful purpose in an era of détente.

This tendency to identify new functions for NATO in accordance with the political trends of the day was not limited to taking on a role for NATO in détente. At the time that détente came onto the agenda, for example, environmental awareness was on the rise in North America and Western Europe. As political pressure began to build in response to media coverage of oil spills and other environmental disasters, NATO quickly identified a role for itself as an ideal coordinator for environmental safety studies. The concept was suggested in 1969 by Nixon, who, at ceremonies celebrating the twentieth anniversary of the signing of the North Atlantic Treaty in Washington, invoked Article 2 of the treaty, which allowed for cooperation in nonmilitary fields, and called for a "third dimension—a social dimension to deal with our concern for the quality of life" to be added to NATO's traditional military and political functions.[51] As a result of this proposal, *ecology* entered the alliance lexicon, the permanent NATO Committee on the Challenges of Modern Society (CCMS) was created, and the alliance laid yet another plank in its expanding conceptual platform.[52] Although the creation of the CCMS was a minor sideshow to NATO's vigorous attempts to perform the role of détente management, it nevertheless illustrates the tendency of the organization continuously to expand its conceptual repertoire. The claims that NATO was able to adapt to changing circumstances were not completely rhetorical.

The German View

The West Germans had perhaps the most to gain from the conception that NATO was conducting détente. By 1972, Chancellor Willy Brandt's overtures to the East had produced substantial results, including the Basic Treaty between the two Germanys and a nonaggression treaty with Moscow.[53] A demonstrative commitment to NATO, which took the form of support for the notion that NATO should manage détente and formulate proposals in multilateral negotiations, helped assuage fears among the FRG's Western allies that the German commitment to NATO had weakened. It also provided substantial political cover for *Ostpolitik*—cover, that is, both from allied claims of unilateralism and from Soviet or Eastern European attempts to coerce the FRG into neutrality or isolation.

Behind Brandt's policy of *Ostpolitik* lay the appealing vision of a peacemaking Germany beginning to make amends for the destruction caused by Hitler. If Brandt could not reunite Germany, then he was determined to lessen the pain and social costs of its division.[54] The division of Germany, however, highlighted the tension that existed between two basic facts: on the one hand, there was the West German commitment to Western Europe and North America, which was expressed through NATO and the EEC and which was based on liberal democratic politics; on the other, there was Germany's geopolitical position at the center of Europe, which placed the FRG on the front line of the Cold War and which compelled its leaders to seek improved relations with the East. Brandt sought to ease this tension through a combined policy of *Ostpolitik* and a reaffirmation of the FRG's commitment to the West.[55]

Ostpolitik marked a substantial departure from the policies of Adenauer and his immediate successors, who eschewed individual German initiatives in favor of following the lead of Germany's major NATO partners, and particularly the United States.[56] Brandt did however share Adenauer's belief that a more tightly integrated Western Europe could serve the cause of eventual German reunification.[57] In addition, Brandt, like Adenauer, viewed

German membership in NATO as an essential precondition to reunification. By embracing the conception that NATO could manage détente, he sought a measure of protection, both from his allies and from his adversaries, as he undertook the potentially risky venture of an opening to the East.[58]

The British View

Although there was no British equivalent of *Ostpolitik*, the United Kingdom was nevertheless undergoing major adjustments in its geopolitical orientation. Until the late 1960s, British policymakers endeavored to nurture a global role for Britain while minimizing the costs and scope of its European obligations. Remnants of the empire and a shift to dependence on the Anglo-American special relationship helped for a time to sustain the image.[59] However, by the late 1960s, the growing tension between Britain's imperial and European commitments had been settled in favor of Europe.[60] The solution combined the withdrawal of British forces east of Suez, a renewed and ultimately successful attempt in 1973 to join the European Community,[61] and a continuing security focus on NATO.

British leaders at first resisted retrenchment, fearing that it would result in the withdrawal of U.S. economic support.[62] As economic realities continued to undermine policy preferences, the 1966 White Paper on Defense noted with dismay British global overextension.[63] Economic woes were compounded by the growing American commitment to the war in Vietnam— a development that seemed further to undercut the rationale of Britain's global deployment and its unstinting support for the United States. The November 1967 devaluation of the pound was the final blow to the British vision of global power: early the following year the Wilson government announced that all British bases in the Persian Gulf region would be evacuated by the end of December 1971.[64] Early in 1969 the government declared that:

> The basis of our defense policy is now fully established. It is to ensure the security of Britain by concentrating our major effort on the Western Alliance.... the task is irreducible; we can withdraw from East of Suez but not from our situation in Europe, on which our national security depends.[65]

A renewed commitment to NATO thus helped Britain mask what appeared to be the final acceptance of its second-rank status.[66] It also gave the United Kingdom some slight measure of participation in the détente process—a process that, with the exception of the multilateral MBFR and

CSCE proposals and the four-power negotiations on Berlin, was by 1972 being conducted largely through the bilateral efforts of the United States and West Germany. By embracing the notion that NATO was the best mechanism for managing the West's approach to détente, the United Kingdom could at least appear to be involved in the great political trend of the day. Finally, support for NATO's new role in détente may have helped persuade Britain's future EEC partners that the United Kingdom was more serious than before about its stated desire to join the European Community.[67]

The French View

By April 1967, France's formal break with NATO's integrated military structure was complete.[68] However, the strategic basis for limited mutual cooperation remained, and France retained its membership in the alliance as a bulwark against an expansive Soviet Union or a revanchist Germany. After the August 1968 Soviet invasion of Czechoslovakia, when de Gaulle's dream of the emergence of a post-bloc Europe appeared distant at best, France began to repair damaged relations with the United States and its NATO allies.[69]

As we have seen in the previous chapter, de Gaulle had been largely successful at scoring political points against the United States when the Soviet threat appeared to be receding. But as the Soviets entered Prague in late August 1968, anti-American rhetoric yielded fewer benefits.[70] Georges Pompidou, who succeeded de Gaulle in 1969, sought to craft a pragmatic political strategy more closely matched to France's means and opportunities. Part of this strategy included a softening of his predecessor's anti-U.S. rhetoric.[71]

In addition to an adjustment in rhetoric, the French amended their strategic doctrine—a change that brought French nuclear strategy and the U.S.-inspired NATO strategy of flexible response closer together.[72] Edmond Combeaux, the French *commandant en chef*, wrote in the spring of 1969 that, because the demands of French nuclear strategy "greatly exceed the capacity of our nation, the need for a permanent defense association with France and her neighbors is inescapable."[73]

There followed numerous practical measures that confirmed Pompidou's stated policy of selective cooperation.[74] In a February 1970 visit to the United States, Pompidou reaffirmed France's commitment to the North Atlantic Treaty and declared that it is "normal that there be an American presence in

Europe."[75] Pompidou also met with Nixon in the Azores in 1971 and at Iceland in 1973. Through the late 1960s and early 1970s, France relaxed its strenuous efforts to obstruct U.S. penetration in Europe. While it turned to a policy of seeking to ensure that U.S. forces were available to deter the USSR, it did not stop asserting its independence, and French policymakers continued to invoke Gaullist doctrine when refusing cooperation on nuclear issues.[76]

As for NATO managing détente, France held the view that NATO was not the appropriate forum for détente. It refused, for example, to associate itself with the NAC's 1968 and 1971 communiqués expressing NATO's desire to conduct MBFR, on the grounds that it reinforced the divisive politics of the Cold War and enhanced the hegemonic role of the United States in the alliance. Indeed, France did not participate directly or indirectly in MBFR, and its forces were never a subject of discussion in this context.[77]

Pompidou, like de Gaulle, sought détente not through an alteration in the military balance but through nonmilitary measures of cooperation, which were expected to bring about a deeper, more lasting political détente. This approach helps account for the French embrace of the CSCE process even as they rejected MBFR. France's rejection of the notion that NATO could conduct multilateral détente should thus be viewed as a manifestation of the Gaullist conception of security, which held that security was largely the product of national effort, not multilateral accords or alliances.

French "empty chair" tactics at multilateral discussions like MBFR (and ultimately at NATO) became increasingly ineffective as the Cold War moderated.[78] Pompidou's pragmatism, marked as it was by softer rhetoric and a hesitant return to alignments and multilateral fora, helped France adjust to the narrow limits within which it could operate at a time when détente was thriving.

The Limits of Détente

The key formative years of détente, which lasted roughly from 1969 to 1972, were infused with a sense of practical optimism about what could be achieved through negotiation and linkages. However, this optimism, although based on an unprecedented array of bilateral treaties and multilateral initiatives, was tempered by a sense of limits. There were perceived limits to what could be achieved through dealing with the Soviets: as commentators repeatedly noted, profound East-West ideological differences remained, and the ultimate solution to the Cold War was deemed to require something beyond détente.[79] Indeed, détente itself was viewed as a limited endeavor, conceived as a means to an end, merely the prerequisite to the settlement of the division of the European continent.

But the limits of détente were also governed by how far it was felt the West could go in pursuit of better relations with its adversaries without damaging the fabric of the alliance. As détente gathered pace, American and European policymakers began openly to question the health of NATO. They did so for at least three reasons. First, American and British global retrenchment in the early 1970s helped fuel the perception that the power (and possibly the will) of the NATO allies to influence global events was diminishing. In the context of British retrenchment east of Suez and U.S. troop reductions in Vietnam, which began slowly in 1969 but quickly gathered pace in the early 1970s, it became less certain that NATO would be able to sustain its commitment to maintaining a strong collective defense while conducting détente.[80] In axiomatic fashion, policymakers reasoned that without a continued strong defense, NATO would unravel and détente would fail.[81]

Second, transatlantic relations became strained as Americans began to complain that the European members of NATO were not carrying their fair share of the defense burden.[82] The Americans also viewed with some suspicion the movement toward greater European integration, which in 1973, with the admission of the United Kingdom, Denmark, and Ireland, led to the expansion of the European Community from its original six members to a total of nine.[83] Western Europe seemed increasingly to be defining itself in opposition to the United States, as opposed to the preferred American suggestion, which most recently had been offered under the guise of Kennedy's concept of Atlantic Partnership, for European integration to complement the growth of greater transatlantic cooperation. For their part, Europeans leaders, in addition to fearing a superpower condominium as a result of détente, were increasingly wary of America's distraction in Vietnam and its tendency to dictate the terms and course of détente to its allies. The 1973 Yom Kippur War, as we shall see, offset fears of superpower condominium with fears of nuclear war.

Third, and more generally, there was shared concern among the allies that public support for NATO was waning when détente appeared to produce substantial results. As success in foreign policy began to be associated with agreements with adversaries, policymakers feared the public would withdraw its support for endeavors designed to enhance or maintain relations with allies. As NATO's elite prepared to celebrate the alliance's twenty-fifth anniversary in 1974, their concern focused on whether a new generation of leaders would be as committed to NATO as their predecessors had been.

As in earlier periods when the health of the alliance had been perceived to be at risk, the antidotes purveyed were concocted largely by Americans. However, Europeans played a major role in shaping these initiatives and on at least one occasion launched a program designed directly to address the problems associated with perceived malaise in NATO. We turn now to these initiatives.

The Nixon Doctrine

In advance of an American disengagement from Vietnam, Richard Nixon and Henry Kissinger attempted to shape a new U.S. foreign policy based on a recognition of the limits of U.S. power. Their solution was to attempt to create a framework for global order by developing a triangular relationship with the Soviet Union and China, with the United States at the fulcrum. In conjunction with the conduct of triangular diplomacy, which sought to play the erstwhile communist allies off against each other, the United States hoped to delegate to regional allies the burden of defending themselves against communism. Announced at Guam in July 1969, the policy of devolving responsibility to America's allies became known as the Nixon Doctrine.[84]

As a substantive global policy, the Nixon Doctrine fell short of its objectives, although it was applied with special emphasis in three places.[85] The first was Vietnam, where it was invoked as a means of legitimizing the policy of Vietnamization and American disengagement. The second was Iran, where the Shah spent billions of dollars in oil revenues building an enormous arsenal of American weapons throughout the 1970s, which later was revealed to have been a poor investment, at least as far as protecting America's regional interests went. The third was Israel, to which the U.S. commitment had been a moral one. Under the Nixon Doctrine, Israel came to be viewed as a military and strategic ally in the Middle East.

In a report to Congress written by Kissinger and signed by Nixon, the doctrine was said to be a means of eliciting "more responsible participation by our foreign friends."[86] None of this was new. The Truman Doctrine had said essentially the same thing, promising support for allies and friends who would help themselves. Indeed, this goal formed part of the original rationale behind U.S. support for the North Atlantic Treaty. However, as far as NATO was concerned, the Nixon Doctrine had two objectives. First, it could be invoked to justify the transfer of U.S. troops from Europe to Vietnam and, later, the demobilization of those troops and their return to the United States. Second, it sent a signal to Europeans that the Kennedy era of a United States willing to "pay any price, bear any burden" was clearly over. In this respect, the Nixon Doctrine appears further to have fueled European fears about U.S. withdrawal and prompted a more concerted European effort to increase defense spending.[87]

The EUROGROUP

An effort to enhance the European contribution to NATO's defense began before the enunciation of the Nixon Doctrine, with the formation in 1968 of EUROGROUP, an informal grouping in which European defense ministers could meet, exchange views on political and military issues, and promote practical defense cooperation. The United Kingdom, which hosted the group's secretariat, promoted the initiative as part of its new security commitment to Europe. However, until the Nixon Doctrine was announced, EUROGROUP had done very little by way of improving European defense.

In December 1970, after the enunciation of the Nixon Doctrine, the ten members of EUROGROUP launched the European Defense Improvement Program (EDIP) and pledged one billion dollars to enhance NATO's common infrastructure and improve national NATO-designated forces.[88] These moves notwithstanding, EUROGROUP was formed less to improve European defenses than to impress American leaders and public opinion with the scale of the European contribution to the defense effort.[89] It was not without effect: Nixon soon pledged that the United States would maintain and improve its forces in Europe and would not remove them except in the context of MBFR.[90]

Officials in the Nixon administration invoked the activities of EURO-GROUP in their efforts to defeat the Mansfield Resolution, arguing that Europeans were now doing more for their own defense than ever before and that U.S. reductions would only fail to stimulate additional European effort.[91] Nixon, in a 1971 report to Congress, tried to address criticism that he had reneged on his doctrine of devolving more responsibility to America's allies: "I have repeatedly emphasized," he wrote, "that the Nixon Doctrine is a philosophy of integrated partnership, not a synonym for American withdrawal. Our relationship with Europe proves it."[92] Ironically, the result of the European effort was to make the Nixon Doctrine largely inapplicable to NATO.[93] Because Nixon pledged not to reduce U.S. troop levels, he undercut much of the rationale behind the concept of an "invigorated partnership."

1973—The Year of Europe

Concern over what détente was doing to the health of NATO prompted an American attempt to define more clearly the principles behind the Nixon Doctrine. In April 1973, Henry Kissinger, who in September would be appointed U.S. secretary of state, heralded the arrival of the "Year of Europe" in which the allies would seek to find a framework "for the management of their diversity, to serve the common objectives which underlie their unity." Nineteen seventy-three was to be the Year of Europe "because the era that was shaped by the decisions of a generation ago is ending.... The revival of Western Europe is an established fact, as is the historic success of its movement toward economic unification." Kissinger proposed that the allies seek a "unifying framework" for the Western alliance: "we need," he said, "a shared view of the world we seek to build."[94]

This shared view was to take the form of a general declaration of Atlantic principles—in short, the drafting of a new Atlantic Charter to replace that of 1941.[95] While the allies had common interests that would define the substance of the declaration, Kissinger declared that "the United States has global interests and responsibilities. Our European allies have regional interests."[96] Underlying this statement was the notion that the United States would set the agenda while the Europeans were, by virtue of their more limited interests and power, to serve in the lower ranks. For all the fanfare that surrounded Kissinger's announcement—and there was a great deal—the Year of Europe was a fiasco. As with Kennedy's July 1963 call for an Atlantic Partnership, the latest American proposal was viewed in Europe as yet another U.S. bid to play the role of hegemon.[97]

Throughout the summer and autumn of 1973, Kissinger took his message to Europe, where he received a cool reception.[98] He declared that because progress on détente had lessened the fear of military aggression on which the original transatlantic relationship had been based, there was a need for a "redefinition of relations with our friends."[99] This was the clearest indication yet that the Nixon Doctrine had failed as a device to reform transatlantic relations. Détente had also allowed allied relations to be neglected: Kissinger observed that "the duty of statesmanship in this period is to see that relations among friends keep pace with relations among former adversaries."[100] As we shall see, the pace of allied relations was falling behind.

The Yom Kippur War

By the early 1970s, the strength of Europeanism was even greater than it had been a decade before, and Europeans were more willing to challenge the authority of their superpower ally. This willingness became most apparent during October 1973, when Egyptian and Syrian forces launched a devastating surprise attack on Israel. Because Nixon was preoccupied with the Watergate scandal, Kissinger had a free hand at the White House and made many of the critical decisions during the crisis. With Nixon's approval, he ordered a massive $2 billion U.S. airlift to Israel using western and southern European air bases. With the exception of West Germany, which soon reversed its position, Portugal, and the Netherlands, the European members of NATO refused to assist the airlift and would not give the U.S. overflight rights.[101] As a result, the United States was forced to develop an alternative plan for the airlift using carriers, in-flight refueling and a long 2,000-mile detour around European airspace.

In the third week of October, as the U.S. airlift continued, Soviet aid began to pour into Cairo and Damascus. When a stunningly successful Israeli counterattack left the Egyptian Third Corps surrounded on the Sinai Peninsula, Soviet airborne troops went on alert. On 24 October the United States received a Soviet ultimatum declaring that unless the United States accepted joint intervention to separate the warring parties, the Soviets would intervene unilaterally.[102] In response, Kissinger authorized a worldwide U.S. nuclear alert, which included U.S. bases in Europe. He later declared that U.S. forces were acting as "custodians of Western security."[103] The crisis soon ebbed—not as a result of the nuclear alert but because the situation on the ground had stabilized and, under U.S. pressure, the Israelis had accepted a cease-fire.

Recriminations over what one anonymous observer called a "Suez in reverse" soon began to fly across the Atlantic.[104] The European allies claimed that the United States had risked nuclear war without consulting its allies, while the United States complained about European unwillingness to protect the stability of the strategically vital Middle East.[105] In fact, the Europeans, who depended heavily on Middle East oil supplies, had the most to fear from an Arab oil embargo, which came despite their open break with the United States.

The ensuing energy crisis further strained transatlantic relations, as the Americans and Europeans, with the French leading the European effort, held competing energy conferences on how to come to terms with the embargo. In February 1974, Kissinger convened the Washington Energy Conference, while under a French initiative the EEC convened its own in Copenhagen.[106] French Foreign Minister Michel Jobert used the forum to widen the transatlantic rift.[107] The French also started their own Middle East dialogue, of which the United States strongly disapproved.[108] With the alliance overshadowed by mutual distrust and with the Americans and Europeans working at cross purposes in their attempts to find a solution to the Arab oil weapon, there appeared to be an even greater need for a renewed conception of allied unity.[109]

In the aftermath of the war, Kissinger returned to his Year of Europe theme.[110] He did so partly out of conviction that the original intent behind his proposal had been correct and yet misunderstood. It also offered an opportunity to repair the damage to NATO. He had proposed the Year of Europe, he said, because "it was obvious that the assumptions on which the alliance was founded had been outstripped by events." The emergence of a strong and unified Western Europe and a Soviet Union that had attained strategic parity meant that NATO faced new problems. One of those problems was with the public, who tended to identify "foreign policy success increasingly with relations with adversaries while relations with allies seem to be characterized by bickering and drift."[111] There was also a new generation of leaders in Europe and North America who "did not have the same commitment to [NATO] that the previous generation did."[112]

The solution, for Kissinger, lay in a symbolic act that would display unity and that would, by virtue of its performance, put an end to the suspicion within the alliance that had arisen in an era of détente.[113] Kissinger, who had himself only recently threatened nuclear war without consulting his allies, bristled at the spectacle of a unifying Europe that seemed "to elevate refusal to consult into a principle defining European identity."[114] As a response to this drift and suspicion, a

> major new effort to renew Atlantic relations and to anchor our friendship in a fresh act of creation seemed essential. We hoped that the drama of the

great democracies engaging themselves once again in defining a common
future would infuse our partnership with new emotional and intellectual
excitement."[115]

True, there is much to be said for symbolism among allies, but engaging in
symbolism with the hope that it will resolve differences of substance can be
futile.

The Declaration on Atlantic Relations

The culmination of Kissinger's overselling of the Year of Europe was the
NATO Declaration on Atlantic Relations. Adopted at the NAC meeting at
Ottawa in June 1974 and signed at a special Heads of State and Government meeting later that month in Brussels, the declaration sought to en-
shrine the nebulous concept of allied unity by invoking long-term political
objectives.[116] As in earlier periods when transatlantic discord threatened
the vitality of the alliance, NATO sought revitalization through new
conception. This effort required the alliance to engage in the sort of rhetoric
that had characterized the pre-détente period. It was occasioned, as we have
seen, not by a perceived revival of the Soviet threat, but by a rise in
transatlantic tensions.

   While reaffirming NATO's cherished axioms about the indivisibility of
the security of its members, the inherent value of consultation, and the
necessity of a strong defense for the conduct of détente, the declaration
took note of U.S.-Soviet strategic parity and sought to ease European fears
over a superpower condominium. The United States promised "not to accept
any situation which would expose its Allies to external political or military
pressure likely to deprive them of their freedom."[117] In addition, U.S. nuclear
and conventional forces in Europe were called "indispensable" and the
presence of the North American allies in Europe was said to be
"irreplaceable."[118] For their part, the European allies promised to make the
"necessary contribution" to the common defense, while the United Kingdom
and France undertook to maintain their nuclear forces and "contribute to
the over-all strengthening" of NATO's deterrent.[119] The French characteristically objected to a statement that observed the necessity for "frank and
timely consultation" on political and economic matters.[120]

   The statement about French and British nuclear forces had special
significance. It marked the first time that NATO (and the United States) had
explicitly blessed those forces. Previous U.S. statements in the early to mid-

1960s had called the French force destabilizing and had been mostly silent about the British one. With this important exception, the Declaration on Atlantic Relations contained nothing new. Americans and Europeans had been making similar statements to address similar concerns not only during the era of détente but also before. Similarly, the French continued to balk at any statement that might hint at a rejection of Gaullist principles. What was new was that the allies had managed broadly to package all their fears, concerns, and hopes in one public declaration. As a document designed to reaffirm the dedication of the allies to the principles of mutual cooperation and consultation and the long-term goals of peace and prosperity, the Declaration on Atlantic Relations was a bland piece of rhetorical generality, but it was not without effect. As Kissinger had hoped, the very process of drafting and agreeing to the declaration seems to have brought a new sense of unity to the alliance and, if it failed definitively to resolve some of the outstanding issues over allied commitments, it at least papered them over with high-minded rhetoric about the importance of those commitments.[121]

Because the document was so vague, it could mean all things to all people. The Europeans could take comfort in a general U.S. statement of its intent not to jeopardize the security of it allies in its pursuit of détente with the Soviets. The Americans could point to a renewed European commitment to contribute their fair share to NATO's defense. But beyond this, nothing concrete was spelled out. There was however, in the end, no need to do so: domestic political changes both in Europe and in the United States helped achieve what all the rhetoric could not.

A Change of Leaders

In contrast to the preceding year, 1974 was one of healing and reconciliation within the alliance, as the elected officials at the top of allied governments shifted. In late February, British Prime Minister Edward Heath was replaced by Harold Wilson, who, along with his foreign secretary, James Callaghan, who himself would ascend to the premiership in March 1976, sought to mend fences with the United States and revitalize the special relationship. In early April in France, the death of Pompidou helped remove the difficult Michel Jobert from his role as foreign minister. Valery Giscard d'Estaing, the new French president, was less hostile toward the United States.[122] In West Germany in June, Willy Brandt was replaced by Helmut Schmidt. As finance minister during the energy crisis Schmidt had sought a less confrontational approach with the United States, and his new role as chancellor seemed to hold the promise of better U.S.-German relations. An even more important factor surrounding the potential for improved relations, however, was that Schmidt and Kissinger were old friends; Kissinger had never quite trusted Brandt, thinking him too willing to make concessions to the Soviets over *Ostpolitik*.[123]

In the United States, by the end of July 1974, the House Judiciary Committee had voted in favor of three articles of impeachment against Nixon and sent them to the Senate for trial. He resigned in disgrace in August and was replaced by Gerald Ford, who, while retaining Kissinger's services as secretary of state, publicly distanced himself from Kissinger.[124]

Conclusion: The Demise of Détente

In the spring of 1976, Ford, who hoped to win the upcoming presidential election by responding to domestic criticism of détente, banished the word from his public vocabulary: "We're going," he said, "to forget the use of the word détente." Instead, it would be replaced with "peace through strength."[125] With this utterance, the use of rhetoric to advance conceptual ideas about or propose actual alterations to NATO's form and function came full circle. The decline of rhetoric, which began in 1967 but which had been partially reversed in the aftermath of the 1973 wave of tension within the alliance, was over. As détente soured, the members of NATO found new unity in opposing perceived Soviet designs on the Third World and in criticizing the failure of détente both to head off the 1973 Middle East crisis and to prevent the Soviets from consolidating their hold over Eastern Europe as a result of the 1975 Helsinki Final Act.

A driving force behind détente had been the *realpolitik* approach to international relations, which sought to downplay ideological aims of morality and justice in defense of national interests. For a time, from roughly 1967 to 1972, leaders on both sides of the Atlantic who espoused the realist approach were successful in their pursuit of détente with the Soviets. However, improved bilateral East-West relations put a strain on relations within NATO and provoked a range of disputes from the once-dormant issue of European burden sharing to newer concern over superpower condominium. The Soviets, with their adventuristic forays into Angola and elsewhere in the Third World in the mid-1970s, gave a boost to the return of rhetoric by providing a focus for increased hostility. But even before détente had begun to unravel, NATO leaders, at Kissinger's prompting, had agreed that both the generational change within NATO and the realities of détente required "a fresh act of creation"—an act, that is, that began with the Year of Europe and culminated in the Declaration on Atlantic Relations and that favored axiomatic reference and rhetorical flourish over substance.

The downplay of ideology and rhetoric in foreign policy that accompanied the early years of détente helped undermine the existing rationale for NATO and created an opening for opposition parties within the member states, and particularly the United States, which had embraced a moral crusade against communism. Indeed, future U.S. presidents Jimmy Carter and Ronald Reagan both advanced their careers by criticizing the amorality of the geopolitical calculations inherent in détente. Similarly, both men would work to advance an ideological agenda, which found expression, respectively, either through an emphasis on human rights or the enunciation of a neo-conservative doctrine that depicted the Soviets as the embodiment of evil. Despite these different approaches, the next decade would be characterized by a return to ideology and the rhetoric of the Cold War. The 1974 Declaration on Atlantic Relations and the change of leaders within NATO's principal members marked the onset of this period, when rhetoric served the purpose, as the limits of détente became evident, of arresting disputes within the alliance.

Chapter 5

Arming to Disarm

The years 1976-1985 were ones during which détente gave way to renewed confrontation, principally between the two superpowers.[1] As this occurred, conceptions of NATO and alliance rhetoric had to respond to major changes in politico-military conditions. In so doing, they lost coherence.

The changes to which NATO had to respond were diverse and powerful. For reasons that need not detain us here, by the late 1970s the Soviets had achieved a sweeping buildup of their conventional and nuclear forces, and they had begun to expand their presence in the Third World. Meanwhile, the ideological threat to Europe had been reversed—that is to say that the appeal of Soviet communism in Western Europe had faded;[2] the peoples of Eastern Europe and the Soviet Union were showing an appetite for Western goods, life-styles, and human rights. Détente had produced an opening of relations such that blind fear through complete ignorance had been replaced on both sides by a measure of trust founded on trade, tourism, official contacts, and a greater flow of information. A further result of détente was that in Western Europe the old Cold War fear of an invasion by the Warsaw Pact had receded. But there had been little or no progress on arms control; the arms race rushed on, perhaps redirected a little but not visibly altered.

Because the arms race bore little relation to the political-cum-military threats in Europe, the public in Western Europe (and to a lesser extent in the United States) was skeptical about NATO's plans for rearmament in the 1980s. According to its leaders, the threat to NATO was no longer one of aggressive Soviet political-military intent in Europe, but rather a Soviet arms buildup, which demonstrated the possibility of that intent. In its early days NATO had armed to offset the threat of an invasion; now, invoking the threat of an arms buildup, NATO proposed to rearm to keep up and, it was also said, to bring the Soviets to the bargaining table. But the bargaining chip argument for new weapons—that NATO was arming to disarm—could be read as confirmation of the view that there was no real threat, only an arms race. A further problem was that the arena of superpower political competition moved away from Europe. The United States urged its reluctant allies to take more seriously what it perceived as a renewed Soviet threat to the Third World, but in so doing it opened rifts in NATO of a familiar kind: those associated with readiness to engage in out-of-area operations.

This chapter examines how NATO responded to these powerful tides. It is divided into three sections. The first covers the period from 1976 until June 1979; it follows the demise of détente during the latter half of the 1970s, when, under the prompting of the Carter administration, NATO reluctantly embraced the rhetoric of human rights. It asks why and how far NATO and its principal members sought to include improving human rights conditions in the East as legitimate objectives of the alliance, and it examines how these largely rhetorical commitments on the part of NATO overshadowed more traditional efforts to improve NATO's long-term military posture in the face of a perceived Soviet military buildup and a growing Soviet military threat. Conceptions surrounding NATO's form and function during this period focused largely on practical military issues of long-standing concern, including long-term force goals, spending commitments, modernization, and equipment standardization and interoperability. Important decisions on these issues set the stage for much of the intra-alliance discord that was to follow in the early 1980s, and it is on this state of affairs that section two focuses. How and why did collective decisions that were intended as symbols of allied unity ultimately threaten public support for NATO? How did conceptions of NATO change in response to changing perceptions of the Soviet threat in Europe and beyond? The third section draws some conclusions.

NATO Prepares for a New Cold War

Carter, Human Rights, and NATO

Jimmy Carter entered the White House in January 1977, intent on restoring the moral credibility and international leadership of the American presidency, which had been eroded by the combined effects of the war in Vietnam, the Watergate scandal, and the disgrace of Richard Nixon. His agenda, which placed human rights and arms reduction at the forefront of U.S. foreign policy objectives, was designed to steer the conduct of U.S. foreign policy in new directions, away from Nixon's *realpolitik* approach, with its perceived lack of concern for moral values, and toward a more humane approach to international affairs. Although he was later strongly criticized for being naive and for neglecting the realities of the Soviet threat, Carter did in fact attempt to strengthen America's defenses, including ties with NATO, even as he sought to elevate human rights as an instrument of foreign policy.[3]

In his inaugural address, Carter called on Americans to embrace a "special obligation: to take on those moral duties which, when assumed, seem invariably to be in our own best interests." America's commitment to human rights, he declared, "must be absolute." Peace should be built not on the weapons of war "but on international policies which reflect our own most precious values."[4] A few weeks into his presidency, Carter told the nation that U.S. foreign policy "should be based on close cooperation with our allies and worldwide respect for human rights, a reduction in world armaments, and it must always reflect our own moral values. I want our nation's actions to make you proud."[5] Jimmy Carter would soon press upon NATO a rhetorical vision that exceeded even the sweeping conceptions of its founders. His was a similar vision in the sense that it sought to portray NATO as something far more than a military and political alliance. However, whereas the early NATO had been conceived as a bulwark to protect the freedom and democracy of the West, the new NATO would be an alliance that could help secure human rights on a global scale.[6]

Carter himself twice carried this message to NATO, on both occasions addressing an NAC Heads of State and Government meeting—the first time in London in May 1977 and the second twelve months later in Washington. Carter urged his London audience to embrace a more "humane vision" in its approach to East-West relations.[7] In Washington in May 1978, Carter's oratory was reminiscent of an earlier era, and he invoked the traditional notion that NATO could help build a better world: "Our alliance," he observed, "has never been an end in itself. It is a way to promote peace and stability in Europe and, indeed, peace in the world at large." Human rights and human values, said Carter, are "the final purpose and meaning of our alliance."[8]

With this prodding, "human rights" entered the alliance lexicon. The final communiqué from the London meeting included the statement that the "allies recognize as wholly legitimate the aspirations of people throughout the world to human rights and fundamental freedoms." In accordance with the UN Charter and the Helsinki Final Act—and on the foundation of NATO—the allies promised to "persevere in the task of building a more just and peaceful world."[9] Despite NATO's new rhetorical commitment to human rights, the reality surrounding human rights as foreign policy was more complex. Carter's European partners were concerned that too forceful an approach would undermine détente by provoking confrontation with the Soviets.[10] It was not that West European governments did not value human rights, but rather that they rejected making human rights the centerpiece of foreign policy; and they opposed the American tendency to make East-West cooperation explicitly dependent on Soviet observance of human rights. They preferred instead the softer approach of working through the CSCE.[11] These differences notwithstanding, NATO members, following the American lead, do appear to have become more willing, as the decade came to an end, to pressure the Soviets on upholding the Helsinki Final Act.[12] Although NATO as an organization never fully embraced Carter's message, its members did come eventually to regard both human rights and the CSCE as political weapons in the coming second Cold War.

The Carter administration was one marked by the rhetoric, and in many cases the substance, of concern for human rights and human values.[13] By addressing perceived domestic and international concern about the strength of America's commitment to upholding moral values, the rhetoric of human rights served Carter's domestic political and international purposes, and it almost certainly sprung from his own strong personal beliefs about what was decent and proper.[14] After one year in office, Carter announced to Congress, "We are a confident nation. We've restored the moral basis of our foreign policy. The very heart of our identity is our firm commitment to human rights."[15] But alongside the rhetoric and substance of Carter's human rights agenda the traditional approach to foreign policy lived on: a close eye was kept on the movements of adversaries, the concerns of allies, and the instruments of war. To this approach NATO was more willing and perhaps better equipped to respond.

NATO Prepares for the 1980s

Although the rhetoric of human rights had lent an air of higher purpose to the 1977 and 1978 NATO summits, the central focus of the meetings was to begin to fashion a response to Soviet improvements in conventional and theater nuclear weapons, and to seek consensus on how best to prepare NATO for the political and military challenges of the 1980s. At the May 1977 London summit, Carter made three proposals that were endorsed by the NAC and approved in May 1978 at Washington. The first of these proposals was that NATO should undertake a special review of East-West relations to assess future trends in the Soviet Union and Eastern Europe and to analyze the implications of these trends for the alliance. The Study of Long-Term East-West Trends, announced in a communiqué that noted "Soviet disregard for the indivisibility of détente," was seen to confirm the continuing value of the Harmel formula of pursuing détente on the basis of a strong defense.[16] As détente began to crumble, the need for a strong defense appeared to become ever more important. In the absence of cooperation, it was argued, NATO would need to be prepared for a return to confrontation.

Carter's second proposal attempted partially to address this need by calling for more cooperation and less waste in transatlantic defense production and procurement.[17] With this move, Carter had reaffirmed a long-standing U.S. commitment to the objectives of equipment standardization and interoperability, and his proposal was in line with recent European efforts to achieve similar goals.[18] At the 1977 London summit the so-called two-way street concept of arms procurement, which called for both sides to accept some of the other's equipment, was heartily endorsed.[19] As had happened before, policy aims were negotiated but the competitive strength of national arms industries was such that not much was achieved in this area.[20] It was a quixotic effort—who, after all, could be for waste?—but it did illustrate the desire to integrate the alliance further and also that détente had not ended the arms race.

The military problems facing NATO were as diverse and divisive in the late 1970s as they had been when NATO was founded. The quest for standardized equipment and single weapon systems—long an alliance objective—was still unrealized, and arguments over conscription service length, the amount of defense expenditures, and the number of troops each member would contribute still simmered.[21] However, these problems were overshadowed at the end of the decade by questions over how NATO could respond to the rapid modernization of Warsaw Pact conventional and theater nuclear forces.[22]

Carter's third proposal, which called on NATO to develop its long-term defense capabilities, represented the most significant of his 1977 initiatives; it sought to prepare NATO for a revitalized Soviet military threat and laid the foundation for the momentous dual-track decision of 1979. Citing "concern at continual expansion of Warsaw Pact offensive capabilities," the allies declared at the conclusion of the 1978 summit that they had "no option" but to improve NATO's defenses while pursuing détente.[23] These improvements, formally known as the Long-Term Defense Program (LTDP) and intended to last for fifteen years, focused largely on conventional forces.[24] The politically more divisive issue of NATO's long-term theater nuclear force requirements was sent for discussion to the Nuclear Planning Group (NPG). Carter described the LTDP as

> an unprecedented attempt by NATO to look across a longer span of years than ever before. It seeks a more cooperative course as the only sensible way to improve our defenses without unnecessary increases in defense spending. It lays out specific measures of alliance cooperation. It is the blueprint we need, and we must carry it out vigorously.[25]

In addition to force improvements and a decision later to address nuclear force modernization, Carter had wrung from his colleagues a commitment to increase their defense expenditures by 3 percent per year in real terms. While it formalized a shared aspiration to increase defense expenditures, the so-called 3 percent solution represented merely a ministerial "guidance" to the allies' legislatures, and its meaning was interpreted differently by different countries; what began as a symbolic expression of resolve became a major source of dispute.[26] Heartily endorsed, as for example by West German Chancellor Helmut Schmidt, who called them "indispensable for NATO," the LTDP and the 3 percent commitment later became sources of friction as intra-alliance disputes erupted over their application and as NATO itself came under attack from Western European peace movements.[27] At the time, however, these plans were justified both by the notion that NATO was *compelled* to respond to a more menacing Soviet threat and by reference to the *Harmel Report*.[28]

Although Carter's assertion that the LTDP and its related commitment to increase defense spending were "unprecedented" has some truth to it, there was nothing unprecedented about the alliance seeking to stay upright by moving forward.[29] Indeed, the notion that NATO had continuously to seek (or respond to) change to remain strong was as prevalent in the late 1970s as it had been in previous decades, though this time NATO's relevance was challenged by the shift in the Soviet political threat.[30]

NATO and the Politics of Peace

NATO entered its fourth decade with a renewed commitment to improve its defenses, but it also faced the troubling evidence that the *Harmel Report*, which had enunciated the axiom that a strong defense would create the conditions for a reduction of East-West tensions, was hollow: peace through strength remained a cold peace, détente was collapsing,[31] and attention to NATO's long-term conventional needs appeared useless as a means of influencing Soviet behavior in the Third World.[32] Even as NATO pledged itself to devote more resources to a stronger defense, transatlantic relations became strained as Americans and Europeans differed over roles and responsibilities in the Third World and over the alleged benefits of détente.[33] It was in this context of emerging transatlantic discord and the demise of détente that NATO decided, in December 1979, to extend the alliance's LTDP to the nuclear sphere.

The 1979 Dual-Track Decision

Soviet deployments of intermediate-range nuclear missiles (SS-20s) in the European theater and the knowledge that the United States had a new generation of missiles ready for deployment had prompted NATO's leaders to pursue the creation of a similar force for Western Europe.[34] After a special meeting of NATO foreign and defense ministers in Brussels in December 1979, the NAC formally approved a plan advanced by the Nuclear Planning Group. Known as the dual-track decision, the plan called for the deployment in 1983 of 108 Pershing II ballistic missiles in West Germany and 464 ground-launched cruise missiles (GLCMs) in the United Kingdom, Italy, the Netherlands, and Belgium.[35] At the same time, NATO announced the pursuit of a second track along which it would seek to place arms control initiatives parallel to force modernization and deployment. These moves were justified by reference to the *Harmel Report*, which had outlined the "twin path along the road to security," and by reference to NATO's earlier decision, which had been reaffirmed in May 1978, to meet the challenge represented by the new Soviet missiles.[36] The decision was praised by U.S. Secretary of State Cyrus Vance as giving "evidence of the central vitality and cohesion of the alliance."[37] This would not long remain the case. To see why, we must note important developments in three areas—nuclear weapons, strategy, and political engagement.

In terms of nuclear-weapon development, it is clear, at least in retrospect, that both superpowers were long past the point of saturation; the accumulation of thousands of nuclear warheads, after taking account of the effects of increased accuracy, meant that both sides could be seen to have a clear capacity for overkill. The Soviet SS-20s and the American cruise and Pershing missiles were additions to vast, redundant nuclear arsenals.

Two important points need to be recognized about this situation, though as we shall see they were not generally acknowledged at the time. First, there was no possibility that either side could be disarmed by preemption, which meant that the military rationale for new missiles was weak. Second, the arguments over whether new missiles would couple or de-couple NATO's nuclear deterrent on the European continent from the threat that the United States would use nuclear weapons against the Soviet Union was inherently ambiguous. On the one hand, it could be claimed that cruise and Pershing missiles would couple: with them the United States was more likely to use, or threaten to use, the intermediate-range nuclear forces (INF) option—and thereby defend Europe—rather than jump to strategic weapons and risk the U.S. homeland; on the other, the missiles might de-couple: with them the United States was more likely to use nuclear weapons in Europe only (and thereby destroy Europe) without threatening the Soviet Union or risking a counterstrike on U.S. territory.[38] In logic, there is nothing to choose between these contrary propositions; each could be and was deployed with conviction by those whose case it supported. This ambiguity, added to the apparent excessiveness of the nuclear arsenals of the superpowers, lies beneath the schism that opened between NATO's leaders and public opinion in their countries.[39]

But these factors alone would not suffice to explain why a wide schism developed between NATO leaders and their peoples: the leaders might have seen that public perceptions were different from their own, that the arguments for the dual-track decision would not carry the same weight as the arguments for more weapons they had used in earlier decades. That they failed to foresee these things appears to have been caused, in part at least, by the fact that as regards their view of nuclear threats and nuclear-weapon policy the leaders lived in a different world from many of their people.

Out of office the European political leaders who took an interest in military affairs learned the vocabulary of nuclear weapons and the ways of reasoning about nuclear strategy from the established nuclear strategic community at meetings of the IISS and at similar forums. In office they were advised by civilians and military officers who represented the same community in the sense that they all used the same modes of reasoning; they all belonged to the school of nuclear deterrence developed in the United States. Deterrence theory assumes that there is a political-military threat; and it could always be made to yield the answer that to acquire more nuclear weapons was the correct response to any Soviet deployment. It led people to feel, when in doubt acquire more nuclear weapons.

The European nuclear experts joined their American counterparts, to whom they are very close, and responded to the SS-20s by talking of the risk of de-coupling and by taking the line that cruise and Pershing deployments would recouple (and hence strengthen the axiom of transatlantic security linkage).[40] The political leaders in Europe listened to their military advisers, nuclear planners, and the nuclear strategic community and decided to adopt the dual-track approach, hoping that the promise of more arms control talks would keep the public happy.[41]

In contrast to their leaders, a large part of the West European people did not embrace the arcane world of deterrence theory. Having accepted nuclear weapons reluctantly in the late 1950s, they had come since then, aided by détente, to be (1) skeptical about the Soviet desire to invade Western Europe; (2) repelled by the nuclear arms race and the idea that more nuclear weapons were needed when tens of thousands had been accumulated, and fearful of the risks of nuclear accident or preemption; and (3) impatient at the slow progress in arms control.

Wrapped in their world of deterrence reasoning, with its assumptions about a threat and the coupling of allies, the political leaders miscalculated what the people of Western Europe felt and believed. Perhaps it is true to say that the error occurred because the European nuclear advisers used

American deterrence reasoning, which made assumptions that were largely accepted by the public in the United States (e.g., that there was a strong Soviet threat to Western Europe), and failed to see that they were not accepted at home. The result was an angry debate over deployment between the public and NATO's political-military elite; the issue of the Euro-missiles took on a political importance that overshadowed the military interests involved; and the dual-track decision became a test of alliance cohesion, rather than a symbol of allied unity, as it had originally been intended.

In addition to concern over how to respond to new Soviet missiles, the decision by the NATO leaders appears to have been linked with uneasiness in the nuclear strategic community in Europe over the credibility of the American nuclear guarantee.[42] Although the deployment of the new Soviet missiles elicited much American rhetoric reaffirming the U.S. commitment to NATO, this proved insufficient reassurance, and the dual-track decision thus became a political symbol among the European elite of U.S. support for NATO.[43] British Secretary of State for Defense Francis Pym, for example, hailed it as a "dramatic reaffirmation of American commitment to Europe."[44]

Once the political decision had been made, it was felt to be essential to follow through with deployment. Failure to deploy would result in a Soviet victory and a loss of prestige for NATO's leaders vis-à-vis their domestic constituencies. Helmut Kohl, for example, claimed that support for the decision was "synonymous with the survival of democratic Europe, the preservation of the Atlantic Alliance and the continuation of relations on an equal basis with the Soviet Union."[45] Public opinion was skeptical.

The interlocking credo of the political-military community had found expression in nuclear issues, as had transatlantic political relations. But these relations came under increasing pressure as European and American leaders fell out over whether and how to pursue détente and as the United States appeared unable effectively to respond to new challenges to its influence in the Third World, most recently in Iran in November 1979, where revolution had overthrown the Shah and where militants had seized the American embassy and held hostage its personnel. The Soviet invasion of Afghanistan late in December 1979, which followed directly on the heels of the announcement of the dual-track decision, prompted both renewed fear of Soviet designs on the unstable Persian Gulf region and a reaffirmation of NATO's commitment to meet strength with strength.[46] In response to the invasion, Carter strongly warned the Soviets from proceeding further, announced trade sanctions and a boycott against the 1980 Moscow Olympic Games, and withdrew the SALT II Treaty, which now faced almost certain defeat, from the ratification debate before the Senate.[47]

Once the phase of implementation had been entered, the dual-track decision invited controversy of a new kind. While the first track (deployment) had been a multilateral decision, the second track (arms control) was to be bilateral in the form of U.S.-Soviet negotiations. NATO's European leaders had control over deployment but, once this had been agreed, found themselves shut out from the negotiating process and facing growing public and parliamentary opposition. This cleavage between control over the two tracks created a special dilemma for French and British leaders, who hoped to influence any future INF negotiations while insisting that their own nuclear forces would not become the subject of those negotiations.[48] In an ironic role reversal, European public opinion blamed the United States—and not the Soviets, who had upped the ante in the first place—for increasing the likelihood of nuclear war in Europe.[49] Thus, West German Chancellor Helmut Schmidt chastised members of the Bundestag who supported the peace movement for acting "as if existing Soviet SS-20 missiles directed at targets in Germany and elsewhere were less dangerous than American missiles that are not even here yet."[50]

The arms control link had been designed to ensure European public support for deployment, but it also made deployment more difficult.[51] The peace movement took the position that deployment was inimical to arms control, and that arms control was an alternative to deployment. Public resistance was further hardened by the ambiguous timetable that surrounded arms control (in contrast to the definite deployment dates) and by the lack of dual-key arrangements over GLCMs, which raised questions about European sovereignty and U.S. willingness unilaterally to commit its allies to nuclear war.[52]

In support of the dual-track decision, the old rhetorical notion of peace through strength was revived. But whatever solace "peace" could give was soon balanced by the anxiety that "strength" created—that is to say that a formula that had been uncontroversial in the past now seemed to threaten the very objective it sought to uphold. New, more accurate and powerful missiles in the heart of Europe seemed the very antithesis of peace. For those uncomfortable with the formula, strength held a very tragic power indeed if the desire for peace could lead NATO to imperil the existence of the societies it was pledged to defend.

Reagan, Anticommunism, and Alliance Relations

NATO's response to the public outcry over the dual-track decision was to launch a massive public relations program aimed at reversing the growing tide of antinuclear and anti-American sentiment in Europe.[53] As this effort got under way, Ronald Reagan, who replaced Jimmy Carter in January 1981, embarked on a flood of anticommunist hyperbole not seen since the early days of the Cold War. An inveterate red baiter and outspoken critic of détente, Reagan combined a self-righteous style of crusading moralism with an unprecedented increase in U.S. defense spending. The short-term result of all this was to complicate NATO's efforts to sway public opinion in favor of the notion that NATO really stood for peace; in the longer term, Reagan would claim that peace through strength (and strong words) had brought the Soviets not only to the bargaining table but ultimately to their knees.[54] However, we are getting ahead of events. On the river of history, détente lay behind and the end of the Cold War ahead, but leaders tend to see what is immediately at hand and what they saw at the opening of the 1980s was an alliance beset by internal bickering and public hostility and a desperate need to reunite.[55]

The solution was to attempt to take the initiative away from the peace movement by cloaking NATO's dual-track decision in the rhetoric of peace. Before we examine these moves, however, we turn briefly to an examination of the style and substance of Reagan's leadership—both of which had important consequences for alliance relations and for the dubious notion, soon to be advanced, that NATO was a peace movement.[56]

During the election of 1980, Reagan had criticized Carter for presiding over an American withdrawal from global leadership that had contributed to a dramatic shift in the balance of power.[57] In response, Reagan engineered a substantial buildup in U.S. nuclear and conventional capabilities, and he employed strong anticommunist rhetoric both to justify the need for these measures and to help combat the short-lived nuclear freeze movement in the United States.[58] The Soviets, he said, "reserve unto themselves the right to commit any crime, to lie, to cheat."[59] Communism was but "a sad, bizarre chapter in human history whose last pages are even now being written."[60] Even so, the Soviet Union was "an evil empire" and "the focus of evil in the modern world."[61]

This language was designed not only to vilify and depersonalize the Soviet adversary, but also to reassert American prestige and American global leadership.[62] "The reassertion of American self-confidence," declared U.S. Secretary of State Alexander Haig, "is the very basis of the President's foreign policy."[63] The Soviets were depicted as an implacable, untrustworthy foe who understood only force—force, that is, expressed not only in American might but also in allied (meaning NATO) power. Under this conception, the dual-track decision formed part of a resolute demonstration of collective will among the allies that would pave the way for new East-West relations.[64]

This strong anti-Soviet language was matched on some occasions by NATO, but only in reference to specific Soviet actions: NATO's rhetoric, reflected in NAC final communiqués in the early 1980s, had neither the vehemence nor the moralism associated with Reagan's.[65] While these communiqués reflected both genuine disgust with Soviet behavior and the impact of U.S. pressure to be more outspoken against such behavior, the European allies, who hoped to hang on to the benefits of détente, were wary of intensifying the war of words. Helmut Schmidt's March 1980 remarks to the Bundestag are representative of this view: "In regard to our relations with Eastern countries, it is our wish in agreement with our Allies, to maintain what has already been achieved."[66] A Franco-German communiqué of February 1980 made a similar appeal, declaring that the European members of NATO had a "special interest" in avoiding confrontation.[67] The dissenting leader in Europe was Margaret Thatcher, whose New Right convictions closely matched those of Reagan and who employed similar anticommunist rhetoric.[68]

Transatlantic relations became increasingly strained as the war of words was extended into the realm of economic sanctions. This extension had begun with Carter's response to the Iranian revolution and the invasion of Afghanistan.[69] The U.S. response to the imposition of martial law in Poland in December 1981 brought troubled transatlantic relations to a new low. Although the NAC called a special meeting, which strongly condemned martial law and warned the Soviets not to interfere,[70] Reagan went a step further and ordered a ban on the sale of oil and gas equipment to the Soviet Union. In June 1982, the ban was extended to cover foreign subsidiaries of U.S. companies.

The U.S. reaction gave rise to a crisis in the alliance because it interfered with the building of a gas pipeline from Siberia to Western Europe from which NATO's European members, especially France and Germany, would benefit. In more general terms, the crisis underscored European reluctance to jettison détente. To some, like Helmut Schmidt, the sanctions appeared symptomatic of an American reluctance to engage in dialogue with the Soviets.[71] He also warned that "a trade war with the Soviet Union ... could usher in a new era of the Cold War."[72] French Foreign Minister Claude Cheysson was more explicit: "we should not," he said, "punish ourselves with sanctions because there are developments in Eastern Europe that cannot be put up with. We need that gas."[73] The European Community also issued a strong condemnation.[74]

The crisis ended in November 1982, when Reagan lifted the sanctions.[75] But allied relations had been severely strained, and both conservatives and liberals in the United States invoked the European response as yet another sign of ungrateful allies.[76] The crisis had at least one other important outcome: it produced a U.S. review of Western economic relations with the Soviet Union and brought new prominence to the conception that NATO should regard those relations as falling within its purview. Because East-West trade was now seen by the United States less as a concomitant of détente and more as an indirect subsidy for the Soviet defense buildup, U.S. leaders urged NATO to consider trade as part of security.[77] Even the French succumbed to this pressure: Cheysson, speaking in reference to the role of NATO's Economic Committee, declared that "NATO is the proper place to consider, to coordinate action for any matter, including economic subjects, insofar as they concern security."[78] The outcome, however, was somewhat different than the rhetoric suggested, with the Coordinating Committee for Multilateral Export Controls (COCOM) and the OECD taking the lead role in responding to this new willingness to examine the strategic aspects of trade.[79] Nevertheless, East-West trade was now an accepted part of NATO's agenda for the 1980s.[80]

Both transatlantic and East-West relations were further strained by Reagan's March 1983 Strategic Defense Initiative (SDI), popularly known as Star Wars, which promised to provide a space-based defense against Soviet missiles. The Soviets claimed that SDI was a violation of the Anti-Ballistic Missile (ABM) Treaty and an escalation of the arms race. Although the notion of complete protection from nuclear missiles was illusory, the proposal caused much consternation in Europe because it seemed to offer a completely new nuclear technology that could undermine mutual deterrence. For the United States, SDI appears to have offered a means of reasserting its leadership in NATO, whose European members might be induced to seek protection under the new U.S. system. In return for acknowledging the renewed U.S. strategic leadership, Washington implied that European industries would receive valuable defense contracts. In addition, because it was claimed to have the power of making nuclear weapons "impotent and obsolete," SDI also provided political leverage against domestic critics of Reagan's defense budget and against the peace movement.[81]

NATO as Peace Movement

Despite the growing public furor over NATO's new nuclear missiles, allied leaders remained wedded to the notion of peace through strength—the validity of which seemed to be confirmed by the opening of intermediate nuclear forces (INF) talks in Geneva in November 1981.[82] Even so, apocalyptic talk within the Reagan administration about nuclear warning shots and the effectiveness of limited nuclear war added to the public frustration with NATO and to the widening transatlantic rift that had erupted over gas sanctions.[83] These troubles were later exacerbated by fantastical talk about the benefits of SDI—talk that appeared to raise the thorny issue of whether SDI, if it were ever built, would have the same effect as that which had been ascribed to the SS-20s: the strategic de-coupling of Western Europe from North America.

Efforts by allied leaders on both sides of the Atlantic to generate public and legislative approval for deployment of new missiles in Europe focused on several themes, including the notions that peace would follow strength, that a demonstration of collective will would hasten negotiations, that deterrence (which now needed strengthening) was the only way to preserve security and freedom, and that NATO had no alternative.[84] None of these proved entirely persuasive, and the situation was further aggravated by Soviet propaganda and so-called active measures, which sought to play on European fears of nuclear war and to portray NATO and the United States as warmongers.[85] The East-West propaganda war prompted U.S. Secretary of State and former SACEUR Alexander Haig to declare that "the nuclear debate in Europe has become a battle for the soul of Europe."[86]

U.S. leaders tended to stress the need for their European counterparts to follow through on their commitment to deploy the missiles by achieving swift parliamentary ratification, while European leaders focused on American promises to engage in arms control negotiations. The U.S. effort reflected both the relative lack of antinuclear sentiment in the United States (which was taken to mean that arms control was less politically important) and a tendency to view with skepticism the commitment of the United States'

NATO partners, who were regarded as dragging their feet over deployment.[87] The European elite, for their part, emphasized arms control both as a means of deflecting domestic criticism of the deployment decision and to pressure the United States to stay the course of the second track.[88]

These efforts came to head at the June 1982 NATO summit in Bonn, where the alliance issued its Program for Peace in Freedom, a political maneuver reminiscent of earlier attempts to patch up differences within the alliance and counter criticism of NATO by finding common cause in the drafting of political hyperbole. In this respect, the Program for Peace in Freedom outdid its predecessors, including even the vapid 1974 Declaration on Atlantic Relations.

The program and its attached documents reaffirmed the principles and purposes of the alliance as stated in the Washington Treaty, proclaimed NATO's desire for arms control and disarmament, and called on NATO further to integrate its political, economic, and security assets to elicit Soviet restraint, both within and beyond NATO's formal area.[89] The program, which referred to NATO as the "essential instrument for peace" and which vowed that NATO's nuclear weapons would never be used except in response to attack, pointedly set out to contrast NATO with the Warsaw Pact in an unsubtle effort to offset the growing influence of the peace movement—a movement that had mustered more than 350,000 antinuclear demonstrators in Bonn on the day the program was issued.[90]

Nothing that was said was new or even very remarkable. The program was what it said it was, an assertion of goodwill, but it was also intended as a consolation for those in the West who now felt threatened by NATO, a reassurance of the alliance's commitment to peace. Schmidt, who hosted the summit, described it thus: "The Bonn Declaration does not contain any new military strategy, nor does it formulate any new policy. Rather it updates and preserves the policy pursued by the alliance since the Harmel Report. The Alliance will continue to follow this course."[91] At the official level, the doctrine of peace through strength remained as strong as ever.

In the wake of the declaration, the rhetorical onslaught continued.[92] At Berlin early in 1983, U.S. Vice President George Bush somewhat bitterly declared that "the NATO countries have fought and paid the price for the framework of freedoms within which those anti-nuclear groups march and demonstrate and speak their minds."[93] A few weeks earlier, NATO Secretary General Joseph Luns had announced with great sincerity that "NATO is the real peace movement."[94] This notion was invoked by allied leaders on both sides of the Atlantic and became a rallying cry for those in favor of deployment. Margaret Thatcher, for example, later called NATO "the greatest peace movement in history."[95]

West Germany, whose leaders had agreed to accept all the new Pershing II missiles, quickly became the center of the critical public relations war.[96] Helmut Kohl, who took power when Schmidt's government fell in October 1982, waged and ultimately won this battle, but not without great effort and not without resorting to portents of impending doom. Kohl found much ammunition in NATO's rich conceptual lore. Calling for a "psychological and moral offensive," he declared that

> NATO in the first place is a community of ideas, not a community of arms. As a matter of fact, the community of arms is there to protect the community of ideas. [Our common values] have to be defended by the alliance. Hence it is vital that these common ideas be stressed again and again, in particular with a view to the younger generation.[97]

Before the final vote in the Bundestag, Kohl, who like his predecessors viewed NATO as a means to an independent and unified Germany, warned that failure to endorse the dual-track decision would undermine the Federal Republic's standing as a dependable ally, destroy NATO, and end any hope of arms control negotiations: "Our country's orientation in external affairs is at stake.... Whoever revokes the dual-track decision and thereby breaks the linkage between defense and arms control is to all intents and purposes putting at risk the alliance itself, its free will and its viability."[98] On 22 November 1983, by a vote of 286 to 225 (with one abstention), the Bundestag endorsed deployment. By the end of the year, deployment had begun in the United Kingdom, Italy, and the FRG.[99]

While the peace movement failed to reverse the deployment of new missiles in Europe, it succeeded, through massive and wholly unexpected pressure, in compelling NATO, an organization long proud of its public support, to embrace rhetorically the dubious notion that it was a peace movement.[100] True, NATO's leaders had always claimed that NATO stood for peace—and that a strong NATO would in fact compel the Soviets to seek peace on Western democratic terms—but this is not quite the same thing as claiming that NATO was a "peace movement." The assumption of grass-roots political and social activism that underlay the concept of a peace movement sat uneasily with even the most farfetched aspects of NATO's conceptual canon; and there was something rather feeble about the sight of NATO trying to take over the label of its opponents.

Out-of-Area Issues

With the year of the missile at an end, 1984 marked softer tones in East-West relations. These improved relations were the combined result of election-year pressures in the United States (during the election Reagan was criticized for being the first president in fifty years not to have met with a Soviet leader), the death of Yuri Andropov in the Soviet Union, and renewed high-level East-West contacts at the CSCE Stockholm Conference.[101] NATO, which celebrated its thirty-fifth anniversary in Washington, was urged by the United States now to turn its attention to improving conventional forces and to helping Third World nations resist Soviet adventurism.[102] While both the NAC and European leaders endorsed these calls for improved conventional forces, out-of-area concerns were more politically sensitive, and Americans continued to chafe over European failure to follow the U.S. lead on out-of-area issues.[103]

As noted earlier, Europeans were reluctant to jeopardize East-West relations over issues beyond Europe, and Carter's plans for rapid intervention in the Persian Gulf raised the additional possibility of a diversion of manpower and matériel from NATO. Under both Carter and Reagan, the United States tried to use the specter of Afghanistan to prod its European allies to increase conventional forces in Europe to compensate for this diversion and to free U.S. resources for use elsewhere.[104]

Though out-of-area concerns had been of great importance since NATO's founding, the term "out-of-area" formally entered the alliance lexicon only in 1980. The partial success of U.S. efforts to raise awareness of out-of-area threats and the need to meet them was reflected in the language of NAC and Defense Planning Committee (DPC) communiqués, as was the need for allied compensatory measures to balance the growing U.S. commitment to Southwest Asia.[105] However, the United States' European partners and Congress were reluctant to transform the rhetoric into reality (this would have to wait until the 1990-1991 Gulf War). A rising federal deficit and domestic pressure in favor of cutting defense expenditures, which followed the bruising and often anti-American battle with the European peace movement, helped foster a revival in Congress of sentiment in favor of a possible U.S. withdrawal from NATO.[106]

With regard to out-of-area assistance, Britain was the most sympathetic of the United States' principal allies—due in large part to Margaret Thatcher's solidarity with Reagan and to the debt incurred by the British during the 1982 Falklands campaign, where the United States provided much assistance.[107] In the aftermath of the Falklands and despite the growing disparity between resources and interests, Britain moved to reverse its global withdrawal by giving support to its allies on out-of-area issues and by increasing the flexibility of its forces and defense spending for out-of-area action.[108]

France viewed out-of-area concerns as an issue not appropriate for NATO, but at the same time declared the intention to enhance its capability to act beyond Europe.[109] In 1984, France formed the *Force d'Action Rapide* with an eye to French interests outside Europe.[110] France shared the British view that future out-of-area threats were more likely to come from regional instability and interstate war than from Soviet aggression.[111] France was not in the IMO and therefore not subject to U.S. calls for compensation in NATO. It did, however, coordinate a military response with the United States to the Libyan invasion of Chad in 1983-1984, reinforce French forces in West Germany, host the first NAC meeting in Paris since 1966, and publicly reaffirm the commitment to NATO.[112]

Out-of-area commitments were particularly difficult for the FRG, which cited constitutional constraints and fears about increasing Cold War tensions on the German border.[113] Germany did, however, sign the 1982 Host Nation Support Agreement with the United States, which provided greater German assistance for the payment of basing costs associated with U.S. troops. The FRG also increased economic assistance to Greece, Turkey, and Portugal.[114]

The December 1984 NAC communiqué formed a watershed in NATO's long dilemma over how to balance out-of-area concerns, which were not covered by the North Atlantic Treaty but which nevertheless existed, with more obvious and legitimate in-area obligations and responsibilities. It observed that "events outside the treaty area may affect [the allies'] common interests…. They will engage in timely consultations on such events if it is established that their common interests are involved."[115] Past references to out-of-area issues had always referred to individual interests, and the notion of common interests now reflected a new willingness, rhetorically speaking at least, to look collectively beyond NATO's formal purview.[116]

Out-of-area concerns remained important to NATO, but March 1985 brought two important changes that shifted the focus back to Europe: first, Mikhail Gorbachev came to power in the Soviet Union; second, with the arrival of the last of the American cruise missiles in Europe, Moscow reopened the INF talks, which it had suspended when deployment began in November 1983. Not since 1972 had a politically strong U.S. president been in office at the same time as a physically strong Soviet secretary general. Reagan had been reelected by a huge margin the previous November; and Gorbachev, a relatively young man and the first Soviet leader since Lenin to have a university education, became the fourth Soviet leader in less than three years.[117] They met in November 1985 at Geneva for a summit that concluded only minor bilateral agreements but that was surprisingly friendly—a result presaged perhaps by Thatcher's own impressions of Gorbachev as being a man with whom the West "could do business."[118]

Conclusion

The late 1970s ushered in a period of muddled rhetoric from NATO. The primary purpose for which NATO had been devised—protection against Soviet invasion—was less telling at a time when détente had broken down old fears and when the excesses of the arms race had paradoxically made the threat of invasion appear even more remote. The apparent absence of any real threat to NATO helped weaken the political cohesion of the alliance. Although plans for a new generation of missiles seemed to offer unity through arms racing, they actually served further to weaken the alliance and strengthen the peace movement.

Jimmy Carter's laudable efforts to rise above power politics failed: despite his clear commitment to human rights, traditional foreign policy concerns (and their traditional solutions) took precedence. Ronald Reagan placed rearmament above human rights and revived the old rhetorical notion of peace through strength to achieve that objective. Reagan in his first term (until 1984) was remarkably bellicose—but, it could also be said, so were the Soviets, who stuck to a hard line over the SS-20s.[119] NATO as an organization tried to resist both the bellicosity on the part of its principal member and the public hostility to its plans for new nuclear missiles by cloaking itself in the rhetoric of the peace movement. It also sought to cast itself as a new force for the consideration of strategic economic concerns and as an invigorated forum for creating a collective approach to out-of-area problems, including state-sponsored terrorism.[120]

NATO's leaders regarded these conceptions as proof of the alliance's vitality and relevance. But compared to earlier periods, their rhetoric was confused and lacked conviction. As NATO's leaders sought endorsement for their actions at home by holding out the lure of arms control, their rhetoric assumed a strong domestic slant. NATO's claim to be the true peace movement was particularly feeble: to adopt the label of the opposition was an act of weakness, perhaps desperation, and it looked like it.

Détente had broken the clear distinctions between East and West, and to some degree it had even broken the Iron Curtain. No matter how shrill the rhetoric about the existence of an evil empire to the East, few in Western Europe warmed to such rhetoric, let alone went along with the notion that more arms were the answer to the evil. Although the threat of an arms buildup was invoked to justify the deployment of new missiles, what most people saw was an arms race.

Politically crippled by its own decisions, by rising public hostility, and by a host of problems on the alliance's periphery, NATO stuck together by wrangling with the peace movement. Any threatening noises from Moscow, let alone any threatening moves, would have provided a familiar, perhaps even welcome, pretext for restoring unity. In the next few years, however, allied leaders were faced with the unprecedented spectacle of a Soviet Union led by a genuine and determined reformer who sought not confrontation but cooperation. It would be in response to this challenge that conceptions of NATO provided their greatest utility.

Chapter 6

Consolidating European Security

The final years in office of Ronald Reagan, the inveterate cold warrior, were characterized by a remarkable shift away from the politics of ideology to the politics of pragmatism.[1] The reasons for this shift need not detain us here. Suffice it to say that domestic political imperatives and a keen desire to make history met head-on with the breathtaking diplomatic overtures of Mikhail Gorbachev. These combined forces helped produce the stunning events that led to an unprecedented relaxation of East-West tensions and laid the foundation for the end of the Cold War.[2] The events that preceded the end of the Cold War and the manner in which it ended were seen to confirm both the wisdom of NATO's axiomatic approach to international political life and the relevance of its conceptual canon. This confirmation was to have profound implications for the way in which NATO's leaders tried to shape the immediate post-Cold War era.

This chapter examines how conceptions of NATO and their rhetorical expression changed in response to the events of the years 1986-1996. The period began with signs of significant reform in the Soviet Union. As Mikhail Gorbachev assumed power, he resumed arms control negotiations with the

West, eased internal repression, began retreating from commitments in the Third World, and loosened constraints on his Warsaw Pact allies in Eastern Europe. By 1990, the Eastern European states had rejected communism, the Iron Curtain disintegrated, Germany was reunified, and the geopolitical and ideological confrontation that was the Cold War had ended—in spectacular, peaceful fashion and almost overnight. On Christmas day 1991, the Soviet Union ceased to exist.

The early NATO reaction to these events was a familiar one: as in previous periods of uncertainty about the threat from the East, the allies, with the Americans in the lead, urged collective restraint and unity, and they pushed for continued vigilance in all areas of East-West relations. Conceptions of NATO's form and function during the late 1980s were largely consistent with forty years of alliance rhetoric, and in many instances the rhetoric articulating those conceptions closely resembled that of the first decade of the Cold War. As the Cold War wound down in rapid and peaceful fashion, NATO's leaders sought to sustain the alliance by publicly reaffirming their faith in the notions of commonly held values and of an Atlantic Community that those values were perceived to have helped create.

By the early 1990s, the end of the Cold War and the collapse of the Soviet empire were seen to present new uncertainties and threats. They also generated public skepticism about the relevance of the alliance. In response, NATO's leaders rhetorically invoked a wide range of well-entrenched notions about the continuing utility of the alliance. These conceptions were accompanied by a set of new strategic and political concepts designed to meet the particular challenges of the post-Cold War era, though they too were often wrapped in recognizable rhetoric. In the first years of the post-Cold War period, old notions of partnership and community found new relevance, and they were purveyed as a conceptual framework that could support NATO's proclaimed goal of consolidating pan-European security well into the twenty-first century.

This chapter is divided into four sections. The first covers the period 1986-1990. It begins by examining how NATO responded to indications that the Soviet Union under Gorbachev was becoming less threatening, and it then turns to the series of events that led to the end of Soviet power in Eastern Europe and the reunification of Germany. How were the final years of the Cold War reflected in alliance rhetoric? How did conceptions of NATO change in response to these powerful events? In what ways were conceptions of NATO and their rhetorical expression consistent with earlier periods? Section two examines the period 1991-1996. What are the post-Cold War conceptions of NATO's form and function? How and where do they fit within the spectrum of images of NATO held during the Cold War? How did these conceptions originate and what purposes do they serve? With these questions in mind, section three takes a closer look at national conceptions of NATO in the post-Cold War era. Section four draws some conclusions.

Conceptions of NATO at the End of the Cold War

In the wake of the November 1985 Geneva summit, new Soviet proposals early in 1986 for conventional force reductions and the signing of the Stockholm Document[3] later that year helped produce widespread optimism that encouraging developments in East-West relations were finally at hand. However, as in the immediate post-Stalin period when a new Soviet leader had also seemed to offer the promise of real change, NATO remained wary.

With the Americans characteristically leading the public relations counterattack, the alliance began to focus its response on two time-honored tactics. The first was to take credit for these new developments. Repeatedly, NATO's leaders, both individually and through the NAC, claimed that improved relations had come about as a result of the alliance's policy of peace through strength. These claims, citing the recent Soviet return to arms control negotiations, referred to the most recent compelling success of the dual-track decision, but they also recalled nearly forty years of alliance solidarity in the face of changing Soviet tactics. In December 1985, for example, the NAC declared that encouraging developments in East-West relations "demonstrate the validity of our policy" of peace through strength and political unity.[4] At the same time, allied leaders urged caution and warned against weakened resolve. These warnings, as for example in the case of Reagan's impassioned plea to the American people in February 1986, often accompanied efforts to prevent defense spending cuts: "strength," declared the president, "is the most persuasive argument we have to convince our adversaries to negotiate seriously and to cease bullying other nations."[5] American leaders also continued to call attention to Soviet noncompliance with previous arms control agreements.[6] As in the mid-1950s, changes in the Soviet stance were perceived to be tactical rather than substantive, and alliance rhetoric reflected a combination of guarded optimism, self-congratulation, a preoccupation with the nebulous concept of strength, and deep distrust of Soviet intentions.[7]

The Lessons of Reykjavik

Prospects for more sweeping changes in East-West relations were improved substantially at the October 1986 Reykjavik summit, where Reagan and Gorbachev came tantalizingly close to reaching an agreement on reducing strategic nuclear forces. The talks ultimately broke down over the acceptable limits of SDI research, but the two leaders' wide-ranging discussions about the possibilities for the complete elimination of ballistic missiles, the reduction of intermediate nuclear forces (INF), new measures for verification, and limits on nuclear testing revealed that the potential for superpower cooperation on arms control was now greater than it had been since perhaps the famed détente of Nixon and Brezhnev.[8]

Despite the inevitable comparisons with the era of high détente, American leaders were keen to discourage use of the terminology of détente. U.S. Secretary of State George Schultz later revealed that, just before the 1985 Geneva summit, he had admonished a group of White House planners who were talking about arranging a tête-à-tête between Reagan and Gorbachev. "You have got to knock this off," he told them. "You keep using these French words, and the next thing you know, you'll be talking about détente."[9]

Alongside widespread support for these new U.S.-Soviet engagements, however, lay official West European anxieties of a familiar kind; those associated with the prospects for superpower condominium, the possible denuclearization of Europe, and, in France and Britain, fear that superpower accord on INF would threaten the future of national deterrents.[10] The West Germans, for their part, resented the idea that the only post-INF nuclear weapons in Western Europe would be of the short-range variety, those designed to fall on German territory.[11]

To these fears the United States responded in predictable fashion: it strove to present the Reykjavik summit, where a deal was nearly done over the heads of the United States' NATO partners, as a summit in NATO's interests and one that could only have gone as far as it did as a result of previous NATO policy. "We went to the Iceland meeting," Reagan told a group of executive branch officers soon afterward, "in a position of strength. The Soviets knew that we had the support, not only of a strong America but a united NATO alliance that was going ahead with deployment of Pershing II and ground-launched cruise missiles. So, yes, it was this strength and unity that brought the Soviets to the bargaining table."[12] The accepted lesson of Reykjavik, like that of the dual-track decision, was that the Soviets would negotiate seriously only in the face of a "broad base of U.S. and allied strength and resolve."[13] Such rhetoric did little to ease official European concern about U.S. willingness to act without the full support of its allies— a tendency that had been most recently confirmed by the April 1986 U.S. air strike against Libya.[14]

The end of 1986 and the early months of 1987 marked the emergence of what was to become the accepted pattern for NATO's response to Soviet overtures. Hereafter and under American tutelage, NATO would present a mix of initiatives—each increasingly bolder than the last—and warnings about the dangers of seeking rapid change. In December 1986, NATO issued its Declaration on Conventional Arms Control—a document that endorsed in principle recent Soviet proposals for large troop cuts and that directly incorporated Gorbachev's rhetoric concerning the creation of stability "from the Atlantic to the Urals."[15] At the same time, however, the NAC noted with concern Soviet improvements in conventional forces and called on the alliance to maintain its conventional and nuclear capabilities.[16] Thus, on the one hand, NATO offered a testament about its desire for improved relations, even as on the other it declared its intentions to meet any Soviet force improvements with those of its own.

On the verge of an INF success, talk turned toward improving conventional forces—a measure meant both to enhance deterrence and to strengthen the hands of the West's negotiators. A strong alliance, it was claimed, would not only bring the Soviets to the negotiating table; it also would ensure that they would arrive with a weak hand.[17] The objective, then, was not simply to meet with the Soviets or even to reach agreement with them, but to walk away from negotiations in a position of strength and leave the Soviets weaker.

Throughout the spring and summer of 1987, U.S. officials continued to warn against undue complacency. Vice President George Bush, for example, declared in May that "the Soviets have unstated political objectives … [they] have not abandoned their political strategy" of de-coupling Western Europe from North America and of weakening NATO. He called on the alliance to modernize its conventional and short-range nuclear forces (SNF), and he recalled the lessons of the dual-track decision: "strength and solidarity are the keys to success." "NATO," declared Bush, "is the best investment in Peace we have ever made."[18]

By characterizing the Soviets as intent on de-coupling the alliance, U.S. officials sought to create an environment more amenable to a U.S.-brokered deal on INF, one in which the United States could cast itself in the role of protecting transatlantic links even as it engaged in what could be perceived as a potentially de-coupling exercise.[19] As in the mid-1950s, when the Soviet threat had also begun to appear less menacing, American leaders sought to promote the concept that NATO was a good investment, an asset that required ongoing vigilance so that it would continue to pay dividends.

Conceptions of NATO after the INF Treaty

When the INF Treaty was finally signed between the United States and the USSR in Washington in December 1987, Washington hailed it as "a NATO triumph."[20] In the treaty both sides agreed for the first time completely to eliminate all land-based missiles with ranges between 500 and 5,500 kilometers.[21] Its effect on NATO was profound, for the treaty was perceived by the members of the alliance to have confirmed the wisdom of their Cold War political strategy. This strategy, we recall, had been enunciated in axiomatic fashion in the 1967 *Harmel Report;* it called on NATO to pursue negotiations with the Soviets on the basis of military strength and political solidarity. The 1979 dual-track decision had been the latest doctrinal manifestation of this formula, and the success of the INF negotiations now appeared to justify the heavy political price that the deployment decision had exacted in terms of public opposition throughout the early 1980s. The treaty, Schultz told a news conference at NATO headquarters, "has proceeded very much from the tradition, philosophy, and concept of the *Harmel Report....* This is an alliance treaty."[22]

In terms of conceptions of NATO, the importance of the INF Treaty cannot be underestimated. It did far more than confirm the foresight and intelligence of Pierre Harmel. NATO's leaders had staked their political careers on the questionable assumption that the introduction of new U.S. missiles in Europe was the correct response to similar Soviet deployments. With all land-based intermediate-range missiles on both sides now being removed and destroyed, NATO's leaders sought to take credit for the arrival of a new era in international relations.[23] They did so by reasserting both the rightness of their cause and the prescience of past prophecies about the diverse nature of NATO's form and function. These assertions were supported by the historical coincidence that the INF Treaty was signed one week short of the twentieth anniversary of the adoption of the *Harmel Report.*[24]

The success of the INF Treaty meant that peace through strength was no longer simply another alliance motto: a more peaceful (or at least somewhat less threatening) world did appear to be at hand. More important, and despite initial European concern about the strategic implications of the treaty, NATO remained cohesive. As such, it could continue to perform its various tasks. In the eyes of its leaders, NATO had demonstrated its central role as a vehicle for improving East-West relations.[25] It remained, much as Harmel said it would, an effective forum for the exchange of ideas between NATO and the Warsaw Pact, as well as among the allies themselves. Put crudely, it now appeared that NATO had been right all along: its political strategy had worked; and NATO had shown itself to be far more than a military alliance—it was a force for good in the world.

There was, however, one exception to the general tendency to perceive the treaty as a NATO victory. The French, who had never subscribed to the Harmel axiom linking political and military solidarity with successful negotiations, could not of course follow their allies and find vindication in its apparent success. Though they supported the INF Treaty, which after all did not apply to French nuclear weapons, they drew their own conclusions from it: if Western Europe wished to be taken seriously, then it would have to begin addressing directly the problems of common security. In the wake of the INF Treaty, France renewed its efforts to create a European alternative to U.S. leadership.[26]

For those who believed in it, the perceived success of NATO's strategy would have far-reaching implications. It instilled a tendency toward triumphalism that became more pronounced as the Soviet grip weakened in Eastern Europe and ultimately at home.[27] A central element in the strategy of peace through strength had been the use of public discourse, which was viewed as having played an important role in forcing Soviet change: "this candor," declared Reagan, "made clear to the Soviets the resilience and strength of the West; it made them understand the lack of illusions on our part about them or their system."[28] NATO's leaders would soon claim that they had "won" the Cold War by sticking firmly to the basic principles of the *Harmel Report.*[29]

But the belief that NATO's strategy was the correct one had other, more immediate outcomes. The notion that strong nuclear forces had paved the way for an important new nuclear treaty gave further impetus to the alliance's long-standing preoccupation with the perceived need always to improve conventional forces. Even as Gorbachev was talking about unprecedented reductions in Soviet troop strength, NATO planners called for more and better conventional forces.[30] If the dual-track approach had worked with nuclear forces, so the reasoning appears to have been, why not with conventional ones, too?[31] Though rendered inconclusive by subsequent events, the INF Treaty also engendered a rich debate about its impact on flexible response and the future status of NATO's conventional forces.[32]

Reaffirming NATO's Role

The signing of the INF Treaty elicited a ritualistic round of warnings about the continued existence of the Soviet threat, and it evoked a curious though not unprecedented response by NATO's leaders.[33] Times of uncertainty within the alliance had always eventually produced some form of rhetoric that sought to bind the allies together. The tactic of finding common cause in the drafting of political hyperbole was well respected and seemed to work. The late 1980s produced no exception to this pattern. With the European allies worried about de-coupling and superpower condominium, and with the United States concerned lest its European partners fall prey to Soviet lures or unilaterally reduce defense expenditures, it was almost inevitable that a document would emerge that enunciated shared hopes and concerns without too tightly committing any one member to a specified course of action. In other words, it was time for another of NATO's periodic declarations, where ambiguous rhetoric could be made to serve the ends of public diplomacy and alliance unity.

The summit took place at NATO headquarters in Brussels early in March 1988. It was the first NATO Heads of State and Government meeting in six years (the last had been held in Bonn just weeks before the arrival in West Germany of the new American-made GLCMs). The summit produced two documents. The first dealt with conventional arms control, and was essentially a reformulation of the long-standing NATO position that Soviet armor and troop concentrations needed reducing and the removal of the capacity for surprise attack. It also made oblique but familiar references to the need for allied burden sharing, adequate defense expenditures, and increased cooperation.[34]

The summit's second document is, for our purposes, the more interesting of the two. It was entitled "A Time for Reaffirmation," and its intent was precisely that.[35] (To reaffirm is to repeat a declaration formally, without oath.) The allies had come together in Brussels to take stock of rapidly changing events, to voice their concerns, and to remind themselves and the public just what NATO was all about. Little of the document was new, and therein lies its significance. It made strong and prominent references to the ideals and common purposes of the allies, to the shared principles and objectives of the North Atlantic Treaty, and to the vital and continuing importance of NATO.[36] Security was proclaimed to be indivisible, which implied at least two things: (1) that arms control was only part of the East-West equation; and (2) that the other elements of the equation, including the economic aspects of security and human rights, would, if they were ever to be resolved, have to fall within NATO's purview.[37]

The document reaffirmed the importance of several NATO axioms. The security of North America and Europe remained inextricably linked.[38] Similarly, the Harmel formula remained as relevant as it had ever been: the political solidarity and military strength of the alliance would provide the basis for negotiations between East and West, and it would continue to inform future cooperation, dialogue, and arms control.[39] In terms of transatlantic relations, the document invoked the axiom of security linkage to hail recent efforts to strengthen the European pillar of NATO. It noted the need for a "major contribution from Europe" and declared that "the alliance cannot be strong if Europe is weak." A strong and independent Europe was declared to be as vital to the security of North America as the presence of North American troops on the continent was to the security of Europe.[40]

The public relations aspects of the summit are fairly obvious. True, it was meant to reaffirm, but it was also meant to reassure. The Americans tried to reassure their partners that the United States continued to view NATO as a collective forum through which East-West relations would be conducted. Hence President Reagan's explicit pre-summit claim that "we will never sacrifice the interests of this partnership in any agreement with the Soviet Union."[41] He also told the allies in open session that "the alliance is the most dynamic force for improving East-West relations."[42]

In conceptual terms, the summit served as a form of alliance therapy. These were uncertain times. Gorbachev seemed sincere and some progress had been made, but the Soviet threat remained and many of the outstanding issues that divided East from West had yet to be addressed. NATO's act of summitry and reaffirmation was part of a conscious effort to recall the enduring traditions and purposes of the alliance.

NATO's conceptual canon had always performed several functions. Produced by events internal and external to the alliance and propagated in rhetoric, conceptions could be called on when there was a perceived need to restrain unruly members, promote unity, or soften the hegemonic tendencies of the United States.[43] On the eve of the end of the Cold War, just such a time presented itself.

The conceptions reaffirmed at this important juncture were several: NATO embodied the U.S. commitment to European security; it had preserved the peace for more than forty years; it had deterred Soviet aggression and enhanced the security of all the allies; it was the principal means of the United States' consultation with its European partners, and vice versa.[44] Allied cohesion was now said to be essential: NATO should improve its conventional forces and, in accordance with the Montebello decision, modernize its short-range nuclear weapons.[45] As they had in the past, political solidarity and military strength would do more than bring the Soviets the negotiating table. They would confirm NATO's central role as the authoritative voice of the West.[46]

Responding to the Gorbachev Challenge

By December 1988 two events had helped further to erode Western suspicions about the nature of change in Soviet foreign relations. The first was the Soviet agreement, announced in April 1988, to withdraw from Afghanistan.[47] The second was Gorbachev's December speech to the UN General Assembly, where, as part of a declaration that the Soviet Union was unilaterally adopting a defensive military doctrine, he announced the unilateral removal of 500,000 troops and 10,000 tanks from Eastern Europe.[48] These initiatives produced three important responses. First, most commentators in the West now accepted that Soviet change was real, and not merely a change in tactics designed to seduce the West.[49] This acceptance occasioned renewed expert debate about the relevance of NATO.[50] There was also, apparently for the first time, public discussion by senior U.S. officials that the end of the Cold War might be at hand.[51]

Second, the announced Soviet troop cuts had a major impact on the question of nuclear modernization. Plans to modernize NATO's short-range nuclear weapons had been justified on the ground that they would be useful against large concentrations of Soviet armor. With a large portion of this armor now being unilaterally withdrawn, and with NATO-Warsaw Pact negotiations to reduce significant portions of the remaining forces on both sides about to begin at the Conventional Forces in Europe (CFE) talks in Vienna, the political and financial costs of modernization suddenly seemed less necessary or even acceptable. Hans-Deitrich Genscher, the West German foreign minister, declared that the cuts "make the question of nuclear arms modernization even less center stage in the alliance than it already was."[52]

Third, and characteristically, NATO sought to take credit for Gorbachev's bold advances. In an ingenious formulation that illustrated the emerging tendency to regard NATO as the harbinger of all change, allied leaders now asserted that NATO had provided the external incentive for internal change in the Soviet Union.[53] It is perhaps possible that the strength and solidarity of NATO had helped somehow to foster Soviet reforms. Indeed, one important conception of NATO had always been that the alliance could serve as a powerful counterattraction to communism and, by displaying the superiority of the West, erode totalitarian instincts. Thus, the vaunting claims of NATO's central role in the Soviet reform process were entirely consistent with forty years of alliance rhetoric. But they also revealed a deep and growing unease within the alliance over how exactly to respond to the increasingly popular, friendly, and cooperative Soviet leader. It was one thing to follow Margaret Thatcher's advice in 1985 and "do business" with him; it was something else entirely to permit a friendly takeover. President Bush warned against "a growing complacency throughout the West."[54]

The phenomenon of "Gorbymania" was now sweeping the world. Public appearances by Gorbachev on the streets of Western capitals often elicited a degree of cheering and joy heretofore reserved for popes and pop stars. Gorbachev, bright and articulate, and possessing none of the bombastic tendencies of his predecessors, presented a genuine dilemma to Western leaders.[55] Every few months he seemed to offer unprecedented proposals for improving relations. He had talked about a "common European home" and about security for all from "the Atlantic to the Urals." He had loosened constraints on his Eastern European allies and had made important human rights gestures.[56] He had ordered the Soviet military to adopt a defensive strategic posture based on the notion of "reasonable sufficiency." He had announced massive unilateral troop reductions, engaged the West in negotiations for further cuts on an alliance-to-alliance basis, agreed to an INF Treaty, and tabled important new proposals for a strategic arms reduction treaty (START) and for a chemical weapons ban. Domestically, he had done what no other Soviet leader had ever dared: his economic and human rights policies of *glasnost* and *perestroika* allowed for public and open debate on television.

These initiatives made Western leaders both giddy and nervous. On the one hand, they wished patiently to pursue these proposals and to seek agreement on a broad range of issues; on the other, they feared the unraveling of the postwar order that might accompany the end of the Cold War.[57] In domestic political terms, no Western leader was prepared to surrender either the spotlight or the acclaim to Mr. Gorbachev. This combination of Western political self-interest, strategic calculation, and growing optimism helped produce a virtuous cycle that met Soviet diplomacy head-on and hastened the end of the Cold War.[58]

NATO's Fortieth Anniversary Summit: The Countervision of Common Values

NATO's leaders felt threatened by the growing public fascination with Gorbachev; they feared that his popularity might somehow erode NATO's effectiveness and control over events.[59] Their response, which came at NATO's fortieth anniversary summit in Brussels in May 1989, was to go on the diplomatic offensive. NATO, which early in its life had come to be conceived partly as a showcase for the superiority of the West, now sought to transform an event of self-celebration into an effort to steal the initiative away from the dynamic Soviet leader.[60] It offered what U.S. Secretary of State James Baker—George Bush was now president— called NATO's "countervision."[61] This countervision was based on the conceptual framework of common values, a time-honored notion that had first been used to justify the signing of the North Atlantic Treaty and that subsequently and periodically had been invoked to support the perceived emergence of an Atlantic Community. President Bush told the NATO summit that, by focusing on the values that brought and held them together, "the nations of the West [would have] both an anchor and a course to navigate for the future."[62]

At the end of the summit, the NATO Heads of State and Government declared that "NATO seeks to establish a new pattern of relations between the countries of East and West."[63] With this objective in mind, they unveiled their Design for Cooperation—a loosely worded plea that called on NATO to overcome the division of Europe by acting as a forum for the establishment of joint policies with regard to Eastern Europe.[64] Significantly, cooperation with the East was seen to be contingent on the creation of a collective NATO response. Recalling one of NATO's central axioms, the allies declared that the challenges and opportunities presented by recent events "transcend the resources of either Europe or North America alone."[65] The axiom surrounding the perceived futility of independent national action remained a powerful one in the closing years of the Cold War.

The Design for Cooperation looked toward the creation of internal unity as a precondition for the opening of new relations with the East, and it foresaw, under the guidance of NATO, the eventual emergence of broader East-West contacts and cooperation. This concept had its origins in the perceived lessons of history. NATO had long been viewed as a community within which Franco-German reconciliation could be engendered and sustained, and it now sought to turn this ability toward healing the division of the continent. President Bush, speaking in Mainz the day after the summit, declared that "a Europe whole and free [is] the new mission of NATO."[66] Secretary Baker later told the Senate Foreign Relations Committee that NATO sought "a Europe whole and free ... a unity based on Western values."[67]

But the summit offered more than rhetoric. The allies responded favorably to a U.S. proposal and endorsed the Conventional Parity Initiative, which sought asymmetrical reductions from the WTO with the aim of reaching a level of 275,000 troops on both sides from the Atlantic to the Urals; limits on tanks, armored personnel carriers and artillery; and a 15 percent cut below current NATO levels of land-based combat aircraft and helicopters. The initiative also accompanied an agreement to enter into talks for partial reductions in SNF once a CFE agreement had been implemented. In conjunction with this move, the question of Lance modernization was deferred until 1992, largely as a result of pressure by Helmut Kohl, who faced elections in 1990 and who feared a return of the strong public opposition that had been aroused over the dual-track decision.[68]

In addition to the launching of an integrated approach to arms control, the alliance identified new problems and challenges, ranging from the environment to terrorism, weapons proliferation, and drugs, which it would address alongside its more traditional pursuits.[69] The summit's final declaration made the traditional plea for the enhancement of the transatlantic partnership and the promotion of a European security identity.[70] In the wake of these declarations, Baker announced that NATO had "regained the initiative."[71] Striking a similarly triumphant chord, Margaret Thatcher observed that the world was witnessing "freedom on the offensive."[72]

the days prior to the summit, the popular assault on communism in rn Europe and the likelihood that democracy would result had prompted r resident Bush to call on his allies to celebrate the West's "moral and spiritual community." There was now, he observed, "a precious opportunity to move beyond containment." It was time for NATO to help "integrate the Soviet Union into the community of nations."[73] He later declared that by moving beyond containment NATO could project "the idea that we are out front as an alliance."[74]

The Origins and Implications of the Rhetoric of Common Values

The May 1989 summit was infused with the image that NATO was a shield to protect and nurture common values. Early alliance rhetoric, we recall, had focused not only on the Soviet threat but also on the unifying properties of common values and shared history. To ease the passage of public and legislative approval, the North Atlantic Treaty had been promoted partly on the basis of its potential to attain the higher ends of Western civilization. As John Foster Dulles had declared in 1956, one of the more compelling conceptions of NATO was that it should work *for* something, not merely against an adversary. Thus, NATO had been historically justified and sustained by conceptions that held that it was far more than a military alliance or a bulwark against communist aggression. With the military threat and Soviet communist dogma rapidly receding, the notion of common values came to the fore.

The Americans supplied the rhetorical thrust behind the familiar and reassuring theme of common values. The alliance as a whole embraced this theme even as it sought to claim responsibility for recent changes in the Soviet position. At the end of the May summit, NATO declared that while it did not claim "exclusive responsibility" for the promising evolution of East-West relations, it did regard major Soviet initiatives, such as those surrounding the transparency of forces, reasonable sufficiency, verification, and stability, as "Western-inspired."[75] The assumption here was that the democratic, liberal, and open values of the West had provided the basis on which a new Soviet approach to international relations could emerge.

In addition to common values, one other important concept helped guide NATO's response to Gorbachev.[76] NATO had long viewed itself as an organization with organic properties, capable of changing to meet the multifaceted challenges of the Cold War. Now the challenge to be met was that the Soviets were seeking not to widen their sphere of political, military, and ideological competition but to narrow it. It was necessary for

NATO to transform itself into an agent of change, and it did so by referring back to its origins and by finding guidance through the invocation of its conceptual history.[77]

The intent of the rhetoric of common values was to counter the Gorbachev challenge. His notion of a common European home disturbed allied leaders; the region from the Atlantic to the Urals did not seem to include a place for the United States or Canada. Nor did it seem to accept the notion of a separate West European defense identity. Thus, in a rare moment of rhetorical harmony, both the French, who continued their long-standing efforts to wean Europe away from U.S. dependency and who sensed new opportunities with the weakening of Soviet power, and the Americans found common ground in the rhetoric of common values. As one senior U.S. policymaker observed, a strong West European defense identity within NATO "maintains essential balance in Europe, and it provides the light to guide Eastern Europe along the path of Western values."[78]

These common values, in contrast to the notion of a common European home, had, according to James Baker, "a much broader reach."[79] As a guiding concept for European security after the Cold War, a common European home was rejected as being too narrow; it was "an idea bounded by geographic borders and without a particular, substantive content."[80] The concept of Western values was also (though perhaps not equally) ambiguous, but it served as a convenient rhetorical tool that had the added attraction of being potentially borderless. The Americans, worried about being excluded from Gorbachev's new Europe, pushed the theme of common values in an effort to remind both their allies and the Soviets that U.S. interests were at stake in any discussions about the future of Europe.[81] Common values implied common interests, and the United States hoped that by focusing on the former, it would remain implicit that the latter might also be defined by the United States. The French, for their part, tacitly joined in this conception as a way to elicit American acquiescence in and West European support for their emerging plans for the creation of a more independent European (and hence less American) defense organization.[82]

When Poland, Hungary, Czechoslovakia, and the GDR rejected communism and embraced democratic governments in the summer and autumn of 1989, NATO again appeared to be "out front": its theme of common values had struck a favorable chord in the East, as well as in the West. In this new era of intensified negotiation and cataclysmic change in Eastern Europe, NATO proclaimed its central role. In accordance with the Harmel axiom, it would provide the military deterrent essential for successful negotiations. It would synchronize the Western approach to the East, and it would seek to draw its former adversaries into the Western orbit by pushing for a conception of European security based not on geography but on values— values, that is, that had become synonymous with NATO and the Atlantic Community. In the words of one State Department report, NATO would work to "remove old obstacles from Europe's path to the future."[83] NATO would also address the problems of the environment, drugs, weapons proliferation, and terrorism.

As had happened in the mid-1950s, wider and looser conceptions of NATO were generated and embraced as a partial response to the receding Soviet threat. The purpose of these conceptions was to provide NATO with a post-Soviet agenda. As Soviet power slowly eroded and then washed away in a tide of largely peaceful revolution, the theme of common values surfaced to support NATO's post-Cold War claims to relevance. In reference to these values, German Defense Minister Volker Rühe, for example, declared as late as March 1993 that "this, and not the presence of an existential threat … is the hub of our alliance."[84] With these values ever in mind, NATO hoped to identify and address new threats, challenges, roles, and opportunities— and to perpetuate itself.

In addition to enunciating its new mission to the East, by the summer of 1989, NATO had made clear its intention not to abandon its central objective of achieving lasting peace among the Western European states. As West European integration proceeded, NATO reaffirmed the conception that it could serve intra-Western political purposes by acting as the forum for transatlantic dialogue and security. NATO would keep the United States engaged in Europe, and it would protect the Europeans from themselves. The Atlantic links and character of the alliance, it was now claimed, should be strengthened in the face of a new, democratizing Europe.[85]

Common Values and the End of the Cold War: German Reunification and NATO

The weakening or collapse of all East European communist governments in the autumn of 1989 gave increased weight to official views in Western Europe and North America surrounding the primacy of NATO. In November 1989 the Berlin Wall fell and, in December, a U.S.-Soviet joint statement from the shipboard summit at Malta solemnly announced that the "epoch of the Cold War" had ended.[86] It was at this time that some Western observers began to declare NATO's "total victory in the ideological Cold War."[87]

Amid this momentary euphoria, two questions confronted NATO. Both had been asked in the past, but had never *required* an answer. The first asked whether NATO could survive without an enemy.[88] The second considered the future status of Germany: would it, once reunified, remain in NATO and, if so, how would this be achieved? We turn now to the second of these questions, for in answering it NATO would begin to answer the first.

The complex process of negotiating the new Germany's entrance into NATO need not detain us here, for it has been well covered elsewhere.[89] What concerns us is what impact the reunification of Germany had on conceptions of NATO.

German reunification was a reminder that NATO could serve intra-Western political purposes; and the rhetoric of common values helped provide NATO and its leaders with a platform on which to negotiate the entrance into NATO of a reunified Germany. "The issue," declared James Baker late in 1989, "is the normalization of relations between the two Germanys *on the basis of Western values.*"[90] The statement could be easily and without contradiction rephrased to read: "… on the basis of NATO membership."

Thus, the rhetoric of common values helped ease Germany's passage into NATO on two occasions: the first being when West Germany entered NATO in 1955; and the second in 1990, as the so-called Two-plus-Four Talks, endorsed by both superpowers, swept aside allied concern about the effects after reunification of German NATO membership on Soviet threat perceptions.[91] Both France and Britain, under U.S. pressure, overcame early fears about a resurgent Germany and eventually lent their full support to the plan for immediate German membership in NATO.[92] It was at this time that the image of a reunified Germany, acting as the continent's leading power and possibly unrestrained by Cold War rivalry, lent new relevance to old conceptions about NATO's capacity to act as a brake on German ambition. At the same time, however, it remained uncertain whether NATO could balance a German prominence based not, as in the past, on militarism but largely on economic and political might.

The preferred response to questions arising from the reunification of Germany, as well as to those concerning the possibilities for upheaval in Central and Eastern Europe and uncertainty about the Soviet Union, was to push for a stronger and more politically oriented NATO alliance.[93] Addressing these issues in May 1990, George Bush declared that "our enemy today is uncertainty, and instability."[94] The conception of NATO as a force for stability both within and beyond Western Europe was gaining credibility, and the acceptance of this notion was hastened by the rapid decline of Soviet power. By June 1991, James Baker would declare that NATO "provides one of the indispensable foundations for a stable European security environment."[95]

Post-Cold War Conceptions of NATO

Once the Cold War had been declared officially over, the NATO elite began to ponder the question of how to deal with the collapse of Soviet power, and they sought to consolidate the gains of victory while stabilizing the East. As we have seen, the Americans under Bush took the lead and called on NATO, including a reunified Germany, to stand at the core of the development of pan-European security institutions. The debate over NATO's proper role in the new Europe, its relation to other European security organizations, and how or whether it could stabilize the East soon replaced the issue of whether NATO could continue to exist now that its adversary had withdrawn.[96] This internal alliance debate occurred within the context of important external change.

NATO's first post-Cold War summit, held in London in May 1990, sought to adapt NATO to the changed conditions in Europe. NATO's political leaders ordered a fundamental strategic review, the results of which were announced at Rome in November 1991, sixteen months later. Between the two summits, German reunification was completed, the Gulf War was fought and won, CFE and START treaties were signed, the Warsaw Pact was dissolved, and the Yugoslavian wars erupted. Meanwhile, the Soviet Union swayed from reaction to coup to democratic revolution and, in December 1991, ceased to exist. The period also marked further strides toward European political union. We turn now to an examination of the effects of these powerful events on conceptions of NATO.

London, Rome, and the Transformation of NATO

At the London summit, NATO's leaders declared that the alliance was being transformed into an "agent of change."[97] By the time they met again in Rome in November 1991, this notion had taken on even greater importance. NATO had been conceived as a vehicle for positive change, as a way to promote the agenda of the West in the Cold War. The end of the Cold War merely altered that agenda; it was deemed not to have broken the transatlantic link or to have obviated the need for the West to work together.[98] Some commentators, however, began openly to question whether the concept of the West was relevant in the post-Cold War world.[99]

But NATO's leaders remained wedded to this notion. As President Bush told his colleagues at Rome: "This Alliance has been more successful than any of us dared to dream. It was designed to defend our freedom, but in fact it triumphed over totalitarianism. What we have built is not some military pact but a community of values and trust—unique in history, perpetual, and vital for the new order."[100] Other allied leaders concurred.[101] On the combined basis of its values, military strength, and past success, NATO was thus called on to shape the new era. The Rome summit, which completed the conceptual work begun at London, was designed to provide NATO with an increased capacity to achieve this task.

The summit produced three documents: the New Strategic Concept; the Declaration on Peace and Cooperation; and a communiqué on developments in the Soviet Union. The first two of these were lengthy documents that devoted much space to reaffirming the litany of C old War NATO axioms and conceptions. While building on previous notions about the nature of NATO, they also contained important new strategic and political conceptions. The third document, as we shall see, was a controversial attempt to manipulate the outcome of affairs in the tumultuous Soviet Union. All three documents provide insight to an understanding of conceptions of NATO in the post-Cold War era.

The New Strategic Concept

The demise of the Warsaw Pact and German reunification made NATO's previous guiding strategic concept of flexible response, with its corollary of forward defense, invalid. There was no longer an enemy at the eastern frontier of NATO, let alone an enemy beyond it. The former central front now ran through the middle of one of its members, and under the terms of the four-power agreement concerning the reunification of Germany, NATO forces could not be moved forward into the territory of the former GDR. To address these new realities and to reflect the expected decline in defense expenditures that the end of the Cold War had occasioned, the New Strategic Concept jettisoned flexible response and forward defense in favor of a new force posture based on smaller, more mobile forces that stood at lower levels of readiness.[102] The declaration that defined the concept also announced the creation of an alliance Rapid Reaction Corps (RRC) comprised of multinational units that were to operate under British command.[103]

With regard to nuclear forces, the allies announced the complete elimination of all ground-launched SNFs and nuclear artillery, which amounted to an 80 percent cut in the NATO nuclear stockpile.[104] In September, Bush had announced the unilateral withdrawal of all American SNFs from Europe.

This new force structure was designed to help NATO achieve its goal of relying less on nuclear weapons while it turned its attention to meeting lower-level threats that might arise from instabilities in or between the states of Eastern and Central Europe.[105] Both the war in Yugoslavia and the Gulf War were invoked as powerful examples to justify these changes— changes that in turn were used to support NATO's shift away from the military defense of a front and toward increased political engagement in the affairs of its former adversaries.[106]

Alongside the new force posture, the New Strategic Concept contained a list of four "core security functions." These were: (1) "to provide one of the indispensable foundations for a stable security environment in Europe"; (2) "to serve ... as a transatlantic forum for Allied consultations"; (3) "to deter and defend against any threat of aggression against the territory of any NATO member states"; and (4) "to preserve the strategic balance within Europe."[107] While these four tasks lacked the precision required to serve as meaningful policy guidance, they did reveal the growing importance of the conception that NATO had a central role to play in post-Cold War security.

Having analyzed the new strategic setting in Europe and the rest of the world, NATO drew two conclusions:

> The first is that the new environment does not change the purpose or the security functions of the alliance, but rather underlines their enduring validity. The second, on the other hand, is that the changed environment offers new opportunities for the Alliance to frame its strategy within a broad approach to security.[108]

This second conclusion provided NATO with the rationale to extend its interests into the new spheres of crisis management and conflict prevention. It also allowed the alliance to update its previous goals of promoting dialogue and cooperation with its former adversaries by widening the range of issues to include environmental and humanitarian ones.[109] Thus, NATO, invoking the radically changed European political and strategic landscape and finding guidance in its self-attributed role as an agent of change, latched on to a broad, new concept of security that embraced nearly every challenge of the post-Cold War era. In so doing, the alliance found a way of perpetuating itself. As British Prime Minster John Major told the House of Commons soon after the summit: "We have agreed a wider role for NATO. Henceforth, NATO will not just be keeping the peace; it will be actively promoting the peace…. The primacy of NATO is secure."[110]

The Rome Declaration on Peace and Cooperation

At Rome the allies loosened the Harmel formula, which had established NATO's dual approach of dialogue and defense, by adding the task of cooperation and partnership with former adversaries. Defense remained an important alliance task, but, declared the assembled allied leaders,

> in a world where the values which we uphold are shared ever more widely, we gladly seize the opportunity to adapt our defenses accordingly; to cooperate and consult with our new partners; to help consolidate a now undivided continent of Europe; and to make our alliance's contribution to a new age of confidence, stability and peace.[111]

In the Rome Declaration, the NATO Heads of State and Government announced that they had gathered "to open a new chapter" in the history of NATO.[112] The alliance was declared to be "an agent of change, a source of stability and the indispensable guarantor of its members' security."[113] In reference to the new Europe, NATO declared its intention to play a key role at the center of the "interlocking institutions" of the CSCE, the European Community, the WEU, and the Council of Europe; it would help build "cooperation and prosperity" throughout Europe.[114] While NATO sought simultaneously to strengthen the CSCE and to encourage the development of the European pillar of the alliance, it would remain "the essential transatlantic link."[115]

The declaration, in addition to proclaiming NATO's central role as guarantor of European security, announced an important new change in the way the NATO allies viewed their former adversaries. The development of democracy in the Soviet Union and the other states of Central and Eastern Europe had instilled the "conviction that our own security is inseparably linked to that of all other states in Europe."[116] This formulation represented an important extension of the central NATO axiom concerning the security linkage of North America and Western Europe.

The extension of this axiom to include all of Europe had at least three implications. First, with the security of the entire European continent now declared to be inextricably tied to NATO, the alliance had a conceptual basis for claiming primacy over all other European security organizations, including even the CSCE, which already embraced the states of both Cold War blocs and the neutral and nonaligned states of Europe. France's leadership, which believed the CSCE to be better prepared than NATO to act as a forum for pan-European security, joined in signing the Rome Declaration and the New Strategic Concept only after receiving concessions that strengthened the language concerning the importance of the CSCE and the development of a West European security identity. Second, the extension of the axiom of security linkage created high expectations for NATO membership among the former Warsaw Pact states. Third, it contributed to the gradual erosion of the distinction between in- and out-of-area issues. These last two points are more fully developed below.

NATO had devoted forty-two years to worrying about the Soviet threat. At Rome, it worried about the collapse of its erstwhile enemy, and about the implications of that collapse for its own future.[117] Both the Rome Declaration and the New Strategic Concept reflected an expansive conception of NATO's roles and objectives in the post-Cold War world. They contained subjective assessments of post-Cold War security challenges, and they served as a rationale to justify alliance policy, past and future. As General John Galvin, SACEUR, observed soon after the summit: "The world is changing and NATO is changing with it. In fact, NATO has been instrumental in bringing about the changes."[118] While they failed to inaugurate a concrete plan of action, the Rome documents did embrace the geopolitical concerns of NATO's leaders and illuminate the now continental scale of allied interests. Conceived and distributed for public consumption, as well as for policy guidance, the documents set forth NATO's priorities and proclaimed NATO's significance as a point of reference in a changing world.[119] In the coming months the allies would restate the same objectives and hopes and lay out similar recommendations for cooperation, partnership, and dialogue.

In the wake of Rome, it became clear that there were to be no geographical or political limitations on NATO's claims to expertise. Describing the significance of the summit, NATO Secretary General Manfred Wörner declared that "we have to think ahead if we want to stay ahead."[120] At the same time, NATO would keep the past in mind: the conception of

NATO as a strategic counterweight to the Soviet Union (and later Russia) did not die with the Cold War. Similarly, the perceived importance of NATO's capacity for transatlantic bridgebuilding retained its potency.[121] NATO, it was claimed, would prevent the emergence of any post-Cold War neo-isolationism in the United States, and it would sensitize Europeans and North Americans to each other's concerns and problems.[122]

The Rome Communiqué on Developments in the Soviet Union

An immediate example of NATO's expansive view of its role in European security came with the Rome communiqué on developments in the Soviet Union. The communiqué, signed by all the NATO members except France, called on the Soviet Union to continue on its path to democracy, respect its international agreements, adopt a market economy, and pay its foreign debt.[123] The failed August 1991 coup against Mikhail Gorbachev had briefly raised the specter of a return to the Cold War and lent a new sense of urgency to NATO's plans for consolidating democracy in the East.[124] The Rome communiqué, a public pronouncement intended to express NATO's concern, revealed the extent to which the conception of NATO as an organization with a pan-European mission had taken root.

France, however, angrily denounced the communiqué and refused to sign. French President François Mitterand declared that NATO should not seek to become "a holy alliance," and he dismissed the actions of its "preacher monks." "NATO," he continued, "has no evangelical mission. France does not want NATO to become a theological institution … dictating its policies."[125] Mitterand was mistaken: the theological character of NATO had been established for decades, and in the early 1990s its leaders, joined at times by even the French, embarked on a crusade to expand NATO's mission.

The NACC and the Partnership for Peace

Once NATO had proclaimed its pan-European agenda, it proceeded at Rome to offer to its former adversaries membership in a new North Atlantic Cooperation Council (NACC), a political mechanism designed to provide an institutional basis for the extension of Western defense cooperation eastward.[126] The call for these more formal links between NATO and the

East was led by the United States and Germany.[127] At the same time, however, NATO continued to resist the idea that the new democracies would be allowed to join the alliance.[128] The NACC was devised as a half-measure; it allowed NATO as an institution to open bilateral contacts without extending the binding commitment of a security guarantee.

Under the NACC format, the defense and foreign ministers of the former Warsaw Pact states (and later the Soviet successor states) could come to Brussels and meet with their NATO counterparts. They could discuss arms control and disarmament, defense planning, and other military matters, including civilian-military relations, crisis management, training and exercises, and the problems of defense conversion. In addition, NATO would lend its expertise with regard to economic, scientific, and environmental issues, air traffic management, and the dissemination of information and the formulation of foreign policy in a democracy.[129] The NACC forum would also be used to tackle problems surrounding the proliferation of weapons of mass destruction and the implementation of arms control treaties.[130]

In conceptual terms, the NACC was viewed as proof of NATO's new commitment to partnership with its former adversaries.[131] A vigorous alliance, working for peaceful change in Europe, was said to illustrate the continued relevance of NATO.[132] But as this perceived relevance grew, so did the expectations of the members of NACC for full NATO membership.[133] These expectations turned increasingly into pleas, as events in the former Soviet Union, and particularly in Russia, suggested that the states of Central and Eastern Europe might soon become the target of revived Russian nationalism.[134]

The concept of cooperation that underlay NATO's bid for new links with its former adversaries presupposed Soviet and, later, Russian acceptance of fundamental allied objectives. However, as Russian leaders began to voice objections to plans by Poland, Hungary, and the Czech and Slovak Republics to seek full NATO membership, NATO itself began to ponder the question as to whether it was wise to permit the Russians a veto on decisions concerning the expansion of NATO. Fear of strategic entanglement made NATO's leaders additionally wary. Neither did they wish to undermine democracy in Russia by igniting old fears of strategic encirclement.[135] And yet they sought to respond to the calls by some members of the NACC for more formal ties.

Their response, launched in October 1993 and led by American initiative, took the form of the Partnership for Peace.[136] Approved by a NATO

Heads of State and Government summit at Brussels in January 1994, the Partnership built on the NACC format and was designed to help the alliance and its prospective new members move from the symbols of partnership to the substantive mutual obligations of membership. It explicitly endorsed the idea that NATO was open to membership of other European countries, only not just yet.[137] For now, any European state—including Russia—could join the Partnership, and each would determine the scope and pace of its relations with NATO.[138] Within the NACC format, there could now be a further strengthening of the loose bilateral ties established in 1991, especially in terms of joint training, peacekeeping, and humanitarian operations.[139] One senior U.S. defense official called the Partnership "a sort of training program for NATO membership."[140]

The Partnership for Peace was intentionally ambiguous. NATO had only opened the door; it had set neither guidelines nor a timetable for membership. Nor was full participation in the military and political aspects of the Partnership deemed the only requirement for possible future membership in NATO. Prospective members would need "a shared set of values [that] proves that these new members are worth defending."[141] The Partnership proposal, compromise though it was, also served further to undermine the distinction between in- and out-of-area issues. The West was slowly going East.

The Gulf War and Conceptions of NATO

The 1990-1991 Gulf War lent a sharp realism to the debate over NATO's future form and function and was in many ways a timely occurrence for the alliance. The Americans sent the largest contingent to the Gulf, followed by the British and the French, who, after some initial hesitation, agreed to assign their forces to U.S. command. However, NATO as an alliance was only indirectly involved in the Gulf War.[142]

The perceived threat of Iraqi attacks against Turkey, a NATO member state that borders Iraq, triggered the dispatch of the Allied Command Europe (ACE) Mobile Force to Turkey. Germany, citing constitutional constraints, belatedly sent support forces to Turkey and, later, mine-sweeping forces to the Eastern Mediterranean to relieve NATO-designated forces sent to the Persian Gulf. Although the Germans contributed financial assistance, their alleged preference for "checkbook diplomacy," which had the effect of keeping German troops out of harm's way, angered Germany's allies and caused a minor temporary breach in alliance relations.[143]

For the military and political leaders of NATO, the Gulf War proved both the continuing importance of NATO for European security and the relevance of its New Strategic Concept. According to John Galvin, the operations by NATO members during the Gulf War represented "the symbol of the new emerging NATO strategy of flexibility, multinationality, and the capability to act in a crisis."[144] In addition, the perceived failure of Western Europe to respond quickly and collectively to the Iraqi invasion of Kuwait helped focus increased interest on the development of multinational rapid reaction forces among the European members of NATO.[145] This interest, as we have seen, was reflected in the alliance's New Strategic Concept and was enhanced by post-Cold War budgetary constraints and impending large cuts in troop levels and defense expenditures. The Gulf War also gave increased impetus to efforts to forge a West European defense identity.[146]

The Gulf War became a central feature of NATO's claims for continued relevance, especially regarding its role in defense and deterrence. It was also, some said, proof that NATO continued to be an essential forum for transatlantic cooperation: NATO's logistics, basing support, and IMO had played a major role in moving American, British, and French military assets to the Gulf and, later, in helping them to fight effectively.[147] These claims contrasted with those made in 1987 during the Iran-Iraq war, when a multinational naval effort, led by the United States and its European allies, was undertaken to protect international shipping in the Persian Gulf. In that instance, all action had been unilateral, and the operation was said to have exposed the weakness of NATO in addressing out-of-area problems.[148]

With regard to the NATO contribution to the Gulf War, one scholar of NATO affairs commented that

> As far as NATO is concerned, it has shown the great value of a functioning military organization, even if it did not go to war under its flag. Information flowed right from the start, consultation was uninterrupted and, as a consequence, action could be and was taken rapidly. Bases were supplied and reorganized, over-flying arranged, cargo ships and aircraft made available, and fighting elements integrated. The systems were available, the procedures had been practiced and the wheels turned smoothly.... The treaty limitation, which prevented NATO from acting as such, seemed almost irrelevant.[149]

NATO was perceived to have played an invaluable behind-the-scenes role, not so much by direct action as by furnishing the vast and accumulated experience of coordinated operations in an international environment that its members brought to the conflict. NATO practices and procedures guided the deployment of allied forces, which flowed as much from Germany as from the United States and United Kingdom, and continued throughout the crisis.

Thus, in addition to the support role played by NATO forces in Turkey and the Mediterranean, the alliance contributed in significant ways. The ease with which the coalition in the Gulf was formed, deployed, and operated was seen to stem in part from the familiarity of the allies in working through NATO's integrated military command structure for more than forty years. Naval command, control, and communications in particular were completely international and, according to one defense expert, "wherever possible in the Gulf NATO procedures were used and if improvement was needed equipment was quickly made available to achieve it."[150] In a similar vein, a British House of Commons Defense Committee report declared that, despite the important contributions made by WEU and Arab nations,

> the war was fought and won primarily on NATO principles.... The rewards of greater interoperability have never been more clearly demonstrated. NATO practices and procedures enabled an *ad hoc* alliance of NATO national forces to fight together out-of-area as a coherent unit; those nations not participating as members of the Alliance cannot expect to be able to play a full part in future conflicts.[151]

This view ignores the possibility that in the future the NATO allies will continue to play the major role while others benefit as free riders.

In the wake of the Gulf War and the ensuing breakup of Yugoslavia, the formal distinction between in- and out-of-area concerns became increasingly moot, and NATO's leaders moved both through rhetoric and the promotion of new concepts to erode the distinction. Not only did they claim that the out-of-area debate had become "increasingly irrelevant" in light of these events, they also invoked them to justify the extension of NATO's functions into peacekeeping, peacemaking and humanitarian roles.[152] The implied corollary to the diminished distinction between in- and out-of-area issues was that NATO could now concern itself with events far beyond its traditional purview.

NATO and the Breakup of Yugoslavia

NATO's leaders used the example of the Gulf War, powerful rhetoric, and a combination of both old and new conceptual frameworks to fashion a new role for the alliance. This new fabric faced a serious practical test when war broke out in Yugoslavia in 1991.

There was a major difference of opinion within official NATO circles over how to respond to the war. The Americans under George Bush were reluctant to intervene in any way, and they preferred to leave the search for a solution to the Europeans, who in turn sought through mediation and humanitarian intervention under the UN and the EC to end the crisis. Beginning in 1992, France and Britain sent large contingents of lightly-armed peacekeeping troops to the former Yugoslavia as part of the United Nations Protection Force (UNPROFOR). Their policy preferences for dealing with the war came to be shaped by the perception that any forcible Western intervention would have dangerous implications for their soldiers on the ground.[153]

As official U.S. opinion shifted under Bush's successor, Bill Clinton, toward a more forceful approach to diplomacy, the prospect of U.S. air strikes against Serbian positions and the lifting of the arms embargo against the Bosnian Muslims seemed imminent. This so-called lift and strike policy was supported by Germany, which, like the United States, had sent no ground troops, but it was rejected by the other European members of NATO, led by those who had troops on the ground. In the face of this opposition, the United States in the spring of 1993 again reversed its position and claimed that it would now support whatever solution the Europeans could mediate among the three warring factions in the former Yugoslavia. In conjunction with this policy shift, the United States became engaged in air-dropping humanitarian assistance to the civilian population. It also sent several hundred troops under the UN flag to the former Yugoslavian republic of Macedonia as a deterrent against Serbian aggression.

As the political leaders wrangled over how or whether to intervene, NATO and the WEU, taking their cues from angry political rhetoric that suggested the imminence of a collective response to the war, prepared for intervention. In April 1993, NATO approved its first military operation outside Western Europe and began the enforcement of the UN no-fly zone over Bosnia-Herzegovina.[154] In June 1993, NATO and WEU vessels in the Adriatic, sent under separate commands one year earlier to enforce UN sanctions, were placed under single NATO command—a move that helped to ease the Franco-American controversy over the relationship between the two organizations. Also in June, NATO, seeking to fulfill its recent commitment to peacekeeping, offered to lend its air power to the UN to establish and protect UN-organized safe havens.[155] In August, NATO military planners prepared plans for air strikes to relieve the siege of Sarajevo and to permit the flow of UN aid to other areas of Bosnia. "The Serbs," declared U.S. Secretary of State Warren Christopher, "are on notice, and whether air power is used depends on their deeds."[156]

In terms of conceptions of NATO, the war in Yugoslavia had mixed implications. On one hand, it suggested that NATO did indeed have both an interest and a role to play in building stability in the neighboring territories beyond its frontiers. Whether on humanitarian principles, the desire to uphold international law, or out of more self-interested notions surrounding the threat of massive refugee flows into Western Europe or the chance that the war might widen and draw in other states, including NATO members, NATO could construct, on a broad conceptual foundation, a strong case in favor of intervention. But because the alliance failed to match its rhetoric with action, the credibility of its post-Cold War conceptual canon was thrown into doubt.

The experience of Yugoslavia made a poor advertisement for conceptions of a European security identity and of NATO as a force for stability. Moreover, it did little to enhance confidence that either European institutions or NATO could effectively respond to the new types of ethnic, religious, or nationalist conflicts that might be let loose in Europe by the ending of the Cold War. NATO's rhetoric about crisis prevention and peacekeeping now seemed hollow.

When faced with a crisis at the gates of Western Europe, NATO's political leaders were unwilling to act.[157] This unwillingness, in turn, was perceived as a failure of NATO. To such criticism NATO officials responded by pointing out that the Western response to Yugoslavia was a failure of political will, not of NATO. "The alliance is there," declared Wörner. "It is transformed. It is ready to act. It is the job of the political leadership to use it."[158] This reasoning implied that NATO could have intervened effectively and that only political will was missing. But the effectiveness of intervention was very doubtful, given that the political hesitation was based on military advice that held that Yugoslavia was a classic quagmire situation along the lines of Vietnam, Afghanistan, Algeria, Northern Ireland, etc. The fear of commitment to a bloody but inconclusive, and hence interminable, military engagement was undoubtedly a powerful reason for political restraint.

Despite the inadvisability of intervention, growing concern among Western political leaders about NATO's weakening credibility became a major factor in what happened next. A particularly gruesome (and particularly well-filmed) mortar-bomb attack on a market in Sarajevo on 4 February 1994—just three weeks after NATO's latest threat of air strikes—added to the public pressure on NATO's leaders to act. On 9 February the alliance issued an ultimatum to the Serbian forces around Sarajevo, demanding that they remove their guns from within range (20 kilometers) of the city within ten days or face air strikes.[159] The French government, which now feared increasingly for the safety of its peacekeeping troops in Bosnia and which faced growing domestic pressure to act, had reversed its earlier caution and begun to call on the United States to intervene militarily.[160] The visual impact of dead and dying civilians—many of them children—that was carried around the world by CNN seems to have tipped the balance, and France and the United States convinced a still-hesitant Britain to join in formulating the ultimatum. Within one week, most of the Serbian guns had been withdrawn—but whether this was due to NATO's fiery rhetoric and military posturing or to the arrival of 400 Russian peacekeepers, who had been ordered to Sarajevo by Moscow from their UN duties in Croatia and whose presence almost assured that no NATO air strikes would be launched, is unclear. Nevertheless, the alliance claimed for itself a major victory in its efforts to bring peace to Bosnia.

NATO's credibility seemed further restored later in February when two U.S. F-16s shot down four Serbian jets that were in violation of the UN-mandated no-fly zone over Bosnia. What would happen next, whether NATO would try to extend the ultimatum to other parts of the region and whether its political leadership could build momentum for a negotiated peace among the warring factions, remained, for the moment, an open question. Though the problems associated with military intervention continued to bedevil policymakers, NATO had nevertheless fashioned an active role for itself in the former Yugoslavia, which included the maintenance of an air exclusion zone; the enforcement, in conjunction with the WEU, of a naval blockade; the employment of combat aircraft to support UN forces; and the development of contingency plans for wider peacekeeping (or peace enforcement) activities.

UNPROFOR, however, continued to play the lead role in the Yugoslavian tragedy, where 25,000 "blue helmets" had been deployed to escort aid convoys, provide humanitarian relief, and enforce UN resolutions, which required military intervention in tandem with NATO air support. In August 1994, NATO began a series of air strikes, code-named Operation Deliberate Force, which was designed to protect UN safe havens and deter the Bosnian Serbs from further aggression. The Bosnian Serb response was to take UN peacekeepers hostage, chaining them to fences, bridges, and street lamps as human shields against further strikes. In November, dozens more UN personel were taken hostage—a hint of things to come and a clear indication that the policy of air strikes was ineffective without ground troops to consolidate the gains. In May 1995, further air strikes against Serb ammunition depots prompted the taking of 370 UN hostages. The final insult to UN and NATO credibility occurred in July 1995, when the safe haven of Srebrenica was overrun by the Bosnian Serbs as a small contingent of Dutch peacekeepers watched helplessly. Belated NATO air strikes did nothing to deter this aggression: the peacekeepers were withdrawn and refugees began to stream out of Srebrenica, making a mockery of the safe haven concept and seriously undermining NATO's credibility. Thousands of Bosnian Muslims were executed as the safe haven collapsed.

The fall of Srebrenica marked a turning point in the war for Bosnia; and it was matched by similarly decisive military outcomes throughout the former Yugoslavia, where a stalemate of sorts had begun to emerge among the three warring factions. The Bosnian Sebs in particular soon suffered a serious military reverse, as the Croats overran the Serb enclave in the Krajina region, prompting a massive exodus of Serbian civilians.

In response to further Serb shelling of Sarajevo late in August 1995, NATO launched its most effective and sustained air campaign of the war. During the two-week bombing campaign, NATO air power was targeted against Bosnian Serb command and control facilities; and NATO leaders threatened to continue the campaign until the Serbs agreed to negotiate an end to the war.[161] The military changes on the ground and NATO's new willingness to employ force in the pursuit of diplomacy coincided with a new American effort to broker a peace plan. Meanwhile, there were indications that concern over the tarnished credibility of NATO now took precedence in debates about U.S. interests in Bosnia.[162] After nearly four years of transatlantic dispute over whether and how far NATO should respond to the Balkan crisis, and after divisive quarrels over the future of NATO, peace in Bosnia and a wider role for NATO seemed finally at hand.

NATO to the Rescue: Dayton and the Implementation Force

The changed military situation in Bosnia, concerns over NATO's credibility as a stabilizing force in post-Cold War Europe, and a new American willingness to lead diplomatic efforts to end the war help explain how NATO came, in December 1995, to deploy 60,000 troops to the former Yugoslavia. Under the leadership of U.S. Assistant Secretary of State Richard Holbrooke, the presidents of Bosnia, Croatia, and Serbia initialed a peace agreement in Dayton, Ohio, late in November 1995. The Dayton Accords were signed in Paris on 14 December 1995.[163] They encompassed a broad agreement for peace, ranging from cease-fire provisions to the setting up of a new democratic political order. They also called for the transfer of authority, on 20 December 1995, from UNPROFOR to the NATO-led Implementation Force (IFOR), which consisted of troops from NATO member states, as well as from sixteen non-NATO states, including Russia.

The withdrawal of UNPROFOR was significant: it allowed the West to take a tougher line without having peacekeepers in the way to serve as tempting targets of retaliation if military force was employed in pursuit of diplomacy. Accordingly, IFOR was a powerful military force, operating under robust rules of engagement, with a UN mandate to keep the peace. IFOR troops did not wear blue helmets and ride around in white vehicles—they could shoot back.

The 1995-1996 NATO operation in the Balkans reflected an unprecedented degree of defense cooperation; it was the largest military operation in alliance history; and it appeared to answer some of the questions surrounding the future of NATO. IFOR was under U.S. command and NATO auspices—arrangements that seemed to resolve the political and military problems that had been associated with the earlier UN operation—and it had a definite objective and a clear withdrawal date. This would be no open-ended commitment or exercise in nation-building, as in Somalia. Under the Dayton Accords, the warring parties had agreed to a cease-fire, which would be followed by their withdrawal to defined areas and the removal of heavy weapons along a demilitarized zone (DMZ) that traversed the borders of the Bosnia-Serbian Republic and the Croat-Bosnian Federation—the two successor units to Bosnia. IFOR's primary mission, code-named Joint Endeavor, was a military one: to police the DMZ. Equally soothing to military commanders, who worried about "mission creep," and to political leaders was IFOR's clear commitment to withdraw after twelve months, in December 1996.[164]

The perceived success of IFOR was said to illustrate the importance of NATO and its essential future role in European security. Alliance leaders publicly argued that without NATO, there would be no IFOR; and without IFOR, there would be no end to the conflict.[165] True, the IFOR deployment had achieved a measure of success where other international efforts had failed; and it had arguably proved the desirability of NATO-led cooperative ventures for peace. But the peace in Bosnia remained uncertain. Would a lasting peace be achieved? And would the nonmilitary goals of Dayton be pursued? IFOR had designedly played a minor role in resolving problems surrounding human rights, displaced persons, and war criminals; and it had left the crucial tasks of political reform and civil and economic reconstruction to the UN, OSCE, and EU—simmering issues that had the potential to undermine the peace once IFOR had withdrawn. Nevertheless, NATO leaders pointed to IFOR as proof of the alliance's enduring validity. Secretary General Javier Solana proclaimed in the spring of 1996 that IFOR was "a model for future operations and demonstrated the practial value of partnership for peace."[166] Klaus Kinkel, the German foreign minister, declared that "IFOR is proof of the adaptability of the alliance."[167] It was also proof of the adaptability of Germany, whose Constitutional Court—at the request of the Kohl government—had in 1994 reached the conclusion that the Constitution did not bar Germany from participating in military deployments beyond the geographical purview of the Washington Treaty.

The NATO operation in the Balkans thus served as much as a statement on conceptions of future security arrangements as on the peace agreement itself. For advocates of the alliance, NATO's mixed record in Bosnia did not prove its irrelevance or point to the suitability of other organizations in performing similar tasks. Rather, it provided lessons about how NATO should continue to adapt.[168]

The Balkan tragedy was said to have proved the essential value of American leadership, which when absent had left NATO adrift and rudderless.[169] Similarly, it highlighted long-standing conceptions within Europe—mostly French generated but gaining an increasing constituency—that Europe must continue to prepare for scenarios in which the United States was unwilling or unable to take part. For European states, national military action on the scale of IFOR was severely constrained by logistical impediments.[170] Thus, Bosnia gave further impetus to those parties who promoted the concept of combined joint task forces as a means of one day ensuring a degree of European autonomy in security affairs.

IFOR was said to demonstrate the practical value of the Partnership for Peace (PfP) concept, in which NATO's former adversaries could begin the process of integration into NATO and other Western arrangements for military cooperation, defense, and security.[171] There was indeed some justification for this claim, given that thirteen of the sixteen non-NATO states participating in IFOR were also signatories to PfP.[172] The IFOR included, for example, a Nordic brigade, comprised of NATO-designated Danish and Norwegian troops, non-NATO Swedish, Polish, and Finnish forces, and contingents from the Baltic states.[173] More remarkably, these troops were fully integrated alongside NATO troops, including those from France, and 1,500 Russian troops. This was the first time since 1966 that French troops operated under direct NATO command, marking a further rapprochement between France and its allies. Russian participation was deemed particularly noteworthy, as it seemed to suggest that a strategic partnership with Russia was still possible, even as NATO sought to expand the alliance eastward to embrace states within the former Soviet sphere of influence. Russian objections to NATO expansion nevertheless remained vociferous.[174]

More broadly, IFOR seemed to represent an explicit demonstration of the value of practical defense cooperation between NATO and its former adversaries. It was a tangible example of how integration between East and West could serve the broader goals of peace and security; and it intensified the enlargement debate. The IFOR mission in Bosnia provided an opportunity for the Eastern and Central European states to demonstrate their suitability as players in the European security arena and as prospective members of NATO. Hungary, for example, was a particularly important partner for NATO in the IFOR mission, serving as a major staging point for the deployment of U.S. troops on their way from Germany to Bosnia.[175] Similarly, IFOR allowed NATO to test the mettle of prospective partners and to further the practical, institutional cooperation that membership entailed and that had been foreseen in the PfP proposals.[176] In conceptual terms, then, the NATO operation in the Balkans seemed to restore, momentarily at least, NATO's claim to primacy over European security. To proponents of NATO expansion, the alliance had begun to prove itself adaptable to the changed conditions of the post-Cold War period, ready for new challenges further to the east.

European Integration and Conceptions of NATO

The most powerful external events that shaped conceptions of NATO in the immediate post-Cold War years were the collapse of the Soviet Union, the Gulf War, and the Yugoslavian wars. But events internal to the alliance, in particular the continuing movement to integration in Western Europe, also shaped conceptions.

Acting on the conviction that increased military cooperation among the European members of NATO would contribute to politico-economic integration, France, strongly backed by West Germany, moved, beginning in 1984, to revitalize the Western European Union (WEU).[177] In conjunction with this move, in 1988 they created the Franco-German brigade, which was upgraded to corps level in 1991.[178] With the advent of German reunification, these moves were justified on the grounds that they would serve to bind the powerful new state more tightly to Western Europe and prevent Germany from acting without the consent of its European partners. Integration, which once had been embraced for its perceived ability to put an end to Franco-German rivalry, was now touted as the best way to check German power. "I advise anyone afraid of the Germans," declared Helmut Kohl, "to join in building a firm roof over this Germany, over this Europe, then these fears will be completely overcome."[179] The integration of French and German military units also provided France with an excuse to continue basing its forces on German soil.

The movement toward European Union (EU) was interrupted briefly by the Gulf War.[180] Even so, the war seemed to prove both the inadequacy of West European provisions for defense not tied to NATO and the need for the development of a common foreign and security policy (CFSP).[181] At Maastricht in December 1991, one month after the Rome NATO summit and in the face of rising hostilities in Yugoslavia, the eleven European Community members of NATO (plus Ireland) announced their intention to create a CFSP by developing further the WEU.[182] By March 1992, the Franco-German corps, now dubbed the Eurocorps in the wake of expressions of intent to join by Belgium, Luxembourg, and Spain, was declared ready to form the nucleus of a European army under the aegis of the WEU.

The effect of these events on conceptions of NATO was threefold. First, they challenged the notion, laid down at NATO's founding and reaffirmed at Rome, that NATO would remain the "essential forum" for transatlantic security consultations. NATO might still remain the forum, but other institutions might come to play a larger role in European security. An independent European army, the instrument of a common West European foreign and security policy, could mean that North America was no longer a primary participant in European security. Taken to an extreme, this might result in the atrophy of organizational and conceptual transatlantic links to such an extent to mean the end of NATO.[183]

Thus, the development of the EU had a second, more philosophical impact on NATO. The collapse of the Soviet Union had freed the Eastern European states, but it also opened the possibility that Western Europe might now shake off the sometimes heavy hand of American leadership.[184] If the Soviet threat had created NATO, would its disappearance, which coincided with the rise of the EU, then also mean the end of NATO?[185] Would NATO, which had done so much to foster European integration, serve merely as an interim stabilizing force, existing only until the West Europeans could create a mechanism to defend themselves?[186] Or would it, as the Americans seemed to prefer, evolve into a pan-European security order that provided for the continuation of American influence even as it reflected the new realities of European integration, both economic and political?[187] Answers to these questions, which went to the heart of the debate about conceptions of NATO, remained elusive throughout the early 1990s. As we have seen, by early 1994, NATO had made impressive rhetorical strides, backed by some small practical measures contained in the NACC and the Partnership for Peace, to support its claims to increased jurisdiction over pan-European security. Its record in Yugoslavia, until the deployment of IFOR, had been decidedly mixed.

When it came to Yugoslavia, however, purely European institutions arguably had a more tarnished record than NATO. There was a stark contrast between early views in favor of Europe's leading role in the Yugoslavian crisis, to which the Americans in particular initially deferred, and the reality of comparative European impotence. To those familiar with the history of the alliance, the European response to Bosnia had special resonance; and the debate over it seemed vaguely to recall Kissinger's discussion of the "Year of Europe" in the early 1970s. In the wake of moves toward further European integration in foreign and security policy, this was to be "Europe's Hour," in which doubts about continental capacity to handle problems such as Bosnia and the long-term capacity for European self-reliance were to be extinguished.

The third and more immediate effect that the development of the European Union had on conceptions of NATO was that it revealed the degree to which the allies themselves differed about the nature of NATO in the post-Cold War world.

National Conceptions of NATO in the Post-Cold War Era

The development of a European security identity was a concept that during the Cold War fitted fairly easily with the development of NATO; the two were generally believed to proceed hand in hand—to be, in the NATO parlance, "mutually reinforcing."[188] In conceptual terms, NATO represented the outer ring of European security structures, with the WEU and the European pillar, which found additional expression in the EUROGROUP, playing a supporting, subservient role.[189] The end of the Cold War, however, seemed to offer the possibility that the European members of NATO, acting under the WEU, would seek to distance themselves from American leadership and undermine NATO.[190]

The United States and Britain

The Americans viewed the post-Cold War development of purely European security initiatives as a threat to NATO.[191] Joined by Britain, U.S. leaders urged that NATO retain its primacy; the WEU was viewed as an adjunct to, and not a replacement for, NATO.[192] Britain and the United States, representing the more conservative wing of the alliance, promoted expansive conceptions of NATO that they hoped would maintain its primacy. Until January 1994, they maintained the view that France sought to undermine NATO by generating alternative, European-centered conceptions of security.[193]

In January 1994, the Clinton administration reached an accommodation with the French, and both agreed to endorse the concept of Combined Joint Task Forces (CJTFs) for NATO and the WEU.[194] This concept allowed for the creation of "separable but not separate" military capabilities to be employed by NATO or the WEU.[195] With the collective assets of NATO now made available to its main potential rival, subject to consultations within the NAC, the Franco-American dispute over the primacy of NATO eased. Britain, with the exception of its initial refusal to endorse the American plan for air strikes in Bosnia, followed the U.S. lead.[196]

France

Nationalist sentiments of the kind fostered by Charles de Gaulle continued to exert a powerful influence in France in the post-Cold War era.[197] France felt the need to stand up to the United States, and to be seen to be doing so. In contrast to the Anglo-American position, France argued that, with the end of the Cold War, the United States would eventually leave Europe and that Europeans should begin to think more seriously about the security implications of their impending political union.[198]

The French plan for a European army was, according to the French Foreign Minister Roland Dumas, "in no way directed against NATO and cannot be." The Eurocorps, he argued, was a way to strengthen NATO in the short term by providing a more coherent European element. In the long term, it would provide the basis for the WEU to act more independently of NATO and the United States.[199]

France thus sought to export to its European partners the central Gaullist axiom that self-defense was necessary to sovereignty. This effort, as demonstrated by Helmut Kohl's public remarks in November 1991, was not without effect: "I want," he declared, "clearly to emphasize that a united Europe without a joint European defense is unthinkable."[200] As Western Europe moved toward political union and gained the capacity for self-defense, NATO, under the French conception, would end its role as an interim stabilizing force. In the quest to ease Europe away from the American political and military shadow, France focused on proposals to turn the CSCE into a defense organization and the development of a West European army under the WEU.[201]

At the same time, however, France did not wish altogether to do away with NATO, which was still regarded as having retained some of its original promise as a hedge against both a resurgent Germany and an unstable Russia. "NATO," declared former Prime Minister Michel Rocard in July 1992, "is a solid reference point in a world of turmoil."[202] In keeping with these views, France approved the agreement setting up more formal links between NATO and the WEU in November 1992.[203] It also agreed to place French forces that were helping to enforce the UN no-fly zone over Bosnia under NATO command.[204]

The renunciation of flexible response by NATO in November 1991 had particular importance for France.[205] Coupled with the new American willingness to pay at least rhetorical support to the notion of a European security identity, the abandonment of flexible response ended the Franco-American doctrinal dispute over deterrence that had erupted in the 1960s and that culminated in the French withdrawal from the IMO.[206] France did not return to the IMO, but the end of the strategic dispute seemed to offer the promise that French isolation from NATO's Defense Planning Committee would soon end.[207] As Defense Minister Pierre Joxe claimed after the Rome summit, "I could soon be the last defense minister in Europe not to participate in NATO meetings. NATO has some missions that are going to evolve ... [France] will be more active."[208]

After a right-wing coalition ousted the Socialists in March 1993, rapprochement between France and its allies accelerated. In April 1993, France returned to discussions in NATO's Military Committee when it discussed peacekeeping issues that affected French forces. In September 1995, the first NATO exercises since 1966 were held on French soil, as allied forces simulated air strikes in Bosnia.[209] In December, Foreign Minister Hervé de Charette informed the NAC of the French intention to resume its role in NATO military bodies "which do not encroach on her sovereignty," to participate in the Council of Defense Ministers, and to be fully involved in the Military Committee.[210] Three weeks later French troops joined IFOR in the former Yugoslavia under NATO command.

French leaders from de Gaulle through Mitterand had emphasized an independent foreign policy based on nuclear autonomy and national assertiveness. Although France spoke out against the Cold War and bloc politics, these conditions provided the perfect setting for the declarations and practice of notional independence.[211] However, as the Cold War ended and NATO itself began to reform, France underwent a major geopolitical adjustment. The perceived decline in the importance of nuclear weapons and the inadequacy of French conventional forces in the Gulf War raised questions about French influence and prestige; and the reunification of Germany rekindled old fears about German domination. It was in this context that the high cost of French absence from NATO's decision-making and consultative bodies became apparent. A partial response, as we have seen, was to promote initiatives designed to restore French leadership over European defense cooperation and integration; and the situation seemed, initially, to call for hostility to an increased political role for NATO. But as it became apparent to French leaders that NATO, true to its claims, would retain its primacy in European security, new forms of accommodation were needed if France was to exert some influence over the course of events.[212]

Opposition had ceased to be a practical basis for relations with NATO, though French leaders retained their emphasis on the need for a European security identity.

Germany

The Germans, faced with the enormous costs of unification and having moved from their former position on the front line of the Cold War to one confronting an emerging security vacuum in Central Europe, sought to accommodate their dreams of European unity within an American-led conception of European security.[213] On the one hand, Germany wanted to strengthen its ties with France and accelerate the process of European unification; on the other, it worked to maintain the importance and cohesion of NATO. For German leaders, these goals were not regarded as irreconcilable. As Chancellor Helmut Kohl observed, "It is not longer a question of either-or, but of one alongside the other."[214]

Nevertheless, the twin goals of European Union and the development of NATO placed the Germans in a difficult position, and German leaders subsequently went to remarkable lengths in their efforts to placate the French while not alienating the Americans.[215] For example, German support for the development of a European army around the expanded Franco-German corps was cloaked in the notion that it would have the effect of bringing France closer to NATO.[216] This assertion soon proved itself to be correct, due largely to the fact that the Germans had the clout to make sure that it was. Although France remained out of the IMO, it did agree, in January 1993, to the establishment of formal links between the Franco-German corps and NATO, which had the effect of allowing NATO to call on and command the corps in times of crisis.

Meanwhile, German political leaders stressed the enduring validity of NATO.[217] It remained, declared Defense Minister Volker Rühe, "the foundation of our security."[218] Having made good on the promise, endorsed by every West German politician since Adenauer, that NATO would serve as the vehicle for reunification, German leaders were not now willing to abandon an organization that had so well served German interests. With grave threats of instability on the horizon in Central Europe and with the Balkans once again in flames, NATO remained at the heart of German foreign policy.[219] Germany now feared mass migration and environmental disaster from the East, was struggling with the costs of unification, and feared neo-isolationist tendencies in the United States.[220] A transformed NATO, in conjunction with renewed efforts to build a European security identity, seemed to offer a mechanism for confronting the challenges presented by the end of the Cold War.[221] German leaders unequivocally endorsed the conception of NATO as an agent of change: "if NATO is to build on its success and stand up to new challenges," declared Rühe, "it must change.... NATO itself has always been an agent of change."[222]

Additional concerns occupied the minds of German leaders. One was the perception among Germany's allies that the Germans might return to their past and seek to impose their will on neighboring states.[223] This image, though playing more on past fears than current realities, was given new life when German Foreign Minister Hans-Deitrich Genscher insisted on the recognition of Croatia and Slovenia in December 1991—a move widely credited with having flamed the fires of war in the disintegrating Yugoslavia.[224] Disturbing signs of rising neo-Nazism also tarnished Germany's image. In response to widespread criticism over these events, German leaders stressed their postwar record of "responsible politics."[225] They also pointed out that the demands of unification made it unlikely that Germany could, even if it wanted to, act alone or in contravention of the wishes of its allies. "We have enough to do at home," declared Kohl, "and the best we can do in these years to the end of the century is to put our own house in order and offer help and solidarity to others."[226]

In the wake of events in the Persian Gulf and Yugoslavia, German leaders declared a willingness to amend the Basic Law to allow German troops to participate in out-of-area operations. "Adopting a passive strategic role," declared Defense Minister Rühe, "would harm vital German interests."[227] Thus, as NATO began to cast its conceptual net ever wider and move beyond its traditional role as a defense organization, Germany followed—despite the domestic political risks inherent in challenging a fundamental tenet of postwar German foreign policy. By early 1994, small contingents of German troops had been dispatched beyond the NATO area.[228] At the same time, many German constitutional lawyers argued that the Basic Law in its existing form would allow for German participation in out-of-area operations.[229] These arguments proved persuasive: in July 1994 the Federal Constitutional Court clarified the constitutional basis for the deployment of German forces out of area; and ruled that the Bundeswehr could legally and fully participate in UN, NATO, and WEU missions.[230] Accordingly, a German contingent of 4,000 troops joined IFOR in the former Yugoslavia in 1995.[231]

In the aftermath of the Cold War, Germany moved swiftly not only to integrate itself more firmly into Western Europe but also to begin the wider integration of the entire continent.[232] Germany became both a leading proponent of NATO membership for the states of the former Warsaw Pact and a major aid donor to the East.[233] By supporting French initiatives for strengthening the WEU, Bonn could help Paris maintain claims of parity with Germany and ease French concern about the new power of its once-divided and formerly weaker ally.[234] Like their French counterparts, German leaders believed in the development of a CFSP, but they thought it could be done without alienating the United States or undermining NATO.[235] In alliance-political terms, Germany played a delicate balancing act, moving between the two conceptual poles of European security; one French, the other American.[236] As one anonymous policymaker in Bonn observed, "every time we give Washington something for NATO, then we give Paris something to feeds its vision of a European defense identity."[237]

Conclusion

Those who foresaw the death of NATO in the end of the Cold War—and there were many—appear to have been unaware of the alliance's remarkable history of perpetuating itself through new rhetoric and conception. In the eyes of its political masters, for NATO there was indeed life after threat. As Manfred Wörner observed early in 1992: "An alliance like ours needs to adapt continuously if it wants to survive."[238] And so, like a bicycle, NATO moved forward to stay upright.

Formed to defend the peace, NATO as the Cold War ended tried to transform itself into an organization committed to promoting peace. This was a dynamic conception. NATO's leaders, led by the Americans, envisaged a day when political Europe, united by shared values and stabilized and protected by the transatlantic link embodied in NATO, would more closely resemble its geographical entity. NATO projected itself as the ultimate guardian of pan-European security, committed to the creation of a stable and prosperous environment for its former adversaries, as well as for its members. In this capacity, it would work to keep the peace, forge new partnerships, control weapons of mass destruction, and even help clean up the environment. It was a wonderful but fleeting scenario, quickly tarnished by the bloody stain of Yugoslavia, the specter of chaos in the former Soviet bloc, and heretical talk about replacing NATO with something more European.

The uncertainties facing the alliance at the end of the Cold War were more political than military. Its leaders tried to respond by changing NATO's force structure and by finding a new strategic doctrine based on less nuclear reliance, enhanced mobility, and increased political engagement. Whether or how the security vacuum in Central and Eastern Europe could be filled by bringing the states of that region into NATO remained an open question. The issue turned not only on the possible risks of expanded membership, but also on whether a military-political instrument could be used to bring stability to a historically volatile region. Whether Russia would evolve into a peaceful, friendly neighbor was largely beyond the control of the West; insofar as the West had any influence it has been through the flow of economic advice and economic aid given to Russia. NATO as an institution seems to have played a very small role, if any, in shaping Western policy toward Russia. Nevertheless, NATO's leaders were driven to begin forging ties with their former adversaries out of the conviction that the alliance had achieved a great moral victory in the Cold War, that it was therefore morally obliged to continue to serve the interests of peace and security. But the alliance acted equally out of a deep sense of uncertainty about the future and from a natural institutional imperative to perpetuate itself.

The key factors shaping conceptions of NATO in the post-Cold War era were thus both internal and external to the alliance. Internally, German reunification, declining defense budgets, the withdrawal of U.S. troops from Europe and the rise of the European Union helped foster a revival of old conceptions and led to the emergence of new ones surrounding the extraordinary nature of NATO's form and function. Institutional inertia also played a crucial role in this process. In the immediate aftermath of the Cold War, NATO bureaucrats appeared eager to imply that NATO had a life of its own, and was not simply a creature of its member governments. One important factor keeping NATO alive has clearly been the body of civil servants who work for it; and one element shaping conceptions of NATO has been its body of permanent employees. Externally, the complete collapse of Soviet power and communism in Central and Eastern Europe helped generate conceptions that held that NATO could continue to defend the West while working to stabilize the East. The experience of the Gulf War, though not likely to be repeated, seemed to support NATO's claims to continued relevance. With regard to Yugoslavia, genuine humanitarian impulses often clashed with domestic political considerations about the electoral costs and military efficacy of intervention, creating a strong rhetorical vision of NATO that lacked substance. NATO's role in Yugoslavia, when it found one, was initially limited to indecisive intervention. Although the belated deployment of IFOR seemed to confirm NATO's claims to continued utility, the overwhelmingly military nature of the mission raised questions about whether and how far NATO was capable of living up to its wider aspirations.

NATO had been anointed at its birth with the notion that it embodied Western values. One compelling scenario of the Cold War held that, if the West was patient, the superiority of its system would eventually become apparent and then NATO, its highest organizational manifestation, would serve as a counterattraction to communism.

None of the United States' allies argued publicly against this value-based conception of NATO. How could they? There was much evidence that seemed to support the scenario. The attraction of the West did appear to be magnetic, the Soviet satellites did gravitate westward, German reunification did take place on American terms, and the Communist bloc disintegrated. But NATO did not resolve the problems of the East-West geopolitical and ideological confrontation called the Cold War. Nor did it resolve the major intra-alliance disputes over burden sharing and out-of-area operations, which had become a source of intermittent transatlantic friction. Rather, NATO simply survived long enough for these problems to disappear. As Mikhail Gorbachev worked to erode the politico-military landscape within which they had been posed, the Soviet Union went from superpower to superpauper almost overnight, and then it collapsed and ceased to exist.

Thus, NATO, though principally the Americans, can perhaps be forgiven for declaring victory in the Cold War. For those who had spent their professional lives waging it, the idea of claiming a total moral and political victory was irresistible.[239] But these leaders spoke mostly to themselves and to their constituents. Nothing remained of the Soviet Union and its ideological and military allies in the Warsaw Pact. Their remnants, NATO's new partners, were clamoring for NATO membership and the promise of all the good things that alliance could bring.

Chapter 7

The Promise of Alliance

The onset and rapid intensification of Cold War rivalry in the immediate postwar years helped establish firmly in the minds of NATO's leaders the notion that, if it was to endure, the Atlantic alliance would require their constant attention, effort, and sacrifice. As John Foster Dulles accurately predicted in December 1957, the endeavor to revitalize NATO would become an ongoing concern that necessitated the clear identification and firm public enunciation not only of what NATO was against—everyone knew that— but also of what NATO was for. From its earliest inception NATO was principally identified with the task of standing tall against the Soviet threat, but it gradually accumulated an extraordinary range of additional attributes that suggested that NATO represented—as in fact its leaders had declared from the very beginning—far more than a military alliance.

The question, of course, is why they felt compelled to do so. If the Soviets were so thoroughly hostile and if communism truly represented such a clear and present danger, why was it felt necessary to invest NATO with conceptual assets other than those associated with military defense? What purposes were served by the multiple and sometimes rather farfetched conceptions surrounding the alliance's tasks and objectives? Did the enunciation of wider and looser conceptions of NATO's form and function mean that its leaders over time became less convinced about the nature of the Soviet threat, or were there other forces at work that helped to promote the acceptance of notions surrounding NATO's nonmilitary utility? Before we turn to these questions, it is useful briefly to review conceptions of NATO.

This work has identified and analyzed some forty conceptions that have been used to describe the nature and promise of the Atlantic alliance. As we have seen in the preceding chapters, NATO has been conceived as having the ability to:

- Form the vanguard in the fight against communism and keep the Soviets out of Western Europe;

- Bind the United States to Western Europe;

- Protect U.S. national security interests and prevent Soviet preponderance in Europe;

- Guarantee Western European defense against the Soviet threat;

- Identify, operationalize and manage the guiding strategic concepts for conventional defense and nuclear deterrence, including the notions of massive retaliation, the trip-wire and shield conceptions of conventional defense, flexible response, and the New Strategic Concept;

- Prevent renewed German militarism while securing a West German contribution to Western defense;

- Promote German reunification and provide West Germany with an international role;

- Serve as a vehicle for European political, social, and economic integration, and shield Western Europe for postwar economic recovery;

- Put an end permanently to European political antagonisms, and particularly to Franco-German rivalry;

- Serve as the foundation for the security efforts of the free world;

- Influence events beyond the geographical purview of the North Atlantic Treaty and serve Western interests out of area;

- Help the European allies retain their colonial possessions or, in the case of the United States, help to justify the extension and defense of U.S. sphere of influence;

- Act as an instrument of human rights, diplomacy, and democracy;

- Illustrate the democratic and moral superiority of the West during the Cold War, and serve as a counterattraction to communism;

- Revitalize the UN and permit it to function as originally conceived;

- Complement the ERP and other basic goals of U.S. foreign policy;

- Help enforce a new Monroe Doctrine for Europe;

- Embody the shared concepts of mutual aid and self-help, and demonstrate the benefits of a unified approach and the futility of independent national action;

- Stabilize the world by promoting peace both in Europe and beyond;

- Stand as the formal manifestation of a North Atlantic Community founded on common interests and shared political and cultural ideals;

- Promote Western civilization and help fulfill humankind's greater aspirations by serving as a repository and defender of moral values;

- Promote public understanding about the danger, nature, and scope of the Soviet threat, and lead the fight against communist propaganda by coordinating psychological warfare;

- Manage détente and serve as a political forum for East-West as well as for intra-allied diplomacy, negotiation, and consultation;

- Help create consensus about how to manage the strategic aspects of economic relations between East and West;

- Negotiate, verify, and enforce compliance with arms control treaties;

- Help forge an Atlantic Partnership wherein the United States and Western Europe would share more equally the roles and responsibilities of alliance;

- Illustrate the opportunities and obligations of international political life in an interdependent world;

- Become the focus of a genuine peace movement that could negotiate with the Soviets on a realistic foundation of peace through strength;

- Act as a vehicle for U.S. hegemony;

- Help smaller and weaker members of the alliance influence the United States;

- Prevent the outbreak of World War III;

- Provide the rationale for defense expenditures, conventional and nuclear modernization and deployments, and overcome the reluctance of democracies to rearm in peacetime;

- Serve as a study in long-range political engineering;

- Perform the functions of an environmental alliance devoted to improving the quality of life in the East, as well as in the West;

- Act as a peacekeeper or peacemaker under UN political authority;

- Assist the international community by helping to prevent or manage crises, and to provide humanitarian assistance during such crises;

- Work to prevent the proliferation of weapons of mass destruction;

- Coordinate scientific research and development among its members and between the alliance and its new partners;

- Act as a force for stability and the growth of democracy in all of Europe;

- Create a new Partnership for Peace under the guise of a new North Atlantic Cooperation Council that would help to integrate former adversaries into the community of nations;

- Help the Western European Union perform more effectively without undermining NATO;

- Balance a resurgent Russia in the post-Cold War world.

The Role of Changing Conceptions: Propaganda, Political Aims, and Alliance Cohesion

Multiple conceptions—and the established habit of changing or adding to those conceptions every few years—provided NATO's leaders with a sense of forward momentum and progress, a measure of their success, and an element of guidance during the decades of the Cold War and also during the years that immediately followed. Repeated reconsideration and repetition of NATO's goals and objectives became an integral part of an ongoing process of renewal within the alliance; and it was an important mechanism in creating an elastic bond that held NATO together. Changing conceptions fed back into the organization and were purveyed to the public, whose support or at least acquiescence was required, to give NATO life. The sheer diversity of conceptions of NATO contributed to alliance unity by preventing any member from feeling too tightly constrained by any one of them.

A comparison between the declarations and aims of NATO and those of the Allies during the Second World War yields interesting results. In a hot war, once it has begun, the objective is simple: it is to defeat the enemy's armed forces before he defeats yours. In fact, the objective is more complicated than that, because the point at which the enemy will yield will depend on the terms of surrender offered. In the Second World War the terms were unconditional surrender, which emphasized that the Allies would not negotiate with Hitler or his associates. A second war aim, for which a precedent had been set in 1918, was the commitment to create a new world order in the form of the United Nations. These aims were intended to serve as guidance to the military and to act as a rallying cry for the people, who were invited to make sacrifices, to fight all-out in the effort to achieve unconditional surrender, and to look forward to the creation of a better world afterward. Roosevelt and Churchill consciously fashioned their rhetoric to vilify the enemy, to make the people hate him or them ruthlessly, and to rally the Allied nations by claiming success and holding out the prospect of victory. In short, the function of war aims and war propaganda is clear: it is to improve the chances of victory.

In the Cold War the aims were essentially the same: to mobilize the people of the NATO allies, possibly to demoralize the Soviets and their allies, and so to hasten the day of "victory." In this context, the problems faced by NATO's leaders become instantly clear. Because there was no hot war to indicate objectively what progress was being made, a wide variety of elements could be adduced to indicate whether the Cold War was being won or lost. For example, quantities of arms could be referred to or political changes; and rhetoric—or propaganda—could be adjusted accordingly. Moreover in a cold war the very concept of victory is nebulous, and there is no clear means of bringing it to an end. NATO began with a purely defensive objective; it maintained its defensive nature throughout the Cold War; and yet it claimed, with some justification, victory in the politico-economic competition of the Cold War.

In the environment of cold or nonwar, it was impossible for conceptions and the rhetoric that described them to remain unchanged; one set of conceptions could become temporarily or permanently out of step with changing reality, or ineffectual as a rallying cry through repetition. In this sense, declarations of aims, assessments of achievement, and the propaganda of the Cold War were further removed from reality and more susceptible to change and mythmaking than the rhetoric and propaganda of hot wars.

The forces that influenced and shaped conceptions were internal to the alliance and internal to the member states, where peaceful economic development and changes in government went on normally. They were also external to the alliance, and conceptions of NATO often changed in response to evolution inside the Soviet Union and the Warsaw Treaty Organization (WTO) or in response to events in areas beyond the geographical purview of either bloc.

Unlike the rigid and Soviet-dominated WTO, NATO was informal and flexible and so was forced to seek consensus for its actions and in its deliberations. Changing conceptions were the expressions and instruments of that consensus. Although some members could apply political or economic pressure more easily or effectively than others when attempting to forge a consensus that best accommodated their interests, there was no risk that resistance to these combined forces would provoke an invasion from the alliance's leading power. In contrast to the Soviet Union, the United States never forcibly invaded or attacked its allies; conception—not invasion—became the preferred means of wielding influence in the alliance. It was the combination of the two—the relatively democratic and cooperative rather than coercive organization of NATO and its lack of formal rules and voting procedures, together with the ability to keep changing notions of what NATO was for and the substance of what it was doing (e.g., strategy)—that kept the alliance together with such remarkable unity for so long. Of course there were other real forces of unity at work, including bureaucratic, economic, political, and cultural ones, as well as threat perceptions. But changing conceptions were a key mechanism. For all the elements of propaganda that they contained, conceptions of NATO were essential statements of political aims without which the alliance would have fallen apart.

The American diplomat and scholar George Kennan, in his memoirs, provided his readers with a characteristically eloquent and intellectually appealing description of the environment of international relations:

> International political life is something organic, not something mechanical. Its essence is change; and the only systems for the regulation of international life which can be effective over long periods of time are ones sufficiently stable, sufficiently pliable, to adjust themselves to constant change in the interest and power of the various countries involved.[1]

NATO's history epitomizes Kennan's view.

The Sources of Conceptions

France, Germany, the United States, and the United Kingdom have been the main sources of conceptions of NATO. France, whose leaders sought politically and intellectually to distance themselves from the United States and United Kingdom, was frequently in opposition. This was particularly the case when it came to the formulation of strategy because, in comparison to political conceptions, strategic concepts had some precision. In addition, France's nuclear arsenal allowed it the luxury of formulating its own deterrence strategy (i.e., one that was French and for France). French conceptions of NATO have, since the late 1960s, moved increasingly close to those held by the United States and United Kingdom. Nevertheless, France, for both domestic and international consumption, continues to view NATO as having limited utility.

In the immediate post-Cold war era, French leaders have chosen publicly to denigrate the long-term utility of NATO in favor of the creation or enhancement of their own (or at least non-American dominated) sources of influence, for example the Franco-German corps, the OSCE, and the WEU. But in promoting expansive conceptions of other organizations, they have had influence on conceptions of NATO. Official French commentary, by turning away from NATO and focusing on other organizations, has done much to set in relief the differences *between* French and American conceptions of NATO. But it has not lent a great deal to a discussion of how the French view NATO, except to say that they view other organizations as being more effective—which is to say that while France and the United States may share some of the same general objectives for European security, they differ on roles and means. When focusing on conceptions of NATO, the official French view of what NATO cannot do is important, if only to show that there are and have been alternatives to what has been proposed and promoted by the United States (often supported of course by the United Kingdom and Germany). Lastly, French conceptions of European security, like American ones for NATO, are often as vague and uninstructive as they are expansive.

The Germans have long preferred to follow where their main allies led—an act that has brought about some curious balancing as Germany strove to deepen connections with France even as it sought to reassure the United States. German leaders historically have been kept (and have studiously kept themselves) at arms length regarding both the formulation of new views of NATO, and the creation of new functions for it. One exception was the German desire, expressed in the early 1960s, for a greater say over the control over the use of nuclear weapons. This was mistaken by the United States for possible evidence of a German appetite for possession of nuclear weapons, and the result was the multilateral force, conceived both as a nonproliferation device and as a means of perpetuating U.S. nuclear control.

Although the Germans have shied away from formulating new conceptions, they have been the most consistent of all when it came to upholding the conceptions of others. Thus, we find that Germany has been a consistently strong proponent of American conceptions—not because German leaders always believed the rhetoric from Washington, but because adherence to those conceptions was in line with larger German goals.

Germans viewed their role in NATO and their conceptions of NATO as two sides of the same coin. Germans would be good allies and, in turn, the good alliance would restore (and later sustain) an international role for West Germany that would lead to reunification. It was also sometimes claimed, by both Germans and non-Germans, that NATO would protect Germany from its darker side. The post-Cold War (and hence postunification) period has somewhat disturbed this rosy scenario, and the Germans are now faced with having to redirect their expectations of what NATO can do for them and what they can do for NATO. The recent focus on peacekeeping and out-of-area actions has been particularly controversial, but as German deployments to the former Yugoslavia, the Adriatic, Somalia, and the Mediterranean (during the Gulf War) show, there has been an erosion of constitutional restraints. But there remain many psychological restraints that suggest that alliance policy will continue to guide German policy.

Germany, despite its large land forces, its recently unified country within NATO, its central geopolitical position, and its strong economy, is, today at least, saddled with the baggage of having to defer to its allies. The reasons for this seem clear. Germany wants to reassure its allies as well as its former adversaries, play the part of a good ally, get along with unification, and appear to be neither too far out front nor too far behind. Fritz Erler's 1963 assessment of German foreign policy remains true today. It should, he said,

> make as little noise as possible.... The Germans should not press forward too ambitiously, but examine the initiatives and reservations of others, and adapt themselves to these as far as they are reasonable. They should not appear to be the element which is continuously disturbing and pushing and driving the alliance.[2]

Thus, German objectives so far remain basically similar to those held since the 1950s, and official German policy embraces any conceptions of NATO that promise to maintain Germany's rank within Europe and within NATO without antagonizing its major partners.

American and British leaders, because they have been at the center of the alliance, have held more constant conceptions than their French and German counterparts, but they (though principally the Americans) have also taken the lead in generating new conceptions in response to changing events or interests. The main British contribution to conceptions was interdependence, which was rather short-lived and which had more to do with the international economy than with NATO. But the British role in steadfastly supporting American conceptions was crucial for both states and for their influence within the alliance. The Americans learned to expect British endorsement for U.S. conceptions in return for the symbols and rhetoric (and nuclear weaponry) that characterized the special relationship.

It was the Americans who generated the largest number of conceptions and who were the most proficient at propagating those conceptions through rhetoric. Whether this was due to national character, to the strong American tradition of infusing foreign policy with missionary zeal, or to the relatively larger size of its governmental bureaucracy is unimportant. As alliance leader, it was the U.S. role to lead through word and action. As one U.S. official recently declared: "A military alliance consists of two things. It consists of words and deeds.... Words and deeds together are nice, but the words are necessary."[3]

This strategy of leadership through words and deeds produced an ever-expanding spectrum of images of the alliance—some of which at first blush seemed ridiculous but which later provided an important focus for unity and action. Thus it was that Richard Nixon, in an age of rising environmental awareness, proposed in the late 1960s that NATO, through its new Committee on the Challenges of Modern Society (CCMS), could serve an environmental function. Even as the CCMS continued, from that time onward, to receive its annually allotted share of the NATO budget, produce papers, and hold workshops, it lay essentially dormant, reaffirming the notion that bureaucrats never die; they just run out of ink. All this changed at the Cold War's end, when the conception of NATO as environmental alliance was revived to justify NATO's continued relevance. Thus, the effectiveness or suitability of some conceptions may tend to weaken over time. Nevertheless, having once been enunciated they hold the status of doctrine—however faded—and many conceptions await revival. Changing conceptions have been a key mechanism of alliance unity; and a future in which NATO remains politically cohesive will been one in which conceptions continue to proliferate.

The Future of NATO

Why did NATO not disband at the end of the Cold War? The answer lies partly in the fact that NATO had managed to weather the changing tides of the Cold War, outlive its adversaries, and emerge into the Cold War's aftermath with, if not a clear idea of what it should do in the future, at least a proud record of past achievement. In the immediate aftermath of the Cold War, when there were many doubts about the future viability of the alliance and before its leaders had crafted a new conceptual basis for NATO's transformation, the rationale for NATO's continued existence was based largely on its record. The unprecedented degrees of institutionalized cooperation, consultation, and politico-military integration that formed the core of the alliance's vast network of transnational links were not to be discarded lightly. NATO, then, was a form of insurance that guaranteed a measure of continuing influence and security for its member states—insurance, that is, that could be called on if scenarios like the Gulf War and the Yugoslavian crisis ever were to arise. NATO's longevity into the post-Cold War era can also be accounted for by institutional inertia: organizations created over a period of four decades are not easily dismantled overnight; and the servants of such organizations are naturally to be expected not to surrender without a fight.

But NATO was not a mammoth, lingering in the post-Cold War thaw, awaiting extinction. Indeed, the remarkable conceptual history of the alliance suggests that NATO has been a rather malleable instrument that has meant many things over the years. The alliance adequately served the needs of its members by changing conceptions of its form and function to meet those needs. NATO's demonstrated flexibility helps account for its longevity.[4]

When studying conceptions of NATO and their rhetorical represent-ation it is important to be skeptical about the overblown hyperbole of alliance leaders. Their repeated exhortations to unity and suggestions of community, and the dogmatic emphasis on common values and shared interests, were often simply clichés, masking a more complicated reality. As we have seen, notions of unity were a key feature in efforts to induce conformity; and shared values appeared most important when those values were under assault by the actions or opinions of recalcitrant allies. While skepticism may help us to attain a measure of objectivity, we need not take it too far and be unduly critical. For at the heart of the alliance there were shared values and common interests, even if those values and interests were occasionally manipulated by some members to gain leverage over alliance policy. The things the allies had in common were far stronger than those that threatened to pull them apart. Common values could, in the end, promote common solutions; and NATO continued to exist because it was rightly viewed as a mechanism by which this process could occur.

From its inception NATO was driven by the notion that it was an organic institution, able—indeed obliged—to change to meet the changing require-ments of international political life. As such, the alliance would either live or die; grow or wither away. This powerful biological conception of the animate nature of the alliance continues to shape thinking about the nature and function of NATO. Released from the relative stability of the Cold War competitive environment, the organic alliance is, as it were, out of the laboratory. During the Cold War "growth" was undertaken largely within the clearly defined parameters of the status quo, nuclear stalemate and bipolarity. Today "growth" has become synonymous with the enlargement of the alliance—the addition of new members from the former Soviet sphere of influence. That NATO has been viewed as organic undoubtedly helps account for its longevity—for why let something that you have created die when you can nurture it toward your own ends?—but it may also have fueled the enlargement debate, with potentially catastrophic results.

Most historians will wisely avoid making predictions, but some tentative speculation about the implications of NATO enlargement seems in order here. Substantial risks inhere in the plan to expand NATO to include its former adversaries, while excluding Russia without provoking it. The rationale behind enlargement is based on the idea that NATO membership can help to stabilize the East and promote democracy and market economies by extending the benefits of common defense and integration. The objective is an undivided Europe, with an organic NATO having adapted and expanded to play the lead role in organizing Europe's security. But Moscow's greatest concern is further marginalization, and many Russian leaders openly view NATO expansion with contempt and hostility. Expansion, in Moscow, is considered a form of preemptive containment or encirclement.

With a weak and distracted Russia unable to do more than protest, and with most former adversaries clamoring for admission, NATO seems set on expansion some time after the millennium, perhaps even as early as 1999.[5] The perceived organic nature of NATO, with its underlying credo of "growth or decay" (or, in this case, "go East or go out of business"), has helped underpin a policy that is unnecessary and counterproductive.[6] It is unnecessary because the states of Central and Eastern Europe need, not the Article 5 security guarantee contained in the North Atlantic Treaty and a nuclear umbrella, but social and political and, above all, economic stability. NATO's former adversaries do now require integration with the West and its politico-economic institutions, and particularly the EU, but any lasting integration will be dependent on the maintenance of good relations with the East, namely Russia. Enlargement is counterproductive because it seems to ignore Russian sensitivities.

Opponents of NATO enlargement claim that it is likely to antagonize Moscow, give hope to revanchist nationalists in Russia, endanger the conventional and nuclear arms control treaties that marked the end of the Cold War, create a security vacuum around those states not initially allowed to join (e.g., the Baltic states), and restore Cold War divisions in Europe. In short, expanding NATO may bring about the very conditions that expansion is meant to prevent. In addition, it remains uncertain whether enlargement can solve minority issues and border disputes among or within new members.

The implications of NATO's Cold War history for a changed world are difficult to determine with precision, but one thing seems clear. The conceptual history of the alliance provides its leaders with a broad-based rationale to perpetuate NATO by enlarging it. For example, proponents of enlargement assert that NATO will consolidate pan-European security, much in the same way as it shielded Germany for democratic development during the Cold War. The relationship between domestic political stability and alliance membership is far from certain, but that, evidently, does not detract from the lure of the conception that NATO is a stabilizing force.

At the heart of such conceptions lies the assumption of a threat, that prospective new members need protection from an adversary or enemy, that only membership in a politico-military alliance can ensure their future peace and prosperity. The rationale for an expanded NATO thus rests, in part at least, on an axiomatic belief in the relationship between military defense and political and economic security—a belief, that is, that underwrote the drafting of the North Atlantic Treaty, the creation of NATO, and the perpetuation of the Cold War.

Today presents a new opportunity to address George Kennan's early concerns for a too military orientation in foreign and defense policies. Looking toward the future, it seems possible to conceive a European security system that places less emphasis on military might. Significantly, many of the conceptions explored in this book were generated by concern for NATO's public image within the member states. Should NATO be expanded there would be, as in the past, great pressures to justify its actions and expenditures by turning to its conceptual history and promoting the alliance as a broad-based, multifaceted organization, capable of providing security while promoting change. Allied leaders would increasingly rely on the promise of what NATO can do and what it stands for, rather than what it is against. The process of changing conceptions of NATO will begin again, with fundamental political consequences for our own times.

Notes

Chapter 1: Introduction

1. A revival of the Russian/Soviet threat might restore to NATO the role of a traditional alliance. See Robert Jervis, "The Future of World Politics: Will it Resemble the Past?" *International Security* 16 (Winter 1991-1992): 39-73. See also Otto Pick, "New Roles for Old Alliances?" *World Today* 46 (October 1990): 193-95; and Robert B. McCalla, "NATO's Persistence after the Cold War," *International Organization* 50 (Summer 1996): 445-75.

2. Quincy Wright, *A Study of War* (Chicago: Chicago University Press, 1965), 131; Hans J. Morgenthau, *Politics among Nations* (New York: Knopf, 1967), 175. See also Edwin H. Fedder, "The Concept of Alliances," *International Studies Quarterly* 12 (1986): 65-86.

3. Stephen M. Walt, *The Origins of Alliances* (Ithaca, N.Y.: Cornell University Press, 1987), 5, 21-32. See also Kenneth N. Waltz, *Theory of International Politics* (Reading, Mass.: Addison-Wesley, 1979), 168-69.

4. George Liska, *Nations in Alliance: The Limits of Interdependence* (Baltimore: Johns Hopkins University Press, 1962), 30.

5. Glenn Snyder, "The Security Dilemma in Alliance Politics," *World Politics* 36 (July 1984): 461-95; and Glenn Snyder, "Alliances, Balance, and Stability," *International Organization* 41 (Winter 1991): 121-42.

6. Robert Jervis, "Hypotheses on Misperception," *World Politics* 3 (Summer 1968): 454-79.

7. Francis A. Beer, *Alliances: Latent War Communities in the Contemporary World* (London: Holt, Rinehart, Winston, 1970), 5-6; and Robert E. Osgood, *Alliances and American Foreign Policy* (Baltimore: Johns Hopkins University Press, 1968), 19.

8. Ole Holsti, Terrence Hopmann, and J. D. Sullivan, *Unity and Disintegration in International Alliances: Comparative Studies* (New York: Wiley, 1973); Susan Groennings, E. W. Kelly, and M. Lieserson, eds., *The Study of Coalition Behavior* (New York: Holt, Rinehart, Winston, 1970); Mancur Olson and Richard Zeckhauser, "An Economic Theory of Alliances," *Review of Economics and Statistics* 48 (August 1966): 266-79; R. Harrison Wagner, "The Theory of Games and the Balance of Power," *World Politics* 38 (July 1986): 546-76. For a similar approach with an emphasis on legislative coalitions, see William H. Riker, *The Theory of Political Coalitions* (New Haven: Yale University Press, 1962). For an application of behavioral theory to pre-1939 systems, see Barry Posen, *The Sources of Military Doctrine: France, Britain and Germany between the Wars* (Ithaca, N.Y.: Cornell University Press, 1984). For recent works in the genre of rational choice, see Michael D. McGinnis, "A Rational Model of Regional Rivalry," *International Studies Quarterly* 34 (March 1990): 111-37; and Michael F. Altfeld, "The Decision to Ally: A Theory and Test," *Western Political Quarterly* 37 (December 1984): 523-44.

9. For an interesting discussion about the implications of the end of bipolarity and the end of the Cold War, see Kenneth N. Waltz, "The Emerging Structure of International Politics," *International Security* 18 (Fall 1993): 44-79.

10. Robert E. Osgood, *NATO: The Entangling Alliance* (Chicago: University of Chicago Press, 1962); Timothy P. Ireland, *Creating the Entangling Alliance: The Origins of the North Atlantic Treaty Organization* (Westport, Conn.: Greenwood Press, 1981); J. Robert Schaetzel, *The Unhinged Alliance: America and the European Community* (New York: Harper and Row, 1975); and Lawrence Freedman, ed., *The Troubled Alliance: Atlantic Relations in the 1980s* (New York: St. Martin's Press, 1983).

11. Henry A. Kissinger, *The Troubled Partnership: A Reappraisal of the Atlantic Alliance* (New York: McGraw Hill, 1965); Josef Joffe, *The Limited Partnership: Europe, the United States and the Burdens of Alliance* (Cambridge, Mass.: Ballinger, 1987); Walter F. Hahn and Robert L. Pfaltzgraff, Jr., eds., *Atlantic Community in Crisis: A Redefinition of the Transatlantic Relationship* (Elmsford, N.Y.: Pergamon, 1979); and Joseph Godson, ed., *Transatlantic Crisis: Europe and America in the 1970s* (London: Alcove Press Ltd., 1974).

12. Lawrence S. Kaplan, *NATO and the U.S.: The Enduring Alliance* (Boston: Twayne, 1988); Harlan Cleveland, *NATO: The Transatlantic Bargain* (New York: Harper and Row, 1970); and Stanley R. Sloan, *Toward a New Transatlantic Bargain* (Washington: National Defense University Press, 1985).

13. John Baylis, *The Diplomacy of Pragmatism: Britain and the Formation of*

NATO, 1942-1949 (Kent, Ohio: Kent State University Press, 1993); Don Cook, *Forging the Alliance: NATO, 1945-1950* (London: Seckler and Warburg, 1989); and André de Staercke, ed., *NATO's Anxious Birth: The Prophetic Vision of the 1940s* (London: C. Hurst, 1985).

14. Ireland, *Entangling Alliance.*

15. Baylis, *Diplomacy of Pragmatism.*

16. Sir Nicholas Henderson, *The Birth of NATO* (London: Weidenfeld and Nicolson, 1982); and Lord Ismay, *NATO: The First Five Years* (Paris: NATO Press and Information Division, 1954). Henderson's work, declassified and published in 1982, is the British Foreign Office official history of the North Atlantic Treaty negotiations. Lord Ismay served as NATO's first secretary general from 1952 to 1957.

17. Kissinger, *Troubled Partnership*; Cleveland, *Transatlantic Bargain*; and David M. Abshire, *Preventing World War Three: A Realistic Grand Strategy* (New York: Harper and Row, 1988). See also David P. Calleo, *Beyond American Hegemony: The Future of the Western Alliance* (New York: Basic Books, 1987).

18. John Baylis, *Anglo-American Defence Relations, 1939-1980: The Special Relationship* (London: Macmillan, 1981); Walter Goldstein, ed., *Reagan's Leadership and the Atlantic Alliance: Views from Europe and America* (Washington: Pergamon-Brassey, 1986); Alastair Buchan, *NATO in the 1960s: The Politics of Interdependence* (London: Weidenfeld and Nicolson for the IISS, 1959); Philip H. Gordon, *A Certain Idea of France: French Security Policy and the Gaullist Legacy* (Princeton: Princeton University Press, 1993); James L. Richardson, *Germany and the Atlantic Alliance: The Interaction of Strategy and Politics* (Cambridge, Mass.: Harvard University Press, 1966); and Rudolf Steinke and Michael Vale, *Germany Debates Defense: The Atlantic Alliance at the Crossroads* (Armonck, N.Y.: Armonck Press, 1983). See also F. W. Mulley, *The Politics of Western Defence* (London: Thames and Hudson, 1962).

19. Elizabeth D. Sherwood, *Allies in Crisis: Meeting Global Challenges to Western Security* (New Haven: Yale University Press, 1990); and Douglas Stuart and William Tow, *The Limits of Alliance: NATO Out-of-Area Problems since 1949* (Baltimore: Johns Hopkins University Press, 1990).

20. Jane E. Stromseth, *The Origins of Flexible Response: NATO's Debate over Strategy in the 1960s* (London: Macmillan, 1988); Katherine Kelleher, *Germany and the Politics of Nuclear Weapons* (New York: Cornell University Press, 1975); and Paul Buteux, *The Politics of Nuclear Consultation in NATO* (Cambridge: Cambridge University Press, 1983). See also Carl H. Amme, Jr., *NATO without France: A Strategic Reappraisal* (Stanford: Hoover Institution on War, Revolution, and Peace, 1967).

21. I have drawn heavily here and in what follows on Lynn Boyd Hinds and Theodore Otto Windt, Jr., *The Cold War as Rhetoric: The Beginnings, 1945-1950* (New York: Praeger, 1991). See also Robert Funk, *Language, Hermeneutic, and the Word of God* (New York: Harper and Row, 1966), 4; and Kenneth Burke, *Philosophy of Literary Form* (Baton Rouge, La.: Louisiana State University, 1941), 4.

22. Hinds and Windt, *Cold War as Rhetoric*, xiv.

23. See, for example, Wayne E. Brockriede and Robert L. Scott, *Moments in Rhetoric of the Cold War* (New York: Random House, 1970).

Chapter 2: Creating Western Defense

1. The question of how best to secure the future peace and prosperity of Europe was a central concern of the architects of the international postwar order, and the question of how best to anchor a defeated and divided Germany within the confines of European unity was paramount. A number of issues surrounded the so-called German question. These included whether to seek the continued division of Germany along the lines of the postwar occupation, whether to dismember the country and break it up into smaller states, or whether to seek its unification. This last issue became academic once four-power rule fell apart and the Council of Foreign Ministers became, by 1947, little more than a forum for the continuation of the emerging rivalry between the Western allies and the Soviets. Dismemberment of Germany was considered unwise in light of the experience of the First World War Versailles settlement, which imposed harsh reparations and international oppro-brium on the Germans and was believed to have been a primary impetus behind the rise of Hitler. Thus, the question was not whether to seek a unified Germany—because, at least in the short term, this appeared to be ruled out by Soviet intransigence—but the nature and scope of German participation in the process of reconstituting and ruling Germany and in postwar European unification. Questions about the future of Germany were initially complicated by uncertainty about how the Allies should treat Germany while the occupation continued, whether to regard the Germans as an enemy on parole, as a security problem, or in some other manner. See Anne Deighton, *The Impossible Peace: Britain, The Division of Germany and the Origins of the Cold War* (Oxford: Clarendon, 1993); Robert McGeehan, *The German Rearmament Question* (Urbana: University of Illinois Press, 1971); and Gregory F. Treverton, *America, Germany and the Future of Europe* (Princeton: Princeton University Press, 1992), 65-78.

2. Dean Acheson, *Present at the Creation: My Years in the State Department* (New York: W. W. Norton, 1968), 395.

3. For Marshall's speech, see *Foreign Relations of the United States* [hereafter *FRUS*] 1947, 3:234-36.

4. See John Gimbel, *The Origins of the Marshall Plan* (Stanford: Stanford University Press, 1976); and Michael J. Hogan, *The Marshall Plan: America, Britain, and the Reconstruction of Western Europe, 1947-1952* (Cambridge: Cambridge University Press, 1987). For a view that questions the necessity of the plan, see Allan Millward, "Was the Marshall Plan Really Necessary?" *Diplomatic History* 13 (Spring 1989): 231-53.

5. For the legislative aspects of the Truman Doctrine, see U.S. Senate, *The Legislative Origins of American Foreign Policy* 3, *The Legislative Origins of the Truman Doctrine* (New York: Garland, 1979).

6. See House of Commons, Parliamentary Debates (London: HMSO, 1948) [hereafter *Hansard*], 22 January 1948, col. 397. See also John Baylis, "Britain, the Brussels Pact, and the Continental Commitment," *International Affairs* 60 (August 1984): 615-31.

7. The text can be found in: United Nations, Treaty Series, *Treaties and Other International Agreements Registered or Filed and Reported with the Secretariat of the United Nations*, 19, no. 304 (1948): 51. "Treaty for collaboration in economic, social and cultural matters, and for collective self defense [The Brussels Treaty]," 17 March 1948. For a detailed discussion of Bevin's role in the creation of a Western Union, see Baylis, *Diplomacy of Pragmatism*, 63-75.

8. For Bevin's public warning about the dangers of German revanchism, see *Hansard*, 22 January 1948, col. 408.

9. For an interesting article that questions this view, see Nikolaj Petersen, "Who Pulled Whom and How Much? Britain, the United States and the Making of the North Atlantic Treaty," *Millenium* 11 (Summer 1982): 93-113.

10. Henderson, *Birth of NATO*, ix.

11. See Gimbel, *Origins of the Marshall Plan*, 220-33; Irwin. M. Wall, *The United States and the Reshaping of Postwar France, 1945-1954* (Cambridge: Cambridge University Press, 1991), chapters 2, 3; and Sean Greenwood, "Ernest Bevin, France, and 'Western Union,' August 1945-February 1946," *European History Quarterly* 14 (January 1984): 319-35.

12. *Public Papers of the Presidents: Harry S. Truman, 1945-1953* (Washington, D.C.: Government Printing Office, 1961-66), 147.

13. See Allan Bullock, *Ernest Bevin: Foreign Secretary, 1945-1951* (London: Oxford University Press, 1985), 513-30; John W. Young, *Britain, France, and the Unity of Europe, 1945-1951* (Leicester, England: Leicester University Press, 1984), 79-92; Henderson, *Birth of NATO*, 1-12; and William C. Cromwell, "The Marshall Plan, Britain, and the Cold War," *Review of International Studies* 8 (October 1982): 233-51.

14. The debate within U.S. policymaking circles about the need for a treaty can be followed in John Lewis Gaddis, *The Long Peace: Inquiries into the History of the Cold War* (London: Oxford University Press, 1987), 48-71. See also Olav Riste, ed., *The Formative Years: European and Atlantic Defense, 1947–1953* (New York: Columbia University Press, 1985), 60-91.

15. An excellent primary source guide to what follows in this section is U.S. Senate. *The Legislative Origins of American Foreign Policy* 6, *The Vandenburg Resolution and the North Atlantic Treaty* (New York: Garland, 1979).

16. A good source for Vandenburg's thinking about European security during this period is Arthur H. Vandenburg, Jr., ed., *The Private Papers of Senator Arthur H. Vandenburg* (London: Gollancz, 1953).

17. For two excellent works on Kennan's tenure on the PPS, see Wilson D. Miscamble, *George F. Kennan and the Making of American Foreign Policy, 1947-1950* (Princeton: Princeton University Press, 1992); and David Mayers, *George Kennan and the Dilemmas of U.S. Foreign Policy* (New York: Oxford University Press, 1989).

18. George F. Kennan, *Memoirs, 1925-1950* (Boston: Little, Brown, 1975), 1: 308.

19. An excellent guide to official American attitudes toward the future of Europe in the immediate postwar era is John L. Harper, *American Visions of Europe: Franklin D. Roosevelt, George F. Kennan, and Dean G. Acheson* (Cambridge: Cambridge University Press, 1994).

20. For Kennan and containment, see X [George F. Kennan], "The Sources of Soviet Conduct," *Foreign Affairs* 25 (July 1947): 566-82; Lloyd C. Gardner, *Architects of Illusion: Men and Ideas in American Foreign Policy, 1941-1949* (Chicago: Quadrangle, 1970), 270-300; and Gaddis, *Strategies of Containment*, 25-53.

21. *FRUS* 1948, 3:283-88.

22. Kennan also had practical reasons for opposing a treaty: he had little faith in the value of written treaties, which had often been ignored, distorted, or forgotten in times of crisis. What was required was a clear definition of interests: military policy should follow political necessity; legal undertakings were likely to be distracting and superfluous. Kennan's views were not widely shared by his State Department colleagues, by the executive branch, or by the European elite. Nicholas Henderson reports that he viewed Kennan's ideas as "heresy." See Kennan, *Memoirs*, 1:407-8. For Henderson's views, see Henderson, *Birth of NATO*, 9.

23. See Baylis, *Diplomacy of Pragmatism*, 75.

24. *FRUS* 1948, 3:46-48.

25. *FRUS* 1948, 3:47.

26. *FRUS* 1948, 3:47.

27. Henderson, *Birth of NATO*, 40. The U.S. history is best followed in the *FRUS* series (1948-1949, various vols.) and in Kennan's *Memoirs*. An excellent synthesis of primary source material pertaining to the Washington Talks is Ireland, *Entangling Alliance*. See also Carl Weibes and Burt Zeeman, "The Pentagon Negotiations, March 1948: The Launching of the North Atlantic Treaty," *International Affairs* 59 (Summer 1983): 351-63; and Escott Reid, *Time of Fear and Hope: The Making of the North Atlantic Treaty, 1947-1949* (Toronto, Ontario: McCelland and Stewart, 1977).

28. Henderson, *Birth of NATO*, viii. Henderson's view was typical of Western political elites, who repeatedly complained that theirs was but a reaction to Soviet actions. Although the documentary literature of the period is filled with expressions of anxiety over Soviet intentions, there were few, if any, initiatives that were not justified as necessary—or even essential—responses to Soviet aggression or intransigence.

29. See Ireland, *Entangling Alliance*, 80-113; and Baylis, *Diplomacy of Pragmatism*, 98-106.

30. The evolution of American thinking on the issue of how to restrain Germany by integrating it into the Western alliance and the European community is admirably dealt with in Jeffrey M. Diefendorf, Axel Frohn, and Herman-Joseph Rupieper, eds., *American Policy and the Reconstruction of West Germany, 1945-1955* (Cambridge: Cambridge University Press, 1994).

31. See John L. Harper, *America and the Reconstruction of Italy, 1945-1948* (Cambridge: Cambridge University Press, 1986), 124-28.

32. Acheson, *Present at the Creation*, 279. See also George F. Kennan, *Memoirs, 1950-1963* (Boston: Little, Brown, 1967), 2:417; and Henderson, *Birth of NATO*, 68-72.

33. Ireland, *Entangling Alliance*, 109.

34. Henderson, *Birth of NATO*, 37.

35. Henderson, *Birth of NATO*, 68.

36. As we have seen, France was successful in its efforts to include the Algerian departments in the treaty. The clauses referring to the Algerian departments were declared inapplicable in January 1963, when the NAC was informed by the French representative that France had recognized Algerian independence.

37. This area included Turkey, even though it was not an original signatory to the treaty.

38. Ireland, *Entangling Alliance*, 161-62. The British and the Americans, however, continued to engage in bilateral postwar defense planning. See Baylis, *Anglo-American Defense Relations*, 28-33.

39. Henderson, *Birth of NATO*, 101. The preamble reads as follows:

> The Parties to this Treaty reaffirm their faith in the purposes and principles of the Charter of the United Nations and their desire to live in peace with all peoples and all governments.
>
> They are determined to safeguard the freedom, common heritage and civilization of their peoples, founded on the principles of democracy, individual liberty and the rule of law.
>
> They seek to promote stability and well-being in the North Atlantic area.
>
> They are resolved to unite their efforts for collective defense and for the preservation of peace and security.
>
> They therefore agree to this North Atlantic Treaty. (Text of the North Atlantic Treaty, signed in Washington on 4 April 1949.)

40. Kennan, *Memoirs*, 2:335-36. Though he made no concessions to the effects such actions may have had on the Soviets, Acheson made a similar confession about the process of simplification that had been deemed necessary to communicate the urgency of the Soviet threat to the public. "The problems which concern us in the relations between the free nations are so manifold, so complex, and so difficult that we all have a natural tendency to oversimplify." See Secretary Acheson's remarks to the Canadian Club, Ottawa, reprinted in the *Department of State Bulletin* [hereafter *DOSB*] (1 December 1952): 848.

41. An excellent guide to this process as it occurred in the United States is Richard M. Freeland, *The Truman Doctrine and the Origins of McCarthyism: Foreign Policy, Domestic Politics and Internal Security, 1946-1948* (New York: New York University Press, 1985). See also Robert S. Griffith, *The Politics of Fear: Joseph R. McCarthy and the Senate* (Lexington: University of Kentucky Press, 1970); and Melvyn P. Leffler, *A Preponderance of Power: National Security, the Truman Administration, and the Cold War* (Stanford: Stanford University Press, 1993), 100.

42. See Robert Jervis, *Perception and Misperception in International Politics* (Princeton, N.J.: Princeton University Press, 1976), 383-406.

43. In his memoirs, Acheson wrote that the treaty was released "for public

discussion before final acceptance of it by governments (*but, in reality, to force it*)." Emphasis added. Of the release, Acheson observed in retrospect: "Never before has a debutante been presented with more fanfare, appearing simultaneously in twelve capitals." Acheson, *Present at the Creation*, 282.

44. See Dean Acheson, "The North Atlantic Pact: Collective Defense and the Preservation of Peace, Security and Freedom in the North Atlantic Community," transcript of radio address, *DOSB* (27 March 1949): 384.

45. See Acheson, "The North Atlantic Pact," 384. See also Truman's inaugural address of January 1949, *DOSB* (23 January 1949): 124.

46. *DOSB* (20 March 1949): 347.

47. *DOSB* (20 March 1949): 348.

48. *DOSB* (20 March 1949): 348.

49. Dean Acheson, "The Meaning of the North Atlantic Pact," *DOSB* (27 March 1949): 384.

50. Acheson, "The Meaning of the North Atlantic Pact," 385.

51. Acheson, "The Meaning of the North Atlantic Pact," 388. On the following day, Truman sent Acheson a telegram congratulating him on his address. Truman called it "clear, lucid and forceful" and "an admirable expression" of the principles and objectives of the North Atlantic Treaty. Truman telegram to Acheson, *DOSB* (27 March 1949): 388.

52. See *Hansard*, 18 March 1949, cols. 2533-36. According to Henderson, Bevin's case for an Atlantic pact "largely rested on its psychological value to the North Atlantic community." Henderson, *Birth of NATO*, 29.

53. The United States and United Kingdom had already unified their two zones, creating Bizonia in 1946. This move has been viewed as the first conscious step toward the Cold War division of the continent. See Anne Deighton, "The 'Frozen Front:' The Labour Government, the Division of Germany and the Origins of the Cold War, 1945-1947," *International Affairs* 63 (Summer 1987): 449-65. The bilateral negotiations on Bizonia are in *FRUS* 1946, 5:589-659.

54. The roots of Anglo-American accord on conceptions of security are explored in Henry B. Ryan, *The Vision of Anglo-America: The United States-United Kingdom Alliance and the Emerging Cold War, 1943-1946* (Cambridge: Cambridge University Press, 1987).

55. Bullock, *Bevin*, 513.

56. For two early formulations of this goal, see "Minute from Sir G. Jebb to Sir W. Strang," 10 March 1950; and "Brief for the U.K. Delegation," 24 April 1950, in *Documents on British Policy Overseas* 2, Roger Bullen and M. E. Pelly, eds. (London: HMSO, 1986-1987), 18-20, 95-106.

57. Truman, however, attended the signing ceremony. Acheson later reported that as the participants waited for the ceremony to begin, the Marine Corps band "added a note of unexpected realism" by playing two songs from the popular musical *Porgy and Bess:* "I've got plenty of nothin" and "It ain't necessarily so." Acheson, *Present at the Creation*, 284.

58. Remarks made at the signing ceremony of the North Atlantic Treaty, *DOSB*

(17 April 1949): 475.

59. The pricipal congressional publications are: U.S. Congress, Senate, *Executive Sessions of the Senate Foreign Relations Committee* 2 (81st Cong., 1st and 2d sess., 1949-1950) *Historical Series,* 1976; U.S. Congress, Senate, *The North Atlantic Treaty. Hearings before the Committee on Foreign Relations* (81st Cong., 1st sess., 1949, 3 parts).

60. Acheson testimony to Senate Committee on Foreign Relations, Executive Report no. 8 (81st Cong., 1st sess., 6 June 1949): 286-308.

61. Acheson testimony to Senate Committee on Foreign Relations, 288.

62. Acheson testimony to Senate Committee on Foreign Relations, 308.

63. See Leffler, *Preponderance of Power*, 345-46.

64. Acheson testimony to Senate Committee on Foreign Relation in U.S. Senate. *Reviews of World Situation: 1949-1950. Historical Series* (81st Cong., 1st and 2d sess., 1974), 304.

65. *Congressional Record* (5 July 1949): 8984.

66. See, for example, Catherine M. Kelleher, "America looks at Europe," in *Troubled Alliance,* Lawrence Freedman, ed., 44-66.

67. *Congressional Record* (5 July 1949): 8984. The concept of a Monroe Doctrine for Europe did not die with the ratification of the treaty. As late as February 1952, Acheson apparently told Eden that the United States had been considering "a new Monroe Doctrine for Europe" in the form of a promise that if one European state threatened the peace, then the United States would come to the aid of the others. This idea ultimately took the form pledges of American support for the European Defense Community (EDC). See Anthony Eden, *Full Circle: The Memoirs of Anthony Eden* (London: Cassel, 1960), 40. See also the section on the EDC later in this chapter.

68. George F. Kennan, "Disengagement Revisited," *Foreign Affairs* 37 (January 1959): 206-7. See also George F. Kennan, *Russia, the Atom Bomb, and the West— The BBC Reith Lectures, 1957* (London: Oxford University Press, 1958), 94-95.

69. Kennan's views were not shared by many of his State Department colleagues, including Secretary of State Dean Acheson and his successor John Foster Dulles, or by Presidents Truman and Eisenhower. Whereas Kennan hoped for the eventual emergence of a broad and united European community, these two successive administrations dismissed what was, in their view, a nebulous concept of European unity. They looked instead to the creation of a strong Atlantic community with the United States tied to Europe and with Germany, as continental Europe's potentially greatest power, tied to its neighbors through military, political, and economic institutions. Despite the defeat of the EDC in 1954, which dealt a blow to American conceptions of European unity, NATO was viewed by its leaders as the center of this seamless web. A strong NATO would safeguard the development of other international institutions by ensuring the defense of the West.

70. *Congressional Record* (6 July 1949): 9065.

71. *Congressional Record* (6 July 1949): 9065.

72. For an outstanding study of the Korean War, see Bruce Cummings, *The*

Origins of the Korean War, 2 vols. (Princeton: Princeton University Press, 1990).

73. See Walter La Faber, "NATO and the Korean War: A Context," *Diplomatic History* 13 (Fall 1989): 461-78.

74. For an account of changes in Western defense preparations immediately after Korea, see Leffler, *Preponderance of Power,* 371-74.

75. Ministerial meetings of the NAC are normally attended by the foreign ministers. On occasion they have also been attended by defense and/or finance ministers.

76. For further discussion of the integration of NATO-designated forces, see Francis A. Beer, *Integration and Disintegration in NATO: Processes of Alliance Cohesion and Prospects for Atlantic Community* (New York: Columbia University Press, 1969), 47-58.

77. Acheson, *Present at the Creation,* 352.

78. Transcript of Radio Address by Secretary Acheson over the Canadian Broadcasting Corporation network, *DOSB* (1 October 1951): 526-28.

79. *DOSB* (1 October 1951): 527.

80. For an explicit critique of what Kennan called "military fixations," see Kennan, *Russia, The Atom Bomb, and the West,* 94-95.

81. Kennan believed that the emphasis on the military power of the alliance was disastrous, because it risked perpetuating the division of the continent and alienating the Soviets by confirming their suspicions about aggressive encirclement by the West. See Kennan, *Memoirs,* 1:407-9, 464; and 2:348.

82. See Leffler, *Preponderance of Power,* especially chapters 2, 3.

83. Acheson address to Congress, *DOSB* (12 June 1950): 931-37.

84. *DOSB* (12 June 1950): 932.

85. Transcript of Acheson press conference, *DOSB* (22 December 1950): 528.

86. Transcript of Acheson press conference, *DOSB* (22 December 1950): 528. Some commentators argued that, because the Atlantic community was defined by common culture and common interests, it could include Australia, South Africa, and New Zealand. See B. K. Sandwell, "North Atlantic—Community or Treaty," *International Journal* 8 (Summer 1952): 162-72; and Sir Percy Spender, "NATO and Pacific Security" in *The National Interest—Alone or with Others,* Norman D. Palmer, ed. (The Annals of the American Association of Political and Social Science, 1952): 115.

87. *DOSB* (1 October 1951): 527. Eden expressed a similar view, claiming that "the Atlantic association ... is the expression of the [Western democratic] cause." Eden, *Full Circle,* 36.

88. F. H. Hinsley, *Power and the Pursuit of Peace: Theory and Practice in the History of Relations between States* (Cambridge: Cambridge University Press, 1963).

89. See Canada, House of Commons Debates, 1948:4 (Ottawa: Edmond Cloutier, 1948), 3449.

90. NAC final communiqué, Lisbon, 20-25 February 1952, para. 1. The Lisbon summit has been widely regarded as a watershed in the development of NATO. The summit finalized the accession of Greece and Turkey to the treaty, and its final

communiqué called for "reciprocal security undertakings" between the members of the proposed EDC and NATO. The NAC also announced the acceptance of minimum force goals for the alliance, set at 50 divisions, 4,000 aircraft, and unspecified naval improvements.

91. Acheson comments made at the opening of the ninth NAC session at Lisbon, 20 February 1952, *DOSB* (10 March 1952): 370-71. Emphasis in original.

92. Harriman address on the third anniversary of the signing of the North Atlantic Treaty, *DOSB* (14 April 1952): 570-72.

93. *DOSB* (14 April 1952): 571.

94. *DOSB* (14 April 1952): 570-71. See also Charles Bohlen, "Creating Situations of Strength," address at Colgate University, *DOSB* (4 August 1952): 167.

95. *DOSB* (14 April 1952): 572. Not everyone took this view. Walter Lippman, for example, wrote that NATO was primarily a military community "and little more." See Walter Lippman, *Isolation and Alliances: An American Speaks to the British* (Boston: Little, Brown, 1952), 43-44.

96. See Dean Acheson, "Chief Imperatives Bearing upon the Atlantic Coalition," address before the Canadian Club, Ottawa, *DOSB* (1 December 1952): 848-49.

97. See Theodore Draper, "Problems Facing the North Atlantic Community," address to the Atlantic Council Conference at Oxford University, *DOSB* (22 September 1952): 438.

98. Draper, "Problems Facing the North Atlantic Community," 439. See also "U.S. Information Programs at Home and Abroad," *DOSB* (22 December 1952): 971-79.

99. Ismay, *NATO*, 153-55. By 1954 NATO's information program included tours to NATO and Supreme Headquarters, Allied Powers Europe (SHAPE) for journalists, students and politicians, a large mobile exhibition called the "NATO Caravan of Peace" (its one-millionth visitor was a French plumber), films entitled *The Atlantic Community: Know Your Allies*, and the SHAPE film *Alliance for Peace*. At the end of 1953, NATO began publication of the *Information Letter* (later *NATO Review*) and *The NATO Handbook*. Ismay, *NATO*, 143.

100. A protocol attached to the treaty stipulated that an attack on any member of the EDC would be regarded as an attack on a member of NATO, which would activate Article 5 of the North Atlantic Treaty. The EDC Treaty also contained contractual agreements, which would come into effect after the treaty had been ratified, ending the occupation of Germany and granting it sovereignty. The text of the EDC Treaty and its supplementary protocols can be found in *American Foreign Policy: Basic Documents* (Washington, D.C.: Department of State, 1957), 1:1107-96. For a detailed account of the EDC, see Edward Fursdon, *The European Defense Community: A History* (New York: St. Martin's, 1979).

101. Excerpts from Pleven's proposal are in Jean Monnet, *Memoirs*, trans. Richard Mayne (Garden City, N.Y.: Doubleday, 1978), 347; see also Fursdon, *European Defense Community*, 86-91.

102. NAC final communiqué, Lisbon, para 6. For Acheson's comments, see

DOSB (10 March 1952): 365.

103. Quoted in Konrad Adenauer, *Memoirs: 1945-1953* (London: Weidenfeld and Nicolson, 1966), 348-49.

104. *DOSB* (5 January 1953): 7.

105. Dean Acheson, "The Nature of the Atlantic Pact," farewell press conference, *DOSB* (26 January 1953): 131.

106. Acheson, "The Nature of the Atlantic Pact," 131. Both Eden and Adenauer practiced their own brands of determinism about the consequences of a failure to establish unity in Europe: "French negative policy [over German entry into Western defense] would result in driving Germany into the arms of Russia and the U.S. into 'fortress America.'" Eden, *Full Circle*, 160. Adenauer said that without a German contribution to Western defense, Germany would have no sovereignty, no unity, and "it is probable that all of Europe would come under Soviet influence." Adenauer, *Memoirs*, 325-26.

107. Note the contradictory nature of Acheson's corollary to this notion (i.e., that weakness repels strength). The attraction of strength was meant to apply only to the internal workings of the alliance: a "weak" NATO would repel potential allies, but when dealing with the Soviets, a "weak" NATO would "attract" Soviet aggression.

108. Not everyone, however, subscribed to this view. Some commentators viewed NATO as a threat to world federation under the UN and feared that NATO might drive some members of the UN into the Soviet orbit and create the war it sought to forestall. See James Warburg, *Faith, Purpose, and Power: A Plea for a Positive Policy* (New York: Harper, Row, 1950), 108-13, 128-31. Those who opposed this view argued that the UN was dead and that NATO would serve as an instrument for the creation of a base of democracies that would ultimately form a world government. See, for example, Owen J. Roberts, "Atlantic Union Now," *Foreign Policy Bulletin* (7 April 1951): 3-14.

109. The war in Korea had generated a rapid buildup in the strength of the West and in the development of NATO, including the agreement in principle for a West German contribution, an integrated defense under unified command, and the office of a supreme commander. In the first months of the war, Acheson declared that "the period of greatest danger is directly before us. Our defense must not only be strong enough, it must come soon enough." *DOSB* (18 December 1950): 965. The end of the Korean War, the death of Stalin, and the ensuing Soviet "peace offensive" relieved East-West tensions and fostered hopes in the power of diplomacy further to ease tensions. It was in this period that NATO began to be regarded by its leadership as the essential forum for East-West diplomatic relations. For a contemporary account of the "long-haul" concept, see Drew Middleton, "NATO Changes Direction," *Foreign Affairs* 33 (April 1953): 427-44.

110. John Foster Dulles, "A Report on the North Atlantic Treaty Organization," address to the National Press Club, *DOSB* (4 January 1954): 3-7. Dulles also told the Press Club that NATO "comes closer to anything yet to being an effective international police force. It is vital to the defense of freedom." Dulles, "A Report

on the North Atlantic Treaty Organization," 3.

111. Dulles, "A Report on the North Atlantic Treaty Organization," 4.

112. This notion was also referred to as "more bang for the buck." In an address to Congress, Eisenhower declared that the new policies would entail a "shift in emphasis and the dependence upon new types of defensive and offensive mechanisms. The present policies will gradually involve the use of atomic weapons as conventional weapons for tactical purposes." Eisenhower address to Congress, 7 January 1954 (H. doc. 251, 83d Cong., 2d sess.). The evolution of NATO's nuclear strategy is more fully examined in chapter 3.

113. See John Foster Dulles, "A Report to the Nation on European Unity," *DOSB* (23 February 1953): 288. About the EDC, Dulles later stated that "there is no other good solution of the problem of establishing adequate strength and peace in Europe." The EDC was central to the search for "more security for less money." See John Foster Dulles, "Results of the NAC's 11th Meeting," *DOSB* (11 May 1953): 672.

114. Concepts like the EDC and the "long haul," declared Dulles, give "greater defensive strength for the same amount of expenditure in manpower, matériel, and money." *DOSB* (27 April 1953): 628.

115. *FRUS* 1952-1954, 5:1560-61. Since 1946, the French had been receiving massive U.S. financial and military support for the war in Indochina. The NAC had also, in December 1952, publicly declared its support for French efforts, stating that "the resistance of the free nations in South East Asia as in Korea is in fullest harmony with the aims and ideals of the Atlantic Community." See "Resolution on Indochina," North Atlantic Council meeting in ministerial session in Paris, 15-18 December 1952. For an account of France's struggle to secure NATO approval for the war in Indochina, see Sherwood, *Allies in Crisis*, 40-57.

116. See George C. Herring, *America's Longest War: The United States in Vietnam, 1950-1975* (New York: 1985), 23.

117. I have drawn heavily here and in what follows from Daniel Lerner and Raymond Aron, eds., *France Defeats EDC* (London: Thames and Hudson, 1957), 2-23; and Alfred Grosser, *The Western Alliance: European-American Relations Since 1945* (London: Macmillan, 1980), 119-28.

118. Dulles called the defeat "a grave event." Dulles to embassy in France, 30 August 1954, *FRUS* 1952-1954, 5:1114.

119. Dulles to NATO Foreign Ministers' Conference, 14 December 1953, *FRUS* 1952-1954, 5:463. He also made the threat in public. See his speech to the National Press Club (above). Eden and Churchill also warned the French, though in private, of the "grave dangers which France and the whole Western world could incur" if France rejected the EDC. See Eden, *Full Circle*, 148.

120. Lerner and Aron, *France Defeats EDC*, 216.

121. Eisenhower described alternatives to the EDC in December 1953 as "feeble," while the idea of rearming Germany as a member of NATO was described by Dulles as "simply said, but hardly done." *DOSB* (4 January 1954): 7. Dulles complained publicly that the so-called NATO solution asked too much in the form

of an amendment to the North Atlantic Treaty and the required fourteen-nation agreement. He also claimed that it would not promote the goal of "organic unity" in Western Europe. *DOSB* (4 January 1954): 5. See also David Clay Large, "Grand Illusions: The United States, the Federal Republic of Germany and the EDC, 1950-1954," in *American Policy and the Reconstruction of West Germany*, Jeffey M. Diefendorf, Axel Frohn, and Herman-Joseph Rupieper, eds., 375-94.

122. The phrase "NATO solution" was Churchill's. See Churchill to Dulles, 14 August 1954, *FRUS* 1952-1954, 5:1037. British Foreign Secretary Anthony Eden was instrumental in creating an acceptable alternative to the EDC. See Eden, *Full Circle*, 146-74. His role is more fully explored in Rolf Steininger, "John Foster Dulles, the European Defense Community, and the German Question" in *John Foster Dulles and the Diplomacy of the Cold War*, Richard H. Immerman, ed. (Princeton: Princeton University Press, 1990), 79-108. An extended treatment of British policy toward West Germany during this period can be found in Saki Dockrill, *Britain's Policy for West German Rearmament 1950-1955* (Cambridge: Cambridge University Press, 1991).

123. Lerner and Aron, *France Defeats EDC*, 215.

124. The concept of national self-sufficiency was declared to be obsolete because of the odious existence of atomic weapons. Paul Henri Spaak, the Belgian prime minister and later secretary general of NATO, succinctly characterized this view when he wrote: "The atom bomb leaves us no room for neutrality or separate national policies." See Paul-Henri Spaak, "The Atom Bomb and NATO," *Foreign Affairs* 33 (April 1955): 359. For an American view, see Bernard Brodie, "The Atom Bomb as Policymaker," *Foreign Affairs* 27 (October 1948): 17-33. The academic work that explores most compellingly the demise of national self-sufficiency owing to nuclear weapons is John H. Herz, *International Politics in the Atomic Age* (New York: Columbia University Press, 1959).

125. Text of London Communiqué, 17 September 1954, *DOSB* (27 September 1954): 434.

126. "Agreement on the Restoration of German Sovereignty and German Association with Western Defense System. Final Act of the Nine-Power Conference Held at London, 28 September–3 October 1954," *DOSB* (11 October 1954): 515-28.

127. The size and general characteristics of Germany's defense contribution would "conform to the contribution fixed for the EDC." The Germans undertook not to manufacture chemical, biological, or nuclear weapons, and agreed not to build bombers, large naval vessels, or guided missiles. The WEU set maximum defense contributions of all its members, whereas at Lisbon in 1952 NATO had set minimum force levels. The United Kingdom agreed to maintain four divisions and a tactical air force on the continent. Regarding NATO, it was agreed that all forces stationed on the continent would be placed under the authority of SACEUR. See *DOSB* (11 October 1954): 520.

128. This ploy had its origins in an earlier move to soften French resistance to the EDC. It was Eden's idea to "emphasize that the Atlantic community was going

to last and that the EDC was simply a closer union within the wider grouping." Eden, *Full Circle*, 36.

129. For the Paris Agreements, see Cmd. 9304, *Documents agreed by the Conference of Ministers held in Paris*, 20-23 October 1954 (London: HMSO, 1954).

130. Konrad Adenauer, "Germany, the New Partner," *Foreign Affairs* 33 (January 1955): 179. Like many of his allies, Adenauer held similar views about the North Atlantic Treaty, which he described as being "not a purely military document" but one designed to further higher ends. Adenauer, *Memoirs*, 345.

131. Statement by Secretary Dulles on the sixth anniversary of NATO, *DOSB* (25 April 1955): 685.

132. "Protocols on German Occupation and Accession to NATO," transmitted to Senate, 15 November 1954. Presidential message of transmittal (S. Exec. L and M, 83d Cong., 2d sess.).

133. For further discussion see the essays in Riste, *The Formative Years*. Portions of this section are also drawn from the essays in Freedman, *Troubled Alliance*.

134. The concept of a United States of Europe had great appeal in the United States. Eden reports that Dulles at first rejected his idea for a NATO solution because it lacked supranational features. The zealous efforts to justify the EDC to the American public by two successive administrations appear to have returned to haunt them: Dulles told Eden that "it was really immaterial whether a NATO plus Brussels solution was better or worse than EDC. Congress had been 'sold' on the latter as the means of uniting Europe, which would then be capable of standing on its own feet without American help." Eden, *Full Circle*, 163.

135. Eden shared this view. See Eden, *Full Circle*, 32-33.

136. Calleo, *Beyond American Hegemony*, 28-31. Calleo argues that the United States, in assuming NATO leadership, established a hierarchy in NATO and a global *Pax Americana* with NATO as its centerpiece.

137. See Kennan, *Memoirs*, 1:454-55. Eden claimed that one of the appealing features of his plan to expand the Brussels Treaty was that it could be used "as a political instrument to keep alive the idea of European unity." Eden, *Full Circle*, 163.

138. One of these was the American tactic of threatening France publicly over the EDC, whereas the British did so in private. Former Prime Minister Clement Attlee summed up these differences well when he wrote that Americans tend to see things in black and white, "where we see shades of gray." Clement R. Attlee, "Britain and America: Common Aims, Different Opinions," *Foreign Affairs* 32 (January 1954): 190-202.

139. Eden, *Full Circle*, 166.

140. British leaders liked to apply the axiom of inseparable security linkage to the Empire. Eden claimed that the security of each of the members of the Commonwealth was tied to that of the others. See Anthony Eden, "Britain in World Strategy," *Foreign Affairs* 29 (April 1951): 341-50. For the importance of NATO to Britain's global strategy, see Martin Kingsley, "NATO—A British View," *International Journal* 6 (Autumn 1951): 292-99.

141. Eden drew attention to the "supreme importance of Anglo-American unity. This is no longer an idealistic conception of small groups but a practical policy of governments." Eden, "Britain in World Strategy," 348. The immediate practical benefits included the 1954 amendment of the Atomic Energy Act, also known as the McMahon Act, which had prohibited U.S. nuclear sharing. It was amended to allow Anglo-American collaboration, as well as limited information disclosures to NATO commanders about U.S. tactical nuclear weaponry in Europe. Enthusiasm over the strength of the special relationship, however, may have led to British miscalculation about possible American reactions to the invasion of Suez in 1956. See chapter 3.

142. See Adenauer, *Memoirs*, 192-232, 400-427.

143. See John H. Herz, "German Officialdom Revisited: Political Views and Attitudes of the West German Civil Service," *World Politics* 7 (October 1954): 63-83. The reconstruction of Western Europe was possible only through acts of cooperation and unity that would change economic conditions there and also "all the thinking and political feeling of European man as well." Adenauer, *Memoirs*, 329, 331.

144. See Walter Hallstein, "Germany's Dual Aim: Unity and Integration," *Foreign Affairs* 31 (April 1953): 58-69; Konrad Adenauer, "Germany and the Problem of Our Times," *International Affairs* 28 (April 1952): 156-61; and Konrad Adenauer, "Germany and Europe," *Foreign Affairs* 31 (April 1953): 361-66.

145. Quoted in Steininger, "European Defense Community," 107. These sentiments were also expressed in a joint statement issued with Eisenhower, following the completion of the Paris Agreements. NATO membership and German sovereignty, declared the two leaders, "will aid our efforts to bring freedom and unity to all the German people." Statement by the president and the German chancellor, *DOSB* (8 November 1954): 681.

146. Adenauer, *Memoirs*, 326.

Chapter 3: Managing Western Defense

1. In May 1955, when the Soviet government agreed to sign a peace treaty with Austria, many in the West detected a new Soviet approach to international relations, and the ensuing thaw in East-West tensions paved the way for a July summit meeting in Geneva. Eisenhower met with Soviet leaders at Geneva in 1955 and Camp David in 1959. The planned 1960 meeting in Paris was aborted due to the fall out from the U-2 affair. Foreign ministers' meetings were held at Berlin in 1954, Vienna, and, on two occasions, at Geneva in 1955, and yet again at Geneva in 1959.

2. See, for example, General J. Lawton Collins, "NATO: Still A Vital Force for Peace," *Foreign Affairs* 34 (April 1956): 367-79.

3. One senior U.S. official testified to Congress that "it is not a coincidence that the radical transformation of Soviet tactics which paved the way for the two Geneva conferences began concurrently with the ratification of the Paris Agreements,

thus affording a striking demonstration of the validity of our policies." See the testimony of C. Burke Elbrick, deputy assistant secretary of state for European affairs, before the House Committee on Foreign Affairs, 27 March 1956, excerpted as "The Mutual Security Program for Europe," *DOSB* (28 April 1956): 676.

4. See Lester B. Pearson, "After Geneva: A Greater Task for NATO," *Foreign Affairs* 34 (October 1955): 14-23.

5. See General Alfred M. Gruenther, SACEUR, "NATO—Our Greatest Instrument for Peace," address made at the congressional dinner of the VOFW, Washington, D.C., 7 February 1956 (Department of Defense Press Release 74). See also *DOSB* (27 February 1956): 334. President Eisenhower soon made a similar appeal, declaring that "NATO symbolizes the unity of free men in an age of peril." *DOSB* (5 March 1956): 378.

6. They tended to view it through the prism of their own efforts to wage the Cold War. Dulles termed the shift from force to economic and political blandishment as the Soviet "New Look." See *DOSB* (28 March 1956): 550.

7. See J. Samuel Walker, "'No More Cold War': American Foreign Policy and the 1948 Soviet Peace Offensive," *Diplomatic History* 5 (Winter 1981): 75-91.

8. *DOSB* (28 March 1956): 550. See also the remarks made by Under Secretary Herbert Hoover before the House Committee on Foreign Affairs on 20 March 1956 (White House Press Release 150).

9. Of the Soviets, Gruenther declared: "As propaganda experts they are masters. We are far behind them in getting our story told. Our effort is very small; theirs is a massive one, cleverly put over, and it does produce results." *DOSB* (27 February 1956): 335.

10. George Murphy, deputy under secretary of state, "The Foundations of the North Atlantic Treaty Organization," *DOSB* (16 April 1956): 654.

11. See *DOSB* (23 April 1956): 677. Adenauer later put forth a similar justification for the continued relevance of NATO. See Konrad Adenauer, "The German Problem, A World Problem," *Foreign Affairs* 41 (October 1962): 61.

12. NATO was later compared to a club, where "you have got to pay your subscription in full." Sir John Slessor, "Nuclear Power and Britain's Defense," *Survival* 4 (November/December 1962): 253. After the French withdrawal from NATO's Integrated Military Organization in March 1966, former U.S. Secretary of State Dean Acheson described NATO as a fire department. See Dean Acheson, "One of Our Firemen is Resigning," *Atlantic Community Quarterly* 4 (Summer 1966): 160-65.

13. There were, however, states within the alliance that benefited from NATO without ever paying their premiums in full, and hence received a free ride. France was the classic "free rider": NATO could not fail to defend Germany, and therefore, because of France's location, had to defend France as well. The notion is derived from public goods theory, notably from an article by Mancur Olson and Richard Zeckhauser. See Olsen and Zeckhauser, "An Economic Theory of Alliances," 266-79.

14. *DOSB* (23 April 1956): 677.

15. Dwight D. Eisenhower, "Our Quest for Peace and Freedom," White House

Press Release, 26 April 1956. See also *DOSB* (30 April 1956): 704.

16. John Foster Dulles, "Developing NATO in Peace," address at the annual luncheon of the Associated Press at New York City, 23 April 1956, *DOSB* (30 April 1956): 708. Despite Dulles's apparent nostalgia for the adhesive effects of an imminent Soviet threat, he may have changed his ideas on the value of fear by this time. His earlier "agonizing reappraisal," directed toward the French over their reluctance to embrace the EDC, had failed as a device to establish U.S. hegemony within the alliance. On this point see Brian R. Duchin, "The 'Agonizing Reappraisal': Eisenhower, Dulles, and the European Defense Community," *Diplomatic History* 16 (Spring 1992): 201-21.

17. Dulles, "Developing NATO in Peace," 708. Emphasis in original. See also Pearson, "After Geneva: New Tasks for NATO," 18.

18. Dulles, "Developing NATO in Peace," 708.

19. Transcript of Dulles Press Conference, *DOSB* (7 May 1956): 747. Anthony Eden, now Lord Avon, also viewed NATO as organic. "An alliance can only mature or decay. The essential thing is to give NATO the body it lacks today, and some revival of its authority is the only way." Anthony Eden, "The Slender Margin of Safety," *Foreign Affairs* 39 (October 1960): 172.

20. *DOSB* (7 May 1956): 748-49.

21. Before the meeting Dulles declared that "this will be an important meeting because I think it is generally recognized that the North Atlantic Community needs to organize itself into something more than a military alliance." Secretary Dulles's departure statement, *DOSB* (15 May 1956): 791. In light of the early conceptual history of the alliance, which cast NATO from the beginning as more than a military alliance, this was a remarkable confession.

22. NAC final communiqué, 5 May 1956, para. 2 (NATO Information Division, Paris).

23. NAC final communiqué, 5 May 1956, paras. 3-4.

24. See, for example, Richard Neustadt, *Alliance Politics* (New York: Columbia University Press, 1970); Stuart and Tow, *Limits of Alliance*, especially chapter 3; and Sherwood, *Allies in Crisis,* 58-94. The most comprehensive work to date on the crisis is Keith Kyle's excellent *Suez* (London: Weidenfeld and Nicolson, 1991).

25. Unless otherwise noted, all subsequent references in this section are from the *Report of the Committee of Three on Nonmilitary Cooperation in NATO* (NATO Information Division, Paris, 14 December 1956).

26. See Christian A. Herter, "The Desirability of the Atlantic Community," address before the Princeton University Conference on NATO at Princeton, 29 June 1957, *DOSB* (22 July 1957): 135.

27. Herter, "The Desirability of the Atlantic Community," 135.

28. John Foster Dulles, "NATO's Two Interlocking Tasks," transcript of address on ABC/TV (Department of State Press Release 478). Emphasis added.

29. After the December 1956 NAC meeting, which approved the recommendations of the Three Wise Men, Dulles declared that "it was recognized that the unity of the Atlantic Community must be further developed if it is to

surmount the shifting tactics of international communism and if it is to serve the needs of this and coming generations." Arrival statement of the secretary, *DOSB* (21 May 1956): 836.

30. Though broad, the concept's appeal was not unanimous. One author described suggestions for NATO's reform as a reflection of a "desperate desire to build NATO up into something more than it is." Wolfgang Freidman, "New Tasks for NATO?" *International Journal* 2 (Summer 1956): 163.

31. One West German author wrote that "the task of policy in a divided world is not just to preserve the status quo; it is to shape the destiny of communities." See Wilhelm Schutz, "New Initiatives for a New Age," *Foreign Affairs* 36 (April 1958): 465. See also Harold Macmillan, *Riding the Storm: 1956-1959* (London: Macmillan, 1973), 340.

32. See James L. Richardson, "The Concept of Atlantic Community," *Journal of Common Market Studies* 3 (October 1964): 1-22. Much Atlantic literature amounts to political advocacy, with authors providing plans for common action, statements of position, and pleas for unity. See, for example, George G. E. Caitlin, *Creating the Atlantic Community*, Fabian Tract 360 (London: The Fabian Society, 1965); and George G. E. Caitlin, *The Atlantic Commonwealth* (Harmondsworth, U.K.: Penguin, 1969). A more sophisticated assessment of the prospects for an Atlantic Commonwealth is Kissinger, *Troubled Partnership*. For an early proposal for Atlantic federation, see Clarence Streit, *Union Now* (New York: Harper and Brothers, 1949).

33. For further discussion, see "De Gaulle's 1958 Tripartite Proposal and U.S. Response," *Atlantic Community Quarterly* 4 (Fall 1966): 455-58; and McGeorge Bundy, *Danger and Survival: Choices about the Bomb in the First Fifty Years* (New York: Random House, 1988), 476-82.

34. See Charles de Gaulle, *Memoirs of Hope: Renewal 1958-62*, trans. Terrence Kilmartin (London: Weidenfeld and Nicolson, 1971), 203; Réne Couve de Murville, "NATO: A French View," *International Journal* 14 (Spring 1959): 85-86; and Réne Pleven, "France in the Atlantic Community," *Foreign Affairs* 38 (October 1959): 19-30. An excellent guide to de Gaulle's growing displeasure with the Anglo-American relationship is John Newhouse, *De Gaulle and the Anglo-Saxons* (New York: Viking, 1970), 111-19.

35. Secretary Dulles's news conference, 10 December 1957, *DOSB* (30 December 1957): 1024-25.

36. *DOSB* (30 December 1957): 1025.

37. Some analysts justified the need for a diminution of sovereignty by looking to the Soviets. Observing that "the proletariat has no country," Alastair Buchan pressed NATO to counter enemy tactics by placing its faith in interdependence. See Alastair Buchan, "The Changed Setting of the Atlantic Debate," *Foreign Affairs* 43 (July 1965): 586. For a more thorough treatment of the concept of national sovereignty, see John H. Herz, "International Politics in the Atomic Age," *World Politics* 9 (1957): 473-93.

38. For this statement and other official U.S. responses to the news of *Sputnik*, see Dulles's news conference of 5 November 1957, *DOSB* (23 November 1957): 829.

39. Even before it began the meeting was hailed as something unique in NATO history. Dulles declared that "there is a need to give a new emphasis to the purposes of NATO and to broaden its purposes." Dulles news conference, 10 December 1957, *DOSB* (30 December 1957): 1024. General Lauris Norstad, the new SACEUR, remarked that "what we shall presently witness in Paris is a ... furthering of the great conception of the alliance, a tighter union of our efforts and resources." See General Lauris Norstad, "Education, the Citizen, and NATO," *DOSB* (16 December 1957): 954. See also Eisenhower's speech to the opening session, *DOSB* (6 January 1958): 3-4.

40. Text of declaration and communiqué, 19 December 1957 (NATO Information Division, Paris). The communiqué also announced the creation of a NATO atomic stockpile, which would be "readily available" for the defense of the alliance. As part of the effort to strengthen NATO's nuclear defenses, U.S. IRBMs would be placed "at the disposal of SACEUR."

At its conclusion the meeting was hailed as a great success. See, for example, "The NATO Conference at Paris," report to the nation by President Eisenhower and Secretary Dulles over radio and television from the White House, 23 December 1957, *DOSB* (13 January 1958): 47-48; and Dwight D. Eisenhower, "The State of the Union," delivered before a joint session of the Senate and the House of Representatives on 9 January 1958 (H. Doc. 251, 85th Cong., 2d sess.). An authoritative British view is in Macmillan, *Riding the Storm*, 341.

41. See Dwight D. Eisenhower, "The Price of Peace," second inaugural address, *DOSB* (11 February 1957): 211. A joint Anglo-American statement later that year justified atomic collaboration in terms of the mutual recognition that "the concept of national self-sufficiency is now out of date. The countries of the free world are interdependent and only in genuine partnership ... can progress and safety be found." *Declaration of Common Purpose*, signed by President Eisenhower and Prime Minister Macmillan at Washington, 25 October 1957, para. 1.

42. Buchan, *NATO in the 1960s*, 33, 96. See also Malcolm Hoag, "What Interdependence for NATO?" *Survival* 2 (May/June 1960): 94-106.

43. John Foster Dulles, "NATO: Interdependence in Action," *DOSB* (13 October 1958): 570-71.

44. One of many such examples can be found in a private conversation with British Ambassador Sir Roger Makins in February 1955, when Dulles explained that U.S. strategy was to split the communist camp and "create the beginning of a balance of power relationship." Thus, not only did Dulles   not see international communism as monolithic, he also had begun to develop a long-term strategy for encouraging fragmentation within the communist world. Dulles conversation with Sir Roger Makins, 7 February 1955, *FRUS: 1955-57*, 2:236. In addition, Dulles's public rhetoric overshadowed the nuances of his thinking toward Yugoslavia, where since 1949 Tito had enlisted U.S. support in his efforts to distance himself from the Soviets. For more on Dulles, Eisenhower, and Sino-Soviet relations, see David Mayers, *Cracking the Monolith: United States policy Against the Sino-Soviet Alliance, 1948-1955* (Baton Rouge: Louisiana State University Press, 1986); and

John Lewis Gaddis, "The Unexpected John Foster Dulles: Nuclear Weapons, Communism, and the Russians," in *John Foster Dulles*, Richard H. Immerman, ed., 47-78.

45. The Americans were not the only ones to portray the Sino-Soviet bloc as monolithic. The West German foreign minister, Heinrich von Brentano, for example, wrote that "we are faced by a politically fanatical opponent who manipulates his interests of power with an iron hand, with a uniform, concentrated power of command." Heinrich von Brentano, "Goals and Means of the Western Alliance," *Foreign Affairs* 39 (April 1961): 419.

46. Buchan, *NATO in the 1960s*, 33.

47. On the international economic aspects of interdependence, see, for example, Edward L. Morse, *Foreign Policy and Interdependence in Gaullist France* (Princeton: Princeton University Press, 1973).

48. Dulles, "NATO: Interdependence in Action," 572. Buchan also rejected a formal extension of NATO's terms of reference. See Buchan, *NATO in the 1960s*, 103.

49. Dulles, "NATO: Interdependence in Action," 572.

50. Dulles, "NATO: Interdependence in Action," 572.

51. See, for example, Wolfram F. Hanrieder, *Germany, America, Europe: Forty Years of German Foreign Policy* (New Haven: Yale University Press, 1989), 5.

52. Kennedy's remarks before the NATO Assembly at Paris, 1 June 1961, *DOSB* (26 June 1961): 995.

53. DOSB (26 June 1961): 996. See also the two-part State Department report, *A Threat to the Peace: North Vietnam's Attempt to Conquer South Vietnam*, Department of State Publication 7308 (Washington, D.C.: Government Printing Office, 1961).

54. John F. Kennedy, "Europe and the United States," *Atlantic Community Quarterly* 1 (Winter 1963-64): 307.

55. Secretary of State Dean Rusk declared that if the United States were to abandon Vietnam, then "this would cause the allies to wonder what our commitments under such commitments as NATO would mean." See "A Conversation with the Secretary of State," *DOSB* (18 January 1965): 65-66. For President Johnson's views on Vietnam, see "Why we are in Vietnam," remarks by President Johnson, *DOSB* (27 December 1965): 1014-15; and "Vietnam: The Struggle to be Free," *DOSB* (14 March 1966): 390.

56. Fritz Erler wrote that German foreign policy should "make as little noise as possible.... The Germans should not press forward too ambitiously, but examine the initiatives and reservations of others, and adapt themselves to these as far as they are reasonable. They should not appear to be the element which is continuously disturbing and pushing and driving the alliance." Fritz Erler, "Germany and Nassau," *Survival* 5 (May/June 1963), 106.

57. On British reluctance to join the Americans in Vietnam, see Baylis, *Anglo-American Defense Relations*, 93-95.

58. See, for example, John F. Kennedy, "The Goal of an Atlantic Partnership,"

address at Philadelphia, 4 July 1962, *DOSB* (23 July 1962): 132; and Kennedy, "Europe and the United States," 305. Macmillan was an early supporter of the concept of Atlantic Partnership. In his memoirs Macmillan conceded that he was gratified when Kennedy "took up my old theme of the interdependence of the nations of the free world and the partnership which must be maintained between Europe and the United States." See his letter of congratulations to Kennedy after the Philadelphia speech in Harold Macmillan, *At the End of the Day, 1961-1963* (London: Macmillan, 1973), 111.

59. For a more extensive treatment, see Joseph Kraft, *The Grand Design: From Common Market to Atlantic Partnership* (New York: Harper and Row, 1962).

60. At least three leading observers opposed this view and argued that Europeans should be encouraged to develop their own deterrent. See Henry A. Kissinger, *The Necessity for Choice: Prospects of American Foreign Policy* (New York: Harper and Brothers, 1961); Benjamin Moore, *NATO and the Future of Europe* (London: Oxford University Press, 1960); and Buchan, *NATO in the 1960s*, 31. Buchan also argued, however, for the focus to be less on notions of partnership and more on the style of American leadership. See Alastair Buchan, "Partners and Allies," *Foreign Affairs* 41 (July 1963): 632.

61. See *DOSB* (6 February 1961): 175.

62. "President Pledges U.S. Support of NATO," text of message from the president to the NAC, 15 February 1961, *DOSB* (6 March 1961): 333-34. See also Lyndon Baines Johnson, "Enhancing the Strength and Unity of the North Atlantic Community," address by the vice president at ceremonies celebrating the 10th anniversary of SHAPE at Paris on 6 April 1961, *DOSB* (24 April 1961): 581-83. Johnson called on the allies to accept "sacrifices of ancient concepts in the light of growing interdependence."

63. One State Department official cast the challenge of partnership as an imperative: "We cannot survive as a great and influential nation unless we can help forge a working partnership of the non-communist peoples of the world." See Chester Bowles, under secretary of state, "The Foundations of Western Partnership," *DOSB* (1 May 1961): 629. Like many of his colleagues, Bowles viewed the Cold War as a conceptual struggle: "The heart of the struggle … lies in widely differing concepts of certain deeply fundamental values." *DOSB* (1 May 1961): 631.

64. See John F. Kennedy, "A New Foreign Trade Program," *Message of the President to the Congress*, transmitted 25 January 1962 (H. Doc. 314, 87th Cong., 2d sess.). See also (Sen.) J. W. Fulbright, "A Community of Free Nations," *Atlantic Community Quarterly* 1 (Summer 1963): 113-30; and *Problems and Trends in Atlantic Partnership*, report of the Senate Foreign Relations Committee, Sen. Doc. 132 (Washington, D.C.: Government Printing Office, 1962).

65. See, for example, George Ball, "Towards an Atlantic Partnership," *DOSB* (5 March 1962): 366.

66. See Kennedy, "A New Foreign Trade Program," 4. British Prime Minister Harold Macmillan also subscribed to the view that the West should showcase its economic and political strength. See Harold Macmillan, *Pointing the Way: 1959-*

1961 (London: Macmillan, 1973), 334-35. For a more general assessment of the economic aspects of partnership, see Walter Lippman, *Western Unity and the Common Market* (London: Hamish Hamilton, 1962).

67. Treaties establishing a European atomic energy authority (EURATOM) and the European Common Market (EEC) were signed in Rome in March 1957.

68. George C. McGhee, "Atlantic Unity—Key to World Community," *DOSB* (22 January 1962): 134. The OECD was viewed as another step in Atlantic cooperation on an institutional basis. The OEEC, an offspring of the Marshall Plan that embraced only allied European countries, was reorganized in 1960 as the OECD to include eighteen states, including the United States, Canada, and Japan. The development of the OECD gave NATO an institutional counterpart in the economic realm, though this did not put an end to the allied impulse to regard NATO as a means of waging economic cold war. Dean Rusk claimed that "NATO also provides a forum in which these [economic] issues can be weighed against *political* background which lends them the necessary urgency." Dean Rusk, "The State of the North Atlantic Alliance," *DOSB* (5 August 1963): 195. Emphasis in original.

69. Transcript of Rusk interview on CBS "Issues and Answers," *DOSB* (10 July 1962): 342.

70. J. Robert Schaetzel, deputy assistant secretary for Atlantic affairs, *DOSB* (3 September 1962): 354-55.

71. For the German reaction see, for instance, Fritz Erler, "The Basis of Partnership," *Foreign Affairs* 42 (October 1963): 84-85; and Willy Brandt, *The Ordeal of Coexistence* (Cambridge: Cambridge University Press, 1963), 81. For the U.K. response, see Macmillan, *At the End of the Day*, 111. For an explicit discussion of the concept of partnership, see Kissinger, *Troubled Partnership*. For a more upbeat appraisal, see Schaetzel, *Unhinged Alliance*, 162-72.

72. Stanley Hoffmann, "Discord in Community: The North Atlantic Area as a Partial Integration System," *International Organization* 17 (Summer 1963): 539-41; and Altiero Spinelli, "Atlantic Partnership or European Unity," *Foreign Affairs* 40 (July 1962): 545.

73. *DOSB* (3 September 1962): 354-55. See also Buchan, *NATO in the 1960s*, 27.

74. Of Kennedy's conception, former Secretary of State Herter declared: "I believe the present Administration ... holds the ... view, which has come to be termed the 'dumbbell concept'—meaning that an economic and political alliance is stronger if it has been agreed to by partners of equal weight on both sides." Christian A. Herter, "Atlantica," *Foreign Affairs* 41 (January 1963): 304.

75. See, for example, David Halberstam, *The Best and the Brightest* (New York: Random House, 1973), 39.

76. Kennedy himself admitted as much in a March 1962 speech at Berkeley, when he declared his dissatisfaction with the "stale and sterile dogmas of the Cold War." *Public Papers of the Presidents: John F. Kennedy, 1961-1963* (Washington, D.C.: Government Printing Office, 1965-1969), 264.

77. There is a wealth of secondary source material on the crisis. See, for example, Robert F. Kennedy, *Thirteen Days: A Memoir of the Cuban Missile Crisis* (New York: Harper and Brothers, 1969); Graham T. Allison, *Essence of Decision: Explaining the Cuban Missile Crisis* (Boston: Little, Brown, 1971); and Bundy, *Danger and Survival*, 391-462.

The *Department of State Bulletin* is a good primary source for the rhetoric of the period. For the transcripts of the secretly taped conversations of Kennedy's executive committee (ExCom) during the crisis, see McGeorge Bundy and James G. Blight, "October 27, 1962: Transcripts of the Meetings of the ExCom," *International Security* 12 (Winter 1987/88), 30-92.

78. George Ball, "NATO and the Cuban Crisis," *DOSB* (3 December 1962): 831.

79. Ball, "NATO and the Cuban Crisis," 831-35.

80. Ball, "NATO and the Cuban Crisis," 833.

81. Ball, "NATO and the Cuban Crisis," 835.

82. In addition, the crisis had highlighted the dangers of nuclear war, and its negotiated outcome contributed to a relaxation of East-West tensions. A significant element of the exchanges of letters between Kennedy and Khrushchev that resolved the Cuban crisis was the proposal, made by Khrushchev and agreed by Kennedy, that, to calm the public once the crisis was resolved, they should seek rapid progress for disarmament with priority for a nuclear test ban. In due course, the Partial Test Ban Treaty, which restricted nuclear tests to underground, was negotiated and signed in Moscow in August 1963. Khrushchev's fall from power in October 1964 further contributed to a calmer international environment. His successors, Leonid Brezhnev and Alexei Kosygin, rejected a policy of threats and bluster in favor of building the Soviet nuclear arsenal, the inferiority of which appeared to have been demonstrated by the Cuban crisis.

83. William R. Tyler, assistant secretary of state for European affairs, "The Meaning of Atlantic Partnership," *DOSB* (31 December 1962): 1008-12.

84. The most comprehensive (and readable) work on nuclear strategy is Lawrence Freedman, *The Evolution of Nuclear Strategy* (London: Macmillan, 1983). An outstanding guide to the development of U.S. nuclear strategy in the early postwar years is Stephen L. Rearden, *The Origins of U.S. Nuclear Strategy, 1945-1953* (New York: St. Martin's Press, 1993).

85. For an argument favoring a trip-wire force as the only conventional component that a deterrence strategy requires, see Kenneth A. Waltz, "Nuclear Myths and Political Realities," *American Political Science Review* 89 (September 1990): 731-46.

86. This concept was sometimes referred to as the "plate-glass" concept.

87. See, for example, General Lauris Norstad, "NATO—Deterrent and Shield," *DOSB* (18 February 1957): 254. See also Basil Liddel-Hart, "Shield Forces for NATO," *Survival* 2 (May/June 1960): 108-10.

88. For an example of Dulles's early discomfort with the implications of massive retaliation, see John Foster Dulles, "Policy for Security and Peace," *Foreign Affairs*

32 (April 1954): 356-58. See also Samuel F. Wells, "The Origins of Massive Retaliation," *Political Science Quarterly* 96 (Spring 1981): 31-52.

89. See, for example, Dulles, "NATO's Two Interlocking Tasks," 478. Two events marked the introduction of nuclear weapons to NATO. The first was the December 1956 NATO ministerial meeting, where the United Kingdom, France, Germany, the Netherlands, and Turkey requested American tactical atomic weapons. The second was the December 1957 decision, also announced at a NATO ministerial meeting, to station American IRBMs in Europe. Both weapon systems were under "dual-key" controls, with use subject to agreement by the owners of the warheads (the Americans) and the host nations. In addition, the NAC, in December 1957, instructed the NATO Military Committee to draw up a long-term plan (MC/70) establishing detailed arms requirements of each member, including tactical nuclear delivery systems.

90. For more on the development and implications of tactical nuclear weaponry, see David Alan Rosenberg, "The Origins of Overkill: Nuclear Weapons and American Strategy, 1945-1960," *International Security* 7 (Spring 1983): 3-71; and Gregory F. Treverton, "How Different are Nuclear Weapons?" *U.S. Nuclear Strategy: A Reader,* Philip Bobbit, Lawrence Freedman, and Gregory F. Treverton, eds. (London: Macmillan, 1989): 112-21.

91. In 1954 the so-called McMahon Act, passed as the original Atomic Energy Act of 1946, was amended to permit sharing of information with Britain on the types, sizes, and capabilities of nuclear weapons. The 1958 amendment was a much larger step, and real sharing of hydrogen bomb designs began immediately. For the public rationale and the linkage between the shield concept and nuclear sharing, see, for example, John Foster Dulles, "Sharing Nuclear Knowledge with Our Allies," statement before the Subcommittee on Agreement for Cooperation of the Joint Committee on Atomic Energy, 17 April 1958, *DOSB* (5 May 1958): 740. For further analysis, see Baylis, *Anglo-American Defense Relations,* 49-54; and John Simpson, *The Independent Nuclear State: The United States, Britain and the Military Atom* (London: Macmillan, 1986).

92. These weapons, subject to release by presidential authority, were intended for use by the supreme allied commander in the event of hostilities. "This assures," Dulles declared to Congress, "the existence of nuclear-capable NATO forces." See Dulles, "Sharing Nuclear Knowledge," 740.

93. Dulles, "Sharing Nuclear Knowledge," 742.

94. Some analysts argued that the very ambiguity of allied nuclear strategy enhanced deterrence. See, for example, Henry A. Kissinger, *Nuclear Weapons and Foreign Policy* (New York: Harper and Brothers, 1957).

95. An outstanding study on the evolution of flexible response, upon which portions of this section are based, is Stromseth, *Origins of Flexible Response.*

96. Christian A. Herter, "Our Expanding Flexible Response," *DOSB* (26 September 1960): 467.

97. Note that the Western European public and peace movements often had quite different views. What is referred to in this work is establishment opinion.

98. Message from the president to the NAC meeting in Paris, 16-18 December 1960, *DOSB* (9 January 1961): 39.

99. See "Remarks by Secretary McNamara, NATO Ministerial Meeting, 5 May 1962 (Restricted Session), declassified 17 August 1979," reprinted in *U.S. Nuclear Strategy*, Bobbit, Freedman, and Treverton, eds., 205-22. McNamara later delivered a sanitized version of the speech at commencement exercises at the University of Michigan at Ann Arbor. See Robert S. McNamara, "Defense Arrangements of the North Atlantic Community," address at commencement exercises, University of Michigan (Ann Arbor), *DOSB* (9 July 1962): 64-69.

100. General Johannes Steinhoff, "NATO Crisis: A Military View," *Survival* 8 (November 1966): 366.

101. See Baylis, *Anglo-American Defense Relations*, 72-74.

102. Adding an interesting twist to alliance rhetoric, the communiqué stressed the importance of the "non-nuclear sword" and the "nuclear shield," thus reversing the standard formulation of nuclear sword and conventional shield and which reflected the new American tendency to emphasize the importance of conventional forces. See "Macmillan-Kennedy Talks at Nassau, 18-21 December 1962, Joint Communi-qué and attached Statement on Nuclear Defense Systems," 21 December 1962. For the text of the U.S.-U.K. Polaris sales agreement, see *DOSB* (13 May 1963): 760.

103. Fritz Erler, deputy leader of the West German Social Democratic Party, was an enthusiastic respondent to the Anglo-American claims about the alliance-wide benefits of Nassau. See Erler, "Germany and Nassau," 102-6. Macmillan argued that the best course for Britain was to pursue "a combination of independence and interdependence," and justified the British nuclear program on the basis of the United Kingdom's "world-wide commitments." See Macmillan, *At the End of the Day*, 356-62, 553-55. See also his comments as minister of defense in *Hansard*, 2 March 1955; and Sir John Slessor, "Command and Control of Allied Nuclear Forces: A British View," *Adelphi Papers* 22 (London: IISS, 1965).

104. See Charles de Gaulle, "Views on the Nassau Agreement, the Atlantic Alliance and National Nuclear Forces," *Survival* 5 (March/April 1963): 58-59. For further discussion of this whole topic, see Bundy, *Danger and Survival*, 492-94. Macmillan's memoirs are also a good source. See Macmillan, *At the End of the Day*, 345, 354-55. See also Kohl, *French Nuclear Diplomacy*, 249-50.

105. Abraham Chayes, "European Integration and American Foreign Policy," *DOSB* (4 March 1963): 318-22.

106. See, for example, Jacques Vernant, "France and Nassau," *Survival* 5 (May/June 1963): 106-9.

107. For de Gaulle's reasoning behind the veto, see *Major Addresses, Statements and Press Conferences of General Charles de Gaulle, 19 May 1958-31 January 1964* (New York: French Embassy, Press and Information Service 1965), 211-16 [hereafter *Major Addresses*]. For Macmillan's reaction see, Macmillan, *Riding the Storm*, 333-78. For the text of the treaty, see *The Common Declaration and the Treaty between the French Republic and the Federal Republic of Germany*, 22 January 1963 (New York: French Embassy, Press and Information Service, 1965).

108. In responding to such worries, the opposition leader Fritz Erler wrote that, for Germany, Franco-German military cooperation was regarded as a means "to strengthen NATO…. Any transition to the French conception [of military policy] would certainly be dynamite for NATO…. But the German Government has not undertaken in the treaty to adopt the French conceptions." See Erler, "Germany and Nassau," 105.

Adenauer's support—as well as de Gaulle's veto—was opposed by the other four signatories to the Treaty of Rome and by West German political elites. Paul-Henri Spaak, the secretary general of NATO, called the veto "an attack on the Atlantic Alliance and the European Community–an attack, that is, on the two most significant achievements of the free world since the end of the Second World War." Paul-Henri Spaak, "Hold Fast," *Foreign Affairs* 41 (July 1963): 611-20. On the German reaction, see Richard Hiscocks, *Germany Revived: An Appraisal of the Adenauer Era* (London: Victor Gollancz, 1966), 240-41; and Fritz Erler, "The Alliance and the Future of Germany," *Foreign Affairs* 43 (April 1963): 436-46.

109. Rusk interview on NBC/TV "Today," 2 January 1963, *DOSB* (11 February 1963): 206. Emphasis added.

110. W. W. Rostow, "The Cold War—A Look Ahead," *DOSB* (15 April 1963): 553.

111. See "Remarks by Secretary McNamara," in *U.S. Nuclear Strategy,* Bobbit, Freedman, and Treverton, eds., 205-22; Albert Wholstetter, "Nuclear Sharing: NATO and the N+1 Country," *Foreign Affairs* 39 (April 1961): 355-88; Sir John Slessor, "Control of Nuclear Strategy," *Foreign Affairs* 42 (October 1963): 96-106; and Leonard Beaton, "The Western Alliance and the McNamara Doctrine," *Adelphi Papers* 11 (London: IISS, 1964).

112. See Newhouse, *De Gaulle and the Anglo-Saxons*, 159-64, 225-30.

113. See, for example, William R. Tyler, "The Effects of the Projected European Union on NATO," *DOSB* (29 April 1963): 648-52.

114. It was claimed that one advantage of the sea-borne, mixed-crew concept was that, because it would operate in international waters, it could not be withdrawn for national purposes and thus would meet the requirements of keeping nuclear defense indivisible. For an argument along these lines, see Robert R. Bowie, "Strategy and the Atlantic Alliance," *International Organization* 17 (Summer 1963): 709-32. This claim contrasted sharply with the terms of the Nassau Agreement, whereby the British prime minister could withdraw his NATO-assigned Polaris missiles.

115. See, for example, Alastair Buchan, "The Multilateral Force—A Study in Alliance Politics," *International Affairs* 40 (October 1964): 619-37; and W. B. Bader, "Nuclear-Weapons Sharing and 'The German Problem,'" *Foreign Affairs* 44 (July 1966): 682-92.

116. This appears to have been the main reason behind German support for the MLF. See Kai-Uwe von Hassel (German defense minister), "Détente through Firmness," *Foreign Affairs* 42 (January 1964): 189; and Richardson, *Germany and the Atlantic Alliance*, 68-70.

117. See, for example, George C. McGhee, "The Atlantic Partnership: A Vital Force in Motion," *DOSB* (20 May 1963): 771-75; and W. W. Rostow, "The Atlantic Community: An American View," *DOSB* (3 June 1963): 855-60.

118. Arthur Schlesinger, Jr., *A Thousand Days: John F. Kennedy in the White House* (Boston: Houghton Mifflin, 1965): 727-28.

119. See Bundy's masterful account in *Danger and Survival*, 492-98, 501-4.

120. See Harold Wilson, "Speech by the Prime Minister on Britain and the Atlantic Nuclear Force, 16 December 1964," *Survival* 7 (March/April 1965), 52-54; and Harold Wilson, *A Personal Record: The Labour Government, 1964-1970* (Boston: Little, Brown, 1971), 41-51. For more on the ANF, see Baylis, *Anglo-American Defense Relations*, 85-91.

121. Freedman, *Evolution of Nuclear Strategy*, 328.

122. See Buchan, "The Multilateral Force," 636. Macmillan's views expressing support for the MLF are in Macmillan, *Riding the Storm*, 358-59.

123. For further discussion of French opposition to the MLF, see Newhouse, *De Gaulle and the Anglo-Saxons*, 267-78.

124. See Stromseth, *Origins of Flexible Response*, 83.

125. Macmillan's 1959 visit to Moscow had apparently also ruffled German feathers. See Richardson, *Germany and the Atlantic Alliance*, 68-71.

126. See Ludwig Erhard, "Statement After Election as Chancellor of the Federal Republic of Germany," *Atlantic Community Quarterly* 3 (Winter 1963-1964): 501-11.

127. Kelleher, *Germany and the Politics of Nuclear Weapons,* 184-91, 213-14; Freedman, *Evolution of Nuclear Strategy*, 326; Buchan, "The MLF," 630; and Von Hassel, "Détente through Firmness," 189.

128. The "Athen's Guidelines" provided for allied consultation in formulating nuclear policy and initiating the use of nuclear weapons. See Stromseth, *Origins of Flexible Response,* 73. The NPG, formally known as the Nuclear Planning Working Group of the NATO Special Committee of Defense Ministers, was formed on the basis of a proposal by McNamara at the June 1965 defense ministers meeting in Paris. Its first meeting was held on 27 November 1965 at Paris, where three working groups were established to discuss intelligence and data exchange, communications, and planning "to insure that agreed consultation concerning the decision whether to use nuclear forces can take place as expeditiously as advanced technology will permit." See *DOSB* (7 March 1966) 368.

129. See George Ball, "The Nuclear Deterrent and the Atlantic Alliance," *DOSB* (13 May 1963): 739. Lauris Norstad later wrote of the MLF that "from the military stand-point it was not an effective instrument. And it was unfortunate that we spent so much time on it." Lauris Norstad, "Defending Europe without France," *Atlantic Community Quarterly* 4 (Summer 1966): 184.

130. Gallois introduced the concept of "proportional" deterrence, which held that "the thermonuclear force can be proportional to the value of the stake it is defending." Gallois applied a cost/benefit analysis in an effort to identify the degree of force necessary to deter aggression. See Pierre M. Gallois, *The Balance of Terror*

(Boston: Houghton, Mifflin, 1961), 22; and Pierre M. Gallois, "New Teeth For NATO," *Foreign Affairs* 39 (October 1960): 67-80.

131. In an earlier work, Gallois was explicit about the irrelevance of alliances. See Pierre M. Gallois, "Collective Defense," *Survival* 1 (May/June 1959): 49. He later called the concept for a MLF "ridiculous" and castigated the Americans for wanting to integrate their allies' strategic forces but not their own. See Pierre M. Gallois, "The Raison d'Etre of French Defense Policy," *International Affairs* 39 (October 1963): 497-510.

132. André Beaufre, *Deterrence and Strategy* (London: Faber and Faber, 1965).

133. André Beaufre, *NATO and Europe* (London: Faber and Faber, 1967), 57-59.

134. Kennedy declared that "we should face the fact that the fundamental purpose of the French atomic bomb is not to increase French capabilities but to increase its stature in the Alliance. The French bomb is aimed toward Washington rather than Moscow." John F. Kennedy, *The Strategy of Peace* (New York: Harper and Brothers, 1960), 100. See also David H. Popper, "The US, France, and NATO: A Comparison of Two Approaches," *DOSB* (8 February 1965): 180-87; and McNamara, "Defense Arrangements of the North Atlantic Community," 64-69.

135. In March 1959, de Gaulle withdrew the French Mediterranean Fleet from its NATO assignment and, shortly afterward, banned U.S. atomic weapons in France. He also refused to transfer returning French North African troops to NATO-designated status, failed to support the allies on crises in the Congo, Lebanon, and Jordan, censured the United States for its role in Vietnam, and recognized the People's Republic of China. De Gaulle's policy of "Atlantic disengagement" came partly in response to Eisenhower's rejection of his September 1958 directorate scheme. The Suez and the Cuban crises undoubtedly helped form his opinions about the unreliability of allies. These actions were taken, he said, to put France "in control of her destiny." See De Gaulle, *Major Addresses*, 67, 204-6, 223-26. For further discussion of the directorate, see "De Gaulle's 1958 Tripartite Proposal and U.S. Response," *Atlantic Community Quarterly* 4 (Fall 1966): 455-58; and the account in Bundy, *Danger and Survival*, 477-82. An excellent book-length analysis of de Gaulle's early moves away from NATO is Nora Beloff, *The General Says No* (Harmondsworth: Penguin, 1963).

136. De Gaulle was entirely correct. Franco-American nuclear cooperation did not begin until the last year of Pompidou's tenure. See Richard H. Ullman, "The Covert French Connection," *Foreign Policy* 75 (Summer, 1989): 3-33.

137. Of his many speeches on this subject, see, for example, *Major Addresses,* 158-60, 216-19. For further discussion of de Gaulle's foreign policy during the period 1963-1966, see Philip G. Cerny, *The Politics of Granduer: Ideological Aspects of de Gaulle's Foreign Policy* (Cambridge: Cambridge University Press, 1980), 176-225.

138. See Newhouse, *De Gaulle and the Anglo-Saxons*. For a French critique of Gaullism, see François Fontaine, "The Impossible Schism," *Atlantic Community Quarterly* 2 (Fall 1964): 367-76.

139. See Robert R. Bowie, "Tensions within the Alliance," *Foreign Affairs* 42 (October 1963): 49-69; André Fontaine, "What Is French Policy?" *Foreign Affairs* 46 (October 1966): 58-76; Stanley Hoffmann, "De Gaulle, Europe and the Atlantic Alliance," *Atlantic Community Quarterly* 2 (Summer 1964): 262-75; and Harlan Cleveland, *The Atlantic Idea and Its European Rivals* (New York: McGraw-Hill, 1966).

140. See, for example, "De Gaulle's 10th Press Conference (23 July 1964)" in *Major Addresses*, 3-7; Charles de Gaulle, "The Atlantic Alliance," *Survival* 5 (September/October 1963): 238-39, and Charles de Gaulle, "Long Live France," *Atlantic Community Quarterly* 3 (Summer 1965): 155-58.

141. West German and other European leaders argued that French leadership was not a viable alternative to the U.S. commitment. See, for example, Fritz Erler, "The Alliance and the Future of Germany," *Foreign Affairs* 43 (April 1965): 444; Ernst Ulrich Fromm, "President de Gaulle's Vision of Europe: A German View," *Atlantic Community Quarterly* 4 (Summer 1966): 224-25; and Charles De Gaulle, *Memoirs of Hope: Endeavour, 1962* (London: Weidenfeld and Nicolson, 1971), 199.

142. See Paul-Henri Spaak, "Chaos in Europe," *Atlantic Community Quarterly* 4 (Summer 1966): 211-15.

143. See, for example, Richardson, *Germany and the Atlantic Alliance*, 41-44.

144. See, for instance, Paul-Henri Spaak, "New Tests for NATO," *Foreign Affairs* 37 (April 1959): 357-65.

145. Dulles told a British television audience in 1958 that "we are up against a creed which believes almost fanatically in a different concept of the nature of the world, the kind of civilization we should have, and above all the nature of man and the part man plays in it…. We have a totally different concept, always have had." Transcript of Secretary Dulles's interview on ITN (U.K.), 23 October 1958, *DOSB* (10 November 1958): 753. Two months later, in testimony before the Senate Foreign Relations Committee, Dulles asserted that the "free world and communist concepts are mutually antagonistic." Dulles's testimony excerpted as "Freedom—The Dominant Force," *DOSB* (2 February 1959): 155. Paul-Henri Spaak, secretary general of NATO, wrote that the Cold War was "a struggle between two civilizations." See Paul-Henri Spaak, "NATO and the Communist Challenge," *DOSB* (20 October 1958): 607.

146. In his memoirs Harold Macmillan wrote that Adenauer supported NATO, WEU, EDC, the Common Market, and a European Army: "In a word, everything which would range Germany in the ranks of the civilized countries." Macmillan, *Riding the Storm*, 335.

147. Franz Josef Strauss, West German defense minister from 1956 to 1962, wrote that German "independence can only be preserved by a policy of alignment." Franz Josef Strauss, "Europe, America and NATO: A German View," *Survival* 4 (January/February 1962): 7. Political support for the U.S. rhetoric, however, was not matched by Strauss's disparaging view of the tenability of U.S. strategic concepts,

which he criticized as "conceptual aids for the pre-calculation of the inconceivable and the incalculable nature of the specific." Quoted in Kelleher, *Germany and the Politics of Nuclear Weapons*, 282.

Chapter 4: Managing Détente

1. See Raymond Garthoff, *Détente and Confrontation: American-Soviet Relations from Nixon to Reagan* (Washington, D.C.: Brookings, 1985), 24-68.

2. For example, one senior U.S. State Department official declared in April 1966 that in return for cooperative agreements the United States expected "reciprocal actions" and "mutual restraint" from the Soviets. See Lawrence Katzenbach, under secretary of state, "U.S. Relations with the Soviet Union," address before the Foreign Policy Association at New York, 21 April 1967, *DOSB* (15 May 1967): 756; and Robert Hunter, "The Future of Soviet-American Détente," *World Today* 24 (July 1968): 281-90.

3. See, for example, Zbigniew Brzezinski, "The Framework for East-West Reconciliation," *Foreign Affairs* 46 (January 1968): 256-75; David S. Collier and Kurt Glaser, eds., *The Conditions for Peace in Europe: Problems of Détente and Security* (Washington: Public Affairs Press, 1969); Robert Conquest, "The Limits of Détente," *Foreign Affairs* 46 (July 1968): 733-42; Eleanor Lansing Dulles and Robert Dickson Crane, eds., *Détente: Cold War Strategies in Transition* (New York: Praeger, 1965); and William E. Griffith and W. W. Rostow, *East-West Relations: Is Détente Possible?* (Washington, D.C.: American Enterprise Institute for Public Policy Research, 1969).

4. Harlan B. Moulton, *From Superiority to Parity: The United States and the Strategic Arms Race, 1961-1971* (Westport, Conn.: Greenwood Press, 1973), x.

5. Jean Laloy, "Western and Eastern Europe: The Changing Relationship," *Adelphi Papers* 33, (London: IISS, 1967).

6. The December 1966 NAC communiqué declared that NATO's defensive and deterrent strength had "produced the basis for the present marked reduction of tension in Europe." NAC final communiqué, 15-16 December 1966, para. 3. One U.S. official declared that standing tall through NATO "has brought a measure of restraint" in East-West relations. See Foy D. Kohler, deputy under secretary of state for political affairs, "Constructive Initiatives in East-West Relations," *DOSB* (13 March 1967): 408.

7. See, for example, (Maj.) Leslie W. Stewart, Jr., *NATO in a World of Détente—* Research Study (Maxwell Air Force Base, Ala.: Air Command and Staff College, 1974); and Philip Windsor, "NATO and European Détente," *World Today* 23 (September 1967): 361-69.

8. The NAC's December 1966 "Declaration on Germany," for example, declared that the solution to division of Germany could come only "through the creation of an atmosphere of détente on the continent." The NAC also gave its full support to West German Foreign Minister Willy Brandt's efforts to develop human,

economic, and cultural contacts between East and West Germany. See NAC final communiqué, 15-16 December 1966 (Annex B: Declaration on Germany).

9. Vice President Humphrey's address to the NAC, 7 April 1967, *DOSB* (1 May 1967): 681. Senior State Department official Foy Kohler declared one month earlier that "today we can no longer talk of a Sino-Soviet bloc.... The Communist world has ceased to be a monolithic entity." See Kohler, "Constructive Initiatives in East-West Relations," 408.

10. Early in 1967 the Johnson administration extended a cultural agreement with the Soviet Union for an additional two years, initiated direct air flights between New York and Moscow, reached agreement at the UN on the peaceful uses of outer space, and introduced trade legislation designed to remove selected items from export controls. For the announcement of these moves, see Lyndon Baines Johnson, "The State of the Union," 10 January 1967 (H. Doc. 1, 90th Cong., 1st sess.). In Europe, the British had been talking to Moscow about a Friendship Treaty; the new West German foreign minister, Willy Brandt, had been trying to arrange diplomatic relations with the German Democratic Republic and other Eastern European states; the French, in the wake of de Gaulle's 1966 trip to Moscow, were attempting to negotiate scientific and military cooperation agreements with the Soviets; the Poles and Belgians had contacts; and Yugoslavia had been promoting improved East-West relations. For a review of these and other East-West bilateral contacts in and before 1967, see Harlan Cleveland, U.S. permanent representative to NATO, "The Golden Rule of Consultation," *DOSB* (31 July 1967): 141-46.

11. See Johnson, "The State of the Union."

12. *DOSB* (6 April 1970): 442.

13. Transcript of Secretary Rusk's interview on West German television, *DOSB* (6 March 1967): 363.

14. See, for example, President Nixon's February 1969 comments to the NAC, where he declared that "a modern alliance must be a living thing, capable of growth, able to adapt to changing circumstances." *DOSB* (24 March 1969): 251; and also Eugene V. Rostow, under secretary of state for political affairs, "Concert and Consultation: The Next Stage of the Atlantic Alliance," address before the Atlantic Treaty Association at Luxembourg, 11 September 1967, *DOSB* (2 October 1967): 427.

15. NAC final communiqué, 15-16 December 1966 (Annex C: Resolution of the NAC).

16. NAC meeting at Luxembourg, 12-14 December 1967, final communiqué and the attached report of the council, annex to the final communiqué of the ministerial meeting, *The Future Tasks of the Alliance (Harmel Report)*, 14 December 1967 (Brussels: NATO Information Division).

17. See Rostow, "Concert and Consultation," 427.

18. *Harmel Report*, para. 9.

19. Manlio Brosio, "Past and Future Tasks of the Alliance: An Analysis of the *Harmel Report*," *Atlantic Community Quarterly* 6 (Summer 1968): 231-37; Harlan

Cleveland, "The Rejuvenation of NATO," *Atlantic Community Quarterly* 5 (Winter 1967-1968): 512-19; and Philip Windsor, "NATO Confronts Its Future," *World Today* 24 (March 1968): 121-26.

20. See Cleveland, "Golden Rule," 142.

21. See Cleveland, "Golden Rule," 144. These remarks came in the wake of the Glassboro, New Jersey, summit, where Johnson met in June with Soviet Premier Alexei Kosygin. For the text of the joint communiqué and a report on the summit, see *DOSB* (10 July 1967): 35. In addition, the United States had been exploring the possibility for a Non-Proliferation Treaty—the final text of which was completed in June 1968. For the text of the treaty and the UN resolution in support, see UN doc A/RES/2373 (xxii) adopted by the General Assembly, 12 June 1968. The NPT entered into force on 5 March 1970.

22. NAC final communiqué, Reykjavik, 24-25 June 1968, and attached "Declaration on Mutual and Balanced Force Reductions."

23. NAC final communiqué, Brussels, 4-5 December 1969, and attached "Declaration on European Security."

24. NAC final communiqué, Rome, 26-27 May 1970. For a review of the early progress of the MBFR negotiations, see R. J. Hill, "MBFR," *International Affairs Journal* 29 (September 1974): 242-55. For a more detailed assessment, see Christoph Bertram, *Mutual Force Reductions in Europe: The Political Aspects* (London: IISS, 1972); and (Maj.) Allan C. Blaisdell, *NATO and the Warsaw Pact: The Challenge of Mutual and Balanced Force Reductions*—Research Study (Maxwell AFB, Ala.: Air Command and Staff College, 1972). The first seven years of the MBFR negotiations are covered in David S. Yost, ed., *NATO's Strategic Options: Arms Control and Defense* (Elmsford, N.Y.: Pergamon, 1981).

25. For the texts of the two declarations and commentary, see "Declaration on Strengthening Peace and Security in Europe," *Survival* 8 (September 1966): 289-93; "Declaration of Ministers of Foreign Affairs of the Warsaw Pact," *Survival* 11 (December 1969): 394-95; "Call for a European Security Conference," *Survival* 11 (March 1969): 159-61; and Joseph M. A. H. Luns, "NATO's View of Security Conferences," *Atlantic Community Quarterly* 11 (September 1973): 55-64.

26. For more on the Berlin Agreement, see Dennis L. Bark, *Agreement on Berlin: A Study of the 1970-1972 Quadripartite Negotiations* (Washington, D.C.: American Enterprise Institute for Public Policy Research, 1974); Dennis L. Bark, *The Dilemmas of Détente: Negotiation and Agreement on Berlin, 1970-1972* (Washington, D.C.: American Enterprise Institute for Public Policy Research, 1974); and Karl Kaiser, "Prospects for West Germany after the Berlin Agreement," *World Today* 28 (January 1972): 30-35.

27. Karl K. Birnbaum, "Pan-European Perspectives after the Berlin Agreement," *International Journal* 27 (Winter 1972): 32-44.

28. *Harmel Report*, paras. 10-12.

29. Even after the invasion, Johnson had hoped to arrange for a lame-duck summit meeting but was thwarted by President-elect Nixon, who opposed it. See

Lyndon Baines Johnson, *The Vantage Point: Perspectives on the Presidency, 1963-1969* (New York: Holt, Rinehart and Winston, 1971), 448-90; and Henry A. Kissinger, *White House Years* (Boston: Little, Brown, 1979), 49-50. For the contemporary official public reaction to the invasion, see "The Soviet Intervention in Czechoslovakia," statement by President Johnson, 21 August 1968, and Secretary Rusk's news conference, both, *DOSB* (9 September 1968): 301; NAC final communiqué, 16 November 1968, paras. 3-4; and Helmut Schmidt, "The Brezhnev Doctrine," *Survival* 11 (October 1969): 307-11.

30. See "The Inaugural Address of President Nixon," *Public Papers of the Presidents: Richard M. Nixon, 1969* (Washington, D.C.: Government Printing Office, 1971), 3. See also Robert Ellsworth, "Europe, America and the Era of Negotiation," *Survival* 13 (April 1971): 114-22; and Richard M. Nixon, "The Time to Save NATO," *Atlantic Community Quarterly* 6 (Winter 1968-1969): 479-84.

31. U.S. Secretary of Defense Clark Clifford declared that events in Czechoslovakia "have clearly demonstrated that a significant American military presence in Western Europe is still needed." *DOSB* (30 September 1968): 337. This, however, was not a foregone conclusion. Although the invasion did in fact make the European members of NATO nervous about Soviet intentions, it could have had the opposite effect. Viewed in a less rigid way the invasion might have indicated that the Soviets were merely being defensive, rather than expansive.

32. See, for example, Philip Windsor, "The Boundaries of Détente," *World Today* 25 (June 1969): 255-64; and Paul-Henri Spaak, "The Fundamental Reality," *Atlantic Community Quarterly* 6 (Winter 1968-1969): 485-92.

33. See, for example, Leonard Beaton, "NATO after the Soviet Invasion of Czechoslovakia," *Atlantic Community Quarterly* 7 (Spring 1969): 76-77; Harlan Cleveland, "NATO after the Invasion," *Foreign Affairs* 47 (January 1969): 251-65; Andrew J. Pierre, "Implications of the Western Response to the Soviet Intervention in Czechoslovakia," *Atlantic Community Quarterly* 7 (Spring 1969): 59-75; and Robert Ranger, "NATO's Reaction to Czechoslovakia: The Strategy of Ambiguous Response," *World Today* 25 (January 1969): 19-26.

34. See, for example, NAC final communiqué, Brussels, 3-4 December 1970, and the attached annex "Alliance Defense for the Seventies" [AD-70s], which declared that "NATO's approach to security in the 1970s will continue to be based on the twin concepts of defense and détente" (para. 20).

35. See, for example, Peter Jener, "NATOs Solid and Undiminished Defense—Basis for Progress Towards Détente," *NATO Review* 6 (December 1973): 3-5; and Kenneth Rush, deputy secretary of state, "The NATO Alliance: The Basis for an Era of Negotiation," *DOSB* (18 June 1973): 871.

36. See Vice President Humphrey's address to the NAC, 7 April 1967, *DOSB* (1 May 1967): 681.

37. Cleveland asserted that "if NATO did not exist, there would indeed be danger of separate negotiations enabling the Soviets to play one Western ally off

against the others—to use détente as a device for discrimination." See Cleveland, "Golden Rule," 145; and Rostow, "Concert and Consultation," 427.

38. Successive NAC communiqués and declarations throughout the late 1960s and early 1970s, while giving explicit approval to *Ostpolitik*, observed the necessity for continued close consultation among the allies.

39. Martin J. Hillenbrand, assistant secretary for European affairs, "NATO and U.S. Security Interests," statement before the Special Subcommittee on NATO Commitments of the House Committee on Armed Services, 14 October 1971, *DOSB* (8 November 1971): 518.

40. See, for example, Richard F. Pedersen, counselor to the Department, "NATO in the Coming Decade," address before the Naval Academy Foreign Affairs Conference at Annapolis on 21 April 1970, *DOSB* (18 May 1970): 634.

41. Rush, "The NATO Alliance," 868.

42. Elliot Richardson, under secretary of state, "The United States and Western European Security," address before the Chicago Council on Foreign Relations on 20 January 1970, *DOSB* (9 February 1970): 158.

43. For Kissinger's comments disparaging the utility of NATO in détente, see Walter Isaacson, *Kissinger: A Biography* (London: Faber and Faber, 1992), 437.

44. Kissinger, *White House Years*, 399-402, 947-48.

45. Garthoff, *Détente and Confrontation*, 115

46. See, for example, "Abolish NATO—But then What?" *NATO's Fifteen Nations* 15 (February-March 1970): 80-86; and Manlio Brosio, "Will NATO Survive Détente?" *World Today* 27 (June 1971): 231-41.

47. For the text of the resolution, see *Congressional Record* (31 August 1966): 21442. The history of the Mansfield Resolution is discussed in Stanley R. Sloan, *Defense Burdensharing: U.S. Relations with NATO Allies and Japan*, Congressional Research Service (CRS) Report no. 85-101F (Washington, D.C.: CRS, 1985).

48. Sloan, *Defense Burdensharing*, 8.

49. For American protestations concerning the importance of consultation, see, for example, President Nixon's remarks to the NAC, *DOSB* (24 March 1969): 251; and, for a response to European concern about superpower condominium and the impact of Vietnam, see Richardson, "The U.S. and Western European Security," 151, 157.

50. On this trend, see John N. Yochelson, "The American Military Presence in Europe: Current Debate in the U.S.," *Orbis* 15 (Fall 1971): 796-802.

51. "The NAC Celebrates the 20th Anniversary of the Signing of the North Atlantic Treaty," address by President Nixon, *DOSB* (28 April 1969): 254. See also Richard M. Nixon, "NATO: Facing the Truth of Our Times," *Atlantic Community Quarterly* 7 (Summer 1969): 203-8.

52. For a report by the committee's first chairman, Daniel P. Moynihan, see "The NATO Committee on the Challenges of Modern Society," *Atlantic Community Quarterly* 7 (Winter 1969-1970): 530-37. See also James R. Huntley, *Man's Environment and the Atlantic Alliance* (Brussels: NATO Information Service, 1971).

For a more recent account of the CCMS, see *The North Atlantic Treaty Organization: Facts and Figures* [hereafter *NATO Facts and Figures*] (Brussels: NATO Information Service, 1989), 311-15.

53. See, for example, E.H. Albert, "Bonn's Moscow Treaty and Its Implications," *International Affairs* 47 (April 1971): 316-26. As a result of the Basic Treaty, both the FRG and the GDR were permitted to join the United Nations in September 1973.

54. E. H. Albert, "The Brandt Doctrine of Two States in Germany," *International Affairs* 46 (April 1970): 292-303. For examples of Brandt's reasoning behind *Ostpolitik*, see Willy Brandt, "Détente over the Long Haul," *Survival* 9 (October 1967): 310-12; Willy Brandt, *A Peace Policy for Europe* (New York: Holt, Rinehart and Winston, 1968); Willy Brandt, "German Policy towards the East," *Foreign Affairs* 46 (April 1968): 476-86; Willy Brandt, "German Foreign Policy," *Survival* 11 (December 1969): 370-72. Secondary contemporary sources include Karl E. Birnbaum, *East and West Germany: A Modus Vivendi* (Lexington, Mass.: Lexington Books, D.C. Heath, 1973); and Lawrence L. Whetten, *Germany's Ostpolitik* (London: Oxford University Press, 1971).

55. See, for example, Willy Brandt, "Germany's 'Westpolitik,'" *Foreign Affairs* 50 (April 1972): 416-26; Carl H. Amme, Jr., "National Strategies within the Alliance: West Germany," *NATO's Fifteen Nations* 17 (August-September 1972): 76; and Egon Bahr, "German *Ostpolitik* and Superpower Relations," *Survival* 15 (November-December 1973): 296-300.

56. (Maj.) William C. Barnhart, *The Future of Europe and NATO: Ostpolitik and its Implications*—Research Study (Maxwell AFB, Ala.: Air Command and Staff College, 1973).

57. This point is more fully developed in Karl W. Deutsch, *France, Germany and the Western Alliance: A Study of Elite Attitudes on European Integration and World Politics* (New York: Charles Scribner's Sons, 1967). A comprehensive study on West German foreign policy during the Cold War is Hanreider, *Germany, America, Europe*.

58. The need for such protection was deemed to be clear. See, for example, the criticism that *Ostpolitik* was a direct threat to NATO, in Geoffrey Stewart-Smith, ed., *Brandt and the Destruction of NATO* (New York: International Public Service, 1973); and (Lt. Col.) Donald J. Cipra, *Ostpolitik and its Influence on the Malaise in NATO Solidarity*—Professional Study (Maxwell AFB, Ala.: Air War College, 1974).

59. See, for example, Neville Brown, *Arms without Empire* (Harmondsworth: Penguin, 1967); and, for a shorter version, Neville Brown, "Arms and the Switch towards Europe," *International Affairs* 43 (July 1967): 468-82. I have drawn here and in what follows from Sherwood, *Allies in Crisis*, 128-29.

60. This point is more fully explored in L. W. Martin, "British Defense Policy: The Long Recessional," *Adelphi Papers* 61 (London: IISS, 1969); and Philip Darby, *British Defense Policy East of Suez, 1947-1968* (London: Oxford University Press, 1973).

61. For a general discussion of the U.K. negotiations to join the EEC, see Western European Union, *A Retrospective View of the Political Year in Europe* (Paris: annual volumes); and Western European Union, *The British Application for Membership in the European Communities, 1963-1968* (Paris: May 1968).

62. See Wilson, *A Personal Record*, 187; and Richard Crossman, *The Diaries of a Cabinet Minister, 1964-1966* (New York: Holt, Rinehart and Winston, 1975), 1:456.

63. *Statement on the Defense Estimates*, 1966, "Part 1: The Defense Review," cmnd. 2901 (London: HMSO, 1966), 7, para. 9.

64. Under the plan, Aden was to be evacuated and forces in Malaysia, Singapore, and the Persian Gulf region were to be drastically reduced. Britain's carrier force was to be phased out, and the government decided to cancel an order for fifty F-111s from the United States. See *Statement on the Defense Estimates*, 1968, cmnd. 3540 (London: HMSO, 1969), and the prime minister's statements in the House of Commons in *Hansard*, 16 January 1968, cols. 1580-85. See also Edward Heath, "Realism in British Foreign Policy," *Foreign Affairs* 48 (October 1969): 39-50; and Charles Douglas-Home, "British Defense Cuts—1968," *Survival* 10 (March 1968): 70-78.

65. *Statement on the Defense Estimates*, 1969, cmnd. 3927 (London: HMSO, 1969), 9, para. 45.

66. Edward Heath, *Old World, New Horizons: Britain, the Common Market and the Atlantic Alliance—The Godkin Lectures at Harvard* (London: Oxford University Press, 1970); F. S. Northedge, "Britain as a Second-Rank Power," *International Affairs* 46 (January 1970): 37-47; and "Britain Rallies to the Aid of NATO," *NATO's Fifteen Nations* 18 (February-March 1973): 16-20.

67. See Michael Stewart, "Britain, Europe and the Alliance," *Foreign Affairs* 48 (July 1970): 70-78; and the *White Papers* issued by the Wilson and Heath governments, which anticipated a linkage between the change in Britain's defense policy and increased political cooperation in Europe: Great Britain, Command Paper 4289, *Britain and the European Communities* (London: HMSO, 1970); and Great Britain, Command Paper 4517, *Britain and the European Communities* (London: HMSO, 1970). See also the memoirs of U.K. Foreign Secretary George Brown, *In My Way* (London: Gollancz, 1971): 209-223.

68. For an extended discussion of the perceived immediate problems for both NATO and France in the post-1966 period, see Amme, *NATO without France.*

69. French reasoning behind mending ties with NATO is masterfully presented in Michael Harrison, *Reluctant Ally: France and Atlantic Security* (Baltimore: Johns Hopkins University Press, 1981).

70. See, for example, Guy de Carmoy, "The Last Year of de Gaulle's Foreign Policy," *International Affairs* 45 (July 1969): 424-35.

71. R. J. Hill, "French Strategy after de Gaulle," *International Journal* 23 (September 1968): 244-53; Michel Debré, "France's Global Strategy," *Foreign Affairs* 49 (April 1971): 395-406; and Edward A. Kolodziej, *French International Policy under de Gaulle and Pompidou: The Politics of Grandeur* (Ithaca, N.Y.: Cornell University Press, 1974), 12-13, 55.

72. Contemporary scholarly literature on French security policy includes, Kohl, *French Nuclear Diplomacy*; Edward A. Kolodziej, *Patterns of French Foreign Policy, 1958-1967* (McLean, Va.: Research Analysis Corp., 1968); and Wolf Mende, *Deterrence and Persuasion: French Nuclear Armament in the Context of National Policy, 1945-1969* (London: Faber and Faber, 1970).

73. Edmond Combeaux, "French Military Policy and European Federation," *Orbis* 13 (Spring 1969): 151-52.

74. For the policy of selective cooperation, see the remarks of Defense Secretary Michel Debré in Debré, "France's Global Strategy," 395-406; and Michel Debré, "The Principles of Our Defense Policy," *Survival* 12 (November 1970): 376-83. France stayed in the NATO technical weapons development group at The Hague and increased its membership on NATO technical committees. In addition, French ties to the NATO early warning system (NADGE) were strengthened and French air defenses were coordinated with NATO. France joined in building a communications network, participated in antisubmarine research at La Spezia, and conducted conventional joint training exercises with NATO forces. In the autumn of 1968, a French admiral commanded joint NATO air and naval exercises in the Mediterranean. In 1971, the French Air Force "defended" against six combined NATO forces in war games, and French troops in West Germany conducted joint exercises with U.S. forces. See Kolodziej, *French International Policy*, 143; and *Economist*, 24 June 1972, 45. For a more lengthy treatment, see (Lt. Col.) Martin Van Hunn, *NATO and France after de Gaulle*—Professional Study (Maxwell AFB, Ala.: Air War College, 1974).

75. Quoted in *US News and World Report*, 2 March 1970, 44. See also Kolodziej, *French International Policy*, 145.

76. Debré, "France's Global Strategy," 401.

77. *NATO Facts and Figures*, 87.

78. Morse, *Foreign Policy and Interdependence in Gaullist France*, 116-46; and, for further explicit discussion of French "empty chair" tactics, see Kolodziej, *French International Policy*, 135-37.

79. See, for example, George Kennan, "After the Cold War: American Foreign Policy in the 1970s," *Foreign Affairs* 51 (October 1972): 210-27; and F. S. Northedge, *East-West Relations: Détente and Afterwards* (Ife, Nigeria: University of Ife Press, 1975).

80. See, for example, Henry Brandon, *The Retreat of American Power: Nixon and Kissinger's Foreign Policy and Its Effects* (Garden City, N.Y.: Doubleday, 1973).

81. One senior State Department official declared in June 1973 that "strengthening détente and a strong defense, making progress with our adversaries and maintaining close relations with our allies—these are not contradictory concepts. In fact they are essential to one another." See Rush, "The NATO Alliance," 871. The *Harmel Report* drew similar axiomatic linkages. See *Harmel Report*, para. 5.

82. The roots of transatlantic discord are explored in Godson, *Transatlantic Crisis*.

83. For a general discussion of the impact of European union on NATO, see

Margaret M. Ball, *NATO and the European Union Movement* (Westport, Conn.: Greenwood Press, 1974).

84. Richard M. Nixon, "Peace through Partnership—The Nixon Doctrine," *DOSB* (24 November 1969): 437.

85. Robert S. Littwak, *Détente and the Nixon Doctrine* (Cambridge: Cambridge University Press, 1984), 140.

86. Richard M. Nixon, *United States Foreign Policy for the 1970s—A New Strategy for Peace*, A Report to the Congress, 18 February 1970 (Washington, D.C.: Government Printing Office, 1970), 276.

87. From 1970 to 1973, European defense spending increased from $24 billion to $39 billion. See the statement of Arthur H. Hartman, assistant secretary for European affairs, before the Ad Hoc Subcommittee on U.S. Military Commitments in Europe of the House Committee on Armed Services on 15 February 1974, *DOSB* (11 March 1974): 245.

88. For the announcement of the formation of the EDIP, see NAC final communiqué, 3-4 December 1970. In 1973 EDIP announced that its members would spend $2.9 billion for the construction of 1,600 aircraft shelters at 73 NATO airfields. It also announced the creation of the Burdensharing Study Group. In 1974 the ten EUROGROUP members pledged a $2 billion increase over the previous year. See *DOSB* (11 March 1974): 245; and Alv Jakob Fostervolli, "European Defense and the EUROGROUP," *NATO Review* 22 (November 1974): 8-11.

89. *NATO Facts and Figures*, 22.

90. *NATO Facts and Figures*, 79.

91. See, for example, the testimony of Martin J. Hillenbrand, assistant secretary for European affairs, 14 October 1971 in U.S. House of Representatives. *United States Relations with Europe in the Decade of the 1970s.* Hearings before the Subcommittee on Europe of the Committee on Foreign Affairs (91st Cong., 2d sess.), 31-35.

92. Richard M. Nixon, *United States Foreign Policy for the 1970s—Building for Peace*, A Report to the Congress, 25 February 1971 (Washington, D.C.: Government Printing Office, 1971), 358.

93. See, for example, (Col.) Will G. MacLauren, Jr., *"Europeanization:" Some Considerations Concerning the Application of the Nixon Doctrine to NATO—* Professional Study (Maxwell AFB, Ala.: Air War College, 1971); and Werner Kalteflieter, "Europe and the Nixon Doctrine: A German Point of View," *Orbis* 17 (Spring 1973): 75-94.

94. Henry A. Kissinger, "The Year of Europe," address to the Associated Press luncheon at New York on 23 April 1973 in *American Foreign Policy*, 104-5.

95. Henry A. Kissinger, "A New Atlantic Charter," *Survival* 15 (July/August 1973): 188-92. Roosevelt and Churchill signed the original charter at Newfoundland in August 1941. It was essentially a statement of common principles in the national policies of their respective countries. After the United States entered the war in December 1941, the Charter served as guidance for the formulation of common war aims. The text of the Atlantic Charter is in Commager, *Documents of American History,* 2:451.

96. Kissinger, "The Year of Europe," 104.

97. Stanley Hoffmann, *Primacy or World Order?* (New York: McGraw Hill, 1978), 48-49; and A.W. Deporte, *Europe between the Superpowers: The Enduring Balance* (New Haven: Yale University Press, 1979), 216-17.

98. Curt Gasteyger, "Europe Cool to U.S. Suggestions on Revitalized Charter," *Atlantic Community Quarterly* 11 (Fall 1973): 319-21; and Michael Howard, "NATO and the Year of Europe," *Survival* 16 (January/February 1974): 21-27. See also J. Robert Schaetzel, "Some Questions for Dr. Kissinger," *Foreign Policy* 12 (Fall 1973): 66-78.

99. Secretary Kissinger's news conference, *DOSB* (15 October 1973): 481.

100. *DOSB* (15 October 1973): 480.

101. In addition, Britain and France declined to support the U.S.-sponsored cease-fire resolution in the UN. Kissinger, outraged at what he considered a British betrayal, ordered a temporary ban on U.S.-U.K. intelligence information sharing. See Henry A. Kissinger, *Years of Upheaval* (Boston: Little, Brown, 1982), 709; and *Economist*, "The Unfriendly Friends," 9 February 1974, 18. For a penetrating analysis of the war and its impact on NATO's out-of-area debate, see Sherwood, *Allies in Crisis*, 138-44.

102. The text of the letter is in Kissinger, *Years of Upheaval*, 583. For further discussion, see Scott D. Sagan, "The Lessons of the Yom Kippur Alert," *Foreign Policy* 36 (Fall 1979): 160-77.

103. Kissinger, *Years of Upheaval*, 713.

104. Z (Pseud.) "The Year of Europe?" *Foreign Affairs* 52 (January 1974): 237-48; and Andrew J. Pierre, "What Happened to the Year of Europe?" *World Today* 30 (March 1974): 110-19.

105. For a review of these charges, see Arthur A. Hartman, "The Impact of the Middle East Crisis on the Atlantic Alliance," testimony before the joint hearing of the Subcommittee on Europe and the Subcommittee on the Northeast and South Asia of the House Committee on Foreign Affairs, 19 February 1974, *DOSB* (18 March 1974): 279-84. See also William B. Quandt, "The Western Alliance in the Middle East: Problems for U.S. Foreign Policy," in *The Middle East and the Western Alliance*, Steven L. Speigel, ed. (London: George Allen and Unwin, 1982), 10.

106. For Kissinger's account, see Kissinger, *Years of Upheaval*, 896-934. See also the statements of the participants in "The Washington Energy Conference," *Atlantic Community Quarterly* 12 (Spring 1974): 22-54.

107. See *Economist*, "Henry's Thunderbolts," 16 March 1974, 11-12; and *Economist*, "With Such Friends, Who Needs Enemies?" 16 March 1974, 43-44. For Kissinger's views, see Kissinger, *Years of Upheaval*, 930. See also Sherwood, *Allies in Crisis*, 142-44.

108. For U.S. criticism, see Kissinger, *Years of Upheaval*, 930.

109. This point is the topic of a lengthy study by the U.S. Department of Defense. See United States Department of Defense, War College, *Effects of the Middle East War and the Energy Crisis on the Future of the Atlantic Alliance—* Proceedings of the National Security Affairs Conference, July 1974, Panel 8

(Washington, D.C.: National War College, February 1975).

110. See, for example, Henry A. Kissinger, "Creativity Together or Irrelevance Apart," *Atlantic Community Quarterly* 11 (Winter 1973/1974): 413-21.

111. Henry A. Kissinger, "The United States and a Unifying Europe: The Necessity for Partnership," address before the Pilgrim's Society at London, 12 December 1973, *DOSB* (31 December 1973): 777-82.

112. Secretary Kissinger's news conference, *DOSB* (21 March 1974): 354-55.

113. The theme that détente had been imperiled by the war in the Middle East, and that it had led to friction among the allies is discussed in Ed Friedland, *The Great Détente Disaster: Oil and the Decline of American Foreign Policy* (New York: Basic Books, 1975); and Schaetzel, *The Unhinged Alliance*.

114. Kissinger, "The United States and a Unifying Europe," 779.

115. Kissinger, "The United States and a Unifying Europe," 778.

116. NAC final communiqué, Ottawa, 19 June 1974, and the attached "Declaration on Atlantic Relations," signed by the NATO Heads of State and Government in Brussels on 26 June 1974. See also Secretary Kissinger's press conference, *DOSB* (29 July 1974): 196; and "President Nixon Visits NATO Headquarters and the Soviet Union," *DOSB* (29 July 1974): 165-73.

117. Declaration on Atlantic Relations, para. 7.

118. Declaration on Atlantic Relations, paras. 5,9.

119. Declaration on Atlantic Relations, para. 6.

120. Declaration on Atlantic Relations, para. 11.

121. See, for example, Joseph M. A. H. Luns, "The North Atlantic Alliance Commemorates its Twenty-fifth Birthday," address to the NATO Heads of State and Government by the secretary general, *NATO Review* 22 (June 1974): 166-68.

122. See, for example, Valéry Giscard d'Estaing, "French Defense Policy," address to the *Institue des Hautes de Défense Nationale, Survival* 18 (September/October 1976): 225-30.

123. See Hans Dietrich Genscher, "The FRG's Alliance Policy," *NATO Review* 22 (December 1974): 3-5; and Kissinger, *Years of Upheaval*, 909, 933-34.

124. At the May 1975 Heads of State and Government meeting in Brussels, Ford, reversing Nixon's policy of letting Kissinger deal with the media, conducted the press briefings. He also refused to allow Kissinger to pose for photos with other leaders. Kissinger, *Years of Upheaval*, 240, 983; and Garthoff, *Détente and Confrontation*, 24.

125. Ford's speech at Peoria, Illinois, on 5 March 1976 is quoted in Garthoff, *Détente and Confrontation*, 548.

Chapter 5: Arming to Disarm

1. I have not attempted a survey of the new Cold War: there are several excellent books and articles on the subject, and little new material to justify another. I describe the conditions of the new Cold War primarily to show the effect these had on

conceptions of NATO and how they were reflected in rhetoric. See Noam Chomsky, *Towards a New Cold War: Essays on the Current Crisis and How We Got There* (London: Sinclair Brown, 1982); Noam Chomsky, Jonathan Steele, and John Gittings, *Superpowers in Collision: The Cold War Now* (London: Penguin, 1982); Fred Halliday, *The Making of the Second Cold War* (London: Verso, 1983); Tad Szulc, "The New Brinkmanship," *New Republic* (8 November 1980): 18-21; and, for a view from the other side of the political spectrum, Samuel P. Huntington, "Renewed Hostility," in *The Making of America's Soviet Policy*, Joseph S. Nye, Jr., ed. (New Haven: Yale University Press, 1984), 265-90.

2. A partial exception to this trend was the phenomenon of Eurocommunism, which for a short period threatened to become a major stumbling block in transatlantic relations. While West European communist parties did make notable parliamentary gains in France and Italy in the mid- to late-1970s, and while for a time it appeared that communists would rule in Portugal, NATO's European leaders tended to view these gains as signs of healthy democracy and not, like their American counterparts, as a threat to NATO. For Kissinger's warnings about Eurocommunism and European charges of U.S. meddling in their internal affairs, see *DOSB* (21 June 1976): 774. For European views on Eurocommunism, see David Owen, "Eurocommunism, Socialism and Democracy," *NATO Review* 1 (February 1978): 3-11; Pierre Hasner, "Eurocommunism and Western Europe," *NATO Review* 4 (August 1978): 8-12; and James P. O'Leary, "Can NATO Survive Eurocommunism?," *International Security Review* 5 (Spring 1980): 70-90. A more thorough analysis is in James E. Dougherty and Dianne Pfaltzgraff, *Eurocommunism and the Atlantic Alliance* (Cambridge, Mass.: International Foreign Policy Analysis, 1977).

3. For a comprehensive study of the foreign policy of Carter, see Burton I. Kaufman, *The Presidency of James Earl Carter* (Lawrence: University of Kansas Press, 1993).

4. Inaugural address of President Carter, 20 January 1977, *DOSB* (14 February 1977): 121-22.

5. President Carter's Report to the American People, transcript of radio and television broadcast, 2 February 1977, *DOSB* (28 February 1977): 161. See also Jimmy Carter, "Peace, Arms Control, World Economic Progress, and Human Rights: Basic Priorities of United States Foreign Policy," address by the president to the United Nations General Assembly, 17 March 1977, *DOSB* (11 April 1977): 329-33; Cyrus Vance, "Human Rights and Foreign Policy," address by the secretary of state at the University of Georgia at Athens, 30 April 1977, *DOSB* (23 May 1977): 505-8; and Warren Christopher, "Human Rights: An Important Concern of U.S. Foreign Policy," statement by deputy secretary of state before the Subcommittee on Foreign Assistance of the Senate Committee on Foreign Relations, 7 March 1977, *DOSB* (28 March 1977): 284-91.

6. Carter's first action on foreign policy, with his administration less than ninety hours old, was to send Vice President Walter Mondale to address the NAC in

Brussels. This address, which Mondale described as an attempt to respond to "doubts among friends about our will and steadfastness," was the first of many efforts to combine a reaffirmation of the American commitment to NATO with an appeal for the alliance to embrace a human rights agenda. Mondale reaffirmed the American commitment to consultation and called on NATO to renew and promote more vigorously its commitment to "shared political and human values." See Mondale's address to the NAC, 24 January 1977, *DOSB* (7 March 1977): 182; and Arthur H. Hartman, assistant secretary of state for European affairs, "U.S. Policy Towards Our NATO Partners: Traditional Commitments and New Directions," statement before the Subcommittee on Europe and the Middle East of the House Committee on International Relations, 23 May 1977, *DOSB* (13 June 1977): 635-39.

7. President Carter's remarks to the NAC, London, 10 May 1977, *DOSB* (6 June 1977): 597-601.

8. Carter's remarks at the opening ceremonies of the NAC summit meeting in Washington, 30 May 1978, *DOSB* (1 July 1978): 1-3.

9. NAC final communiqué, London, 11 May 1977.

10. In this regard they had some cause for concern, because détente had already been imperiled by the Jackson-Vanik Amendment, which linked trade agreements with the Soviets to the emigration of Soviet Jews to the West. The Soviets objected to this linkage, denounced the amendment, and moved to restrict Jewish emigration.

11. For more on this point, see Brian White, *Britain, Détente, and Changing East-West Relations* (London: Routledge, 1992), 139; and Michael Clarke, "The Implementation of Britain's CSCE Policy, 1975-1984" in *Foreign Policy Implementation*, Steve Smith and Michael Clarke, eds. (London: Allen and Unwin, 1985), 142-65.

12. How this came about is examined in William Korey, *The Promises We Keep: Human Rights, The Helsinki Process and American Foreign Policy* (New York: St. Martin's Press, 1993).

13. In practical terms, Carter, who believed that restrained arms transfers could help shape a new global regard for human rights, moved to curtail sales of American arms to all states except long-standing allies, including of course the United States' European allies. More important, however, were the sanctions, which took the form of aid cutoffs, against some Latin American states for human rights violations. For more on the administration's policy on arms transfers, see "Controlling Arms Transfers: An Instrument of U.S. Foreign Policy," *DOSB* (1 August 1977): 150-55.

14. Jimmy Carter, *Keeping Faith* (New York: Bantam, 1982), 141-43; and Jerel A. Rosati, *The Carter Administration's Quest for Global Community: Beliefs and Their Impact on Behavior* (Charleston: University of South Carolina Press, 1987).

15. President Carter's State of the Union address before a joint session of Congress, 19 January 1978, *DOSB* (February 1978): 20-21. See Warren Christopher, "Human Rights: The Diplomacy of the First Year," address before the American Bar Association in New Orleans on 13 February 1978, *DOSB* (February 1978): 30-33.

16. NAC final communiqué, 31 May 1978, from the NATO Heads of State and Government meeting at Washington.

17. An independent study in 1974 estimated that NATO was wasting $11 billion per annum by failing to reap the benefits of common research and development, joint procurement, and common support. See Thomas A. Callaghan, Jr., *United States/European Economic Cooperation in Military and Civil Technology* (Georgetown: Center of Strategic and International Studies, 1977).

18. In February 1976, for example, the EUROGROUP, with the strong support of its chairman, U.K. Defense Secretary Roy Mason, had moved to include the French in its efforts to rationalize Europe's fragmented defense industries. To get around French sensibilities, a new organization called the Independent European Program Group (IEPG), which comprised the EUROGROUP plus France, was established. For more on the role of Britain in this effort, see Michael Carver, *Tightrope Walking: European Defense Policy Since 1945* (London: Hutchison, 1992), 115. See also Walter LaBerge, "Standardization and Interoperability," *NATO Review* 6 (December 1976): 13-23; D. C. R. Heyhoe, "The Alliance and Europe: Part 6: The European Program Group," *Adelphi Papers* 129 (London: IISS, 1976/1977); Willem Scholten, "The Eurogroup's First Ten Years," *NATO Review* 2 (April 1978): 3-5; and Luciano Radi, "European Armaments Cooperation," *NATO Review* 3 (June 1977): 8-10. An interesting critique of these moves is Geoffrey L. Williams, *The European Defense Initiative: Europe's Bid for Equality* (New York: St. Martin's Press, 1986).

19. This move had a basis in congressional pressure. In the 1976 Department of Defense Appropriations Act (Section 803, c), Congress declared that "a two-way street concept of cooperation in defense procurement between Europe and North America could only work in a realistic sense if the European nations operated on a unified and collective basis." See also Martin Edwards, ed., *International Arms Procurement* (Elmsford, N.Y.: Pergamon Press, 1981); Julian Critchley, "A Common Policy for Armaments," *NATO Review* 1 (February 1979): 10-15; and (Maj.) Dennis M. Drummond, "Getting Traffic Moving on NATO's Two-Way Street," *Air University Review* 30 (September/October 1979): 26-34.

20. See Stephen Kirby, "The Independent European Program Group: The Failure of Low-Profile High-Politics," *Journal of Common Market Studies* 18 (December 1979): 175-96; and Philip Taylor, "Weapons Standardization in NATO: Collaborative Security or Economic Competition?" *International Organization* 36 (Winter 1982): 95-112.

21. See, for example, Lawrence S. Kaplan, "NATO in the Second Generation," *NATO Review* 5 (October 1980), 1-7. Or, in book form, see Sloan, *Toward a New Transatlantic Bargain.*

22. For further information on the magnitude of Soviet force modernization, see Carl G. Jacobsen, ed., *The Soviet Defense Enigma: Estimating Costs and Burden* (London: Oxford University Press for SIPRI, 1987), 144-45.

23. NAC final communiqué, 31 May 1978, Washington.

24. These included improvements in force readiness, the mobility of reserves, strengthened air and electronic warfare defenses, an enhanced maritime posture, improved logistics support, and better command, communications, and control facilities and methods. Rapid deployment plans were approved and the United States agreed to preposition heavy equipment for three divisions in Europe, with the European allies providing support and other facilities. In December 1978, as part of the LTDP, the Defense Planning Committee (DPC) approved the purchase of an AWACs force for NATO, making it the largest single commonly-funded program ever undertaken by the alliance. See NAC final communiqué, 31 May 1978, Washington, part 2—the Long-term Defense Program. On the AWACs decision, see "Airborne Early Warning and Control System," *NATO Review* 1 (February 1979): 6.

25. President Carter's remarks at the closing ceremonies of the NAC summit meeting in Washington, 30 May 1978, *DOSB* (1 July 1978): 3.

26. David Greenwood, "NATO's Three Per Cent Solution," *Survival* 6 (November/December 1981): 252-61.

27. See Helmut Schmidt, "Policy of Safeguarding Peace," excerpts of the government's response to major questions concerning security and defense policy of the FRG in the Bundestag, *Bulletin* 5 (October 1979): 9, para. 33 (Bonn: Press and Information Office of the FRG). Hereafter cited as *Bulletin*.

28. See, for example, President Carter's remarks at the closing ceremonies of the NAC summit meeting in Washington, 30 May 1978, *DOSB* (1 July 1978): 3.

29. See Robert W. Komer, "NATO's Long-term Defense Program—Origins and Objectives," *NATO Review* 3 (June 1978): 9-12.

30. See, for example, Joseph Godson, "Is NATO Still Necessary?" *NATO Review* 4 (August 1976): 18-21; Alexander Haig, SACEUR, "The Challenge for the West in a Changing Strategic Environment," *NATO Review* 3 (June 1976): 10-13; and Alexander Haig, "NATO and the Security of the West," *NATO Review* 4 (August 1978): 8-12.

31. American critics of détente attributed its demise to three main causes: Soviet exploitation of opportunities for expanded influence in the Third World, which was said to violate the 1972 agreement on Basic Principles; the deployment of new strategic and conventional weapons in Europe; and Soviet political actions against dissidents and other violations of the Helsinki Accords. In September 1978, one senior State Department official told Congress that: "It is evident that the difficulties in the U.S.-Soviet relationship in recent months have astringently washed away the remnants of any euphoric expectations from the period of détente as it appeared to exist six years ago." See the statement by Marshall D. Shulman, special advisor to the secretary of state on Soviet affairs, before the Subcommittee on Europe and the Middle East of the House Committee on International Relations on 26 September 1978, *DOSB* (November 1978): 33.

32. See, for example, Sir John Killick, "Is NATO Relevant to the 1980s?" *World Today* 36 (January 1980): 4-10; and Kenneth Adler and Douglas Westerman, "Is NATO in Trouble?" *Public Opinion* 4 (August/September 1981): 8-12. Not

everyone accepted this reasoning, least of all those most closely associated with NATO, who continued to argue that a strong NATO would eventually induce the Soviets to negotiate on a wide range of issues and moderate their behavior in the Third World. NATO Secretary General Joseph Luns declared on the alliance's thirtieth anniversary that "the old axiom of strength in unity which was the base on which the Alliance was built still holds true today." Joseph M. A. H. Luns, "Thirty Years Later—Aims of the Alliance Still Valid," *NATO Review* 2 (April 1979): 8.

33. These problems and how to solve them are discussed in Hahn and Pfaltzgraff, *Atlantic Community in Crisis*.

34. While the allies wrestled publicly with fashioning a conventional response, the Nuclear Planning Group created the High Level Group (HLG) in the autumn of 1977, to undertake the more quiet process of studying NATO's long-term theater nuclear needs. The HLG, comprised of members of the NPG and with the United States acting as chairman, was assisted by the Special Group on Arms Control and Related Matters, which allowed non-NPG members an advisory role in the process. See David N. Schwartz, *NATO's Nuclear Dilemmas* (Washington, D.C.: Brookings, 1983), 194-232; and "Consulting on NATO Nuclear Policy," *NATO Review* 5 (October 1979): 25-28.

35. The FRG appeared most eager to receive the missiles, though it stated that it would not be the only member to do so. British, German, and Italian representatives agreed to seek immediate approval from their parliaments, while those from the Belgian government imposed a six-month caveat, pending developments in arms control. The Dutch adopted a similar stance, promising to decide within two years. The Danes proposed a six-month postponement of any decision, but this found no support from any other members. The United States was to pay for the development and production of the missiles, while all members of the IMO agreed to pay for infrastructure funding.

36. See the final communiqués from Brussels of both the special NATO meeting of foreign and defense ministers, 11-12 December 1979, and the NAC, 13-14 December 1979. See also Paul Buteux, "Theater Nuclear Forces—Modernization Plan and Arms Control," *NATO Review* 6 (December 1980): 1-6; Stephen R. Hanmer, Jr., "NATO's Long-range Theater Nuclear Forces: Modernization in Parallel with Arms Control," *NATO Review* 1 (February 1980): 1-6. Book-length sources are Paul Buteux, *The Politics of Nuclear Consultation in NATO* (Cambridge: Cambridge University Press, 1983); and J. D. Reed, *NATO's Theater Nuclear Forces—A Coherent Strategy for the 1980s* (Washington, D.C.: National Defense University Press, 1983).

37. *DOSB* (February 1980): 15

38. Some people believed that a theater balance existed independently of a strategic balance. For a statement of that rationale, see Richard H. Ullman, "Out of the Euro-missile Mire," *Foreign Policy* 50 (Spring 1983): 39-52.

39. NATO leaders may have underestimated the strength of antinuclear sentiment in Europe, but they were not unaware of the need to enlist early public support for any decision on the deployment of new missiles in Europe. Brzezinski,

for example, boldly declared that: "The true test of NATO's purpose lies with our allied parliaments and publics. Are they willing to pay to the political price required to avoid the infinitely more costly alternative of intimidation at best, and even war at worst?" The public did not quite see it in these stark terms. See Brzezinski's remarks before the 25th Assembly of the Atlantic Treaty Association on 10 October 1979, *DOSB* (November 1979): 36.

40. For this type of rationale, see, for example, the communiqué from the special NATO meeting of foreign and defense ministers, 11-12 December 1979; statement by Secretary Vance, *DOSB* (February 1980): 15; and "NATO's Fourth Decade: Defense and Détente," remarks by Vice President Walter Mondale and Zbigniew Brzezinski before the 25th Assembly of the Atlantic Treaty Association on 10 October 1979, *DOSB* (November 1979): 32-35.

41. The dual-track approach was unique because, for the first time, a U.S. nuclear program had been made dependent on a prior allied commitment to deployment. It was also the first to be directly linked to an arms control agenda. Before the United States would agree to produce the new missiles, the allies had to agree to deploy them—a condition that later served to promote the notion that the United States had forced the missiles on its unwilling allies. This conditional arrangement later was exploited by European antinuclear activists, who tended to ignore the pivotal role played by European leaders both in calling for new missiles and in getting the Americans to produce them. Although the announcement of the dual-track decision received great attention, the public furor surrounding NATO's response to Soviet nuclear force improvements began as early as October 1977, when Helmut Schmidt made a widely publicized speech in London to the IISS. This speech, which made only general references to the so-called problem of "gray area" weapons (i.e., medium-range nuclear systems not covered by the SALT II process), had been presaged by Schmidt's private comments to the NAC in May and by Carter's own warnings about Soviet nuclear forces in February. Schmidt's speech is reprinted in *Survival* 6 (January/February 1978): 2-10. Carter had publicly asked the Soviets in February 1977 to "ease deployment of the mobile missile." See *DOSB* (28 February 1977): 159; and Richard Burt, "The SS-20 and the Euro-strategic Balance," *World Today* 33 (February 1977): 43-51. German concern over the gray-area problem is also outlined in the FRG's *White Paper on Defense* (Bonn, September 1979), excerpted in *Survival* 6 (November/December 1979): 273-77.

42. Christoph Bertram, "The Implications of Theater Nuclear Weapons in Europe," *Foreign Affairs* 60 (Winter 1981/1982): 310.

43. In October 1979 Walter Mondale told a largely European audience that the U.S. commitment was "permanent and lasting and complete in terms of total public support." He was followed by Brzezinski, who denied that de-coupling would ever occur and who claimed that U.S. support for NATO was "unshakable. It is organic. It is complete. There are no conceivable circumstances in which we would not react to a security threat directed at our European allies." See their remarks before the Atlantic Treaty Association on 10 October 1979, *DOSB* (November 1979): 32-35.

44. *Hansard* (13 December 1979): col. 1542.

45. *Bulletin* (20 December 1983): 8.

46. Vance declared that the invasion "underscores the importance of our policies of strengthening conventional and theater nuclear forces." *DOSB* (February 1980): 4. See also the special issue on Afghanistan of *NATO Review* 3 (June 1980): 1-13; Dimitri K. Simes, "The Death of Détente?–Some effects of Russia's Invasion in Afghanistan," *International Security* 5 (Summer 1980): 3-25; U.S. Congress, *NATO after Afghanistan*, Report to the Committee on Foreign Affairs and the Subcommittee on Europe and the Middle East, prepared by the Foreign Affairs and National Defense Division, CRS, Library of Congress, 96th Cong, 2d sess., 27 October 1980 (Washington, D.C.: Government Printing Office, 1980); and U.S. Congress. *East-West Relations in the Aftermath of the Soviet Invasion of Afghanistan, The West European Response: U.S.-Soviet Relations.* Hearings before the Committee on Foreign Affairs and its Subcommittee on Europe and the Middle East, House of Representatives, 96th Cong, 2d sess., 24, 30 January 1980 (Washington, D.C.: Government Printing Office, 1980).

47. For this announcement, which became known as the Carter Doctrine, and for details of the sanctions, see President Carter's address to the nation on 4 January 1980, *DOSB* (January 1980): A-D.

48. French Prime Minister Pierre Mauroy declared that "when a balance of forces has been struck between the two superpowers at the lowest possible level, when the two no longer have the means to destroy each other several times over— then it will be time to talk about all the nuclear forces in the world. Until such time, France will stay away from the negotiations." Pierre Mauroy, "France and Western Security," *NATO Review* 5 (1983): 23. For an almost identical formulation by Margaret Thatcher, see *NATO Review* 3/4 (1983): 10. See also Pierre Lellouche, "SALT and European Security: The French Dilemma," *Survival* 1 (January/February 1980): 2-6; Roy Dean, "The British Nuclear Deterrent and Arms Control," *NATO Review* 3/4 (1983): 9-12; and *Statement on the Defense Estimates* 1983, cmnd. 8951 (London: HMSO, 1983).

49. American and European NATO leaders later complained that Western European public opinion failed adequately to criticize the Soviets for their blatant global disregard for international law and human rights. See, for example, U.S. Secretary of State Alexander Haig's charges of a double standard: "where," he asked a gathering of the West Berlin Press Association, "are the demonstrations against Soviet outrages?" See *DOSB* (November 1981): 45. See also Richard R. Burt, director of the Bureau of Political-Military Affairs, "In Defense of Western Values," address before the Copenhagen Regional Seminar on 5 February 1982, *DOSB* (April 1982): 65-67.

50. Schmidt later told both Reagan and Brezhnev that "such aberrations are not symptomatic of the basic attitude of the German people." *Bulletin* (2 July 1982): 7.

51. Stanley Hoffmann, "NATO and Nuclear Weapons: Reason and Unreason," *Foreign Affairs* 60 (Winter 1981/1982): 327-46.

52. See, for example, the debate in the House Commons late in 1979, when opposition members raised questions about ownership and control of the new

missiles and about the timetable of U.S. arms control initiatives. For the announcement of the decision by U.K. Secretary of State for Defense Francis Pym and the ensuing debate, see *Hansard* (13 December 1979): cols. 1539-62.

53. See, for example, Christopher Jon Lamb, "Public Opinion and Nuclear Weapons in Europe—A Report on the 27th Anniversary Session of the North Atlantic Assembly," *NATO Review* 6 (December 1981): 27-31; Gregory Flynn, "Public Opinion and Atlantic Defense," *NATO Review* 5 (1983): 4-11; and the Special Edition of *NATO Review* 2 (1982), entitled "Peace and Security: Choosing the Right Way."

54. In 1987 Reagan declared: "This candor made clear to the Soviets the resilience and strength of the West; it made them understand the lack of illusions on our part about them or their system." Quoted in Don Oberdorfer, *The Turn: How the Cold War Come to an End—The United States and the Soviet Union, 1983-1990* (London: Jonathan Cape, 1992), 285.

55. See, for example, U.S. Senate, Committee on Foreign Relations, *Crisis in the Atlantic Alliance: Origins and Implications*, CRS, Library of Congress, 97th Cong., 2d sess. (Washington, D.C.: Government Printing Office, 1982); Irving Kristol, "Does NATO Exist?" paper prepared for the conference sponsored by the Center for Strategic and International Studies on *NATO: The Second Thirty Years* (Brussels, 1-3 September 1979); Richard Woyke, "A Crisis in U.S.-West European Relations?" *NATO Review* 5 (October 1981): 14-18; Henry A. Kissinger, "Something is Deeply Wrong in the Atlantic Alliance," *Washington Post*, 21 December 1981, 21; Simon Serfaty, "The Atlantic Crisis–I," *Baltimore Sun*, 12 January 1982, 7; and "Crisis in NATO: A Problem of Leadership?" *NATO Review* 3 (1982): 13-19.

56. The impact of Reagan's leadership on NATO is discussed in Walter Goldstein, ed., *Reagan's Leadership and the Atlantic Alliance: Views from Europe and America* (Washington, D.C.: Pergamon-Brassey, 1986). See also Freedman, *The Troubled Alliance*; and the essays in Richard H. Ullman and Mario Zucconi, *Western Europe and the Crisis in U.S.-Soviet Relations* (New York: Praeger, 1987).

57. Carter had "substituted theology for a healthy sense of self-preservation" and had hid behind a "moralistic smoke screen." These are the comments of a senior Reagan official, but are representative of Reagan's own criticisms. Under Reagan, human rights were deemphasized and global arms transfers to nonessential allies were restored. For these moves and the above quotes, see James L. Buckley, "Arms Transfers and the National Interest," *DOSB* (July 1981): 51-52.

58. See, for example, Caspar Weinberger, secretary of defense, "Requirements of our Defense Policy," address before the UPI luncheon of American Newspaper Publishers Association at Chicago on 5 May 1981, *DOSB* (July 1981): 46-48.

59. President Reagan's press conference, *DOSB* (February 1981): 12. Reagan's first secretary of state, Alexander Haig, voiced similar views, declaring that "Moscow is the greatest source of international insecurity today ... the greatest danger to world peace." See Alexander Haig, secretary of state, "A New Direction in U.S. Foreign Policy," address before the American Society of Newspaper Editors on 24 April 1981, *DOSB* (June 1981): 6.

60. President Reagan's press conference, *DOSB* (August 1981): 23.

61. President Reagan's speech of 8 March 1983 to American Evangelical leaders, *DOSB* (April 1983): 10.

62. For more on the political discourse of those in the United States who campaigned against détente and cooperation with the Soviets, see Simon Dalby, Creating the Second Cold War: The Discourse of Politics (London: Pinter, 1990).

63. Alexander Haig, "NATO and the Restoration of American Leadership," address at Syracuse University on 9 May 1981, *DOSB* (June 1981): 11. See also Alexander Haig "Foreign Policy and the American Spirit," *DOSB* (June 1981): 13.

64. See, for example, Lawrence S. Eagleburger, "U.S. Policy Towards Western Europe and Canada," statement before the Subcommittee on Europe and the Middle East of the House Foreign Affairs Committee on 2 June 1981, *DOSB* (August 1981): 65-72.

65. See, among the many examples, the NAC final communiqués of 26 June 1980, 5 May 1981, and 10 December 1982. See also Robert McGeehan, "The Atlantic Alliance and the Reagan Administration," *World Today* 37 (July/August 1981): 254-62.

66. Helmut Schmidt, "Report of the State of the Union," address before the Bundestag on 20 March 1980, *Bulletin* 4 (25 March 1980): 10; and also Helmut Schmidt, "Common Convictions and Common Policies," address by the chancellor before the Foreign Policy Association at New York on 6 March 1980, *Bulletin* 4 (25 March 1980): 7-10.

67. See "Joint Statement on Franco-German Consultations of 4-5 February," *Bulletin* 4 (25 March 1980): 14.

68. This is not to suggest that domestic opinion in Britain wholly supported Thatcher. Indeed, the opposition Labour Party remained committed to nuclear disarmament, and the United Kingdom, which since the late 1950s had seen periodic revivals of the Campaign for Nuclear Disarmament (CND), became a strong center for antinuclear and peace activism. Thatcher had her own version of Reagan's "evil empire": she called the Soviet Union "a modern version of the early tyrannies of history—its creed barren of conscience, immune to promptings of good or evil." This type of rhetoric earned her the sobriquet of "Iron Lady" from TASS, the Soviet news agency. Quoted in Peter Jenkins, *Mrs. Thatcher's Revolution: The Ending of the Socialist Era* (London: Cape, 1987), 288.

69. U.S. policy toward Iran consisted of two main elements: economic sanctions to keep the pressure on Iran to release the hostages; and diplomatic channels to point out the consequences of holding them. On economic sanctions, U.S. officials complained that the EC didn't go as far as it first said it would. European leaders, for their part, were concerned that U.S. military action against Iran, which was ultimately taken in the form of an aborted rescue mission, would inflame confrontation with the Soviet Union. In addition, the European powers had been reluctant to support the United States on sanctions against Iran for fear that they would face a repeat of the 1973 Arab oil embargo. In response to Carter's post-Afghanistan trade sanctions and the Olympic boycott, the European allies lent much

rhetorical support, but only the FRG, Turkey, Norway, and Canada joined the boycott. NATO's European members did, however, support the grain embargo by agreeing not to replace the shortfall in U.S. deliveries with their own stocks. See Gary Sick, *All Fall Down: America's Tragic Encounter with Iran* (New York: Random House, 1985), 240-42; Carter, *Keeping Faith*, 482-83; and transcript of Brzezinski interview of 27 April 1980 on ABC's "Issues and Answers," *DOSB* (June 1980): 47-49.

70. NAC "Declaration on Events in Poland," 11 January 1982.

71. In reference to this unwillingness, Schmidt said that "it is precisely in times of crisis that dialogue with the Soviet Union must not be cut short." See Schmidt's address to the National Press Club in Washington on 22 May 1981, *Bulletin* 4 (5 June 1981): 6. NATO, however, retained its preeminence for the FRG. At the time of the Polish crisis, Schmidt told the Bundestag that "the unity of the alliance must not be jeopardized." See *Bulletin* 1 (7 February 1982): 3; and William E. Griffith, "Bonn and Washington: From Détente to Crisis," *Orbis* 26 (Spring 1982): 117-33.

72. Governmental Declaration before the Bundestag, 24 June 1982, *Bulletin* 1 (2 July 1982): 6. For more on the importance of East-West trade for the FRG, see Angela Stent, *From Embargo to Ostpolitik: The Political Economy of West German-Soviet Relations, 1955-1980* (Cambridge: Cambridge University Press, 1981).

73. Quoted in *Bulletin* 1 (7 February 1982): 5. French Prime Minister Pierre Mauroy later declared that, "France does not share [the U.S.] interpretation. The logic of the economic blockade is the logic of armed conflict. Throughout history, the two have always been linked." See Mauroy, "France and Western Security," 22.

74. The EEC Council declared that: "this action taken without any consultation with the Community implies an extra-territorial extension of the U.S. jurisdiction which, in the circumstances, is contrary to the principles of international law, unacceptable to the Community, and unlikely to be recognized in courts in the EEC." Quoted, *Bulletin* 1 (2 July 1982): 7.

75. For the announcement, see Ronald Reagan, "East-West Trade Relations and the Soviet Pipeline Sanctions," the president's address to the nation, *DOSB* (January 1983): 28-29.

76. See, for example, Lawrence S. Eagleburger, "America's Role in NATO," testimony before the Senate Foreign Relations Committee on 30 November 1982, *DOSB* (January 1983): 62-64; and Arthur F. Burns, "Economic Health of the Western Alliance," address before the *Deutsche Atlantische Gesellshaft* in Bonn on 9 December 1982, *DOSB* (February 1983): 35-40.

77. Much of this effort was undertaken at three successive G-7 meetings: the first at Ottawa in July 1981, where the allies agreed to ensure that economic policy would be compatible with political and security objectives; at the Versailles summit in December 1982, where the allies discussed European vulnerability to disruptions in Soviet gas exports; and at the May 1983 Williamsburg summit, where the allies announced that "East-West economic relations should be compatible with our security interests." See *DOSB* (July 1983): 13-14.

78. See the joint press conference at Versailles with U.S. Secretary of State

George Schultz on 14 December 1982, *DOSB* (February 1983): 27.

79. The Coordinating Committee for Multilateral Export Controls (COCOM) agreed not to approve new contracts for Soviet natural gas until after it had studied the availability of alternative resources. Controls were also tightened on the export of strategic materials to the East. The OECD, which included Japan, agreed to improve procedures for monitoring financial relations with Eastern Europe and the Soviet Union and provided a forum for the allies to harmonize export credit policies. The Reagan administration used these developments, highlighting especially the new unity within NATO, to argue against a Senate Defense Appropriations Bill that contained provisions to cut back on U.S. participation in NATO defense programs. See Eagleburger, "America's Role in NATO," 62-64; and W. Allen Wallis, "A Collective Approach to East-West Economic Relations," *DOSB* (August 1983): 31-33.

80. See, for example, Schultz's announcement after the 1983 NAC meeting in Paris—the first on French soil since 1966—that there was "a great deal of sentiment for having a broad study, a kind of umbrella study, of East-West economic relations [to take place] within the NATO framework." Schultz press conference of 8 June 1983 at Paris, *DOSB* (August 1983): 39. See also the NAC final communiqué from Paris, 9-10 June 1983.

81. Fred Halliday has observed that: "Dishonest and ominous as it was, this grim initiative was wrapped in the sheep's clothing of peace and enhanced security. It was a new example of the political success of the Big Lie." See Halliday, *Creating the Second Cold War*, 235-36. Two outstanding introductions to SDI are E. P. Thompson, *Star Wars* (Harmondsworth: Penguin, 1985); and Edward Reiss, *The Strategic Defense Initiative: The Development of an Armaments Program* (Cambridge: Cambridge University Press, 1992). For more on the impact of SDI on NATO, see Sanford Lakoff and Randy Willoughby, eds., *Strategic Defense and the Western Alliance* (Lexington, Mass.: Lexington Books, 1987).

82. After the scheduled talks were publicly announced, the NPG, for example, hailed the dual-track decision as the cause for Soviet willingness to negotiate. See NPG communiqué from Gleneagles, Scotland, 21 October 1981, para. 10. A masterful account of the drama surrounding the history of the INF negotiations is Strobe Talbott, *The Master of the Game: Paul Nitze and the Nuclear Peace* (New York: Vintage Books, 1989).

83. For Reagan's remarks on limited nuclear war and for Haig's talk of a nuclear warning shot, see *DOSB* (November 1981): 27.

84. In the spring of 1980, Helmut Schmidt, for example, announced that the introduction of Soviet missiles "has upset the military balance in Europe and created for itself an instrument of political pressure on the countries within the range of the SS-20s, for which the West so far has no counterbalance." This quote and a summation of other official rationales for the dual-track decision can be found in Alexander Haig, "NATO and Nuclear Deterrence," address before the Arms Control Association Conference in Brussels on 23 September 1981, *DOSB* (November 1981): 56-59.

85. In addition, the Soviets proposed a moratorium on the deployment of missiles by both sides. This was rejected by NATO as an attempt to "freeze [the allies] into inferiority." See NAC final communiqué of 5 May 1981, which also decried "Soviet threats and efforts to divide the allies." See also "Soviet Active Measures—An Update," *DOSB* (October 1982): 42-44, which includes documentation of a forged letter supposedly sent from retiring SACEUR Haig to NATO Secretary General Joseph Luns. The letter discussed a possible nuclear first strike and called for "action of a sensitive nature" to "jolt the faint-hearted in Europe." It remains puzzling why the Soviets felt the need to forge letters when many of Haig's actual public comments were not far from those suggested here.

86. See Haig, "NATO and Nuclear Deterrence," 59. See also Morton Halperin, "NATO and the TNF Controversy: Threats to the Alliance," *Orbis* 26 (Spring 1982): 105-16.

87. See Lawrence S. Eagleburger, "The U.S. and Europe: Partnership for Peace and Freedom," address before the European People's Party Conference in Bonn on 7 December 1981, *DOSB* (March 1982): 46-49. Eagleburger stressed NATO's "shared ideals and interests" and urged his listeners to "translate those ideals into the reality of common conduct." See also J. Walter Stoessel, Jr., "Atlantic Prospects, 1981-1990," address before the Atlantic Institute in Brussels on 24 October 1981, *DOSB* (December 1981): 52-55.

The German response to this sort of lecturing was to stress the FRG's history as dependable ally. See, for example, Schmidt Helmut, "A Policy of Reliable Partnership," *Foreign Affairs* 59 (Spring 1981): 743-55; and Robert Strausz-Hupe, "Will West Germany Stay in Step?" *Policy Review* 11 (Winter 1980): 37-49.

88. In a statement typical of this approach, Schmidt told the Bundestag that Reagan seemed "very serious" about negotiations. See "Government Statement on the Chancellor's visit to Washington," *Bulletin* 6 (5 June 1981): 9-10. Schmidt had the strong support of the new French president, François Mitterand, who, after meeting with Schmidt, told German television viewers that, regarding the dual-track decision, "Our views are entirely along the same lines." Both leaders had agreed on the need to restore the nuclear balance *and* to negotiate. *Bulletin* 6 (5 June 1981): 11.

89. See the final communiqué from the Bonn NATO Summit on 10 June 1982 and the attached "Program for Peace in Freedom," "Document on Arms Control and Disarmament," and "Document on Integrated NATO Defense." Haig praised these documents as reaffirming NATO strategy "at a time when it has become fashionable to question something that has kept and preserved the peace" for more than thirty years. Haig press briefing of 10 June 1982, *DOSB* (July 1982): 11-13.

90. For an official report on this demonstration, see *Bulletin* 6 (2 July 1982): 11.

91. *Bulletin* 6 (2 July 1982): 9. See also the remarks by German Defense Minister Manfred Wörner in Manfred Wörner, "The 'Peace Movement' and NATO: An Alternative View from Bonn," *Strategic Review* 10 (Winter 1982): 15-21.

92. This rhetoric accompanied two further moves at demonstrating NATO's commitment to peace. The first was the decision, taken in Montebello, Canada in

October 1983, to announce the withdrawal of 1,400 tactical warheads from Europe, bringing the total of such withdrawals since 1979 to 2,400. The withdrawal of the first 1,000 was announced in December 1979, when the dual-track decision was made public. The Montebello decision also called for further NATO improvements in conventional forces and short-range nuclear weapons. Thus, Montebello was essentially a second modernization decision, taken in the aftermath of one surrounding INF missiles and one that sought later to upgrade aging, short-range systems by referring to the retirement of those systems as a withdrawal. The second move was made in December 1983 in Brussels where, at the initiative of Hans Deitrich Genscher, the German foreign minister, NATO issued the Brussels Declaration. It came in the aftermath of the first deployments of Pershings and GLCMS, was essentially a reformulation of the Program for Peace in Freedom, and called on the Soviets and their Warsaw Pact allies to respond to NATO's repeated calls for the resumption of arms control negotiations. See NAC final communiqués from Montebello, 27 October 1983, and from Brussels, 9 December 1983.

93. Vice President Bush's remarks at Berlin on 31 January 1983, *DOSB* (March 1983): 4.

94. *DOSB* (March 1983): 4.

95. Quoted in Abshire, *Preventing World War Three*, 35. Abshire, who also emphasized NATO's potential to achieve peace, was the American ambassador to NATO from 1983 to 1987.

96. For a concise discussion of domestic opinion in the FRG, see Hans Ruhle, "The Theater Nuclear Issue in German Politics," *Strategic Review* 9 (Spring 1981): 54-60. For a more thorough treatment, see Steinke, *Germany Debates Defense*.

97. *Bulletin* 7 (14 December 1982): 16, 19. For an American argument along the same lines, see Kenneth W. Dam, deputy secretary of state, "The Atlantic Alliance: The Facts and Lessons of History," address before the *Atlantik-Bruecke* and the American Council of Germany in West Berlin on 25 March 1983, *DOSB* (July 1983): 83-86.

98. Kohl statement to the Bundestag, 21 November 1983, *Bulletin* 7 (20 December 1983): 2-10.

99. For the Resolution of the Bundestag in favor of deployment, see *Bulletin* 7 (20 December 1983): 15.

100. A more thorough treatment of the impact of the peace movement on NATO is James E. Dougherty and Robert L. Pfaltzgraff, Jr., eds., *Shattering Europe's Defense Consensus: The Antinuclear Protest Movement and the Future of NATO* (Washington, D.C.: Pergamon-Brassey's, 1985).

101. On Reagan and arms control, see Strobe Talbott, *Deadly Gambits: The Reagan Administration and the Stalemate in Nuclear Arms Control* (New York: Vintage, 1984). The Stockholm Conference worked successfully to expand the provisions for confidence- and security-building measures (CSBMs) in the Helsinki Final Act. See Jane E. Goodby, "The Stockholm Conference: A Report on the First Year," *DOSB* (February 1985): 5-8.

102. See Bush's remarks before the celebrations for the thirty-fifth anniversary of the North Atlantic Treaty at Washington on 29 May 1984, *DOSB* (July 1984): 1-3; and Michael H. Armacost, under secretary of state for political affairs, "NATO and the Challenges Ahead," address before the thirtieth meeting of the Atlantic Treaty Association in Toronto on 10 October 1984, *DOSB* (December 1984): 63-64.

103. See NAC final communiqué, 14 December 1984. Kohl's remarks at Washington on the need for conventional force improvements are in *DOSB* (January 1984): 23-24. Meeting in Lisbon in June 1985, NATO's foreign and defense ministers declared that "we are concerned that the current disparity between NATO's conventional forces and those of the Warsaw Pact risks an undue reliance on the early use of nuclear weapons." They pledged a "special effort" to redress this problem. See NAC final communiqué from Lisbon, 6-7 June 1985.

104. The United States also increased assistance to Portugal and Turkey and sought improved access to air bases on NATO's periphery. See Sherwood, *Allies in Crisis*, 147-54.

105. See DPC communiqués of 13-14 May 1980 and 9-10 December 1980; and NAC final communiqués of 25-26 June 1980 and 11-12 December 1980.

106. During the latter half of the 1970s, burden sharing ceased to be a major political issue, but it returned to the fore in the 1980s. Senator Sam Nunn's 1984 troop cut proposal, which provoked criticism in Europe, was narrowly defeated. The Nunn Amendment demanded that the allies meet the 3 percent target agreed on in 1977 and invoked a penalty clause that stipulated that if the allies failed to meet their commitments, the United States would reduce its troops in Europe by 30,000 annually from 1987 to 1989. For the text of the amendment, see *Congressional Record* (20 June 1984): 57721. See also U.S. Senate, *Europe and the Middle East: Strains on Key Elements of America's Vital Interests* (Report of Senator William S. Cohen to the Committee on Armed Services) 97th Cong., 2d sess. (Washington, D.C.: Government Printing Office, 1982); Phil Williams, *The U.S. Senate and U.S. Troops in Europe* (London: Macmillan, 1985); and, for background up to 1979, see Gavin Kennedy, *Burdensharing in NATO* (New York: Holmes and Meier, 1979). The end of the Cold War seems, for the moment, to have laid to rest the burden sharing debate. See Simon W. Duke, *Burdensharing Debate: A Reassessment* (London: Macmillan, 1993).

107. For further discussion of the Reagan-Thatcher relationship, see Geoffrey Smith, *Reagan and Thatcher* (London: Bodley Head, 1990).

108. See, for example, *The Falklands Campaign: The Lessons*, cmnd. 8758 (London: HMSO, 1982), 31-36; and the *White Paper on the Defense Estimates* (December 1982).

109. See, for example, Mauroy, "France and Western Security," 21-25.

110. Giovanni de Briganti, "Force d'Action Rapide—France's Rapid Deployment Force," *Armed Forces International Journal* 122 (October 1984): 122-23.

111. Dominique Moïsi, "Mitterand's Foreign Policy: The Limits of Continuity," *Foreign Affairs* 60 (Winter 1981/1982): 355; and Sherwood, *Allies in Crisis*, 164.

112. One senior French general wrote that these moves were "tokens of our

determination to be at our allies' side, should a serious crisis develop in Europe." General Georges Fricaud-Chagnaud, "France's Defense Policy—The Law on the Long-range Plan for 1984-1988," *NATO Review* 1 (1984): 6-7.

113. For a cogent expression of these concerns, see Hans Deitrich Genscher, "Toward an Overall Western Strategy for Peace, Freedom and Progress," *Foreign Affairs* 61 (Fall 1982): 42-66; and transcript of Genscher television interview, *Bulletin* 6 (December 1981): 2.

114. Simon Duke, *United States Military Forces and Installations in Europe* (London: Oxford University Press for SIPRI, 1989), 67-68, 75, 77.

115. Extracts from the minutes of the NAC meeting at Brussels on 14 December 1984 attached to the final communiqué, para. 9.

116. Sherwood has observed that "in retrospect, most of the post-Afghanistan measures endorsed by the NAC appear to have been largely rhetorical: the commitments they entailed were not binding and produced few substantial results." Sherwood, *Allies in Crisis*, 155.

117. Brezhnev, who died in November 1982, was replaced by Yuri Andropov, who lasted less than one year. Constantine Chernenko, Andropov's successor, ruled only until March 1985. For an excellent account of Gorbachev's background and rise to power, see Oberdorfer, *The Turn*, 108-11.

118. Margaret Thatcher's first term in office, like that of Ronald Reagan, was marked by anti-Soviet diatribe and skepticism about the benefits of détente. She moved the United Kingdom closer to the United States by deciding to purchase the Trident missile system and she increased defense expenditures, which included endorsing NATO's 3 percent solution. The second Thatcher government, which returned to office in June 1983, marked the creation of Britain's own version of *Ostpolitik*. In the wake of victories at the polls and in the South Atlantic, Thatcher curbed her rhetoric and she and her ministers embarked on a series of trips to meet with Soviet leaders and their allies. Sir Geoffrey Howe, foreign secretary, went to Hungary in September 1983 and met with his Soviet counterpart, Andrei Gromyko, at Stockholm in 1984. Thatcher herself went to Hungary in February 1984, and in 1985 she met and gave early support to Gorbachev just before his elevation to general secretary.

119. An excellent guide to the Soviet position is Jonathan Haslam, *The Soviet Union and the Politics of Nuclear Weapons in Europe, 1969-1987: The Problem of the SS-20* (Basingstoke: Macmillan, 1989).

120. See, for example, the NAC's May 1981 Declaration on Terrorism, which deplored the resurgence of terrorist attacks in Western Europe and agreed on the necessity for bilateral and multilateral cooperation to prevent and combat terrorism. As in other areas, however, the rhetoric failed to match reality. European leaders were reluctant to follow the U.S. approach to terrorism, which sought to use NATO as a coordinating forum and which favored a quick and forceful response. They preferred to use the EEC to coordinate multilateral police and paramilitary action. See Paul E. Gallis, *Combating State-Supported Terrorism: Differing U.S. and West European Perspectives* (Washington, D.C.: Congressional Research Service, 1988).

Chapter 6: Consolidating European Security

1. See, for example, Terry L. Deibel, "Reagan's Mixed Legacy," *Foreign Policy* 75 (Summer 1989): 34-55. For a less objective assessment, see Michael H. Armacost, "Military Power and Diplomacy: The Reagan Legacy," *DOSB* (November 1988): 40-44.

2. A convincing argument detailing Reagan's central role in this process is made by John Lewis Gaddis, *The United States and the End of the Cold War: Implications, Reconsiderations, Provocations* (London: Oxford University Press, 1992), 119-32. An excellent account of Gorbachev's role is Coit D. Blacker, *Hostage to Revolution: Gorbachev and Soviet Security Policy, 1985-1991* (New York: Council on Foreign Relations Press, 1993).

3. The Stockholm Document, signed by the thirty-five member-states of the CSCE, called for prior notification of military activities involving more than 13,000 troops, exchange of observers and annual calendars of military exercises, and introduced strong new measures for compliance and verification of the agreement. For the text, see *DOSB* (November 1986): 20-25.

4. NAC final communiqué, 13 December 1985, Brussels, para. 1. See also George Schultz, secretary of state, "Berlin and the Cause of Freedom," remarks before the Berlin Press Club, 14 December 1985, *DOSB* (February 1986): 29-31.

5. Ronald Reagan, "Strengthening American Security," televised address to the nation, 26 February 1986, *DOSB* (April 1986): 18. The president also declared that defense cuts would be "reckless, dangerous and wrong.... The old shopper's adage is true—they are cheaper by the dozen." *DOSB* (April 1986): 20. See also the White House statement of 3 June 1986 concerning the U.S. strategic modernization program, *DOSB* (September 1986): 82.

6. See, for example, Ronald Reagan, "Soviet Noncompliance with Arms Control Agreements," unclassified report to Congress, *DOSB* (February 1986): 65-72.

7. See, for example, Michael H. Armacost, under secretary of state for political affairs, "Dealing with Gorbachev's Soviet Union," address before the World Affairs Council in Dallas, 8 April 1986, *DOSB* (June 1986): 63-64.

8. For the official U.S. views of the summit, see "Report on Reykjavik," *DOSB* (December 1986): 1-21; and U.S. Congress, House Committee on Foreign Affairs, Subcommittee on Arms Control, International Security and Science, *The Reykjavik Talks: Promise or Peril,* 100th Cong., 1st sess. (Washington, D.C.: Government Printing Office, 1987). The best account of the talks is in Oberdorfer, *The Turn,* 155-219. See also Kenneth L. Adelman, *The Great Universal Embrace: Arms Summitry—A Sceptic's Account* (New York: Simon and Schuster, 1989), 55-62.

9. See George Schultz, "A New International Perspective," address before the Pilgrims of Great Britain in London, 10 December 1985, *DOSB* (February 1986): 24.

10. Schultz publicly addressed these fears two months later in Brussels, following the annual December meeting of the NAC. See Schultz's press conference of 12 December 1986, *DOSB* (March 1987): 44. He returned to these concerns

again in May. See *DOSB* (June 1987): 14. See also Stanley R. Sloan, "NATO after Reykjavik," *National Defense* 71 (May-June 1987): 65-72.

11. French, British, and German concern over INF are discussed in Christoph Bertram, "Europe's Security Dilemmas," *Foreign Affairs* 65 (Summer 1987): 45-57.

12. Reagan's remarks to officers of the Department of State and the Arms Control and Disarmament Agency (ACDA), 14 October 1986, *DOSB* (December 1986): 20.

13. See George Schultz, "Reykjavik: A Watershed in U.S.-Soviet Relations," *DOSB* (December 1986): 23.

14. This night raid on Tripoli, which was made in retaliation against alleged Libyan involvement in terrorist activities in Europe, brought wide condemnation. Despite American efforts to portray Libyan terrorism as a threat to NATO (and hence the American strike as in protection of NATO), Britain was the only major European ally to lend support for the raid. In a parallel to the airlift to Israel during the 1973 Yom Kippur War, the United States, faced with French and Spanish refusal to grant overflight rights, rerouted its British-based F-111s around continental airspace. (Spain joined NATO in 1981.) The raid could have been launched from naval platforms in the Mediterranean, but the United States, which sought allied political support for its actions, chose to include its major allies by using planes that required either their consent as host nations of U.S. bases or their permission for overflight. The event opened only a minor temporary rift in transatlantic relations, but it served to warn U.S. allies that the United States could resort to pressure tactics when it believed its interests to be at stake. See *DOSB* (June 1986): 10-11; Sherwood, *Allies in Crisis*, 168; and Stuart and Tow, *Limits of Alliance*, 237-38.

15. Declaration on Conventional Arms Control, 12 December 1986, para. 9. See also David S. Yost, "Beyond MBFR: The Atlantic to the Urals Gambit," *Orbis* 31 (Spring 1987), 99-134.

16. NAC final communiqué, Brussels, 12 December 1986, para. 3. The NPG also warned of "the unabated expansion of Warsaw Pact military capabilities across the board." See NPG final communiqué, Stavanger, Norway, 15 May 1987.

17. For this reasoning, see John H. Hawes, deputy assistant secretary of state for politico-military affairs, "Improving the Balance of Conventional Forces in Europe," address before the National Defense University symposium entitled "The Future of Conventional Defense Improvements in NATO," 27 March 1987, *DOSB* (July 1987): 18-21.

18. See George Bush, "NATO: The Best Investment in Peace," address at the University of New Hampshire in Durham, 23 May 1987, *DOSB* (August 1987): 27-28. This theme is also the subject of Hugh Hanning, *NATO and Our Guarantee of Peace* (London: Brassey's, 1986).

19. See, for example, George Schultz, "Achievements of the INF Treaty," testimony before the Senate Foreign Relations Committee, 16 May 1988, *DOSB* (July 1988): 6-8. For the inherent ambiguity of the coupling/de-coupling debate, see chapter 5.

20. *DOSB* (November 1987): 21. See also Adelman, *Great Universal Embrace*, 55-62.

21. Under the terms of the INF Treaty, the Soviets agreed to eliminate 1,500 warheads; and the West, 350. The missiles were destroyed over a three-year period. The treaty allowed for unprecedented and highly intrusive verification and inspection measures, which included the monitoring of production facilities and on-site inspections of deployment sites. The treaty entered into force on 1 June 1988. For the text of the treaty and attached protocols, see *DOSB* (February 1988): 22-77. See also Paul H. Nitze, "INF Negotiations and European Security," address before the AAAS, 28 September 1987, *DOSB* (December 1987): 40-43; and U.S. Congress, Senate Committee on Foreign Relations, *The INF Treaty Hearings* (25 January–22 May 1988), 100th Cong., 2d sess. (Washington, D.C.: Government Printing Office, 1988). For a comprehensive history of the treaty, see George L. Rueckert, *Global Double Zero: The INF Treaty from Its Origins to Implementation* (Westport, Conn.: Greenwood Press, 1993).

22. Schultz news conference at NATO Headquarters, 25 November 1987, *DOSB* (January 1988): 13.

23. See, for example, Ronald Reagan, "Prospects for a New Era of World Peace," address before the UN General Assembly on 26 September 1988, *DOSB* (November 1988): 1-8.

24. See Pierre Harmel, "Forty Years of East-West Relations: Hopes, Fears and Challenges," *NATO Review* 4 (August 1987): 1-9; and Eugene Rostow, "A Practical Program for Peace: The Twentieth Anniversary of the Harmel Report," *NATO Review* 4 (August 1987): 9-15.

25. See, for example, Manfred Wörner, "NATO in the post-INF Era: More Opportunities than Risks," *NATO Review* 4 (August 1988): 1-7.

26. See, for example, Georges Fricaud-Chagnaud, "European Security after the INF Treaty: A French Approach," in *NATO in the Fifth Decade*, Keith A. Dunn and Stephen J Flannagen, eds., (Washington, D.C.: National Defense University, 1990), 135-44; and David S. Yost, "Franco-German Defense Cooperation," *Washington Quarterly* 11 (Spring 1988), 173-95.

27. For an early expression of this trend, see Keith A. Dunn, "NATO's Enduring Value," *Foreign Policy* 71 (Summer 1988): 156-75.

28. See Ronald Reagan, "Report on U.S.-Soviet Relations," address before the World Affairs Council of Western Massachusetts, 21 April 1988, *DOSB* (July 1988): 1.

29. Consider, for example, the remarks by General John Galvin, SACEUR, before the Senate Committee on Armed Services. "NATO," declared the general, "is the most successful security organization in history. North Atlantic solidarity and collective defense brought the Cold War to a successful conclusion." Official text from USIS, U.S. embassy, London (5 March 1992), 2.

30. See, for example, John R. Galvin, "The INF Treaty: No Relief from the Burdens of Defense," *NATO Review* 1 (February 1988): 1-7; and Edward L. Rowny, "Hard

Work Ahead in Arms Control," address before the National War College Alumni Association in Colorado Springs, 16 October 1987, *DOSB* (January 1988): 20-22.

31. See, for example, "Conventional Arms Control: The Way Ahead," NAC statement, 2 March 1988, Brussels; and the special edition of *NATO Review*, "The Way Ahead," February 1989.

32. See John Baylis, "NATO Strategy: The Case for a New Strategic Concept," *International Affairs* 64 (Winter 1987): 43-59; Michael J. Bell, "Flexible Response: Is It Still Relevant?" *National Review* 36 (April 1988): 12-17; Robert Neild and Anders Boserup, "Beyond INF: A New Approach to Nonnuclear Forces," *World Policy Journal* 4 (Fall 1987): 605-20; and James A. Schear and Joseph Nye, Jr., "Addressing Europe's Conventional Instabilities," *Washington Quarterly* 11 (Summer 1988): 45-55.

33. For an expression of concern over the Soviet threat after the INF Treaty, see, for example, Ronald Reagan, "National Security Strategy of the United States," report to Congress, *DOSB* (April 1988): 1-31.

34. "Conventional Arms Control: The Way Ahead," NAC statement, 2 March 1988, Brussels, paras. 1-6.

35. "A Time for Reaffirmation," NAC declaration, 3 March 1988, Brussels.

36. "A Time for Reaffirmation," para. 1.

37. "A Time for Reaffirmation," para. 2.

38. "A Time for Reaffirmation," para. 4.

39. "A Time for Reaffirmation," para. 3.

40. "A Time for Reaffirmation," para. 4.

41. The NATO Summit—President Reagan's departure remarks, 1 March 1988, *DOSB* (May 1988): 1.

42. The NATO Summit—President Reagan's remarks to the closing session, *DOSB* (May 1988): 4.

43. For further discussion of the conception concerning American dominance of NATO, see Dan Smith, *Pressure: How America Runs NATO* (London: Bloomsbury, 1989); and Melvyn B. Krauss, *How NATO Weakens the West* (New York: Simon and Schuster, 1986).

44. For an early and more thorough treatment of this last conception, see Cleveland, *Trans-Atlantic Bargain*. On the transatlantic importance of NATO, see Robert S. Jordan, "NATO: Has Anything Really Changed?—An American Perspective," *World Today* 44 (October 1988): 180-82; and Kaplan, *Enduring Alliance*.

45. The Montebello decision of October 1983 announced the withdrawal of aging short-range tactical nuclear warheads from Europe and the intent to replace them with upgraded systems. See chapter 5 and Oliver Ramsbotham, *Modernizing NATO's Nuclear Weapons: "No Decisions Have Been Made"* (London: Macmillan for the Oxford Research Group, 1989).

46. For this formulation, see Reagan, "National Security Strategy of the United States," 21-22.

47. "The Agreements on Afghanistan" are reprinted in *DOSB* (June 1988): 54-60.

48. The speech is excerpted in *New York Times,* 8 December 1988, 1(A).

49. For a view that held that the Soviets had not significantly changed, see Michael Armitage, "NATO: Beyond Present Horizons," *Global Affairs* 4 (Fall 1989): 1-11. For an early discussion about the implications for NATO of a radically reduced Soviet threat, see Lawrence Freedman, "Managing Alliances," *Foreign Policy* 71 (Summer 1988): 65-85. For an official U.S. assessment, see U.S. Department of Defense, *Soviet Military Power, 1989: Prospects for Change* (Washington, D.C.: Government Printing Office, 1989).

50. See, for example, François Heisbourg, "Can the Atlantic Alliance Outlast the Century?" *International Affairs* 63 (Summer 1987), 413-23; Colin S. Grey, "NATO: Time to Call It a Day," *National Interest* 10 (Winter 1987-1988), 13-26; and Christopher Layne, "Atlanticism without NATO," *Foreign Policy* 67 (Summer 1987), 22-45.

51. See Schultz's news conference of 9 December 1988, *DOSB* (February 1989): 48. Among outside analysts, discussion about the end of the Cold War had been under way for some time. See the articles in the special issue of *Foreign Affairs* 65, "Containment: Forty Years Later," (Spring 1987): 827-90. An excellent guide to the whole subject is Terry Deibel and John Lewis Gaddis, eds., *Containment: Concept and Policy* (Washington, D.C.: National Defense University, 1988).

52. Quoted by Schultz, *DOSB* (February 1989): 47.

53. See, for example, Paul H. Nitze, "Security Challenges Facing NATO in the 1990s," address before the Nobel Institute's Leangkollen Seminar in Oslo on 6 February 1989, *DOSB* (April 1989): 48; and the special edition of *NATO Review*, "The Way Ahead," February 1989, where one photo caption (16) reads: "the remarkable change in Soviet behavior … reflects not only the clear-cut superiority of the Western system, but also the solidarity of the Alliance's military position."

54. George Bush, "The Future of Europe," remarks at commencement ceremonies at Boston University, 21 May 1989, *DOSB* (July 1989): 18-19.

55. See, for example, Michael Howard, "The Gorbachev Challenge and the Defense of the West," in *NATO in the Fifth Decade*, Dunn and Flanagan, eds., 31-44.

56. An excellent account of these changes is in Glenn R. Chafetz, *Gorbachev, Reform, and the Brezhnev Doctrine: Soviet Policy towards Eastern Europe, 1985-1990* (New York: Praeger, 1993).

57. See, for example, Manfred Wörner, "A Time of Accelerating Change," *NATO Review* 6 (December 1989): 1-5.

58. For a firsthand account of how this process occurred, see Michael R. Beschloss and Strobe Talbott, *At the Highest Levels: The Inside Story of the End of the Cold War* (New York: Little, Brown, 1993).

59. One senior U.S. official warned that "we must guard against any erosion of the public consensus around long-term alliance defense positions and hard-nosed

realistic arms control policies." See Lawrence S. Eagleburger, "The Challenge of the European Landscape in the 1990s," statement before the Subcommittee on European Affairs of the Senate Foreign Relations Committee on 22 June 1989, *DOSB* (October 1989): 40.

60. NATO's assistant secretary general for public affairs called the summit "a resounding vindication of the alliance." See Henning Wegener, "The Management of Change: NATO's Anniversary Summit," *NATO Review* 3 (June 1989): 1-7.

61. *DOSB* (June 1989): 16.

62. *DOSB* (July 1989): 21. See also Robert L. Phillips, "Is There an Ethos to NATO?" *Ethics and International Affairs* 1 (1987): 211-19.

63. "The Brussles Declaration," issued by the NATO Heads of State and Government participating in the meeting of the NAC at Brussels, 30 May 1989, para. 7 (hereafter "Brussels Declaration").

64. "Brussels Declaration," paras. 24-28.

65. "Brussels Declaration," para. 21.

66. President Bush's remarks at Mainz, 31 May 1989, *DOSB* (August 1989): 38.

67. See James A. Baker III, "Challenges ahead for NATO and Developments in East-West Relations," statement to the Senate Foreign Relations Committee, 20 June 1989, *DOSB* (August 1989): 61.

68. For the SNF accord, see "A Comprehensive Concept of Arms Control and Disarmament," NAC, Brussels, 30 May 1989, paras. 48-49. For the West German stance, see "A Short History of NATO," *DOSB* (August 1989): 5.

69. "Brussels Declaration," paras. 29-35.

70. "Brussels Declaration," paras. 20-23. See also Bush, "The Future of Europe," 18-19.

71. Transcript of Secretary Baker's interview on "Good Morning America" at Brussels, 30 May 1989, *DOSB* (August 1989): 29.

72. Quoted, *DOSB* (August 1989): 41.

73. George Bush, "Security Strategy for the 1990s," address at commencement exercises at the Coast Guard Academy at New London, Connecticut, on 24 May 1989, *DOSB* (July 1989): 19-21.

74. Question and answer session, Brussels, 29 May 1989, *DOSB* (August 1989): 16.

75. "A Comprehensive Concept of Arms Control and Disarmament," para. 11.

76. For an early treatise on how the United States should respond, see Joseph S. Nye, Jr., and Whitney Macmillan, *How Should America Respond to Gorbachev's Challenge? A Report of the Task Force on Soviet New Thinking* (New York: Institute for East-West Security Studies, 1987).

77. See, for example, James A. Baker III, "After the NATO Summit: Challenges for the West in a Changing World," address before the National Press Club, 8 June 1989, *DOSB* (August 1989): 55-59.

78. See Eagleburger, "The Challenge of the European Landscape in the 1990s," 40.

79. *DOSB* (June 1989): 16.

80. Secretary Baker's news conference, 23 May 1989, *DOSB* (June 1989): 21.

81. The need to protect U.S. interests while encouraging European integration was an important theme during this period. For an excellent example, see Eagleburger, "The Challenge of the European Landscape in the 1990s," 40.

82. See, for example, François Mitterand, "On NATO, the CSCE and Germany," remarks by the president following the NATO summit at London, 6 July 1990, reprinted in *Germany and Europe in Transition,* Adam Daniel Rotfeld and Walther Stutzle (London: Oxford University Press for SIPRI, 1991), 118-19.

83. "Western Security: The United States and Its NATO Allies," *DOSB* (August 1989): 10.

84. Volker Rühe, "Shaping European-American Policies—A Grand Strategy for a New Era," Alastair Buchan Memorial Lecture before the IISS, London, 26 March 1993 (text from German embassy, London).

85. James A. Baker III, "A New Europe, A New Atlanticism: Architecture for a New Era," speech before the Berlin Press Club, 12 December 1989 (text from U.S. embassy, London). See also, Thomas A. Callaghan, "Do We Still Need NATO? Achieving Inter-Allied Trust," *Defense and Diplomacy* 8 (April 1990): 51-55.

86. By this time only Albania retained its communist government. See Robert McGeehan, "The U.S. and NATO after the Cold War," *NATO Review* 1 (February 1990): 7-13. An early scholarly attempt to assess the importance of these events is Michael J. Hogan, ed., *The End of the Cold War: Its Meaning and Implications* (Cambridge: Cambridge University Press, 1992).

87. Sir Michael Howard, "Military Grammar and Political Logic: Can NATO Survive if the Cold War Is Won?" *NATO Review* 6 (December 1989): 8.

88. NATO had rhetorically been asked this question by the Three Wise Men in 1956, in their *Report of the Committee of Three on Nonmilitary Cooperation.* See chapter 3. For a contemporary formulation of these questions see, for example, McGeehan, "The U.S. and NATO after the Cold War."

89. See, for example, Rotfeld, *Germany and Europe in Transition*; U.S. Senate, Committee on Foreign Relations, *Legal Issues Concerning the Future Status of Germany* (Washington, D.C.: Government Printing Office, 1990). For a study that places reunification in the context of broader political changes in Europe, see Wolfgang Heisenberg, *German Unification in European Perspective* (London: Brassey's, 1991). Beschloss and Talbott's account is particularly insightful. See Beschloss and Talbott, *At the Highest Levels,* 183-93.

90. See *DOSB* (December 1989): 28. Emphasis added.

91. In February 1990 the Four Powers (the United States, United Kingdom, France, and the USSR), exercising their postwar rights over the whole of Germany and Berlin, agreed to the unification of the GDR and FRG. Under the Two-plus-Four formula, the two Germanys decided on the process of unification and discussed with the four the new state's external relations with the rest of Europe. The Soviets at first called for neutrality for a united Germany, but dropped this demand in April 1990, thus paving the way for NATO membership—a condition advocated by the

FRG. In exchange for Soviet acquiescence, NATO forces, including those of the FRG assigned to NATO, would not move east of the territory of the former GDR once Soviet forces withdrew.

92. For the French view, see, for example, the speech by Foreign Minister Roland Dumas in Berlin, 1 March 1990 (text from French embassy, Washington); and François Mitterand, "A New Europe and Germany," speech before the spring session of the North Atlantic Treaty Association Assembly at Paris, 1 May 1990 (text from French embassy, Washington).

Late in 1989 Margaret Thatcher called on the allies to stall German reunification until the end of the century. Faced with that prospect despite her objections, she reversed position and supported rapid reunification. See Margaret Thatcher, "Great Britain and German Unification," address at the Konigswinter Conference at Cambridge, England, 29 March 1990, reprinted in *Germany and Europe in Transition,* Rotfeld and Stutzle, 110-12.

93. For further discussion of attempts to make NATO more politically effective, see Jamie Shea, *NATO 2000: A Political Agenda for a Political Alliance* (London: Brassey's, 1990).

94. George Bush, "A Europe that is Whole and Free," address at Oklahoma State University, 4 May 1990, *DOSB* (July 1990): 97-99.

95. James A. Baker III, "Euro-Atlantic Architecture from West to East," address to the Aspen Institute at Berlin, 18 June 1991, *Department of State Dispatch* [hereafter *DOSD*] (24 June 1991): 439.

96. See Peter Corterier, "NATO after the Collapse of Bolshevism," *NATO's Sixteen Nations* 36 (September 1991): 17-23. Some commentators, however, continued to question the relevance of NATO. See, for example, François Heisbourg, "The Future of the Atlantic Alliance: Whither NATO? Whether NATO?" *Washington Quarterly* 15 (Spring 1992): 127-39; Hugh de Santis, "The Greying of NATO," *Washington Quarterly* 14 (Autumn 1991): 51-65; and Wallace J. Thies, "The 'Demise' of NATO: A Postmortem," *Parameters* 20 (June 1990): 17-30.

97. "The London Declaration on a Transformed North Atlantic Alliance," issued by the NATO Heads of State and Government participating in the meeting of the NAC at London, 8-9 May 1990. For an assessment of NATO strategy after the London summit, see Paul Buteux, "NATO Strategy: Where Do We Go from Here?" *Canadian Defense Quarterly* 19 (June 1990): 17-22.

98. For a range of views concerning why the United States should stay engaged in Europe after the Cold War, see Sean M. Lynn-Jones, ed., *The Cold War and After: Prospects for Peace—An International Security Reader* (Cambridge, Mass.: MIT Press, 1991); Steven Van Evera, "Why Europe Matters, Why the Third World Doesn't: American Grand Strategy after the Cold War," *Journal of Strategic Studies* 13 (June 1990): 2-12; and Robert J. Art, "A Defensible Defense: American Grand Strategy after the Cold War," *International Security* 15 (Spring 1991): 5-53.

99. See, for example, Owen Harries, "The Collapse of the West," *International Security* 18 (Summer 1993): 41-53.

100. President Bush's remarks at the Rome NATO summit, 8 November 1991, *European Wireless File* (text from USIS, U.S. embassy, London), 7.

101. Klaus Kinkel, the German minister for foreign affairs, later wrote that "NATO is the most successful military alliance in history." See Klaus Kinkel, "NATO's Enduring Role in European Security," *NATO Review* 5 (October 1992): 3-8. For a similar view from an outside analyst, see Keith A. Dunn, *In Defense of NATO: The Alliance's Enduring Value* (Boulder, Colo.: Westview Press, 1990).

102. It was expected that, in conjunction with these moves, NATO would begin to rely more heavily on the reserve forces of its member states. For a discussion of the types and composition of those forces, see Sjouke de Jong, *NATO's Reserve Forces* (London: Brassey's, 1992). See also John R. Galvin, "European Security: A Military Perspective," *RUSI Journal* 136 (Autumn 1991): 5-9. For impending changes in post-Cold War allied defense expenditures, see Christopher Coker, ed., *Shifting into Neutral?: Burden Sharing in the Western Alliance in the 1990s* (London: Brassey's, 1990).

103. See "The Alliance's New Force Posture: Characteristics of Conventional Forces" in "The Alliance's New Strategic Concept," agreed by the NATO Heads of State and Government participating in the meeting of the NAC at Rome, 7-8 November 1991, paras. 40-54.

104. "The Alliance's New Strategic Concept," para. 57.

105. See "Security Challenges and Risks" and "The Characteristics of Nuclear Forces" in "The Alliance's New Strategic Concept," paras. 8-15, 57. For further discussion of the nuclear aspects of NATO's new strategy, see Shaun Gregory, *Nuclear Command and Control in NATO* (London: Brassey's, 1995), chapter 7.

106. See Michael Legge, "The Making of NATO's New Strategy," *NATO Review* 6 (December 1991): 9-14.

107. "The Alliance's New Strategic Concept," para. 21.

108. "The Alliance's New Strategic Concept," para. 15.

109. See, for example, Deniz Yuksel-Beten, "CCMS: NATO's Environmental Program is Expanded and Opened to the East," *NATO Review* 4 (August 1991): 2-7; Paul C. Rambaut, "Environmental Challenges: The Role of NATO," *NATO Review* 2 (April 1992): 24-27; Gerhardt G. von Moltke, "NATO Takes Up its New Agenda," *NATO Review* 1 (February 1992): 3-7; and "Atlanticist Aid: Using NATO to Feed Russia," *Wall Street Journal*, 7 November 1991, 6.

110. Prime Minister Major's remarks to the House of Commons after the Rome Summit are in *Hansard,* 12 November 1991, col. 901-13.

111. "The Rome Declaration on Peace and Cooperation," issued by the NATO Heads of State and Government attending the meeting of the NAC at Rome, 7-9 November 1991, para. 20.

112. "The Rome Declaration on Peace and Cooperation," para. 1.

113. "The Rome Declaration on Peace and Cooperation," para. 2.

114. "The Rome Declaration on Peace and Cooperation," para. 3.

115. "The Rome Declaration on Peace and Cooperation," para. 4. See also Alfred Cahen, "The Western European Union and NATO: Building a European

Defense Identity within the Context of Atlantic Solidarity," *Brassey's Atlantic Commentaries* 2 (London: Brassey's, 1989).

116. "The Rome Declaration on Peace and Cooperation," para. 9.

117. See Edward Mortimer, "European Security after the Cold War," *Adelphi Papers* 271 (London: IISS, 1992); Jan Willem Honig, "NATO: An Institution under Threat?" *Occasional Paper Series* 22 (New York: Institute for East-West Security Studies, 1991); and Peter Corterier, "Quo Vadis NATO?" *Survival* 32 (March/April 1990): 141-56.

118. John R. Galvin, "From Immediate Defense to Long-term Stability," *NATO Review* 6 (December 1991): 15.

119. This last point concerning the significance of NATO is made by William H. Taft IV, "The NATO Role in Europe and the U.S. Role in NATO," *NATO Review* 4 (August 1992): 1-8; and Johan Jorgan Holst, "Pursuing a Durable Peace in the Aftermath of the Cold War," *NATO Review* 4 (August 1992): 9-13. This view was echoed by French Prime Minister Michel Rocard in July 1992, when he called NATO "a solid reference point in a world of turmoil." Quoted in *International Herald Tribune*, 28 July 1992, 4.

120. Manfred Wörner, "NATO Transformed: The Significance of the Rome Summit," *NATO Review* 6 (December 1991): 8.

121. See, for example, Henry A. Kissinger, "The Atlantic Alliance Needs Revival in a Changed World," *International Herald Tribune*, 2 March 1992, 5. Kissinger wrote that "NATO is needed because it remains the sole institutional link between America and Europe and the best protection against nuclear blackmail." See also Jenonne Walker, "Keeping America in Europe," *Foreign Policy* 83 (Summer 1991): 128-42.

122. Manfred Wörner, "A Vigorous Alliance—A Motor for Peaceful Change in Europe," *NATO Review* 6 (December 1992): 5. For earlier expressions of this concept, see Brian Kenny, "A NATO Vehicle for the Road Ahead," *Parameters* 21 (Autumn 1991): 19-27; and Crosbie E. Saint, "Today's NATO—The Indispensable Anvil of Stability and Freedom," *Canadian Defense Quarterly* 19 (February 1990): 19-22.

123. "Developments in the Soviet Union," issued by the NATO Heads of State and Government attending the meeting of the NAC at Rome, 8 November 1991.

124. Christopher Donnelly, "The Coup and Its Aftermath," *NATO Review* 5 (October 1991): 3-7.

125. Quoted in *Wall Street Journal*, 11 November 1991, 1.

126. The NACC held its first meeting on 20 December 1991. Following the breakup of the Soviet Union, its successor states were offered membership. Its current membership, which totals fifty-seven states, includes the sixteen members of NATO, the fifteen Soviet successor states, the states of the former Warsaw Pact, and Finland, which holds observer status.

127. See "U.S.-German Call for Closer NATO Ties to the East," *Financial Times*, 4 October 1991, 1.

128. Trevor Taylor, "NATO and Central Europe," *NATO Review* 5 (October 1991): 17-22.

129. This rather fantastic list can be found in "Work Plan for Dialogue, Partnership and Cooperation," issued by the NACC at Brussels, 10 March 1992.

130. See Lamberto Zanier, "The Proliferation of Weapons and Expertise— NATO Helps Tackle the Problem," *NATO Review* 4 (August 1992): 26-30.

131. See, for example, Manfred Wörner, "From Confrontation to Partnership: The Role of NATO in East-West Relations," *Jane's Intelligence Review* 4 (June 1992): 242-44; and Angus Watt, "The Hand of Friendship—The Military Contacts Program," *NATO Review* 1 (February 1992): 19-22.

132. See Wörner, "A Vigorous Alliance—A Motor for Peaceful Change in Europe," 3-9.

133. Arguments for and against expanded NATO membership can be found in Charles L. Glaser, "Why NATO is Still Best: Future Security Arrangements for Europe," *International Security* 18 (Summer 1993): 5-50; Ronald D. Asmus, Richard L. Kugler, and Stephen F. Larrabee, "Building a New NATO," *Foreign Affairs* 72 (September/October 1993): 28-40; Ronald D. Asmus, Richard L. Kugler, and Stephen F. Larrabee, "NATO Expansion: The Next Steps," *Survival* 37 (Spring 1995): 7-33; and Michael E. Brown,"The Flawed Logic of NATO Expansion," *Survival* 37 (Spring 1995): 34-52.

134. For a cogent expression of these fears, see Jacop Kipp, ed., *Central European Security Concerns: Bridge, Buffer or Barrier?* (London: Frank Cass, 1994).

135. How to accommodate these considerations while working toward partnership with Russia is examined in James E. Goodby and Benoit Morel, *The Limited Partnership: Building a Russian-U.S. Security Community* (London: Oxford University Press for SIPRI, 1993).

136. "The Brussels Declaration (The Partnership for Peace)," issued by the NATO Heads of State and Government attending the meeting of the NAC at Brussels, 11 January 1994. See also the remarks by President Clinton at intervention for the NAC summit, 10 January 1994 (Brussels: White House Press Release). Clinton called NATO "the greatest military alliance in history" and assured his partners that the "security of the North Atlantic region is vital to the security of the United States."

137. The invitation to join the Partnership declared that the members of the alliance "expect and would welcome expansion." See "Partnership for Peace: Invitation," issued by the NATO Heads of States and Government attending the meeting of the NAC at Brussels, 10-11 January 1994. See also the annex to that document, "Partnership for Peace: Framework Document."

138. Including Russia in the scheme was regarded by some observers as a major mistake, and they warned against giving Russia a de facto veto over the expansion of NATO. See, for example, Zbignew Brzezinski, "The Way Forward for an Inspired NATO," *International Herald Tribune,* 2 December 1993, 6; Zbignew

Brzezinski, "The Premature Partnership," *Foreign Affairs* 73 (March/April 1994): 67-82; and Henry A. Kissinger, "Europe Needs a Strong NATO, Not Utopian Gimmicks," *International Herald Tribune*, 24 January 1994, 8.

139. "The Brussels Declaration (The Partnership for Peace)," paras. 13-16.

140. See Joseph Kruzel, deputy assistant secretary of defense for European and NATO policy, "Partnership for Peace Initiative Explained," transcript of Worldnet interview on 7 December 1993, *Wireless File* 233, 8 December 1993, 3.

141. See Kruzel, "Partnership for Peace Initiative Explained," 3-5.

142. For an explicit discussion of NATO's role in the crisis, see Jonathan T. Howe, "NATO and the Gulf Crisis," *Survival* 33 (May/June 1991): 246-59.

143. A Turkish request to NATO for the deployment of alliance troops to Turkey to defend against a possible Iraqi attack was approved on 2 January. Troops were deployed on 10 January. The deployment of German troops more than one month later was the cause of considerable friction, both in Germany and elsewhere. Turkey was annoyed about German hesitancy to "fulfill its alliance obligations," while Germans were concerned about the implications and symbolism of deploying German forces abroad. There were never constitutional restrictions on Germany's ability to deploy troops within the NATO area. See Resit Guerdilek, "View from Ankara," *NATO's Sixteen Nations* 36 (December 1991): 57.

144. Quoted in *The Times* (London), 25 May 1991, 5.

145. See Karl Lowe and Thomas-Durell Young, "Multinational Corps and NATO," *Survival* 33 (January/February 1991): 66-77. For a discussion of the problems afflicting the EC during the crisis, see Carol Reed, "1992: The EC— Inertia in the Midst of Crisis," *Defense* 21 (October 1990): 620-21.

146. See Wilem van Eekelen, "WEU and the Gulf Crisis," *Survival* 32 (November/December 1990): 519-32.

147. See William H. Taft IV, "European Security: Lessons Learned from the Gulf War," *NATO Review* 3 (June 1991): 7-11. For an excellent discussion of the French response, see David S. Yost, "France and the Gulf War of 1990-1991: Political-Military Lessons Learned," *Journal of Strategic Studies* 16 (September 1993): 339-74. For a detailed discussion of logistics, see Martin White, ed., *Gulf Logistics* (London: Brassey's, 1994).

148. See Jed C. Snyder, *Defending the Fringe: NATO, the Mediterranean, and the Persian Gulf* (Boulder: Westview Press, 1987); Charles A. Kupchan, "NATO and the Persian Gulf: Examining Intra-Alliance Behavior," *International Organization* 42 (Spring 1988): 317-46; Amitav Achaya, "NATO and Out-of-Area Contingencies: The Gulf Experience," *International Defense Review* 20 (1987): 569-76; and Michael Chickester, "Allied Navies and the Gulf: Strategic Implications," *Navy International* 93 (June 1988): 318-21

149. David Cooper, "NATO Diary," *NATO's Sixteen Nations* 36 (February 1991): 84.

150. David Miller, "U.K. Forces in the Gulf: Analysis of a Commitment," *Military Technology* 15 (July 1991): 40.

151. See House of Commons Papers 287/I, Defense Committee, 10th Report

(session 1990-1991), "The Preliminary Lessons of Operation Granby," xiii, para. 20. For further discussion of the Arab role in the early stages of the crisis, see Rosemary Hollis, "The Gulf Crisis: The Arab Lineup," *Military Technology* 14 (October 1990): 29-37.

152. Manfred Wörner, "The Atlantic Alliance in the New Era,"*NATO Review* 1 (February 1991): 5. In December 1993, Wörner declared that "the old distinction between 'in-area' and 'out-of-area' has lost all relevance." See Manfred Wörner, "European Security: Political Will Plus Military Might," address to the Philip Morris Institute for Public Policy Research, December 1993 (text from WEU Press and Information Service, Brussels). The German defense minister made a similar statement, declaring that, in the light of the end of the Cold War, the out-of-area debate "has become artificial." See Rühe, "Shaping Euro-Atlantic Policies," 20. See also the comments by General John Galvin in *Guardian*, 18 February 1992, 7.

153. On this whole subject, and for the debate in policymaking circles in the United States and Europe, see the essays in Richard H. Ullman, ed., *The World and Yugoslavia's Wars* (New York: Council on Foreign Relations, 1996).

154. American, British, French, and Dutch planes, joined by NATO's multinational AWACs, which include German crews, participated in the operation.

155. See, for example, Salvo Ando, "Preparing the Ground for an Alliance Peacekeeping Role," *NATO Review* 2 (April 1993): 4-10. For the June announcement, see NAC final communiqué, 10 June 1993, Athens.

156. See *DOSD* (16 August 1992): 584.

157. One commentator declared that failure to act in Yugoslavia made NATO "little more than an expensive fiction." See James Chace, "NATO in Limbo: Clinton Should Transform It or Abandon It," *International Herald Tribune*, 15 June 1993, 9.

158. Manfred Wörner's speech at the Munich Conference for Security Policy, 7 February 1993 (text from NATO Press and Information Division, Brussles), 7. He later declared that "the argument that we should abolish NATO because of Yugoslavia is masochistic in the extreme. It is as if we were to abolish doctors for the persistence of illness or abolish police for the persistence of crime." Quoted in *International Herald Tribune*, 27 November 1993, 5.

159. For the ultimatum, see NAC press release, 9 February 1994, Brussels. The most recent reaffirmation of the NATO threat of air strikes had been contained in the 11 January 1994 Brussels Declaration, outlining the Partnership for Peace (paras. 23-25).

160. See Alan Riding, "France Presses U.S. to Intervene in Bosnia," *International Herald Tribune*, 6 January 1994, 1.

161. I have not attempted a detailed chronology and analysis of the slow, four-year escalation of NATO's involvement in the former Yugoslavia, or of the conflict itself. Both of these topics have been well covered elsewhere. See David C. Gompert, "The United States and Yugoslavia's Wars," in *The World and Yugoslavia's Wars*, Ullman, ed., 122-44; and Susan L. Woodward, *Balkan Tragedy: Chaos and Dissolution after the Cold War* (Washington, D.C.: Brookings, 1995).

162. See, for example, Philip H. Gordon, "Recasting the Atlantic Alliance,"

Survival 38 (Spring 1996): 42.

163. For overview and analysis of the accord, see Marie-Janine Calic, "Bosnia-Hercegovina after Dayton: Opportunities and Risks for Peace," *Aussen Politik* 47 (2/96): 127-35.

164. See the article by IFOR commander Admiral Leighton W. Smith, Jr., "The Pillars of Peace in Bosnia," *NATO Review* 3 (July 1996): 11-16.

165. Javier Solana, "NATO's Role in Bosnia: Charting a New Course for the Alliance," *NATO Review* 2 (March 1996): 6.

166. Solana, "NATO's Role in Bosnia," 3.

167. Klaus Kinkel, "The New NATO: Steps Towards Reform," *NATO Review* (May 1996): 10.

168. See, for example, General George A. Joulwan, SACEUR, "SHAPE and IFOR: Adapting to the Needs of Tomorrow," *NATO Review* 2 (March 1966): 6-9; and David Lightburn, "NATO and the Challenge of Multifunctional Peacekeeping," *NATO Review* 2 (March 1996): 10-14.

169. See Stanley R. Sloan, "U.S. Perspectives on NATO's Future," *International Affairs* 71 (April 1995): 217-32.

170. See Philip Zelikow, "The Masque of Institutions," *Survival* 38 (Spring 1996): 12.

171. See, for example, John Borowski, "Partnership for Peace and Beyond," *International Affairs* 71 (April 1995): 233-45.

172. The PfP signatories participating in IFOR included the Czech Republic, Estonia, Finland, Hungary, Latvia, Lithuania, Poland, Romania, Russia, Sweden, and Ukraine.

173. See Ronald D. Asmus and Robert C. Nurick, "NATO Enlargement and the Baltic States," *Survival* 38 (Summer 1996): 136.

174. On Russian participation in IFOR and objections to NATO expansion, see Vlad Sobell, "NATO, Russia and the Yugoslav War," *World Today* 51 (November 1995): 210-15; Anatol Lieven, "Russian Opposition to NATO Expansion," *World Today* 51 (October 1995): 196-200; and Lightburn, "Challenges of Multifunctional Peacekeeping."

175. See Michael Williams, "The Best Chance for Peace in Bosnia," *World Today* 52 (January 1996): 7.

176. On this trend, see, for example, Nick Williams, "Partnership for Peace: Permanent Fixture or Declining Asset?" *Survival* 38 (Spring 1996): 98-110.

177. By November 1992, the WEU had expanded from its original five, to ten members (Germany, France, Spain, Great Britain, Italy, Belgium, Luxembourg, the Netherlands, Portugal, and Greece). Denmark holds observer status. Turkey and Norway hold associate membership. For the rejuvenation of the WEU, see Western European Union, *The Reactivation of WEU: Statements and Communiqués, 1984 to 1987* (London: Secretariat-General of WEU, 1988); Assembly of Western European Union, *WEU, European Union and the Atlantic Alliance*, Doc. 990 (30 October 1984); and Assembly of Western European Union, *Reactivation of WEU—Its tasks, structure and place in Europe*, Doc. 1058 (29 April 1986). For a more

recent and concise official description of this process, see Western European Union, *Western European Union: History, Structures, Prospects* (Brussels, February 1994). Portions of this section are based on Simon W. Duke, "The Second Death (or the Second Coming?) of the WEU," unpublished paper, February 1994.

178. By 1995 the unit was expected to number some 35,000 men. A concise history of the Franco-German corps and of the official U.S. response to it can be found in David Abshire, Barry Blechman, and Harold Brown, *The Franco-German Corps and the Future of European Security* (Washington, D.C: Policy Consensus Report, Johns Hopkins Foreign Policy Institute, 1992). See also Paul E. Gallis, *Franco-German Security Cooperation: Implications for the NATO Alliance* (Washington, D.C.: Congressional Research Service, 1989).

179. Quoted in *International Herald Tribune*, 25 November 1991, 5.

180. For further discussion of the impact of the Gulf War on the EU, see N. Gnesotto and J. Roper, eds., *Western Europe and the Gulf: A Study of Reactions of the Countries of Western Europe to the Gulf War* (Brussels: WEU Institute for Security Studies, 1991).

181. See Jacques Delors, "European Integration and European Security," text of Alastair Buchan Memorial Lecture to the IISS at London, 7 March 1991, 1 (text from WEU Press and Information Service, Brussels).

182. See Council of the European Communities, Commission of the European Communities, *Treaty on European Union*, as signed at Maastricht, 7 February 1992 (Luxembourg: Office for Official Publications of the European Communities, 1992), title 5, articles J.8, J.3, J.4.

183. See, for example, Olli Kivinen, "French Alarm NATO by Pressing for New Defense Alliance," *The Times* (London), 25 March 1992, 7; and John A. Myers, *The Western European Union: Pillar of NATO or Defense Arm of the EC?* (London: Brassey's, 1992).

184. For further discussion of the impact of the EU on transatlantic relations, see the essays in Henry Brandon, ed., *In Search of A New World Order: The Future of U.S.–European Relations* (Washington, D.C.: Brookings, 1992); and Richard Latter, *The Future of Transatlantic Relations* (London: HMSO, 1993).

185. See John Leech, *Halt! Who Goes Where? The Future of NATO in the New Europe* (London: Brassey's, 1991).

186. For a further discussion of the conception that NATO fostered European integration, see Josef Joffe, "Europe's American Pacifier," *Foreign Policy* 34 (Spring 1984): 64-82. The idea is more fully developed in Joffe, *Limited Partnership*.

187. For an enlightening discussion on how a future European Security Organization might emerge, see Richard H. Ullman, *Securing Europe* (Princeton: Princeton University Press, 1991), 63-72, 75-79, 151-52. See also Hans Binnedijk, "The Emerging European Security Order," *Washington Quarterly* 14 (Autumn 1991): 67-81; Eric A. Kunsman, "The 1990s: A Decade of Transition to a New European Security Order," *Comparative Strategy* 10 (1991): 273-86; and Manfred Wörner, "NATO's Changing Role in a New Security Order," *International Defense Review* 24 (July 1991): 751-53.

188. "Rome Declaration on Peace and Cooperation," para. 6. See also Jenonne Walker, *Fact and Fiction about a European Security Identity and American Interests* (Washington: Atlantic Council of the United States, 1992).

189. See, for example, *Western Defense: The European Role in NATO* (Brussels: EUROGROUP, 1988).

190. See Jane Sharp, "If Not NATO, Who?" *Bulletin of the Atomic Scientists* 48 (October 1992): 29-32; and Josef Joffe, "Collective Security and the Future of Europe," *Survival* 34 (Spring 1992): 45-47.

191. For reports of this concern, see, for example, Jeanne Kirkpatrick, "A Second European Defense Force—To Exclude America?" *Washington Post,* 25 May 1992, 12; and Hella Pick, "U.S. Rejects Plan to Establish European Army," *Guardian*, 31 October 1991, 7.

192. For the official British view of the relationship between the WEU and NATO, see Prime Minister John Major's speech on the European Community, 20 November 1991 (The Prime Minister's Office, Press Office, London), 6-7. See also Malcolm Rifkind, secretary of state for defense, "A Decade of Change in European Security," address to the Center for Defense Studies, London, 14 May 1992 (text from WEU Press and Information Service, Brussels).

193. U.S. Defense Secretary Dick Cheney called the Eurocorps proposal "pernicious" and "extraordinarily undesirable." Quoted in *Armed Forces Journal International,* December 1991, 27. British Foreign Secretary Douglas Hurd called the Eurocorps "useless and dangerous." Quoted in *Financial Times*, 17 October 1991, 5.

194. A framework document for operationalizing the concept was adopted by the NAC in June 1996. See NAC final communiqué from the 3 June 1996 ministerial meeting at Bonn, para. 6. For further overview and analysis of the concept, see Charles Barry, "NATO's Combined Joint Task Forces in Theory and Practice," *Survival* 38 (Spring 1996): 81-97; Anthony Cragg, "The Combined Joint Task Forces Concept: A Key Component of the Alliance's Adaptation," *NATO Review* 4 (July 1996): 7-10. For the role of the WEU, see Sir John Goulden, "The WEU's Role in the New Strategic Environment," *NATO Review* 3 (May 1996): 21-24.

195. "Brussels Declaration (The Partnership for Peace)," paras. 6-8. For an official view of the significance of the move for the WEU, see Willem van Eeklen, "WEU after Two Brussels Summits: A New Approach to Common Tasks," address before the Royal Institute of International Relations in Brussels, 27 January 1994 (WEU press release).

196. For an explicit discussion of Britain's defense choices in the next century, see Michael Clarke and Philip Sabin, eds., *British Defence Choices for the Twenty-First Century* (London: Brassey's, 1993).

197. Such nationalist sentiments are often sweepingly referred to as "Gaullist," but their origins go beyond de Gaulle. They are French, played on and strengthened by de Gaulle. For their perpetuation in the post-Cold War era, see Gordon, *A Certain Idea of France.*

198. See, for example, the speech by French Foreign Minister Roland Dumas, "What Architecture for the New Europe?" Lisbon, 17 January 1992 (text from French embassy, London).

199. See the statement by Roland Dumas with the American press at Washington, 11 May 1992, in *Speeches and Statements* (French embassy, London, 15 May 1992).

200. Quoted in *Guardian*, 7 November 1991, 1.

201. See, for example, David S. Yost, "France and West European Defense Identity," *Survival* 33 (July/August 1991): 327-51; David S. Yost, "France in the New Europe," *Foreign Affairs* 69 (Winter 1990-1991): 107-28.

202. Quoted in *International Herald Tribune*, 28 July 1992, 7.

203. These links were designed to avoid duplication and rivalry. They allowed for information exchanges between the two organizations and the coordination of meetings. The WEU moved its headquarters from London to Brussels in January 1992.

204. See Wörner, "European Security: Political Will Plus Military Might," 4.

205. For a discussion of French strategy before the end of flexible response, see Diego A. Ruiz Palmer, "French Strategic Options in the 1990s," *Adelphi Papers* 260 (London: IISS, 1991). For a post-Cold War assessment, see Gregory, *Nuclear Command*.

206. It is of course possible that flexible response will be revived if Russia asserts itself in too threatening a manner.

207. Meanwhile, some political analysts in France urged the government to return to the IMO and embrace the notion of a leading role for the United States in Europe. See François de Rose, "A U.S.-French Key to a NATO Future," *International Herald Tribune*, 17 February 1993, 8. See also Dominique Moïsi, "The Place for France is in NATO," *International Herald Tribune*, 7 November 1991, 10.

208. John Phillips, "Paris Hints at Rethink on NATO Membership Ties," *The Times* (London), 4 December 1991, 1. See also Michael Meimeth, "France Gets Closer to NATO," *World Today* 50 (May 1994): 84-86.

209. See Robert P. Grand, "France's New Relationship with NATO," *Survival* 38 (Spring 1996): 58-80.

210. See Charles Millon, "France and the Renewal of the Atlantic Alliance," *NATO Review* 3 (May 1996): 13.

211. See Anand Menon, "From Independence to Cooperation: France, NATO and European Security," *International Affairs* 71 (January 1995): 19-34.

212. See Grand, "France's New Relationship with NATO," 63.

213. For an overview of German policy after the Cold War, see Wolfgang F. Schlör, "German Security Policy," *Adelphi Papers* 277 (London: IISS: 1993); and Keith B. Payne and Michael Ruhle, "The Future of the Alliance: Emerging German Views," *Strategic Review* 19 (Winter 1991): 37-45.

214. Helmut Kohl's address to the chiefs of the General Staffs of the WEU member states in Bonn, 27 January 1992 (text from German embassy, London).

215. In spite of these tactics, France and Germany continued frequently to disagree on major issues ranging from trade to security (e.g., GATT and Yugoslavia). German leaders viewed these disagreements as a major hindrance to European unity. Volker Rühe, for example, complained that "France and Germany have not contributed to a conceptual enrichment [of the debate on European unity], above all because they could not coordinate their own national interests in international crises." See Volker Rühe, "Weakened Paris-Bonn Axis Thwarts Greater European Unity," *The Times* (London), 29 June 1993, 13.

216. See, for example, John Eisenhower, "Paris and Bonn Present Plans for European Army," *Independent*, 6 April 1992, 1; and Volker Rühe, "Atlantic Alliance Remains Basis of European Security Identity," *Report* (German embassy, London, 12 November 1992), 3.

217. See Emil Kirchener and James Sperling, "The Future Germany and the Future of NATO," *German Politics* 1 (April 1992): 50-77.

218. Rühe, "Atlantic Alliance Remains Basis of European Security Identity," 3.

219. See, for example, David Gow, "Kohl Affirms Germany's Support for the Alliance," *Guardian,* 7 November 1991, 1. See also Helmut Kohl, "European Security and Germany's Role," remarks to the 31st Munich Conference on Security Policy, 5 February 1994 (Official translation from German embassy, London).

220. For a cogent official German expression of concern over neo-isolationism in the United States, see Klaus Kinkel, "NATO's Enduring Role in European Security," *NATO Review* 5 (October 1992): 3.

221. See Christopher Bluth, "Germany: Towards a New Security Format," *World Today* 48 (November 1992): 196-98.

222. See Rühe, "Shaping Euro-Atlantic Policies," 7.

223. See, for example, David M. Keithly, "Shadows of Germany's Authoritarian Past," *Orbis* 38 (Spring 1994): 207-224.

224. Fears of a resurgent Germany filled the press at this time. See, for example, David Binder, "U.S. is Worried by Bonn's New Assertiveness," *International Herald Tribune*, 7 January 1992, 6; and Hanns W. Maull, "'Assertive' Germany: Cause for Concern?" *International Herald Tribune*, 17 January 1992, 10. For charges that Bonn helped ignite the war in Yugoslavia, see "Bonn Fights Back," *The Times* (London), 22 June 1993, 9.

225. See, for example, the address by Gerhard Stoltenberg, defense minister, "Security Policy in the Process of Changing World Politics," address to the Munich Conference on Security Policy, 8 February 1992 (text from German embassy, London).

226. Quoted in *Guardian*, 11 January 1992, 9. See also William Wallace, "Germany as Europe's Leading Power," *World Today* 51 (August-September

1995): 62-164; and Jochen Thies, "Germany: Europe's Reluctant Great Power," *World Today* 51 (October 1995): 186-90.

227. See Rühe, "Shaping Euro-Atlantic Policies," 4. See also Philip H. Gordon, "Normalization of German Foreign Policy," *Orbis* 38 (Spring 1994): 225-44.

228. In July 1992, Germany sent a destroyer and three surveillance planes to the Adriatic to participate in the NATO/WEU enforcement of UN sanctions against Yugoslavia. In the autumn of 1993, Germany sent 1,700 noncombat troops to Somalia to aid UN humanitarian relief. More significantly, by the spring of that year, the German Luftwaffe had joined in air drops over Bosnia, and German crews, under the command of a German officer, were flying in AWACs in support of the UN no-fly zone.

229. For a brief review of the legal steps taken to contest the issue, see Joseph Fitchett, "Bonn Seeks Expanded Functions for Bundeswehr," *International Herald Tribune,* 20 April 1994, 6.

230. See Klaus Kinkel, "Peacekeeping Missions: Germany Can Now Play Its Part," *NATO Review* 5 (October 1995): 3-7; Gordon, "Normalization of German Foreign Policy," 225-44; and Karsten Voigt, "German Interest in Multilateralism," *Aussen Politik* 47 (2/96): 107-16.

231. See Hanns W. Maull, "Germany in the Yugoslav Crisis," *Survival* 37 (Winter 1995-1996): 99-130; and Kinkel, "The New NATO," 10.

232. On these priorities, see the statement by Hans-Deitrich Genscher in the Assembly of WEU, Paris, 4 December 1991 (WEU press release).

233. By the spring of 1993, Germany had provided more than 60 percent of Western aid to Eastern and Central Europe and the former Soviet Union. For this statistic, see Rühe, "Shaping Euro-Atlantic Policies," 6; and "The Germany That Can Say No," *Economist,* 3 July 1993, 41.

234. See, for example, the address by Hans-Deitrich Genscher to the Foreign Relations Committee of the French National Assembly at Paris, 19 November 1991 (text from German embassy, London).

235. For an argument that claims that Germany chose these tactics in order not to have to make a choice in favor of the development of nuclear weapons, see Jeffrey Bontrell, *The German Nuclear Dilemma* (Ithaca, N.Y.: Cornell University Press, 1990).

236. See, for example, "Bonn Plays Both Sides in Defense Contest," *Independent,* 17 October 1991, 12.

237. Quoted in *International Herald Tribune,* 19 May 1992, 7.

238. Manfred Wörner, quoted in *International Defense Review* 12 (January 1992): 35.

239. For further discussion of the notion of victory in the Cold War, see Matthew S. Hirshberg, *Perpetuating Patriotic Perceptions: The Cognitive Function of the Cold War* (New York: Praeger, 1993).

Chapter 7: The Promise of Alliance

1. Kennan, *Memoirs*, 1: 215.

2. Erler, "Germany and Nassau," 106.

3. See Kruzel, "Partnership for Peace Initiative Explained," 8.

4. For an article that looks at alliance theory to explain NATO's longevity, see McCalla, "NATO's Persistance after the Cold War."

5 The states most likely to be admitted in the first round of expansion are Poland, Hungary, and the Czech Republic. See Brian Knowlton, "Clinton Targets '99 for NATO Growth," *International Herald Tribune*, 1.

6. For a similar argument along these lines, see Asmus and Nurick, "NATO Enlargement and the Baltic States."

Bibliography

Books

Abshire, David M. *Preventing World War Three: A Realistic Grand Strategy.* New York: Harper and Row, 1988.

Abshire, David M., Barry Blechman, and Harold Brown. *The Franco-German Corps and the Future of European Security.* Washington, D.C.: Policy Consensus Report, Johns Hopkins Foreign Policy Institute, 1992.

Acheson, Dean. *Present at the Creation: My Years in the State Department.* New York: W. W. Norton, 1968.

Adelman, Kenneth L. *The Great Universal Embrace: Arms Summitry—A Sceptic's Account.* New York: Simon and Schuster, 1989.

Adenauer, Konrad. *Memoirs 1945-1953.* London: Weidenfeld and Nicolson, 1966.

Allison, Graham T. *Essence of Decision: Explaining the Cuban Missile Crisis.* Boston: Little, Brown, 1971.

Amme, Carl H., Jr. *NATO without France: A Strategic Reappraisal.* Stanford: Hoover Institution on War, Revolution, and Peace, 1967.

Ball, Margaret M. *NATO and the European Union Movement.* Westport, Conn.: Greenwood Press, 1974.

Bark, Dennis L. *Agreement on Berlin: A Study of the 1970-1972 Quadripartite Negotiations.* Washington, D.C.: American Enterprise Institute for Public Policy Research, 1974.

————. *The Dilemmas of Détente: Negotiation and Agreement on Berlin, 1970-1972.* Washington, D.C.: American Enterprise Institute for Public Policy Research, 1974.

Barnhart, William C. *The Future of Europe and NATO: Ostpolitik and Its Implications.* Maxwell AFB, Ala.: Air Command and Staff College, 1973.

Baylis, John. *Anglo-American Defence Relations, 1939-1980: The Special Relationship.* London: Macmillan, 1981.

————. *The Diplomacy of Pragmatism: Britain and the Formation of NATO, 1942-1949.* Kent, Ohio: Kent State University Press, 1993.

Beaufre, André. *Deterrence and Strategy.* London: Faber and Faber, 1965.

————. *NATO and Europe.* London: Faber and Faber, 1967.

Beer, Francis A. *Alliances: Latent War Communities in the Contemporary World.* London: Holt, Rinehart, Winston, 1970.

————. *Integration and Disintegration in NATO: Processes of Alliance Cohesion and Prospects for Atlantic Community.* New York: Columbia University Press, 1969.

Beloff, Nora. *The General Says No.* Harmondsworth: Penguin, 1963.

Bertram, Christoph. *Mutual Force Reductions in Europe: The Political Aspects.* London: IISS, 1972.

Beschloss, Michael R., and Strobe Talbott. *At the Highest Levels: The Inside Story of the End of the Cold War.* New York: Little, Brown, 1993.

Betts, Richard K. *Nuclear Blackmail and Nuclear Balance.* Washington, D.C.: Brookings, 1987.

Birnbaum, Karl E. *East and West Germany: A Modus Vivendi.* Lexington, Mass.: Lexington Books, D.C. Heath, 1973.

Blacker, Coit D. *Hostage to Revolution: Gorbachev and Soviet Security Policy, 1985-1991.* New York: Council on Foreign Relations Press, 1993.

Blaisdell, Allan C. *NATO and the Warsaw Pact: The Challenge of Mutual and Balanced Force Reductions.* Maxwell AFB, Ala.: Air Command and Staff College, 1972.

Blechman, Barry M., and Edward N. Lutwack, eds. *International Security Yearbook, 1983-1984.* New York: St. Martin's Press, 1984.

Bobbit, Philip, Lawrence Freedman, and Gregory F. Treverton, eds. *U.S. Nuclear Strategy: A Reader.* London: Macmillan, 1989.

Bontrell, Jeffrey. *The German Nuclear Dilemma.* Ithaca, N.Y.: Cornell University Press, 1990.

Brandon, Henry, ed. *In Search of a New World Order: The Future of U.S.– European Relations.* Washington: Brookings, 1992.

————. *The Retreat of American Power: Nixon and Kissinger's Foreign Policy and Its Effects.* Garden City, N.Y.: Doubleday, 1973.

Brandt, Willy. *The Ordeal of Coexistence.* Cambridge: Cambridge University Press, 1963.

————. *A Peace Policy for Europe.* New York. Holt, Rinehart, and Winston, 1968.

Brockriede,Wayne E., and Robert L. Scott. *Moments in Rhetoric of the Cold War.* New York: Random House, 1970.

Brown, George. *In My Way.* London: Gollancz, 1971.

Brown, Neville. *Arms without Empire.* Harmondsworth: Penguin, 1967.

Buchan, Alastair. *NATO in the 1960s: The Politics of Interdependence.* London: Weidenfeld and Nicolson for the IISS, 1959.

Bullock, Allan. *Ernest Bevin: Foreign Secretary, 1945-1951.* London: Oxford University Press, 1985.

Bundy, McGeorge. *Danger and Survival: Choices about the Bomb in the First Fifty Years.* New York: Random House, 1988.

Burke, Kenneth. *Philosophy of Literary Form.* Baton Rouge, La.: Louisiana State University, 1941.

Butuex, Paul. *The Politics of Nuclear Consultation in NATO.* Cambridge: Cambridge University Press, 1983.

Caitlin, George G. E. *The Atlantic Commonwealth.* Harmondsworth: Penguin, 1969.

———. *Creating the Atlantic Community.* London: The Fabian Society, 1965.

Callaghan, Thomas A., Jr. *United States/European Economic Cooperation in Military and Civil Technology.* Georgetown: Center of Strategic and International Studies, 1977.

Calleo, David P. *Beyond American Hegemony: The Future of the Western Alliance.* New York: Basic Books, 1987.

Carter, James Earl. *Keeping Faith.* New York: Bantam, 1982.

Carver, Michael. *Tightrope Walking: European Defence Policy Since 1945.* London: Hutchison, 1992.

Cerny, Philp G., *The Politics of Grandeur: Ideological Aspects of de Gaulle's Foreign Policy.* Cambridge: Cambridge University Press, 1980.

Chafetz, Glenn R. *Gorbachev, Reform, and the Brezhnev Doctrine: Soviet Policy Towards Eastern Europe, 1985-1990.* New York: Praeger, 1993.

Chomsky, Noam. *Towards a New Cold War: Essays on the Current Crisis and How We Got There.* London: Sinclair Brown, 1982.

Chomsky, Noam, Jonathan Steele, and John Gittings. *Superpowers in Collision: The Cold War Now.* London: Penguin, 1982.

Cipra, Donald J. *Ostpolitik and Its Influence on the Malaise in NATO Solidarity.* Maxwell AFB, Ala.: Air War College, 1974.

Clark, Ian, and Nicholas J. Wheeler. *The British Origins of Nuclear Strategy, 1945-1955.* Oxford: Clarendon, 1985.

Clarke, Michael, and Philp Sabin, eds. *British Defence Choices for the Twenty-First Century.* London: Brassey's, 1993.

Cleveland, Harlan. *The Atlantic Idea and Its European Rivals.* New York: McGraw-Hill, 1966.

———. *NATO: The Transatlantic Bargain.* New York: Harper and Row, 1970.

Coker, Christopher, ed. *Shifting into Neutral?: Burdensharing in the Western Alliance in the 1990s.* London: Brassey's, 1990.

Collier, David S., and Kurt Glaser, eds. *The Conditions for Peace in Europe: Problems of Détente and Security.* Washington: Public Affairs Press, 1969.

Commager, Henry Steele. *Documents of American History,* 2 vols. Englewood Cliffs, N.J.: 1988.

Cook, Don. *Forging the Alliance: NATO, 1945-1950.* London: Seckler and Warburg, 1989.

Cragan, John F., and Donald Shields, eds. *Applied Communication: A Dramatistic Perspective.* Prospect Heights, Ill.: Waveland, 1981.

Crossman, Richard. *The Diaries of a Cabinet Minister,* vol. 1, *1964-1966.* New York: Holt, Rinehart, and Winston, 1975.

Cummings, Bruce. *The Origins of the Korean War.* 2 vols. Princeton: Princeton University Press, 1990.

Dalby, Simon. *Creating the Second Cold War: The Discourse of Politics.* London: Pinter, 1990.

Darby, Philip. *British Defence Policy East of Suez, 1947-1968.* London: Oxford University Press, 1973.

De Gaulle, Charles. *Memoirs of Hope: Endeavour, 1962.* Translated by Terrence Kilmartin. London: Weidenfeld and Nicolson, 1971.

————. *Memoirs of Hope: Renewal 1958-62.* Translated by Terrence Kilmartin. London: Weidenfeld and Nicolson, 1971.

De Staercke, André, ed. *NATO's Anxious Birth: The Prophetic Vision of the 1940s.* London: C. Hurst, 1985.

DeJong, Sjouke. *NATO's Reserve Forces.* London: Brassey's, 1992.

Deibel, Terry, and John Lewis Gaddis, eds. *Containment: Concept and Policy.* Washington, D.C.: National Defense University, 1988.

Deighton, Anne. *The Impossible Peace: Britain, the Division of Germany, and the Origins of the Cold War.* Oxford: Clarendon, 1993.

Deporte, A. W. *Europe between the Superpowers: The Enduring Balance.* New Haven: Yale University Press, 1979.

Deutsch, Karl W. *France, Germany, and the Western Alliance: A Study of Elite Attitudes on European Integration and World Politics.* New York: Charles Scribner's Sons, 1967.

Diefendorf, Jeffrey M., Axel Frohn, and Herman-Joseph Rupieper. *American Policy and the Reconstruction of West Germany, 1945-1955.* Cambridge: Cambridge University Press, 1993.

Dockrill, Saki. *Britain's Policy for West German Rearmament 1950-1955.* Cambridge: Cambridge University Press, 1991.

Dougherty, James E., and Dianne Pfaltzgraff, *Eurocommunism and the Atlantic Alliance.* Cambridge, Mass.: International Foreign Policy Analysis, 1977.

Dougherty, James E., Dianne Pfaltzgraff, and Robert L. Pfaltzgraff, Jr., eds.

Shattering Europe's Defense Consensus: The Antinuclear Protest Movement and the Future of NATO. Washington, D.C.: Pergamon-Brassey's, 1985.

Duke, Simon W. *Burdensharing Debate: A Reassessment.* London: Macmillan, 1993.

————. *United States Military Forces and Installations in Europe.* London: Oxford University Press for SIPRI, 1989.

Dulles, Eleanor Lansing, and Robert Dickson Crane, eds. *Détente: Cold War Strategies in Transition.* New York: Praeger, 1965.

Dunn, Keith A. *In Defense of NATO: The Alliance's Enduring Value.* Boulder, Colo.: Westview Press, 1990.

Dunn, Keith A., and Stephen J. Flannagen, eds. *NATO in the Fifth Decade.* Washington, D.C.: National Defense University, 1990.

Eden, Anthony. *Full Circle: The Memoirs of Anthony Eden.* London: Cassel, 1960.

Edwards, Martin, ed., *International Arms Procurement.* Elmsford N.Y.: Pergamon Press, 1981.

Enthoven, Alain C., and K. Wayne Smith. *How Much Is Enough? Shaping the Defense Program, 1961-1969.* New York: Harper and Row, 1971.

EUROGROUP. *Western Defence: The European Role in NATO.* Brussels, 1988.

Freedman, Lawrence. *The Evolution of Nuclear Strategy.* London: Macmillan, 1983.

————, ed. *The Troubled Alliance: Atlantic Relations in the 1980s.* New York: St. Martin's Press, 1983.

Freeland, Richard M. *The Truman Doctrine and the Origins of McCarthyism: Foreign Policy, Domestic Politics and Internal Security, 1946-1948.* New York: New York University Press, 1985.

Friedland, Ed. *The Great Détente Disaster: Oil and the Decline of American Foreign Policy.* New York: Basic Books, 1975.

Funk, Robert. *Language, Hermeneutic, and the Word of God.* New York: Harper and Row, 1966.

Fursdon, Edward. *The European Defense Community: A History.* New York: St. Martin's Press, 1979.

Gaddis, John Lewis. *The Long Peace: Inquiries into the History of the Cold War.* London: Oxford University Press, 1987.

————. *Strategies of Containment: A Critical Appraisal of Postwar American National Security Policy.* London: Oxford University Press, 1982.

————. *The United States and the End of the Cold War.* London: Oxford University Press, 1992.

Gallis, Paul E. *Combatting State-Supported Terrorism: Differing U.S. and West European Perspectives.* Washington, D.C.: Congressional Research Service, 1988.

————. *Franco-German Security Cooperation: Implications for the NATO Alliance.* Washington, D.C.: Congressional Research Service, 1989.

Gallois, Pierre M. *The Balance of Terror.* Boston: Hougton, Mifflin, 1961.

Gardner, Lloyd C. *Architects of Illusion: Men and Ideas in American Foreign Policy, 1941-1949.* Chicago, Ill.: Quadrangle, 1970.

Garthoff, Raymond. *Détente and Confrontation: American-Soviet Relations from Nixon to Reagan.* Washington, D.C.: Brookings, 1985.

Gimbel, John. *The Origins of the Marshall Plan.* Stanford: Stanford University Press, 1976.

Gnesotto, N., and J. Roper, eds. *Western Europe and the Gulf: A Study of Reactions of the Countries of Western Europe to the Gulf War.* Brussels: WEU Institute for Security Studies, 1991.

Godson, Joseph, ed. *Transatlantic Crisis: Europe and America in the 1970s.* London: Alcove Press Ltd., 1974.

Goldschmidt, Bertrand. *The Atomic Adventure: Its Political and Technical Aspects.* Oxford: Pergamon, 1964.

Goldstein, Walter, ed. *Reagan's Leadership and the Atlantic Alliance: Views from Europe and America.* Washington, D.C.: Pergamon-Brassey, 1986.

Goodby, James E., and Benoit Morel. *The Limited Partnership: Building a Russian-U.S. Security Community.* London: Oxford University Press for SIPRI, 1993.

Goodspeed, Stephen S. *The Nature and Function of International Organization.* London: Oxford University Press, 1967.

Gordon, Philip H. *A Certain Idea of France: French Security Policy and the Gaullist Legacy.* Princeton: Princeton University Press, 1993.

Gowing, Margaret. *Independence and Deterrence: Britain and Atomic Energy, 1945-1952.* 2 vols. London: Macmillan, 1974.

Gregory, Shaun. *Nuclear Command and Control in NATO.* London: Brassey's, 1995.

Griffith, Robert S. *The Politics of Fear: Joseph R. McCarthy and the Senate.* Lexington: University of Kentucky Press, 1970.

Griffith, William E., and W. W. Rostow. *East-West Relations: Is Détente Possible?* Washington, D.C.: American Enterprise Institute for Public Policy Research, 1969.

Groennings, Susan, E.W. Kelly, and M. Lieserson, eds. *The Study of Coalition Behavior.* New York: Holt, Rinehart, Winston, 1970.

Grosser, Alfred. *The Western Alliance: European–American Relations since 1945.* London: Macmillan, 1980.

Hahn, Walter F., and Robert L. Pfaltzgraff, Jr., eds. *Atlantic Community in Crisis: A Redefinition of the Transatlantic Relationship.* Elmsford, N.Y.: Pergamon, 1979.

Halberstam, David. *The Best and the Brightest.* New York: Random House, 1973.

Halliday, Fred. *The Making of the Second Cold War.* London: Verso, 1983.

Hanning, Hugh. *NATO and Our Guarantee of Peace.* London: Brassey's, 1986.

Hanreider, Wolfram F. *Germany, America, Europe: Forty Years of German Foreign Policy.* New Haven, Conn.: Yale University Press, 1989.

Harper, John L. *America and the Reconstruction of Italy, 1945-1948.* Cambridge: Cambridge University Press, 1986.

———. *American Visions of Europe: Franklin D. Roosevelt, George F. Kennan, and Dean G. Acheson.* Cambridge: Cambridge University Press, 1994.

Harrison, Michael. *Reluctant Ally: France and Atlantic Security.* Baltimore: The Johns Hopkins University Press, 1981.

Haslam, Jonathan. *The Soviet Union and the Politics of Nuclear Weapons in Europe, 1969-1987: The Problem of the SS-20.* Basingstoke: Macmillan, 1989.

Heath, Edward. *Old World, New Horizons: Britain, the Common Market and the Atlantic Alliance—The Godkin Lectures at Harvard.* London: Oxford University Press, 1970.

Heisenberg, Wolfgang. *German Unification in European Perspective.* London: Brassey's, 1991.

Henderson, Nicholas. *The Birth of NATO.* London: Weidenfeld and Nicolson, 1982.

Herken, Gregg. *The Winning Weapon: The Atomic Bomb in the Cold War, 1945-1950.* New York: Alfred A. Knopf, 1980.

Herring, George C. *America's Longest War: The United States in Vietnam, 1950-1975.* New York: Basic Books, 1985.

Herz, John H. *International Politics in the Atomic Age.* New York: Columbia University Press, 1959.

Hinds, Lynn Boyd, and Theodore Otto Windt, Jr. *The Cold War as Rhetoric: The Beginnings, 1945-1950.* New York: Praeger, 1991.

Hinsley, F. H. *Power and the Pursuit of Peace: Theory and Practice in the History of Relations between States.* Cambridge: Cambridge University Press, 1963.

Hirshberg, Matthew S. *Perpetuating Patriotic Perceptions: The Cognitive Function of the Cold War.* New York: Praeger, 1993.

Hiscocks, Richard. *Germany Revived: An Appraisal of the Adenauer Era.* London: Victor Gollancz, 1966.

Hoffmann, Stanley. *Primacy or World Order?* New York: McGraw Hill, 1978.

Hogan, Michael J. *The Marshall Plan: America, Britain, and the Reconstruction of Western Europe, 1947-1952.* Cambridge: Cambridge University Press, 1987.

————, ed. *The End of the Cold War: Its Meaning and Implications.* Cambridge: Cambridge University Press, 1992.

Holsti, Ole, Terrence Hopmann, and J. D. Sullivan. *Unity and Disintegration in International Alliances: Comparative Studies.* New York: Wiley, 1973.

Huntley, James R. *Man's Environment and the Atlantic Alliance.* Brussels: NATO Information Service, 1971.

Immerman, Richard H., ed. *John Foster Dulles and the Diplomacy of the Cold War.* Princeton: Princeton University Press, 1990.

Ireland, Timothy P. *Creating the Entangling Alliance: The Origins of the North Atlantic Treaty Organization.* Westport, Conn.: Greenwood Press, 1981.

Isaacson, Walter. *Kissinger: A Biography.* London: Faber and Faber, 1992.

Ismay, Lionel Hastings. *NATO: The First Five Years: 1949-1954.* Paris: NATO Press and Information Division, 1954.

Jacobsen, Carl G., ed. *The Soviet Defence Enigma: Estimating Costs and Burden.* London: Oxford University Press for SIPRI, 1987.

Jenkins, Peter. *Mrs. Thatcher's Revolution: The Ending of the Socialist Era.* London: Cape, 1987.

Jervis, Robert. *Perception and Misperception in International Politics.* Princeton: Princeton University Press, 1976.

Jervis, Robert, and Severyn Bialer, eds. *Soviet-American Relations after the Cold War.* Durham, N.C.: Duke University Press, 1991.

Jervis, Robert, Richard Ned Lebow, and Janet Gross Stein. *Psychology and Deterrence.* Baltimore: Johns Hopkins University Press, 1985.

Joffe, Josef. *The Limited Partnership: Europe, the United States and the Burdens of Alliance.* Cambridge, Mass.: Ballinger, 1987.

Johnson, Lyndon Baines. *The Vantage Point: Perspectives on the Presidency, 1963-1969.* New York: Holt, Riehart and Winston, 1971.

Jordan, Robert S. *The NATO International Staff/Secretariat, 1952-1957: A Study in International Administration.* London: Oxford University Press, 1967.

Kaplan, Lawrence S. *NATO and the U.S.: The Enduring Alliance.* Boston: Twayne, 1988.

————. *The United States and NATO: The Formative Years.* Lexington: University of Kentucky Press, 1984.

Kaufman, Burton I. *The Presidency of James Earl Carter.* Lawrence: University of Kansas Press, 1993.

Kelleher, Katherine. *Germany and the Politics of Nuclear Weapons.* Ithaca, N.Y.: Cornell University Press, 1975.

Kennan, George F. *Memoirs,* vol. 1: *1925-1950;* vol. 2, *1950-1963.* Boston: Little, Brown, 1975.

————. *Russia, the Atom Bomb, and the West—The BBC Reith Lectures, 1957.* London: Oxford University Press, 1958.

Kennedy, Gavin. *Burdensharing in NATO.* New York: Holmes and Meier, 1979.

Kennedy, John F. *The Strategy of Peace.* New York: Harper and Brothers, 1960.

Kennedy, Robert F. *Thirteen Days: A Memoir of the Cuban Missile Crisis.* New York: Harper and Brothers, 1969.

Kipp, Jacop, ed. *Central European Security Concerns: Bridge, Buffer or Barrier?* London: Frank Cass, 1994.

Kissinger, Henry A. *The Necessity for Choice: Prospects of American Foreign Policy.* New York: Harper and Brothers, 1961.

————. *Nuclear Weapons and Foreign Policy.* New York: Harper and Brothers, 1957.

————. *The Troubled Partnership: A Reappraisal of the Atlantic Alliance.* New York: McGraw Hill, 1965.

————. *White House Years.* Boston: Little, Brown, 1979.

————. *Years of Upheaval.* Boston: Little, Brown, 1982.

Knorr, Klauss, ed. *NATO and American Security.* Princeton: Princeton University Press, 1959.

Kohl, Wilfred L. *French Nuclear Diplomacy.* Princeton: Princeton University Press, 1971.

Kolodziej, Edward A. *French International Policy Under de Gaulle and Pompidou: The Politics of Grandeur.* Ithaca, N.Y.: Cornell University Press, 1974.

————. *Patterns of French Foreign Policy, 1958-1967.* McLean, Va.: Research Analysis Corp., 1968.

Korey, William. *The Promises We Keep: Human Rights, The Helsinki Process and American Foreign Policy.* New York: St. Martin's Press, 1993.

Kraft, Joseph. *The Grand Design: From Common Market to Atlantic Partnership.* New York: Harper and Row, 1962.

Krauss, Melvyn B. *How NATO Weakens the West.* New York: Simon and Schuster, 1986.

Kyle, Keith. *Suez.* London: Weidenfeld and Nicolson, 1991.

Lakoff, Sanford, and Randy Willoughby, eds. *Strategic Defense and the Western Alliance.* Lexington, Mass.: Lexington Books, 1987.

Langer, Peter H. *Trans-Atlantic Discord and NATO's Crisis of Cohesion.* Washington: D.C.: Pergamon-Brassey's, 1986.

Latter, Richard. *The Future of Transatlantic Relations.* London: HMSO, 1993.

Leech, John. *Halt! Who Goes Where? The Future of NATO in the New Europe.* London: Brassey's, 1991.

Leffler, Melvyn P. *A Preponderance of Power: National Security, the Truman Administration, and the Cold War.* Stanford: Stanford University Press, 1993.

Lerner, Daniel, and Raymond Aron, eds. *France Defeats EDC.* London: Thames and Hudson, 1957.

Lippman, Walter. *Isolation and Alliances: An American Speaks to the British.* Boston: Little, Brown, 1952.

————. *Western Unity and the Common Market.* London: Hamish Hamilton, 1962.

Liska, George. *Nations in Alliance: The Limits of Interdependence.* Baltimore: Johns Hopkins University Press, 1962.

Littwak, Robert S. *Détente and the Nixon Doctrine.* Cambridge: Cambridge University Press, 1984.

Lynn-Jones, Sean M., ed. *The Cold War and After: Prospects for Peace—An International Security Reader.* Cambridge, Mass.: MIT Press, 1991.

MacLauren, Will G., Jr. *"Europeanisation": Some Considerations Concerning the Application of the Nixon Doctrine to NATO.* Maxwell AFB, Ala.: Air War College, 1971.

Macmillan, Harold. *At the End of the Day, 1961-1963.* London: Macmillan, 1973.

————. *Pointing the Way, 1959-1961.* London: Macmillan, 1973.

————. *Riding the Storm, 1956-1959.* London: Macmillan, 1973.

Malone, Peter. *The British Nuclear Deterrent.* New York: St. Martin's Press, 1984.

Mayers, David. *Cracking the Monolith: United States Policy against the Sino-*

Soviet Alliance, 1948-1955. Baton Rouge: Louisiana State University Press, 1986.

———. Mayers, David. *George Kennan and the Dilemmas of U.S. Foreign Policy.* New York: Oxford University Press, 1989.

McGeehan, Robert. *The German Rearmament Question.* Urbana: University of Illinois Press, 1971.

Mende, Wolf. *Deterrence and Persuasion: French Nuclear Armament in the Context of National Policy, 1945-1969.* London: Faber and Faber, 1970.

Miscamble, Wilson D. *George F. Kennan and the Making of American Foreign Policy, 1947-1950.* Princeton: Princeton University Press, 1992.

Monnet, Jean. *Memoirs.* Translated by Richard Mayne. Garden City, N.Y.: Doubleday, 1978.

Moore, Benjamin. *NATO and the Future of Europe.* London: Oxford University Press, 1960.

Morgenthau, Hans J. *Politics among Nations.* New York: Knopf, 1967.

Morse, Edward L. *Foreign Policy and Interdependence in Gaullist France.* Princeton: Princeton University Press, 1973.

Moulton, Harlan B. *From Superiority to Parity: The United States and the Strategic Arms Race, 1961-1971.* Westport, Conn.: Greenwood Press, 1973.

Mulley, F. W. *The Politics of Western Defence.* London: Thames and Hudson, 1962.

Myers, John A. *The Western European Union: Pillar of NATO or Defence Arm of the EC?* London: Brassey's, 1992.

Neustadt, Richard. *Alliance Politics.* New York: Columbia University Press, 1970.

Newhouse, John. *De Gaulle and the Anglo-Saxons.* New York: Viking, 1970.

Nixon, Richard M. *United States Foreign Policy for the 1970s—A New Strategy for Peace.* Washington, D.C.: Government Printing Office, 1970.

———. *United States Foreign Policy for the 1970s—Building for Peace.* Washington, D.C.: Government Printing Office, 1971.

North Atlantic Treaty Organization. *The North Atlantic Treaty Organization: Facts and Figures.* Brussels: NATO Information Service, 1989.

Northedge, F. S. *East-West Relations: Détente and Afterwards.* Ife, Nigeria: University of Ife Press, 1975.

Nye, Joseph S. Jr., ed. *The Making of America's Soviet Policy.* New Haven: Yale University Press, 1984.

Nye, Joseph S. Jr., and Whitney Macmillan. *How Should America Respond to Gorbachev's Challenge? A Report of the Task Force on Soviet New Thinking.* New York: Institute for East-West Security Studies, 1987.

Oberdorfer, Don. *The Turn: How the Cold War Come to an End—The United States and the Soviet Union, 1983-1990.* London: Jonathan Cape, 1992.

Osgood, Robert E. *Alliances and American Foreign Policy.* Baltimore: Johns Hopkins University Press, 1968.

————. *NATO: The Entangling Alliance.* Chicago: University of Chicago Press, 1962.

Palmer, Norman D., ed. *The National Interest—Alone or with Others.* New York: The American Association of Political and Social Science, 1952.

Pierre, Andrew J. *Nuclear Politics: The British Experience with an Independent Strategic Force, 1939-1970.* London: Oxford University Press, 1972.

Posen, Barry. *The Sources of Military Doctrine: France, Britain and Germany between the Wars.* Ithaca, N.Y.: Cornell University Press, 1984.

Ramsbotham, Oliver. *Modernizing NATO's Nuclear Weapons: "No Decisions Have Been Made."* London: Macmillan for the Oxford Research Group, 1989.

Rearden, Stephen L. *The Origins of U.S. Nuclear Strategy, 1945-1953.* New York: St. Martin's Press, 1993.

Reed, J. D. *NATO's Theater Nuclear Forces—A Coherent Strategy for the 1980s.* Washington, D.C.: National Defense University Press, 1983.

Reid, Escott. *Time of Fear and Hope: The Making of the North Atlantic Treaty, 1947-1949.* Toronto, Ontario: McCelland and Stewart, 1977.

Reiss, Edward. *The Strategic Defense Initiative: The Development of an Armaments Programme.* Cambridge: Cambridge University Press, 1992.

Richardson, James L. *Germany and the Atlantic Alliance: The Interaction of Strategy and Politics.* Cambridge, Mass.: Harvard University Press, 1966.

Riker, William H. *The Theory of Political Coalitions.* New Haven, Conn: Yale University Press, 1962.

Riste, Olav, ed. *The Formative Years: European and Atlantic Defense, 1947-1953.* New York: Columbia University Press, 1985.

Rosati, Jerel A. *The Carter Administration's Quest for Global Community: Beliefs and their Impact on Behavior.* Charleston: University of South Carolina Press, 1987.

Rotfeld, Adam Daniel, and Walther Stutzle. *Germany and Europe in Transition.* London: Oxford University Press for SIPRI, 1991.

Rueckert, George L. *Global Double Zero: The INF Treaty from Its Origins to Implementation.* Westport, Conn.: Greenwood Press, 1993.

Ryan, Henry B. *The Vision of Anglo-America: The U.S.-U.K. Alliance and the Emerging Cold War, 1943-1946.* Cambridge: Cambridge University Press, 1987.

Schaetzel, J. Robert. *The Unhinged Alliance: America and the European Community.* New York: Harper and Row, 1975.

Scheinman, Lawrence. *Atomic Energy in France under the Fourth Republic.* Princeton: Princeton University Press, 1965.

Schlesinger, Arthur, Jr. *A Thousand Days: John F. Kennedy in the White House.* Boston: Houghton Mifflin, 1965.

Schwartz, David N. *NATO's Nuclear Dilemmas.* Washington, D.C.: Brookings, 1983.

Shea, Jamie. *NATO 2000: A Political Agenda for a Political Alliance*. London: Brassey's, 1990.

Sherwood, Elizabeth D. *Allies in Crisis: Meeting Global Challenges to Western Security*. New Haven, Conn.: Yale University Press, 1990.

Sick, Gary. *All Fall Down: America's Tragic Encounter with Iran*. New York: Random House, 1985.

Simpson, John. *The Independent Nuclear State: The United States, Britain and the Military Atom*. London: Macmillan, 1986.

Sloan, Stanley R. *Defense Burdensharing: U.S. Relations with NATO Allies and Japan*. Washington, D.C.: Congressional Research Service, 1985.

—————. *Toward a New Transatlantic Bargain*. Washington, D.C.: National Defense University Press, 1985.

—————, ed. *NATO in the 1990s*. Washington: D.C.: Pergamon-Brassey's, 1989.

Smith, Dan. *Pressure: How America Runs NATO*. London: Bloomsbury, 1989.

Smith, Geoffrey. *Reagan and Thatcher*. London: Bodley Head, 1990.

Smith, Steve, and Michael Clarke, eds. *Foreign Policy Implementation*. London: Allen and Unwin, 1985.

Snyder, Jed C. *Defending the Fringe: NATO, the Mediterranean, and the Persian Gulf*. Boulder, Colo.: Westview Press, 1987.

Spaak, Paul-Henri. *Why NATO?* Harmondsworth: Penguin, 1959.

Speigel, Steven L., ed. *The Middle East and the Western Alliance*. London: George Allen and Unwin, 1982.

Steinke, Rudolf, and Michael Vale. *Germany Debates Defense: The Atlantic Alliance at the Crossroads*. Armonck, N.Y.: Armonck Press, 1983.

Stent, Angela. *From Embargo to Ostpolitik: The Political Economy of West German-Soviet Relations, 1955-1980*. Cambridge: Cambridge University Press, 1981.

Stewart, Leslie W., Jr. *NATO in a World of Détente*. Maxwell Air Force Base, Ala.: Air Command and Staff College, 1974.

Stewart-Smith, Geoffrey, ed. *Brandt and the Destruction of NATO*. New York: International Public Service, 1973.

Streit, Clarence. *Union Now*. New York: Harper and Brothers, 1949.

Stromseth, Jane E. *The Origins of Flexible Response: NATO's Debate over Strategy in the 1960s*. London: Macmillan, 1988.

Stuart, Douglas, and William Tow. *The Limits of Alliance: NATO Out-of-Area Problems since 1949*. Baltimore: Johns Hopkins University Press, 1990.

Talbott, Strobe. *Deadly Gambits: The Reagan Administration and the Stalemate in Nuclear Arms Control*. New York: Vintage, 1984.

—————. *The Master of the Game: Paul Nitze and the Nuclear Peace*. New York: Vintage Books, 1989.

Thompson, E. P. *Star Wars*. Harmondsworth: Penguin, 1985.

Treverton, Gregory F. *America, Germany and the Future of Europe*. Princeton: Princeton University Press, 1992.

Tucker, Robert W., and Linda Wrigley, eds. *The Atlantic Alliance and its Critics.* London: Praeger, 1983.

Ullman, Richard H. *Securing Europe.* Princeton: Princeton University Press, 1991.

———, ed. *The World and Yugoslavia's Wars.* New York: Council on Foreign Relations, 1996.

Ullman, Richard H., and Mario Zucconi. *Western Europe and the Crisis in U.S.–Soviet Relations.* New York: Praeger, 1987.

Van Hunn, Martin. *NATO and France after de Gaulle.* Maxwell AFB, Ala.: Air War College, 1974.

Vandenburg, Arthur H., Jr., ed. *The Private Papers of Senator Arthur H. Vandenburg.* London: Gollancz, 1953.

Walker, Jenonne. *Fact and Fiction about a European Security Identity and American Interests.* Washington: Atlantic Council of the United States, 1992.

Wall, Irwin. M. *The United States and the Reshaping of Postwar France, 1945-1954.* Cambridge: Cambridge University Press, 1991.

Walt, Stephen M. *The Origins of Alliances.* Ithaca, N.Y.: Cornell University Press, 1987.

Waltz, Kenneth N. *Theory of International Politics.* Reading, Mass.: Addison-Wesley, 1979.

Warburg, James P. *Faith, Purpose, and Power: A Plea for a Positive Policy.* New York: Harper and Row, 1950.

Whetten, Lawrence L. *Germany's Ostpolitik.* London: Oxford University Press, 1971.

White, Brian. *Britain, Détente, and Changing East-West Relations.* London: Routledge, 1992.

White, Martin, ed. *Gulf Logistics.* London: Brassey's, 1994.

Williams, Geoffrey L. *The European Defense Initiative: Europe's Bid for Equality.* New York: St. Martin's Press, 1986.

Williams, Phil. *The U.S. Senate and U.S. Troops in Europe.* London: Macmillan, 1985.

Wilson, Harold. *A Personal Record: The Labour Government, 1964-1970.* Boston: Little, Brown, 1971.

Woodward, Susan L. *Balkan Tragedy: Chaos and Dissolution after the Cold War.* Washington, D.C.: Brookings, 1995.

Wright, Quincy. *A Study of War.* Chicago: Chicago University Press, 1965.

Yost, David S., ed. *NATO's Strategic Options: Arms Control and Defense.* Elmsford, N.Y.: Pergamon, 1981.

Young, John W. *Britain, France, and the Unity of Europe, 1945-1951.* Leicester, England: Leicester University Press, 1984.

Articles

"Abolish NATO—But then What?" *NATO's Fifteen Nations* 15 (February-March 1970): 80-86.

Achaya, Amitav. "NATO and Out-of-Area Contingencies: The Gulf Experience." *International Defence Review* 20 (1987): 569-76.

Acheson, Dean. "One of Our Firemen is Resigning." *Atlantic Community Quarterly* 4 (Summer 1966): 160-65.

Adenauer, Konrad. "Germany and Europe." *Foreign Affairs* 31(April 1953): 361-66.

————. "Germany and the Problem of Our Times." *International Affairs* 28 (April 1952): 156-61.

————. "Germany, the New Partner." *Foreign Affairs* 33 (January 1955): 177-83.

————. "The German Problem, a World Problem." *Foreign Affairs* 41 (October 1962): 59-65.

Adler, Kenneth, and Douglas Westerman. "Is NATO in Trouble?" *Public Opinion* 4 (August/September 1981): 8-12.

"Airborne Early Warning and Control System." *NATO Review* 1 (February 1979): 6.

Albert, E. H. "Bonn's Moscow Treaty and Its Implications." *International Affairs* 47 (April 1971): 316-26.

————. "The Brandt Doctrine of Two States in Germany." *International Affairs* 46 (April 1970): 292-303.

Allen, David. "The Euro-Arab Dialogue." *Journal of Common Market Studies* 16 (June 1978): 323-25.

Amme, Carl H. J. "National Strategies within the Alliance: West Germany." *NATO's Fifteen Nations* 17 (August-September 1972): 74-77.

Ando, Salvo. "Preparing the Ground for an Alliance Peacekeeping Role." *NATO Review* 2 (April 1993): 4-10.

Armitage, Michael. "NATO: Beyond Present Horizons." *Global Affairs* 4 (Fall 1989): 1-11.

Art, Robert J. "A Defensible Defence: American Grand Strategy after the Cold War." *International Security* 15 (Spring 1991): 5-53.

Asmus, Ronald D., Richard L. Kugler, and Stephen F. Larrabee. "Building a New NATO." *Foreign Affairs* 72 (September/October 1993): 28-40.

Asmus, Ronald D., Richard L. Kugler, and Stephen F. Larrabee, "NATO Expansion: The Next Steps." *Survival* 37 (Spring 1995): 7-33.

Asmus, Ronald D., and Robert C. Nurick, "NATO Enlargement and the Baltic States." *Survival* 38 (Summer 1996): 121-42.

Attlee, Clement R. "Britain and America: Common Aims, Different Opinions." *Foreign Affairs* 32 (January 1954): 190-202.

Bader, W. B. "Nuclear-Weapons Sharing and 'The German Problem.'" *Foreign*

Affairs 44 (July 1966): 83-92.

Bahr, Egon. "German *Ostpolitik* and Superpower Relations." *Survival* 15 (November-December 1973): 296-300.

Barry, Charles. "NATO's Combined Joint Task Forces in Theory and Practice." *Survival* 38 (Spring 1996): 81-97.

Baylis, John. "Britain, the Brussels Pact, and the Continental Commitment." *International Affairs* 60 (August 1984): 615-31.

————. "NATO Strategy: The Case for a New Strategic Concept." *International Affairs* 64 (Winter 1987): 43-59.

Beaton, Leonard. "NATO after the Soviet Invasion of Czechoslovakia." *Atlantic Community Quarterly* 7 (Spring 1969): 76-77.

————. "The Western Alliance and the McNamara Doctrine." *Adelphi Papers* 11 (London: IISS, 1964).

Bell, Michael J. "Flexible Response: Is it Still Relevant?" *National Review* 36 (April 1988): 12-17.

Bertram, Christoph. "Europe's Security Dilemmas." *Foreign Affairs* 65 (Summer 1987): 45-57.

————. "The Implications of Theatre Nuclear Weapons in Europe." *Foreign Affairs* 60 (Winter 1981/1982): 310.

Binnedijk, Hans. "The Emerging European Security Order." *Washington Quarterly* 14 (Autumn 1991): 67-81.

Birnbaum, Karl K. "Pan-European Perspectives after the Berlin Agreement." *International Journal* 27 (Winter 1972): 32-44.

Blechman, Barry M. "The Political Utility of Nuclear Weapons." *International Security* 7 (Summer 1982): 132-56.

Bluth, Christopher. "Germany: Towards a New Security Format." *World Today* 48 (November 1992): 196-98.

Borowski, John. "Partnership for Peace and Beyond." *International Affairs* 71 (April 1995): 233-45.

Bowie, Robert R. "Strategy and the Atlantic Alliance." *International Organization* 17 (Summer 1963): 709-32.

————. "Tensions within the Alliance." *Foreign Affairs* 42 (October 1963): 49-69.

Brandt, Willy. "Détente over the Long Haul." *Survival* 9 (October 1967): 310-12.

————. "German Foreign Policy." *Survival* 11 (December 1969): 370-72.

————. "German Policy Towards the East." *Foreign Affairs* 46 (April 1968): 476-86.

————. "Germany's 'Westpolitik.'" *Foreign Affairs* 50 (April 1972): 416-26.

Brentano, Heinrich von. "Goals and Means of the Western Alliance." *Foreign Affairs* 39 (April 1961): 416-29.

"Britain Rallies to the Aid of NATO." *NATO's Fifteen Nations* 18 (February– March 1973): 16-20.

Brodie, Bernard. "The Atom Bomb as Policymaker." *Foreign Affairs* 27 (October 1948): 7-33.

Brosio, Manlio. "Past and Future Tasks of the Alliance: An Analysis of the Harmel Report." *Atlantic Community Quarterly* 6 (Summer 1968): 231-37.

————. "Will NATO Survive Détente?" *World Today* 27 (June 1971): 231-41.

Brown, Michael E. "The Flawed Logic of NATO Expansion." *Survival* 37 (Spring 1995): 34-52.

Brown, Neville. "Arms and the Switch Towards Europe." *International Affairs* 43 (July 1967): 468-82.

Brzezinski, Zbigniew. "The Framework for East-West Reconciliation." *Foreign Affairs* 46 (January 1968): 256-75.

————. "The Premature Partnership." *Foreign Affairs* 73 (March/April 1994): 67-82.

Buchan, Alastair. "The Changed Setting of the Atlantic Debate." *Foreign Affairs* 43 (July 1965): 574-86.

————. "The Multilateral Force—A Study in Alliance Politics." *International Affairs* 40 (October 1964): 619-37.

————. "Partners and Allies." *Foreign Affairs* 41 (July 1963): 621-37.

Bundy, McGeorge, and James G. Blight. "October 27, 1962: Transcripts of the Meetings of the ExCom." *International Security* 12 (Winter 1987/88): 30-92.

Burt, Richard. "The SS-20 and the Eurostrategic Balance." *World Today* 33 (February 1977): 43-51.

Buteux, Paul. "NATO Strategy: Where Do We Go From Here?" *Canadian Defence Quarterly* 19 (June 1990): 17-22.

————. "Theatre Nuclear Forces—Modernization Plan and Arms Control." *NATO Review* 6 (December 1980): 1-6.

Cahen, Alfred. "The Western European Union and NATO: Building a European Defence Identity within the Context of Atlantic Solidarity." *Brassey's Atlantic Commentaries* 2. London: Brassey's, 1989.

Calic, Marie-Janine. "Bosnia-Hercegovina after Dayton: Opportunities and Risks for Peace." *Aussen Politik* 47 (2/96): 127-35.

"Call for a European Security Conference." *Survival* 11 (March 1969): 159-61.

Callaghan, Thomas A. "Do We Still Need NATO? Achieving Inter-Allied Trust." *Defence and Diplomacy* 8 (April 1990): 51-55.

Chickester, Michael. "Allied Navies and the Gulf: Strategic Implications." *Navy International* 93 (June 1988): 318-21

Cleveland, Harlan. "NATO after the Invasion." *Foreign Affairs* 47 (January 1969): 251-65.

————. "The Rejuvenation of NATO," *Atlantic Community Quarterly* 5 (Winter 1967-1968): 512-19.

Collins, J. Lawton. "NATO: Still a Vital Force for Peace." *Foreign Affairs* 34 (April 1956): 367-79.

Combeaux, Edmond. "French Military Policy and European Federation." *Orbis* 13 (Spring 1969): 151-55.

Conquest, Robert. "The Limits of Détente." *Foreign Affairs* 46 (July 1968): 733-42.

"Consulting on NATO Nuclear Policy." *NATO Review* 5 (October 1979): 25-28.

"Containment: Forty Years Later." (Special Issue) *Foreign Affairs* 65 (Spring 1987): 827-90.

Cooper, David. "NATO Diary." *NATO's Sixteen Nations* (February 1991): 84.

Corterier, Peter. "NATO after the Collapse of Bolshevism." *NATO's Sixteen Nations* 36 (September 1991): 17-23.

————. "*Quo Vadis* NATO?" *Survival* 32 (March/April 1990): 141-56.

Couve de Murville, Maurice. "NATO: A French View." *International Journal* 14 (Spring 1959): 85-86.

Cragg, Anthony. "The Combined Joint Task Forces Concept: A Key Component of the Alliance's Adaptation." *NATO Review* 4 (July 1996): 7-10.

"Crisis in NATO: A Problem of Leadership?" *NATO Review* 3 (1982): 13-19.

Critchley, Julian. "A Common Policy for Armaments." *NATO Review* 1 (February 1979): 10-15.

Cromwell, William C. "The Marshall Plan, Britain, and the Cold War." *Review of International Studies* 8 (October 1982): 233-51.

de Briganti, Giovanni. "Force d'Action Rapide—France's Rapid Deployment Force." *Armed Forces International Journal* 122 (October 1984): 122-23.

de Carmoy, Guy. "The Last Year of de Gaulle's Foreign Policy." *International Affairs* 45 (July 1969): 424-35.

De Gaulle, Charles. "The Atlantic Alliance." *Survival* 5 (September/October 1963): 238-39.

————. "Long Live France." *Atlantic Community Quarterly* 3 (Summer 1965): 155-58.

————. "Views on the Nassau Agreement, the Atlantic Alliance and National Nuclear Forces." *Survival* 5 (March/April 1963): 58-59.

"De Gaulle's 1958 Tripartite Proposal and U.S. Response." *Atlantic Community Quarterly* 4 (Fall 1966): 455-58.

DeSantis, Hugh. "The Greying of NATO." *Washington Quarterly* 14 (Autumn 1991): 51-65.

Dean, Roy. "The British Nuclear Deterrent and Arms Control." *NATO Review* 3/4 (1983): 9-12.

Debré, Michel. "France's Global Strategy." *Foreign Affairs* 49 (April 1971): 95-406.

————. "The Principles of Our Defence Policy." *Survival* 12 (November 1970): 376-83.

"Declaration of Ministers of Foreign Affairs of the Warsaw Pact." *Survival* 11 (December 1969): 394-95.

"Declaration on Strengthening Peace and Security in Europe." *Survival* 8 (September 1966): 289-93.

Deibel, Terry L. "Reagan's Mixed Legacy." *Foreign Policy* 75 (Summer 1989): 34-55.

Deighton, Anne. "The 'Frozen Front': The Labour Government, the Division of Germany and the Origins of the Cold War, 1945-1947." *International Affairs* 63 (Summer 1987): 449-65.

Donnelly, Christopher. "The Coup and Its Aftermath." *NATO Review* 5 (October 1991): 3-7.

Douglas-Home, Charles. "British Defence Cuts—1968." *Survival* 10 (March 1968): 70-78.

Drummond, Dennis M. "Getting Traffic Moving on NATO's Two-Way Street." *Air University Review* 30 (September/October 1979): 26-34.

Duchin, Brian R. "The 'Agonising Reappraisal': Eisenhower, Dulles and the European Defence Community." *Diplomatic History* 16 (Spring 1992): 201-21.

Duke, Simon W. "The Second Death (or the Second Coming?) of the WEU." Unpublished paper.

Dulles, John Foster. "Challenge and Response in U.S. Foreign Policy." *Foreign Affairs* 36 (October 1957): 25-43.

———. "Policy for Security and Peace." *Foreign Affairs* 32 (April 1954): 353-64.

Dunn, Keith A. "NATO's Enduring Value." *Foreign Policy* 71 (Summer 1988): 156-75.

Eden, Anthony. "Britain in World Strategy." *Foreign Affairs* 29 (April 1951): 341-50.

———. "The Slender Margin of Safety." *Foreign Affairs* 39 (October 1960): 165-73.

Ellsworth, Robert. "Europe, America and the Era of Negotiation." *Survival* 13 (April 1971): 114-22.

Erhard, Ludwig. "Statement after Election as Chancellor of the Federal Republic of Germany." *Atlantic Community Quarterly* 3 (Winter 1963-1964): 501-11.

Erler, Fritz. "The Alliance and the Future of Germany." *Foreign Affairs* 43 (April 1965): 436-46.

———. "The Basis of Partnership." *Foreign Affairs* 42 (October 1963): 84-95.

———. "Germany and Nassau." *Survival* 5 (May/June 1963): 102-6.

Fedder, Edwin H. "The Concept of Alliances." *International Studies Quarterly* 12 (1986): 65-86.

Federal Republic of Germany. "White Paper on Defence, 1979." *Survival* 6 (November/December 1979): 273-77.

Flynn, Gregory. "Public Opinion and Atlantic Defence." *NATO Review* 5 (1983): 4-11.

Fontaine, André. "What Is French Policy?" *Foreign Affairs* 46 (October 1966): 58-76.

Fontaine, François. "The Impossible Schism." *Atlantic Community Quarterly* 2 (Fall 1964): 367-76.

Fostervolli, Alv Jakob. "European Defence and the EUROGROUP." *NATO Review* 22 (November 1974): 8-11.

Freedman, Lawrence. "Managing Alliances." *Foreign Policy* 71 (Summer 1988): 65-85.

Freidman, Wolfgang. "New Tasks for NATO?" *International Journal* 2 (Summer 1956): 157-64.

Fricaud-Chagnaud, Georges. "France's Defence Policy—The Law on the Long-Range Plan for 1984-1988." *NATO Review* 1 (1984): 6-7.

Fromm, Ernst Ulrich. "President de Gaulle's Vision of Europe: A German View." *Atlantic Community Quarterly* 4 (Summer 1966): 224-25.

Fulbright, J. W. "A Community of Free Nations." *Atlantic Community Quarterly* 1 (Summer 1963): 113-30.

Gallois, Pierre M. "Collective Defense," *Survival* 1 (May/June 1959): 49.

———. "New Teeth for NATO." *Foreign Affairs* 39 (October 1960): 67-80.

———. "The Raison d'Etre of French Defence Policy." *International Affairs* 39 (October 1963): 497-510.

Galvin, John R. "European Security: A Military Perspective." *RUSI Journal* 136 (Autumn 1991): 5-9.

———. "From Immediate Defence to Long-Term Stability." *NATO Review* 6 (December 1991): 14-18.

———. "The INF Treaty: No Relief from the Burdens of Defence." *NATO Review* 1 (February 1988): 1-7.

Gasteyger, Curt. "Europe Cool to U.S. Suggestions on Revitalized Charter." *Atlantic Community Quarterly* 11 (Fall 1973): 319-21.

Genscher, Hans Deitrich. "The FRG's Alliance Policy." *NATO Review* 22 (December 1974): 3-5.

———. "Toward an Overall Western Strategy for Peace, Freedom and Progress." *Foreign Affairs* 61 (Fall 1982): 42-66.

George, Alexander L. "The 'Operational Code': A Neglected Approach to the Study of Political Decision Making." *International Studies Quarterly* 12 (June 1969): 190-220.

Giscard d'Estaing, Valéry. "French Defence Policy." *Survival* 18 (September/October 1976): 225-30.

Glaser, Charles L. "Why NATO is Still Best: Future Security Arrangements for Europe." *International Security* 18 (Summer 1993): 5-50.

Godson, Joseph. "Is NATO Still Necessary?" *NATO Review* 4 (August 1976): 18-21.

Gordon, Philip H. "The Normalization of German Foreign Policy." *Orbis* 38 (Spring

1994): 225-44.

———. "Recasting the Atlantic Alliance." *Survival* 38 (Spring 1996): 32-57.

Goulden, John. "The WEU's Role in the New Strategic Environment." *NATO Review* 3 (May 1996): 21-24.

Grand, Robert P. "France's New Relationship with NATO." (*Survival* 38 Spring 1996): 58-80.

Greenwood, David. "NATO's Three Per Cent Solution." *Survival* 6 (November/ December 1981): 252-61.

Greenwood, Sean. "Ernest Bevin, France, and 'Western Union,' August 1945-February 1946." *European History Quarterly* 14 (January 1984): 319-35.

Grey, Colin S. "NATO: Time to Call it a Day." *National Interest* 10 (Winter 1987-1988): 13-26.

Griffith, William E. "Bonn and Washington: From Détente to Crisis." *Orbis* 26 (Spring 1982): 117-33.

Guerdilek, Resit. "View from Ankara." *NATO's Sixteen Nations* 36 (December 1991): 57.

Haig, Alexander. "The Challenge for the West in a Changing Strategic Environment." *NATO Review* 3 (June 1976): 10-13.

———. "NATO and the Security of the West." *NATO Review* 4 (August 1978): 8-12.

Hallstein, Walter. "Germany's Dual Aim: Unity and Integration." *Foreign Affairs* 31 (April 1953): 58-69.

Halperin, Morton. "NATO and the TNF Controversy: Threats to the Alliance." *Orbis* 26 (Spring 1982): 105-16.

Hanmer, Stephen R., Jr. "NATO's Long-Range Theatre Nuclear Forces: Modernization in Parallel with Arms Control." *NATO Review* 1 (February 1980): 1-6.

Harmel, Pierre. "Forty Years of East-West Relations: Hopes, Fears and Challenges." *NATO Review* 4 (August 1987): 1-9.

Harries, Owen. "The Collapse of the West." *International Security* 18 (Summer 1993): 41-53.

Hasner, Pierre. "Eurocommunism and Western Europe." *NATO Review* 4 (August 1978): 8-12.

Heath, Edward. "Realism in British Foreign Policy." *Foreign Affairs* 48 (October 1969): 39-50.

Heisbourg, François. "Can the Atlantic Alliance Outlast the Century?" *International Affairs* 63 (Summer 1987): 413-23.

———. "The Future of the Atlantic Alliance: Whither NATO? Whether NATO?" *Washington Quarterly* 15 (Spring 1992): 127-39.

Herter, Christian A. "Atlantica." *Foreign Affairs* 41 (January 1963): 299-309.

Herz, John H. "German Officialdom Revisited: Political Views and Attitudes of the West German Civil Service." *World Politics* 7 (October 1954): 63-83.

———. "International Politics in the Atomic Age." *World Politics* 9 (1957): 473-93.

Heyhoe, D. C. R. "The Alliance and Europe: Part 6: The European Programme Group." *Adelphi Papers* 129 (London: IISS, 1976/1977).

Hill, R. J. "French Strategy after de Gaulle." *International Journal* 23 (September 1968): 244-53.

———. "MBFR." *International Affairs Journal* 29 (September 1974): 242-55.

Hoag, Malcolm. "What Interdependence for NATO?" *Survival* 2 (May/June 1960): 94-106.

Hoffmann, Stanley. "De Gaulle, Europe and the Atlantic Alliance." *Atlantic Community Quarterly* 2 (Summer 1964): 262-75.

———. "Discord in Community: The North Atlantic Area as a Partial Integration System." *International Organization* 17 (Summer 1963): 521-49.

———. "NATO and Nuclear Weapons: Reason and Unreason." *Foreign Affairs* 60 (Winter 1981/1982): 327-46.

Hollis, Rosemary. "The Gulf Crisis: The Arab Lineup." *Military Technology* 14 (October 1990): 29-37.

Holst, Johan Jorgan. "Pursuing a Durable Peace in the Aftermath of the Cold War." *NATO Review* 4 (August 1992): 9-13.

Honig, Jan Willem. "NATO: An Institution under Threat?" *Occasional Paper Series* 22 (New York: Institute for East-West Security Studies, 1991).

Howard, Michael. "Military Grammar and Political Logic: Can NATO Survive if the Cold War Is Won?" *NATO Review* 6 (December 1989): 7-12.

———. "NATO and the Year of Europe." *Survival* 16 (January/February 1974), 21-27.

Howe, Geoffrey. "Sovereignty and Interdependence: Britain's Place in the World." *International Affairs* 66 (October 1990): 675-96.

Howe, Jonathan T. "NATO and the Gulf Crisis." *Survival* 33 (May/June 1991): 246-59.

Hunter, Robert. "The Future of Soviet-American Détente." *World Today* 24 (July 1968): 281-90.

Jener, Peter. "NATO's Solid and Undiminished Defence—Basis for Progress Towards Détente." *NATO Review* 6 (1973): 3-5.

Jervis, Robert. "The Future of World Politics: Will It Resemble the Past?" *International Security* 16 (Winter 1991-1992): 39-73.

———. "Hypotheses on Misperception." *World Politics* 13 (Summer 1968): 454-79.

Joffe, Josef. "Collective Security and the Future of Europe." *Survival* 34 (Spring 1992): 45-47.

———. "Europe's American Pacifier." *Foreign Policy* 34 (Spring 1984): 64-82.

Jordan, Robert S. "NATO: Has Anything Really Changed?—An American Perspective." *World Today* 44 (October 1988): 180-82.

Joulwan, George A. "SHAPE and IFOR: Adapting to the Needs of Tomorrow." *NATO Review* 2 (March 1966): 6-9.

Kaiser, Karl. "Prospects for West Germany after the Berlin Agreement." *World Today* 28 (January 1972): 30-35.

Kalteflieter, Werner. "Europe and the Nixon Doctrine: A German Point of View." *Orbis* 17 (Spring 1973): 75-94.

Kaplan, Lawrence S. "NATO in the Second Generation." *NATO Review* 5 (October 1980): 1-7.

Keithly, David M. "Shadows of Germany's Authoritarian Past." *Orbis* 38 (Spring 1994): 207-24.

Kennan, George F. "Disengagement Revisited." *Foreign Affairs* 37 (January 1959): 187-210.

————. "After the Cold War: American Foreign Policy in the 1970s." *Foreign Affairs* 51 (October 1972): 210-27.

Kennedy, John F. "Europe and the United States." *Atlantic Community Quarterly* 1 (Winter 1963-1964): 305-15.

Kenny, Brian. "A NATO Vehicle for the Road Ahead." *Parameters* 21 (Autumn 1991): 19-27.

Killick, John. "Is NATO Relevant to the 1980s?" *World Today* 36 (January 1980): 4-10.

Kingsley, Martin. "NATO—A British View." *International Journal* 6 (Autumn 1951): 292-99.

Kinkel, Klaus. "NATO's Enduring Role in European Security." *NATO Review* 5 (October 1992): 3-8.

————. "The New NATO: Steps Towards Reform." *NATO Review* (May 1996): 8-13.

————. "Peacekeeping Missions: Germany Can Now Play Its Part." *NATO Review* 5 (October 1995): 3-7.

Kirby, Stephen. "The Independent European Programme Group: The Failure of Low-Profile High-Politics." *Journal of Common Market Studies* 18 (December 1979): 175-96.

Kirchener, Emil, and James Sperling. "The Future Germany and the Future of NATO." *German Politics* 1 (April 1992): 50-77.

Kissinger, Henry A. "Creativity Together or Irrelevance Apart." *Atlantic Community Quarterly* 11 (Winter 1973/1974): 413-21.

————. "A New Atlantic Charter." *Survival* 15 (July/August 1973): 188-92.

Komer, Robert W. "NATO's Long-Term Defence Programme—Origins and Objectives." *NATO Review* 3 (June 1978): 9-12.

Kristol, Irving. "Does NATO Exist?" Paper prepared for the conference sponsored by the Centre for Strategic and International Studies on *NATO: The Second Thirty Years* (Brussels, 1-3 September 1979).

Kunsman, Eric A. "The 1990s: A Decade of Transition to a New European Security Order." *Comparative Strategy* 10 (1991): 273-86.

Kupchan, Charles A. "NATO and the Persian Gulf: Examining Intra-Alliance Behavior." *International Organization* 42 (Spring 1988): 317-46.

La Faber, Walter. "NATO and the Korean War: A Context." *Diplomatic History* 13 (Fall 1989): 461-78.

LaBerge, Walter. "Standardization and Interoperability." *NATO Review* 6 (December 1976): 13-23.

Laloy, Jean. "Western and Eastern Europe: The Changing Relationship." *Adelphi Papers* 33. London: IISS, 1967.

Lamb, Christopher Jon. "Public Opinion and Nuclear Weapons in Europe—A Report on the Twenty-seventh Anniversary Session of the North Atlantic Assembly." *NATO Review* 6 (December 1981): 27-31.

Layne, Christopher. "Atlanticism without NATO." *Foreign Policy* 67 (Summer 1987): 22-45.

Legge, Michael. "The Making of NATO's New Strategy." *NATO Review* 6 (December 1991): 9-14.

Lellouche, Pierre. "SALT and European Security: The French Dilemma." *Survival* 1 (January/February 1980): 2-6.

Liddel Hart, Basil. "Shield Forces for NATO." *Survival* 2 (May/June 1960): 108-10.

Lieven, Anatol. "Russian Opposition to NATO Expansion." *World Today* 51 (October 1995): 196-200.

Lightburn, David. "NATO and the Challenge of Multifunctional Peacekeeping." *NATO Review* 2 (March 1996): 10-14.

Lowe, Karl, and Thomas-Durell Young, "Multinational Corps and NATO." *Survival* 33 (January/February 1991): 66-77.

Luns, Joseph M. A. H. "NATO's View of Security Conferences." *Atlantic Community Quarterly* 11 (September 1973): 55-64.

————. "The North Atlantic Alliance Commemorates Its Twenty-fifth Birthday." *NATO Review* 22 (June 1974): 166-68.

————. "Thirty Years Later—Aims of the Alliance Still Valid." *NATO Review* 2 (April 1979): 7-9.

Martin, L. W. "British Defence Policy: The Long Recessional." *Adelphi Papers* 61 (London: IISS, 1969).

Maull, Hanns W. "Germany in the Yugoslav Crisis." *Survival* 37 (Winter 1995-1996): 99-130.

Mauroy, Pierre. "France and Western Security." *NATO Review* 5 (1983): 23.

McCalla, Robert B. "NATO's Persistance after the Cold War." *International Organization* 50 (Summer 1996): 445-75.

McGeehan, Robert. "The Atlantic Alliance and the Reagan Administration." *World Today* 37 (July/August 1981): 254-62.

————. "The U.S. and NATO after the Cold War." *NATO Review* 1 (February 1990): 7-13.

McGinnis, Michael D. "A Rational Model of Regional Rivalry." *International Studies Quarterly* 34 (March 1990): 111-37

McNamara, Robert S. "The Military Role of Nuclear Weapons: Perceptions and Misperceptions." *Foreign Affairs* 62 (Fall 1983): 59-80.

Meimeth, Michael. "France Gets Closer to NATO." *World Today* 50 (May 1994): 84-86.

Menon, Anand. "From Independence to Cooperation: France, NATO and European Security." *International Affairs* 71 (January 1995): 19-34.

Middleton, Drew. "NATO Changes Direction." *Foreign Affairs* 33 (April 1953): 427-44.

Miller, David. "U.K. Forces in the Gulf: Analysis of a Commitment." *Military Technology* 15 (July 1991): 39-50.

Millon, Charles. "France and the Renewal of the Atlantic Alliance." *NATO Review* 3 (May 1996): 13-16.

Millward, Allan. "Was the Marshall Plan Really Necessary?" *Diplomatic History* 13 (Spring 1989): 231-53.

Mortimer, Edward. "European Security after the Cold War." *Adelphi Papers* 271 (London: IISS, 1992).

Moynihan, Daniel P. "The NATO Committee on the Challenges of Modern Society." *Atlantic Community Quarterly* 7 (Winter 1969-1970): 530-37.

Moïsi, Dominique. "Mitterand's Foreign Policy: The Limits of Continuity." *Foreign Affairs* 60 (Winter 1981/1982): 347-57.

Neild, Robert, and Anders Boserup. "Beyond INF: A New Approach to Non nuclear Forces." *World Policy Journal* 4 (Fall 1987): 605-20.

Nixon, Richard M. "NATO: Facing the Truth of Our Times." *Atlantic Community Quarterly* 7 (Summer 1969): 203-8.

————. "The Time to Save NATO." *Atlantic Community Quarterly* 6 (Winter 1968-1969): 479-84.

Norstad, Lauris. "Defending Europe without France." *Atlantic Community Quarterly* 4 (Summer 1966): 178-89.

Northedge, F. S. "Britain as a Second-Rank Power." *International Affairs* 46 (January 1970): 37-47.

O'Leary, James P. "Can NATO Survive Eurocommunism?" *International Security Review* 5 (Spring 1980): 70-90.

Olson, Mancur, and Richard Zeckhauser. "An Economic Theory of Alliances." *Review of Economics and Statistics* 48 (August 1966): 266-79.

Owen, David. "Eurocommunism, Socialism and Democracy." *NATO Review* 1 (February 1978): 3-11.

Payne, Keith B., and Michael Ruhle, "The Future of the Alliance: Emerging German Views." *Strategic Review* 19 (Winter 1991): 37-45.

"Peace and Security: Choosing the Right Way" (Special Edition). *NATO Review* 2 (1982).

Pearson, Lester B. "After Geneva: A Greater Task for NATO." *Foreign Affairs* 34 (October 1955): 14-23.

Petersen, Nikolaj. "Who Pulled Whom and How Much? Britain, the United States and the Making of the North Atlantic Treaty." *Millenium* 11 (Summer 1982): 93-113.

Phillips, Robert L. "Is There an Ethos to NATO?" *Ethics and International Affairs* 1 (1987): 211-19.

Pick, Otto. "New Roles for Old Alliances?" *World Today* 46 (October 1990): 193-95.

Pierre, Andrew J. "Implications of the Western Response to the Soviet Intervention in Czechoslovakia." *Atlantic Community Quarterly* 7 (Spring 1969): 59-75.

————. "What Happened to the Year of Europe?" *World Today* 30 (March 1974): 110-19.

Pleven, Réne. "France in the Atlantic Community." *Foreign Affairs* 38 (October 1959): 19-30.

Radi, Luciano. "European Armaments Cooperation." *NATO Review* 3 (June 1977): 8-10.

Rambaut, Paul C. "Environmental Challenges: The Role of NATO." *NATO Review* 2 (April 1992): 24-27.

Ranger, Robert. "NATO's Reaction to Czechoslovakia: The Strategy of Ambiguous Response." *World Today* 25 (January 1969): 19-26.

Reed, Carol. "1992: The EC—Inertia in the Midst of Crisis." *Defence* 21 (October 1990): 620-21.

Roberts, Owen J. "Atlantic Union Now." *Foreign Policy Bulletin* (7 April 1951): 3-14.

Rosenberg, David Alan. "American Atomic Strategy and the Hydrogen Bomb Decision." *Journal of American History* 66 (June 1977): 62-67.

————. "The Origins of Overkill: Nuclear Weapons and American Strategy, 1945-1960." *International Security* 7 (Spring 1983): 3-71.

Rostow, Eugene. "A Practical Programme for Peace: The Twentieth Anniversary of the Harmel Report." *NATO Review* 4 (August 1987): 9-15.

Ruhle, Hans. "The Theatre Nuclear Issue in German Politics." *Strategic Review* 9 (Spring 1981): 54-60.

Ruiz Palmer, Diego A. "French Strategic Options in the 1990s." *Adelphi Papers* 260 (London: IISS, 1991).

Sagan, Scott D. "The Lessons of the Yom Kippur Alert." *Foreign Policy* 36 (Fall 1979): 160-77.

Saint, Crosbie E. "Today's NATO—The Indispensible Anvil of Stability and Freedom." *Canadian Defence Quarterly* 19 (February 1990): 19-22.

Sandwell, B. K. "North Atlantic—Community or Treaty." *International Journal* 8 (Summer 1952): 162-72.

Schaetzel, J. Robert "Some Questions for Dr. Kissinger." *Foreign Policy* 12 (Fall 1973): 66-78.

Schear, James A., and Joseph Nye, Jr.. "Addressing Europe's Conventional Instabilities." *Washington Quarterly* 11 (Summer 1988): 45-55.

Schlör, Wolfgang F. "German Security Policy." *Adelphi Papers* 277 (London: IISS: 1993).

Schmidt, Helmut. "The Brezhnev Doctrine." *Survival* 11 (October 1969): 307-11.

―――. "The 1972 Alastair Buchan Memorial Lecture." *Survival* 6 (January/February 1978): 2-10.

―――. "A Policy of Reliable Partnership." *Foreign Affairs* 59 (Spring 1981): 743-55.

Scholten, Willem. "The Eurogroup's First Ten Years." *NATO Review* 2 (April 1978): 3-5.

Schutz, Wilhelm. "New Initiatives for a New Age." *Foreign Affairs* 36 (April 1958): 460-71.

Sharp, Jane. "If Not NATO, Who?" *Bulletin of the Atomic Scientists* 48 (October 1992): 29-32.

Simes, Dimitri K. "The Death of Détente?–Some Effects of Russia's Invasion in Afghanistan." *International Security* 5 (Summer 1980): 3-25.

Slessor, John. "Command and Control of Allied Nuclear Forces: A British View." *Adelphi Papers* 22 (London: IISS, 1965).

―――. "Control of Nuclear Strategy." *Foreign Affairs* 42 (October 1963): 96-106.

―――. "Nuclear Power and Britain's Defence." *Survival* 4 (November/December 1962): 250-54.

Sloan, Stanley R. "NATO after Reykjavik." *National Defence* 71 (May-June 1987)): 65-72.

―――. "U.S. Perspectives on NATO's Future." *International Affairs* 71 (April 1995): 217-32.

Smith, Leighton W., Jr. "The Pillars of Peace in Bosnia." *NATO Review* 3 (July 1996): 11-16.

Snyder, Glenn. "Alliances, Balance, and Stability." *International Organization* 41 (Winter: 1991): 121-42.

―――. "The Security Dilemma in Alliance Politics." *World Politics* 36 (July 1984): 461-95.

Sobell, Vlad. "NATO, Russia and the Yugoslav War." *World Today* 51 (November 1995): 210-15;

Solana, Javier. "NATO's Role in Bosnia: Charting a New Course for the Alliance." *NATO Review* 2 (March 1996): 3-6.

Spaak, Paul-Henri. "The Atom Bomb and NATO." *Foreign Affairs* 33 (April 1955): 353-59.

―――. "Chaos in Europe." *Atlantic Community Quarterly* 4 (Summer 1966): 211-15.

―――. "The Fundamental Reality." *Atlantic Community Quarterly* 6 (Winter 1968-1969): 485-92.

————. "Hold Fast." *Foreign Affairs* 41 (July 1963): 611-20.

————. "New Tests for NATO." *Foreign Affairs* 37 (April 1959): 357-65.

Spinelli, Altiero. "Atlantic Partnership or European Unity." *Foreign Affairs* 40 (July 1962): 542-52.

Steinhoff, Johannes. "NATO Crisis: A Military View." *Survival* 8 (November 1966): 365-71.

Stewart, Michael. "Britain, Europe and the Alliance." *Foreign Affairs* 48 (July 1970): 70-78.

Strauss, Franz Josef. "Europe, America and NATO: A German View." *Survival* (January/February 1962): 5-8.

Strausz-Hupe, Robert. "Will West Germany Stay in Step?" *Policy Review* 11 (Winter 1980): 37-49.

Szulc, Tad. "The New Brinkmanship." *New Republic* (8 November 1980): 18-21.

Taft, William H., IV. "European Security: Lessons Learned from the Gulf War." *NATO Review* 3 (June 1991): 7-11.

————. "The NATO Role in Europe and the U.S. Role in NATO." *NATO Review* 4 (August 1992): 1-8.

Taylor, Philip. "Weapons Standardization in NATO: Collaborative Security or Economic Competition?" *International Organization* 36 (Winter 1982): 95-112.

Taylor, Trevor. "NATO and Central Europe." *NATO Review* 5 (October 1991): 17-22.

"The Soviet Invasion of Afghanistan." *NATO Review* 3 (June 1980): 1-13.

"The Washington Energy Conference." *Atlantic Community Quarterly* 12 (Spring 1974): 22-54.

"The Way Ahead" (Special Edition). *NATO Review* 1, February 1989.

Thies, Jochen. "Germany: Europe's Reluctant Great Power." *World Today* 51 (October 1995): 186-90.

Thies, Wallace J. "The 'Demise' of NATO: A Postmortem." *Parameters* 20 (June 1990): 17-30.

Ullman, Richard H. "The Covert French Connection." *Foreign Policy* 75 (Summer 1989): 3- 33.

————. "Out of the Euro-missile Mire." *Foreign Policy* 50 (Spring 1983): 39-52.

Van Eekelen, Wilem. "WEU and the Gulf Crisis." *Survival* 32 (November/ December 1990): 519-32.

Van Evera, Steven. "Why Europe Matters, Why the Third World Doesn't: American Grand Strategy after the Cold War." *Journal of Strategic Studies* 13 (June 1990): 2-12.

Vernant, Jacques. "France and Nassau." *Survival* 5 (May/June 1963): 106-9.

von Hassel, Kai-Uwe. "Détente through Firmness." *Foreign Affairs* 42 (January 1964): 184-94.

von Moltke, Gerhardt G. "NATO Takes up Its New Agenda." *NATO Review* 1 (February 1992): 3-7.

Wagner, R. Harrison. "The Theory of Games and the Balance of Power." *World Politics* 38 (July 1986): 546-76.

Walker, J. Samuel. "'No More Cold War': American Foreign Policy and the 1948 Soviet Peace Offensive." *Diplomatic History* 5 (Winter 1981): 75-91.

Walker, Jenonne. "Keeping America in Europe." *Foreign Policy* 83 (Summer 1991): 128-42.

Wallace, William. "Germany as Europe's Leading Power." *World Today* 51 (August-September 1995): 62-64.

Waltz, Kenneth N. "The Emerging Structure of International Politics." *International Security* 18 (Fall 1993): 44-79.

———. "Nuclear Myths and Political Realities." *American Political Science Review* 89 (September 1990): 371-46.

Watt, Angus. "The Hand of Friendship—The Military Contacts Programme." *NATO Review* 1 (February 1992): 19-22.

Wegener, Henning. "The Management of Change: NATO's Anniversary Summit." *NATO Review* 3 (June 1989): 1-7.

Weibes, Carl, and Burt Zeeman. "The Pentagon Negotiations, March 1948: The Launching of the North Atlantic Treaty." *International Affairs* 59 (Summer 1983): 351-63.

Wells, Samuel F. "The Origins of Massive Retaliation." *Political Science Quarterly* 96 (Spring 1981): 31-52.

Wholstetter, Albert. "Nuclear Sharing: NATO and the N+1 Country." *Foreign Affairs* 39 (April 1961): 355-88.

Williams, Michael. "The Best Chance for Peace in Bosnia." *World Today* 52 (January 1996): 4-7.

Williams, Nick. "Partnership for Peace: Permanent Fixture or Declining Asset?" *Survival* 38 (Spring 1996): 98-110.

Wilson, Harold. "Speech by the Prime Minister on Britain and the Atlantic Nuclear Force, 16 December 1964." *Survival* 7 (March/April 1965): 52-54.

Windsor, Philip. "The Boundaries of Détente." *World Today* 25 (June 1969): 255-64.

———. "NATO Confronts Its Future." *World Today* 24 (March 1968): 121-26.

———. "NATO and European Détente." *World Today* 23 (September 1967): 361-69.

Woyke, Richard. "A Crisis in U.S.-West European Relations?" *NATO Review* 5 (October 1981): 14-18.

Wörner, Manfred. "The Atlantic Alliance in the New Era." *NATO Review* 1 (February 1991): 3-10.

———. "From Confrontation to Partnership: The Role of NATO in East-West Relations." *Jane's Intelligence Review* 4 (June 1992): 242-44.

————. "NATO in the Post-INF Era: More Opportunities than Risks." *NATO Review* 4 (August 1988): 1-7.

————. "NATO Transformed: The Significance of the Rome Summit." *NATO Review* 6 (December 1991): 7-9.

————. "NATO's Changing Role in a New Security Order." *International Defense Review* 24 (July 1991): 751-53.

————. "The 'Peace Movement' and NATO: An Alternative View from Bonn." *Strategic Review* 10 (Winter 1982): 15-21.

————"A Time of Accelerating Change." *NATO Review* 6 (December 1989): 1-5.

————. "A Vigorous Alliance—A Motor for Peaceful Change in Europe." *NATO Review* 6 (December 1992): 3-9.

X [Kennan, George F.]. "The Sources of Soviet Conduct." *Foreign Affairs* 25 (July 1947): 566-82.

Yochelson, John N. "The American Military Presence in Europe: Current Debate in the U.S." *Orbis* 15 (Fall 1971): 796-802.

Yost, David S. "Beyond MBFR: The Atlantic to the Urals Gambit." *Orbis* 31 (Spring 1987): 99-134.

————. "France and the Gulf War of 1990-1991: Political-Military Lessons Learned." *Journal of Strategic Studies* 16 (September 1993): 339-74.

————. "France and West European Defence Identity." *Survival* 33 (July/August 1991): 327-51.

————. "France in the New Europe." *Foreign Affairs* 69 (Winter 1990-1991): 107-28.

————. "Franco-German Defense Cooperation." *Washington Quarterly* 11 (Spring 1988): 173-95.

Yuksel-Beten, Deniz. "CCMS: NATO's Environmental Programme is Expanded and Opened to the East." *NATO Review* 4 (August 1991): 2-7.

Z (Pseud.). "The Year of Europe?" *Foreign Affairs* 52 (January 1974): 237-48.

Zanier, Lamberto. "The Proliferation of Weapons and Expertise—NATO Helps Tackle the Problem." *NATO Review* 4 (August 1992): 26-30.

Zelikow, Philip. "The Masque of Institutions." *Survival* 38 (Spring 1996): 6-18.

Index

About the Author

Ian Q. R. Thomas received a Ph.D. in history from the University of Cambridge in 1995. He also holds degrees from the University of Stockholm and Amherst College.